P9-CKX-372

On the CAMINO

JASON

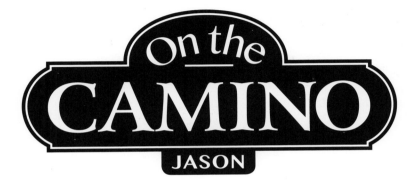

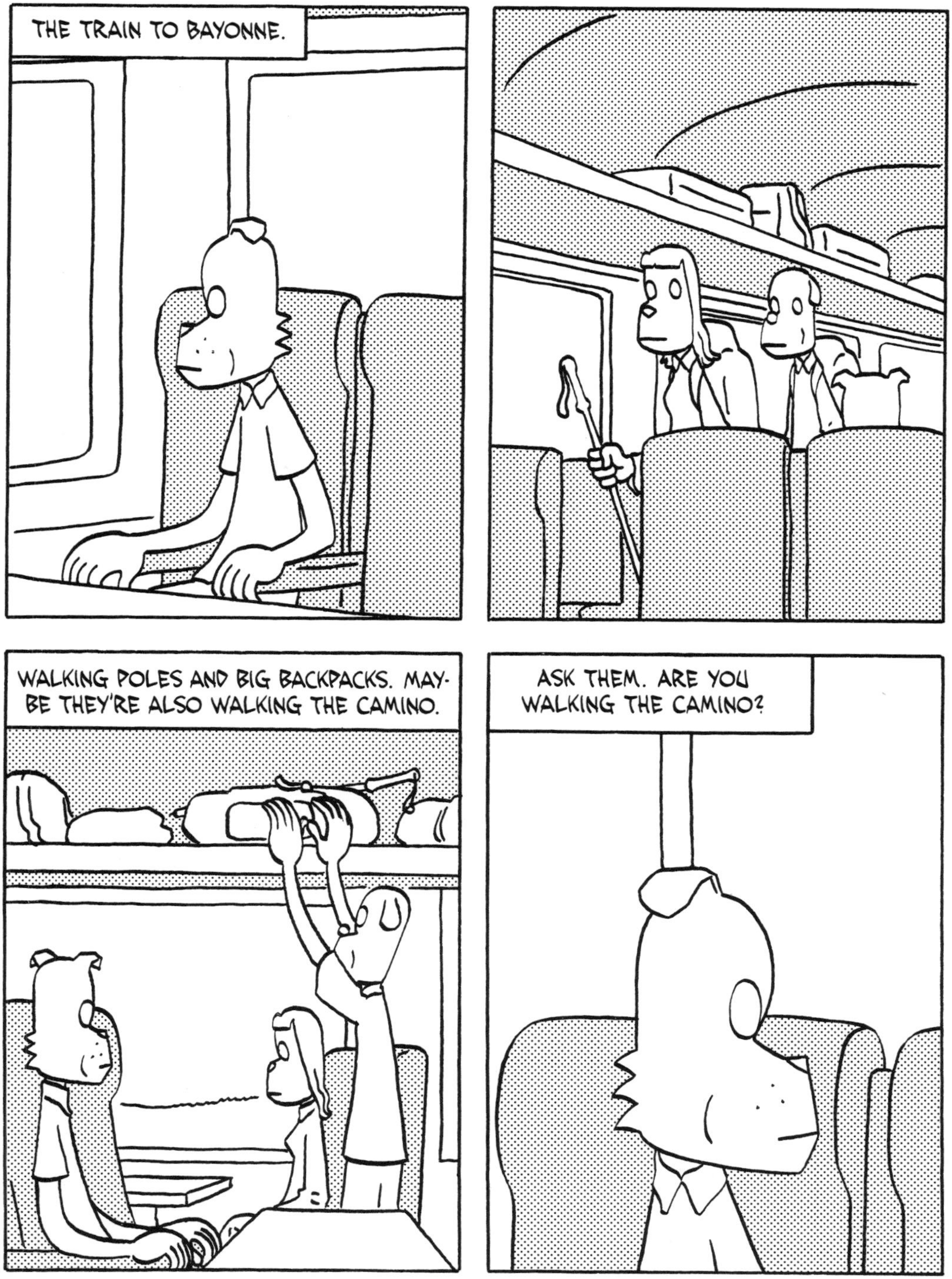
THE TRAIN TO BAYONNE.
WALKING POLES AND BIG BACKPACKS. MAY-BE THEY'RE ALSO WALKING THE CAMINO.
ASK THEM. ARE YOU WALKING THE CAMINO?

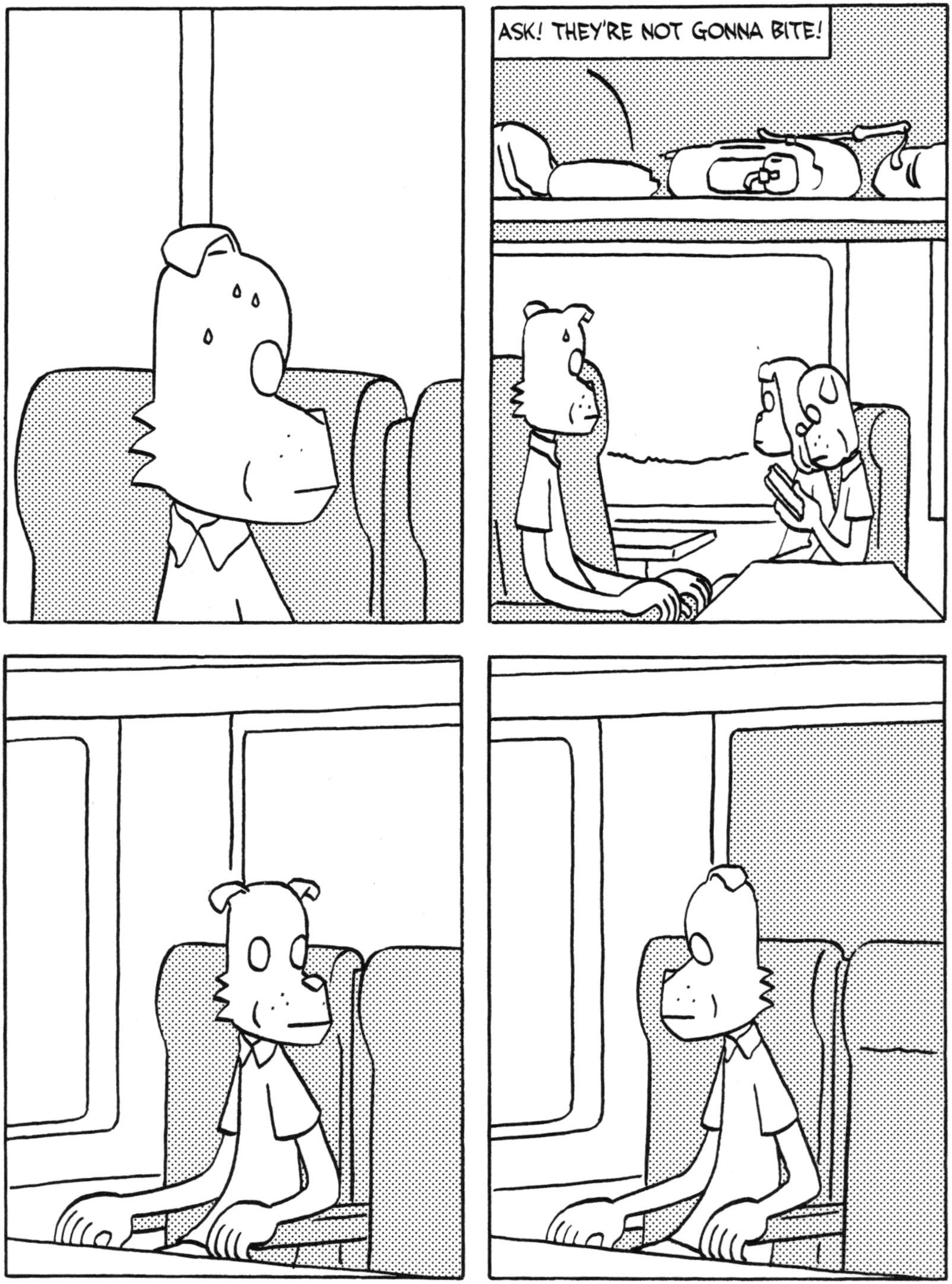
ASK! THEY'RE NOT GONNA BITE!

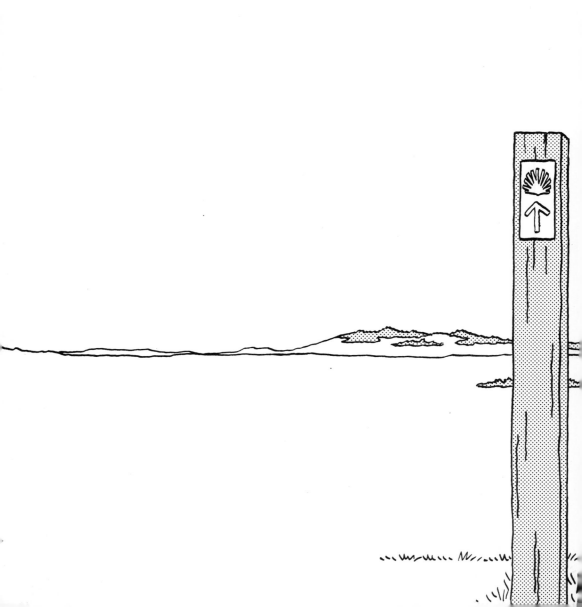

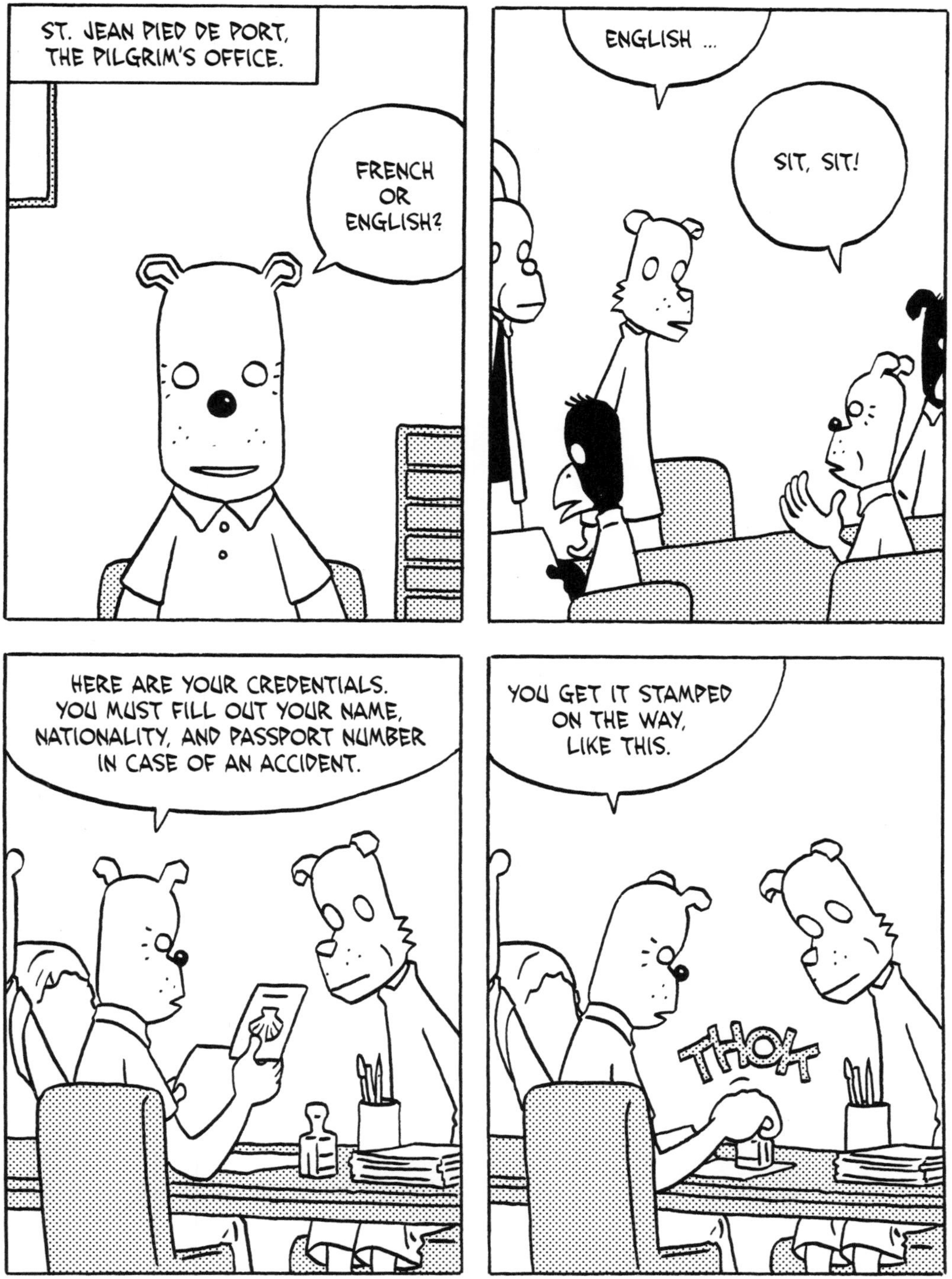
ST. JEAN PIED DE PORT, THE PILGRIM'S OFFICE.
FRENCH OR ENGLISH?
ENGLISH ...
SIT, SIT!
HERE ARE YOUR CREDENTIALS. YOU MUST FILL OUT YOUR NAME, NATIONALITY, AND PASSPORT NUMBER IN CASE OF AN ACCIDENT.
YOU GET IT STAMPED ON THE WAY, LIKE THIS.
THOK

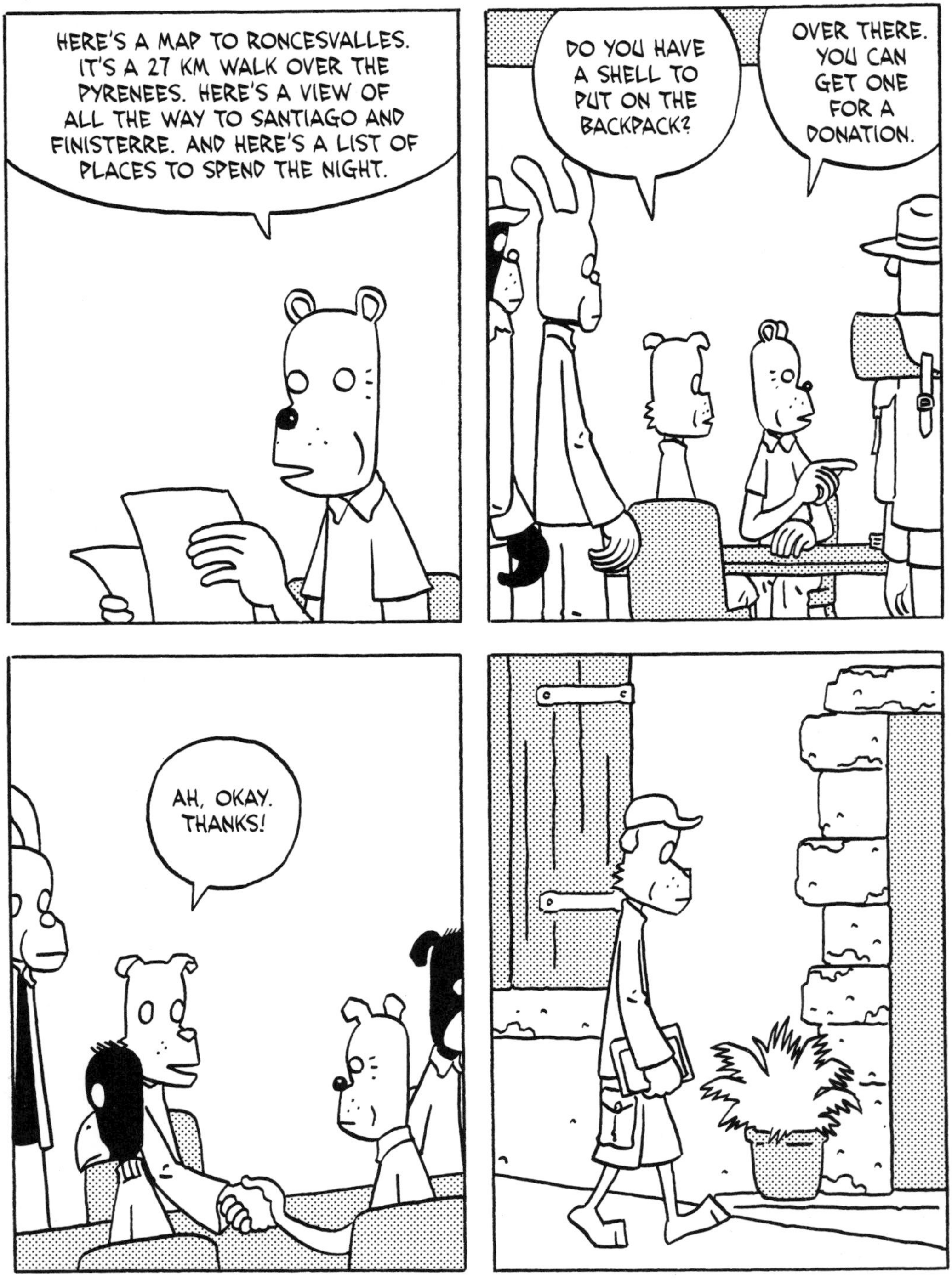
HERE'S A MAP TO RONCESVALLES. IT'S A 27 KM WALK OVER THE PYRENEES. HERE'S A VIEW OF ALL THE WAY TO SANTIAGO AND FINISTERRE. AND HERE'S A LIST OF PLACES TO SPEND THE NIGHT.
DO YOU HAVE A SHELL TO PUT ON THE BACKPACK?
OVER THERE. YOU CAN GET ONE FOR A DONATION.
AH, OKAY. THANKS!

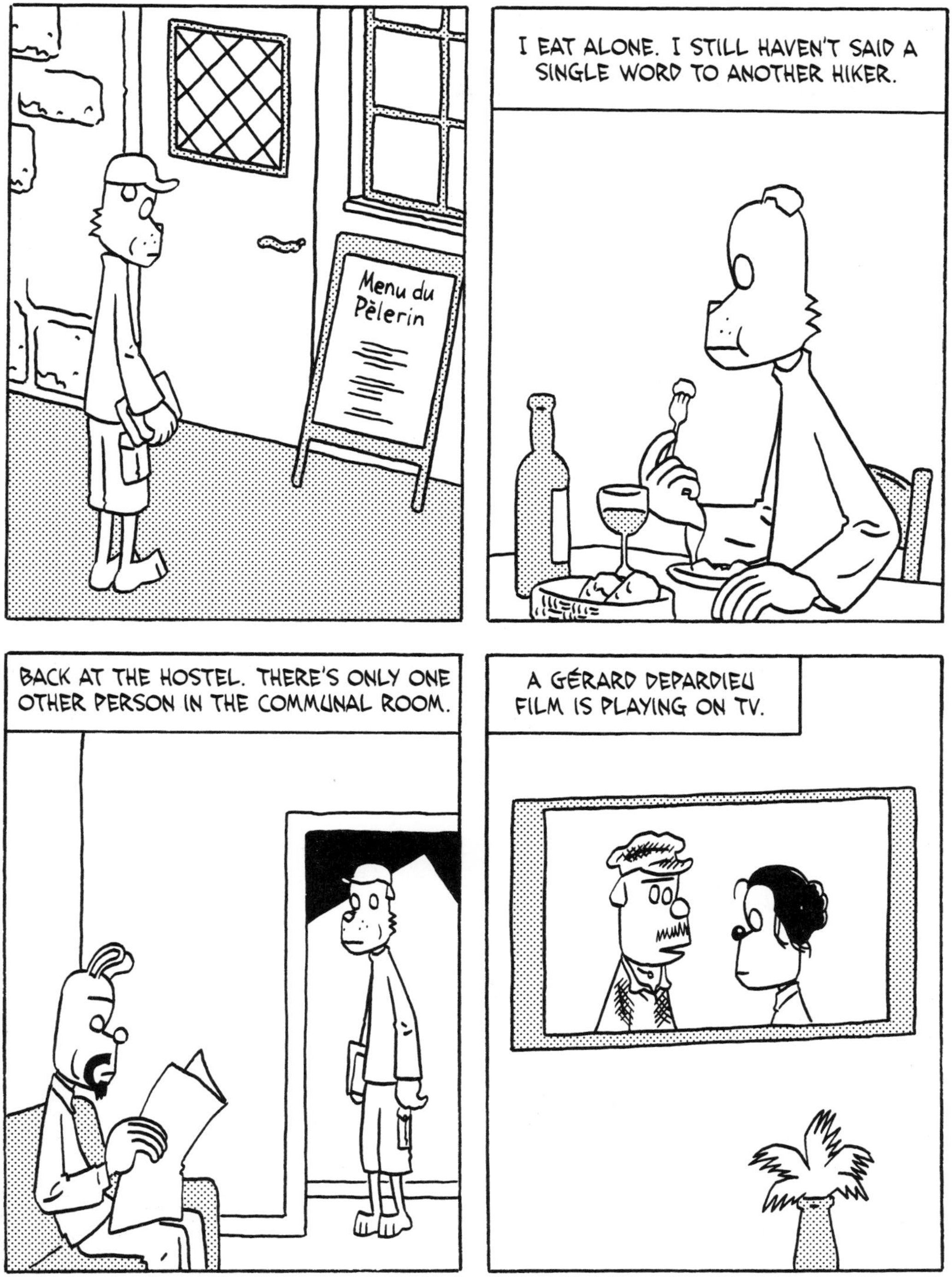
Menu du Pèlerin
I EAT ALONE. I STILL HAVEN'T SAID A SINGLE WORD TO ANOTHER HIKER.
BACK AT THE HOSTEL. THERE'S ONLY ONE OTHER PERSON IN THE COMMUNAL ROOM.
A GÉRARD DEPARDIEU FILM IS PLAYING ON TV.

I CHECK MY GUIDEBOOK. AT THE HOSTEL ACROSS THE STREET FROM THE PILGRIM'S OFFICE, THEY HAVE A GROUP DINNER WHERE EVERYONE INTRODUCES THEMSELVES.

THAT'S WHERE I SHOULD HAVE BEEN. I'M AT THE WRONG HOSTEL!

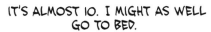

IT'S ALMOST 10. I MIGHT AS WELL GO TO BED.

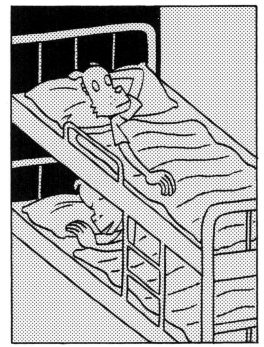

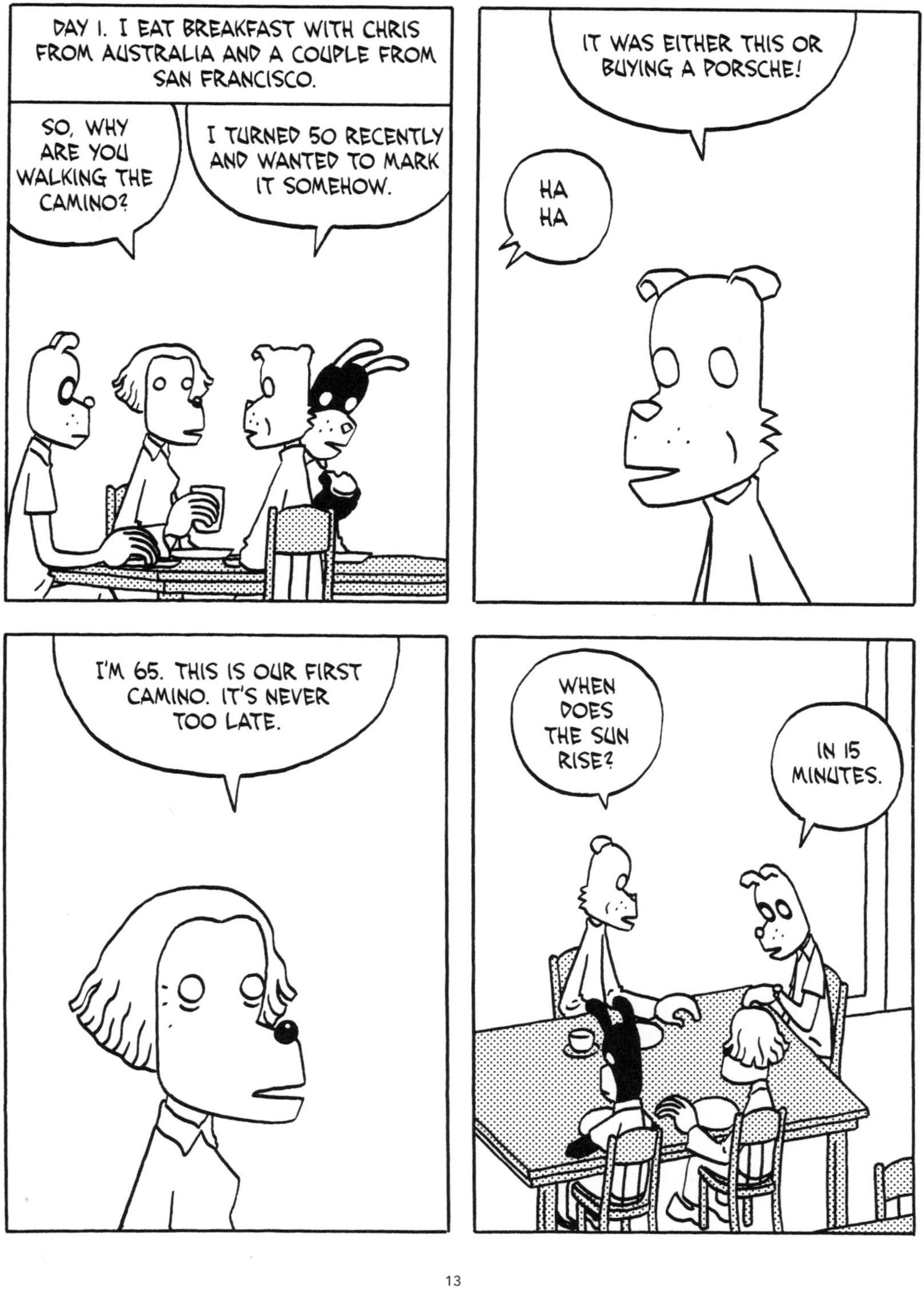
DAY 1. I EAT BREAKFAST WITH CHRIS FROM AUSTRALIA AND A COUPLE FROM SAN FRANCISCO.
SO, WHY ARE YOU WALKING THE CAMINO?
I TURNED 50 RECENTLY AND WANTED TO MARK IT SOMEHOW.
IT WAS EITHER THIS OR BUYING A PORSCHE!
HA HA
I'M 65. THIS IS OUR FIRST CAMINO. IT'S NEVER TOO LATE.
WHEN DOES THE SUN RISE?
IN 15 MINUTES.

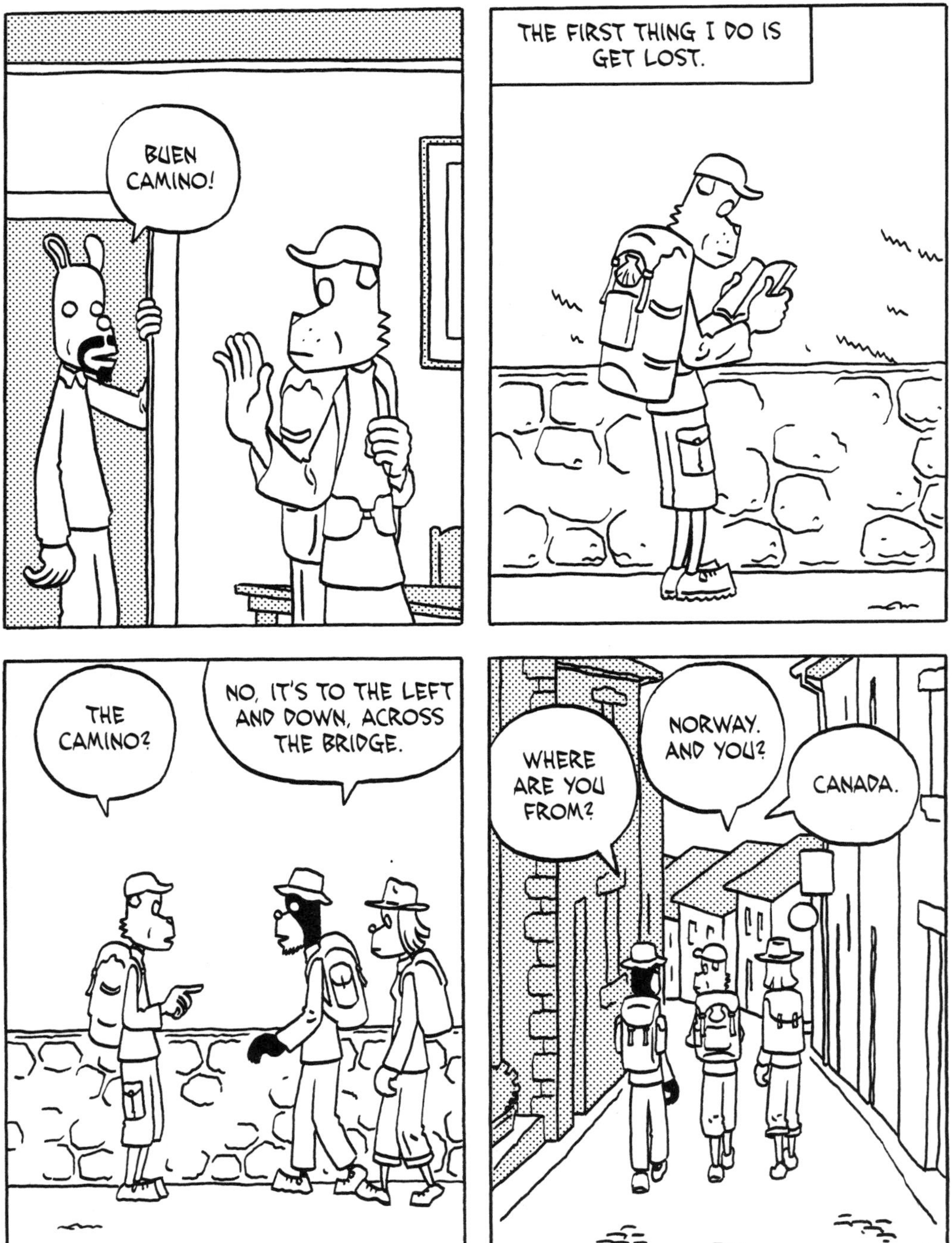
BUEN CAMINO!
THE FIRST THING I DO IS GET LOST.
THE CAMINO?
NO, IT'S TO THE LEFT AND DOWN, ACROSS THE BRIDGE.
WHERE ARE YOU FROM?
NORWAY. AND YOU?
CANADA.

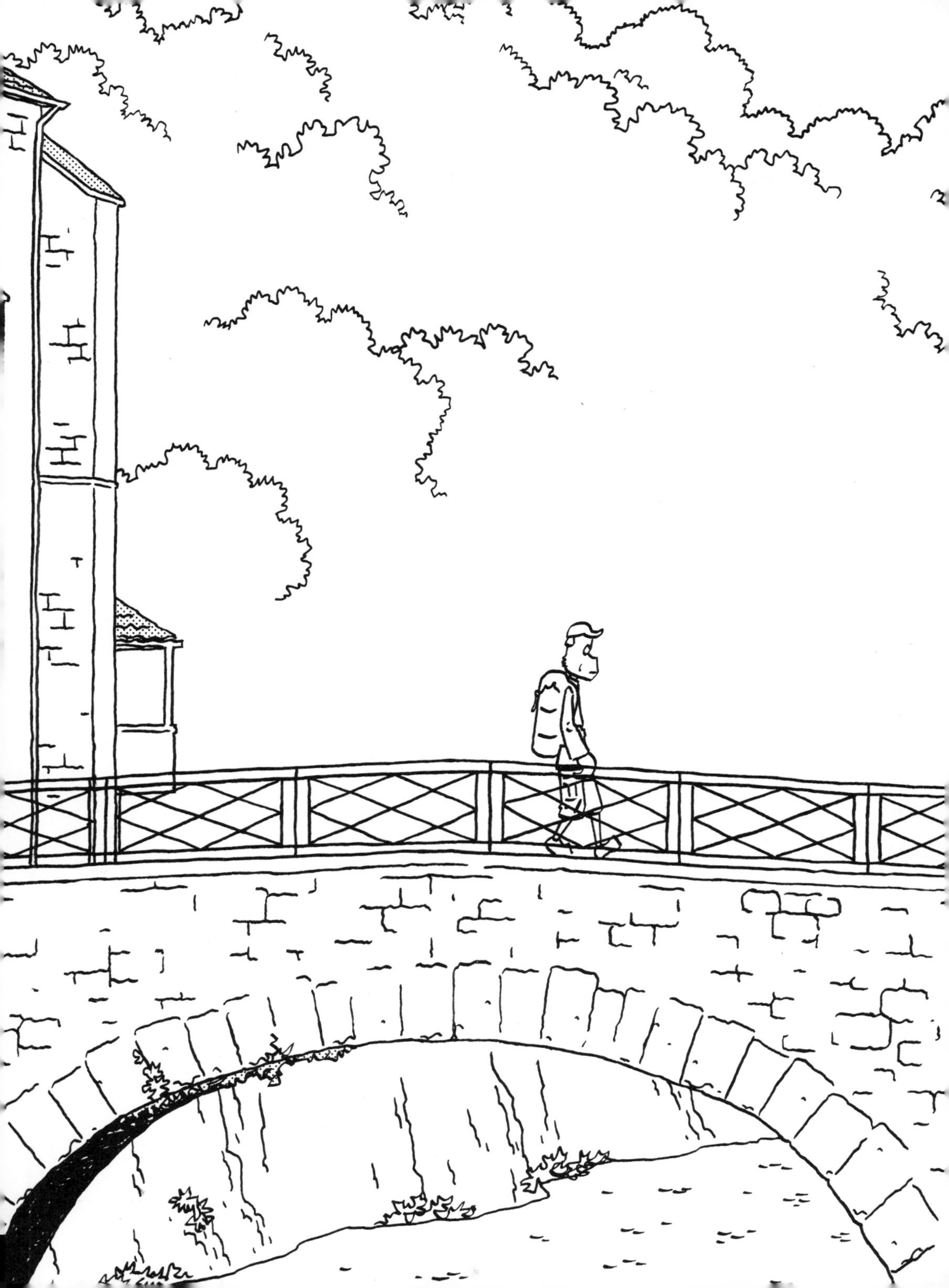

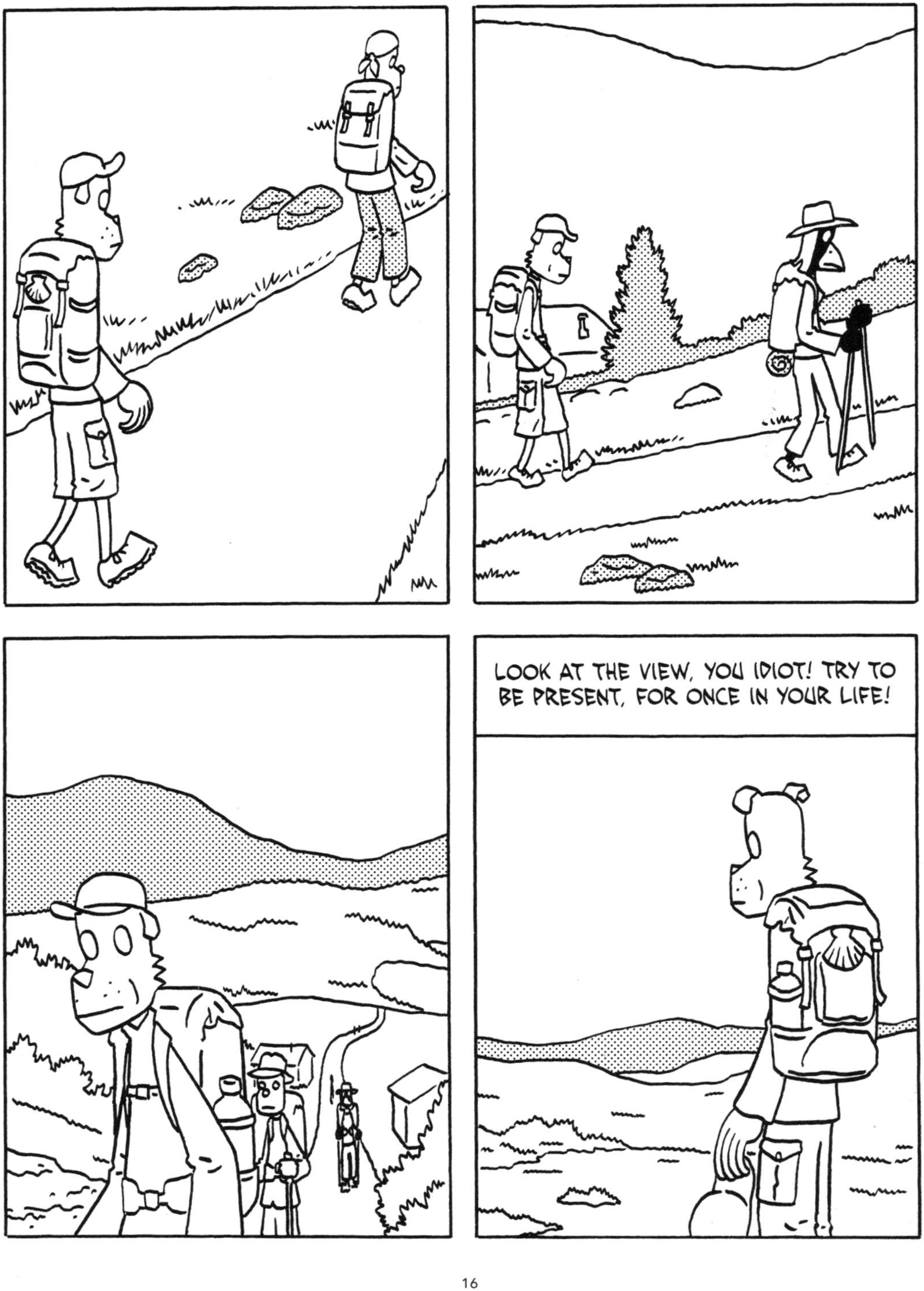
LOOK AT THE VIEW, YOU IDIOT! TRY TO BE PRESENT, FOR ONCE IN YOUR LIFE!

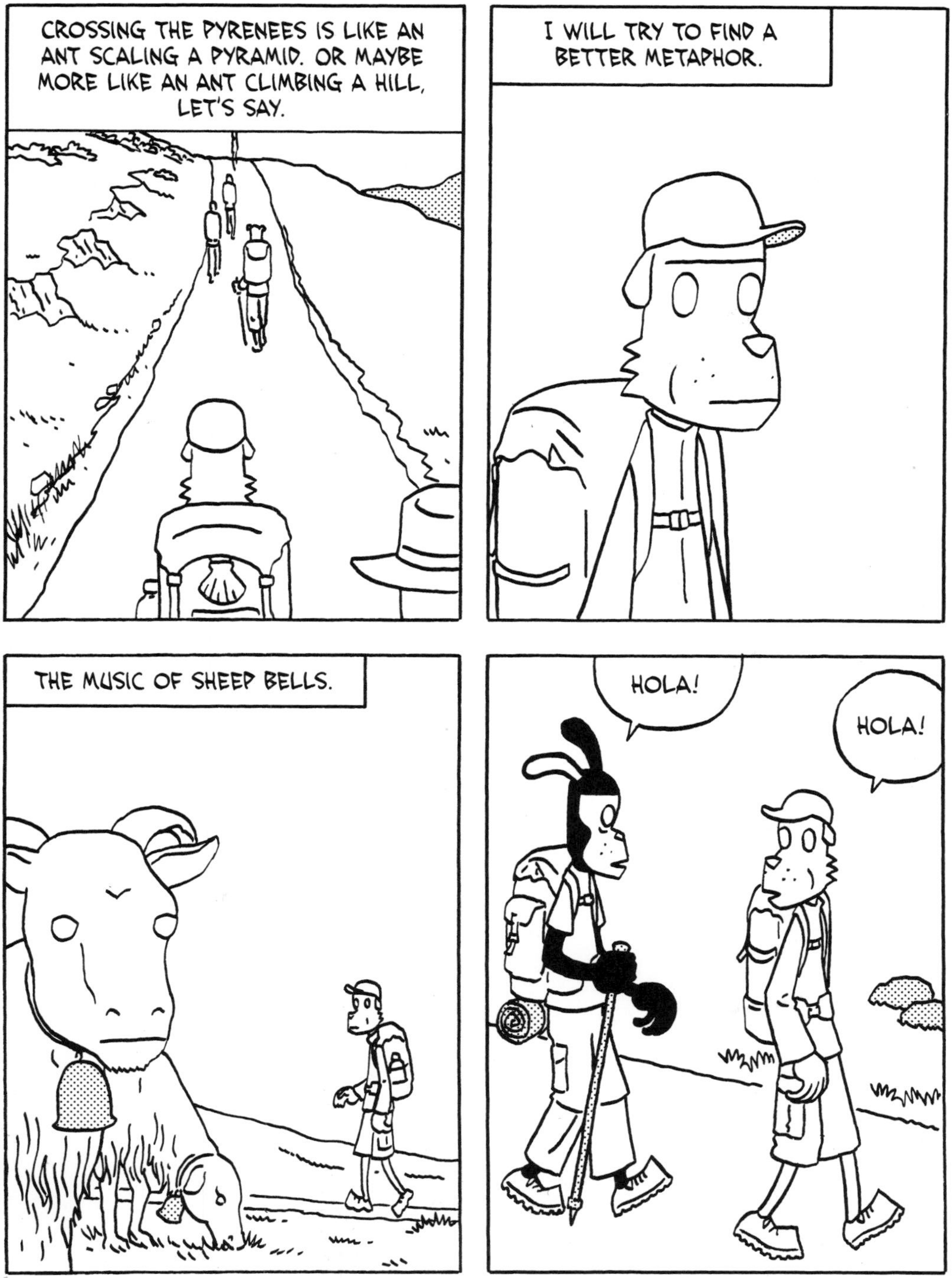
CROSSING THE PYRENEES IS LIKE AN ANT SCALING A PYRAMID. OR MAYBE MORE LIKE AN ANT CLIMBING A HILL, LET'S SAY.
I WILL TRY TO FIND A BETTER METAPHOR.
THE MUSIC OF SHEEP BELLS.
HOLA!
HOLA!

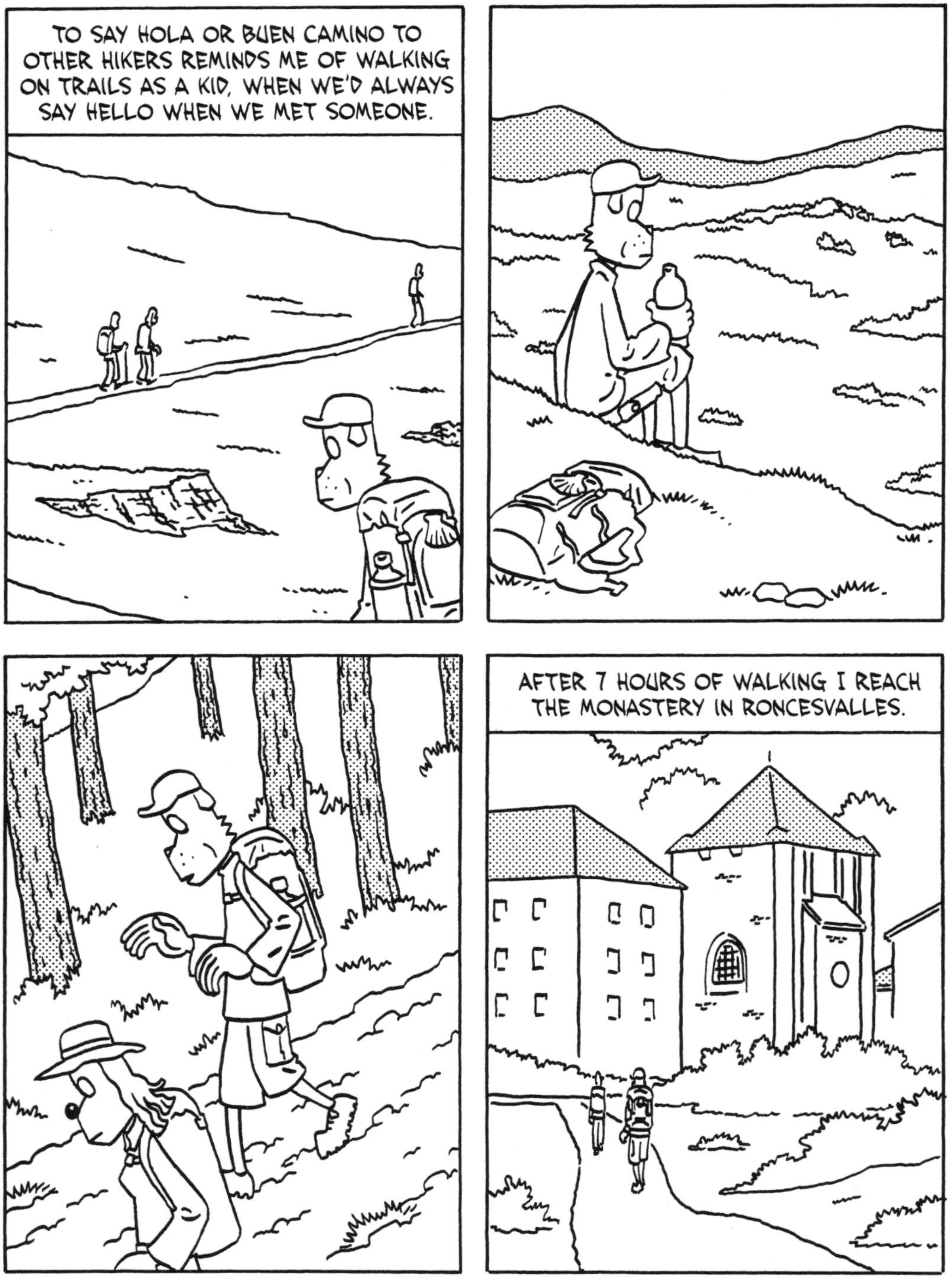
TO SAY HOLA OR BUEN CAMINO TO OTHER HIKERS REMINDS ME OF WALKING ON TRAILS AS A KID, WHEN WE'D ALWAYS SAY HELLO WHEN WE MET SOMEONE.
AFTER 7 HOURS OF WALKING I REACH THE MONASTERY IN RONCESVALLES.

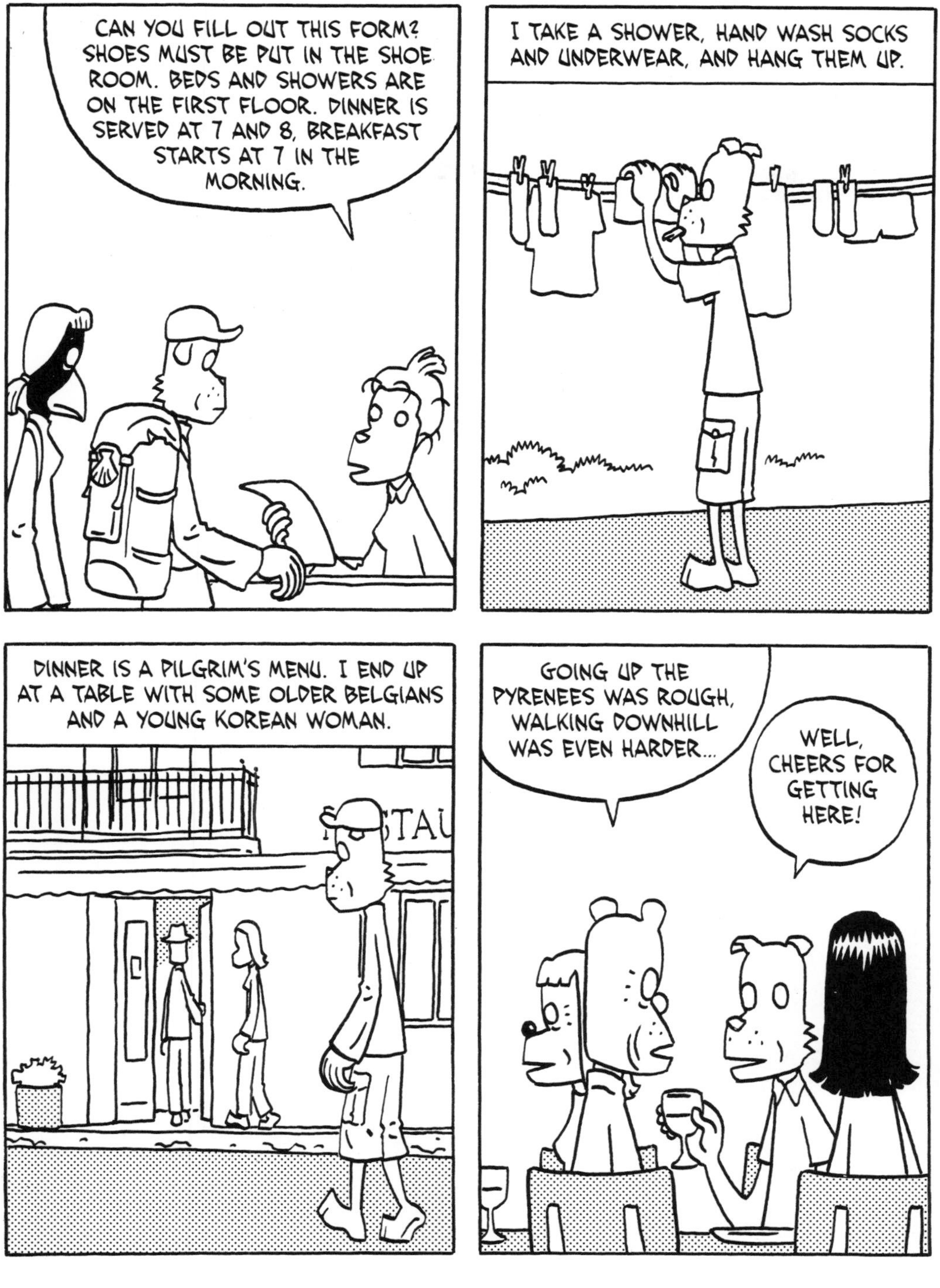

CAN YOU FILL OUT THIS FORM? SHOES MUST BE PUT IN THE SHOE ROOM. BEDS AND SHOWERS ARE ON THE FIRST FLOOR. DINNER IS SERVED AT 7 AND 8, BREAKFAST STARTS AT 7 IN THE MORNING.
I TAKE A SHOWER, HAND WASH SOCKS AND UNDERWEAR, AND HANG THEM UP.
DINNER IS A PILGRIM'S MENU. I END UP AT A TABLE WITH SOME OLDER BELGIANS AND A YOUNG KOREAN WOMAN.
GOING UP THE PYRENEES WAS ROUGH, WALKING DOWNHILL WAS EVEN HARDER...
WELL, CHEERS FOR GETTING HERE!

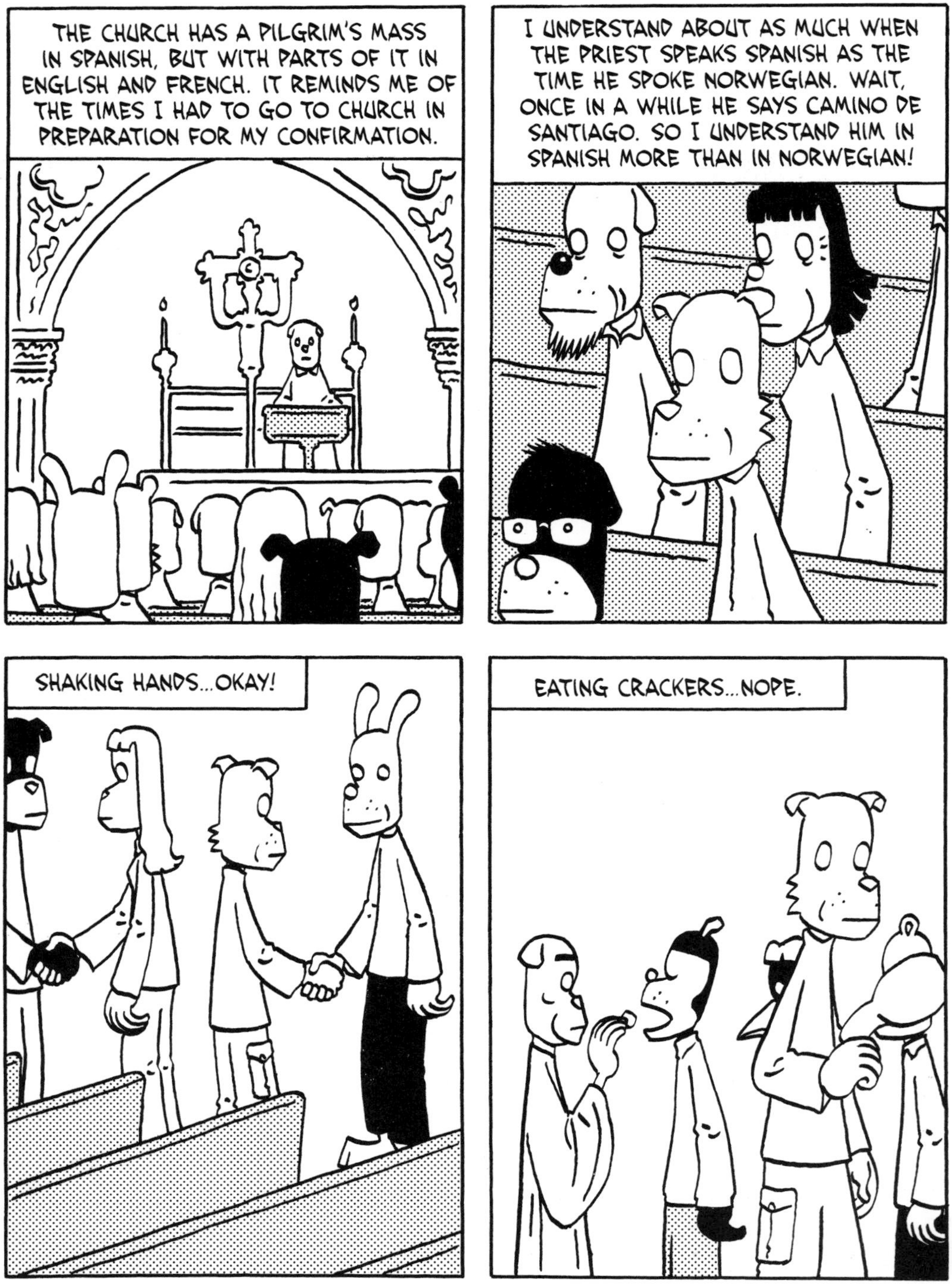
THE CHURCH HAS A PILGRIM'S MASS IN SPANISH, BUT WITH PARTS OF IT IN ENGLISH AND FRENCH. IT REMINDS ME OF THE TIMES I HAD TO GO TO CHURCH IN PREPARATION FOR MY CONFIRMATION.
I UNDERSTAND ABOUT AS MUCH WHEN THE PRIEST SPEAKS SPANISH AS THE TIME HE SPOKE NORWEGIAN. WAIT, ONCE IN A WHILE HE SAYS CAMINO DE SANTIAGO. SO I UNDERSTAND HIM IN SPANISH MORE THAN IN NORWEGIAN!
SHAKING HANDS...OKAY!
EATING CRACKERS...NOPE.

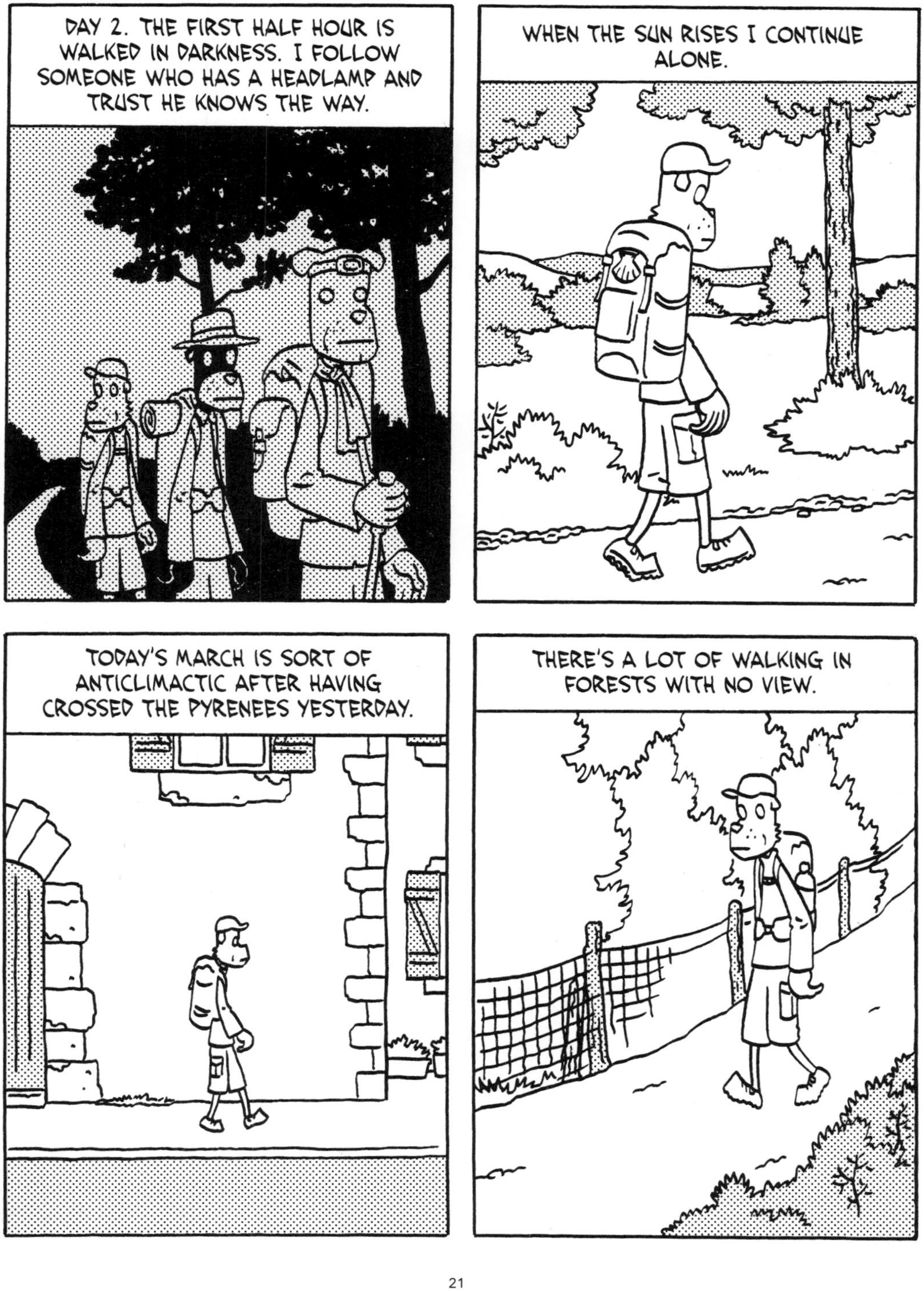
DAY 2. THE FIRST HALF HOUR IS WALKED IN DARKNESS. I FOLLOW SOMEONE WHO HAS A HEADLAMP AND TRUST HE KNOWS THE WAY.
WHEN THE SUN RISES I CONTINUE ALONE.
TODAY'S MARCH IS SORT OF ANTICLIMACTIC AFTER HAVING CROSSED THE PYRENEES YESTERDAY.
THERE'S A LOT OF WALKING IN FORESTS WITH NO VIEW.

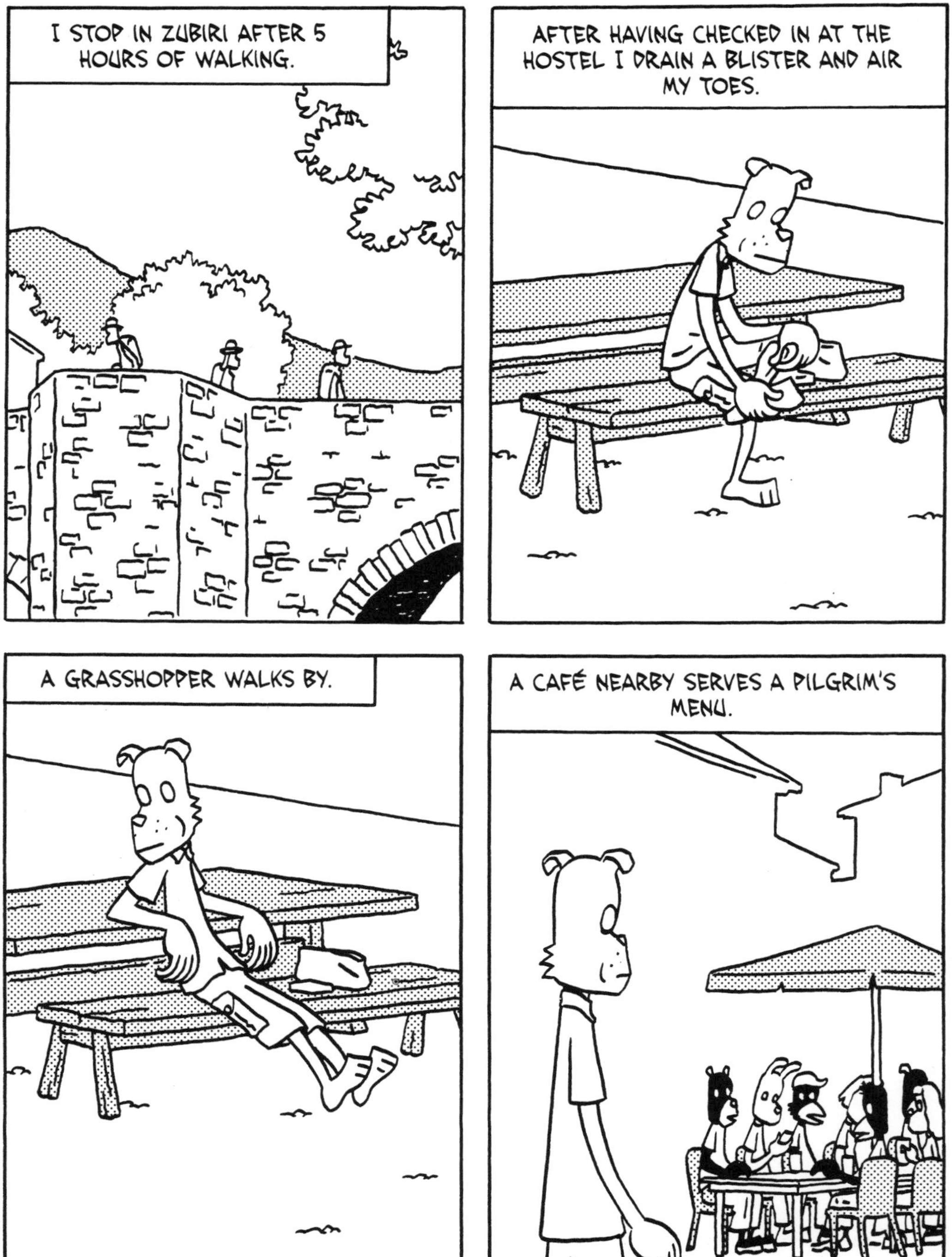
I STOP IN ZUBIRI AFTER 5 HOURS OF WALKING.
AFTER HAVING CHECKED IN AT THE HOSTEL I DRAIN A BLISTER AND AIR MY TOES.
A GRASSHOPPER WALKS BY.
A CAFÉ NEARBY SERVES A PILGRIM'S MENU.

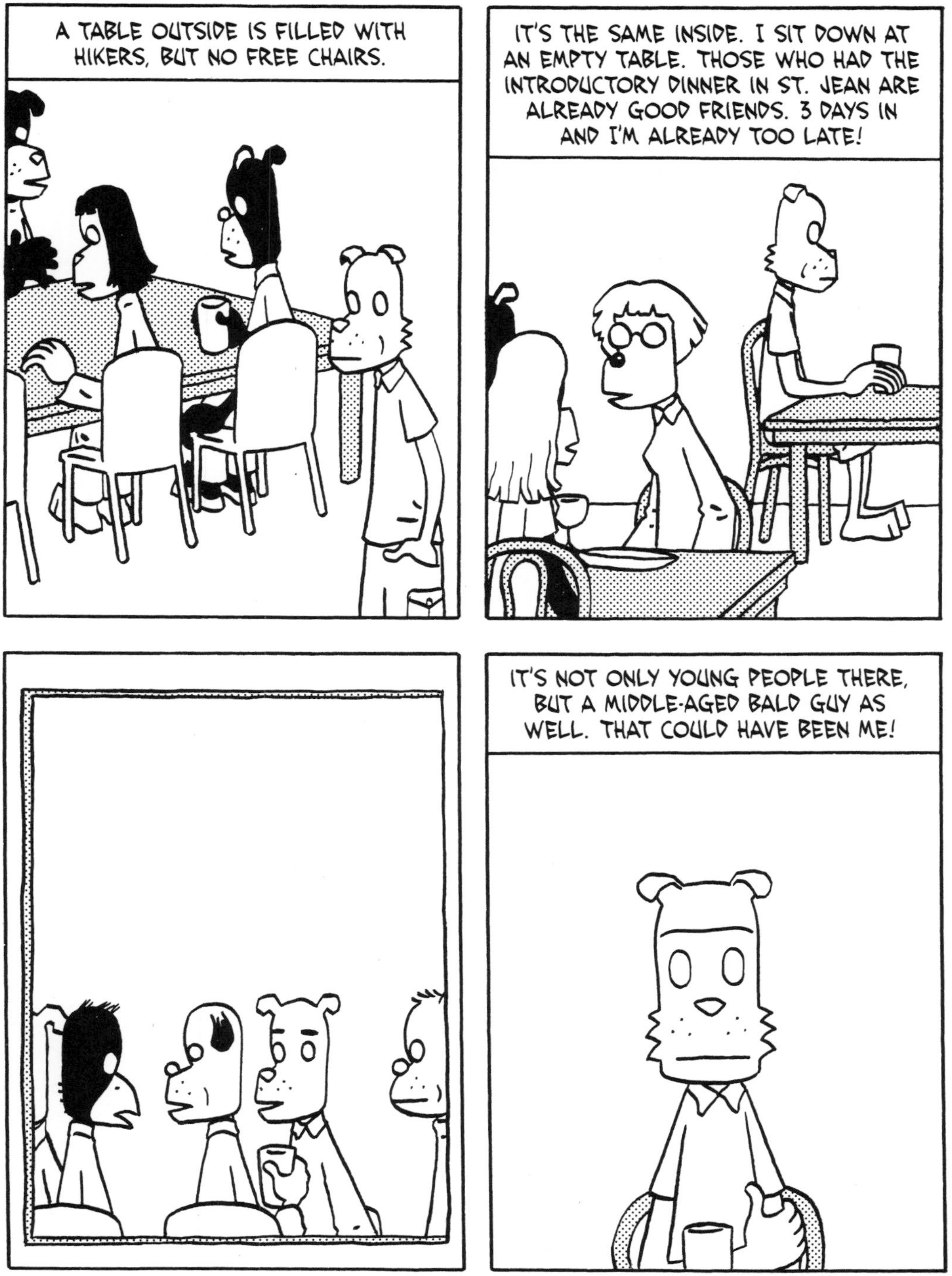
A TABLE OUTSIDE IS FILLED WITH HIKERS, BUT NO FREE CHAIRS.
IT'S THE SAME INSIDE. I SIT DOWN AT AN EMPTY TABLE. THOSE WHO HAD THE INTRODUCTORY DINNER IN ST. JEAN ARE ALREADY GOOD FRIENDS. 3 DAYS IN AND I'M ALREADY TOO LATE!
IT'S NOT ONLY YOUNG PEOPLE THERE, BUT A MIDDLE-AGED BALD GUY AS WELL. THAT COULD HAVE BEEN ME!

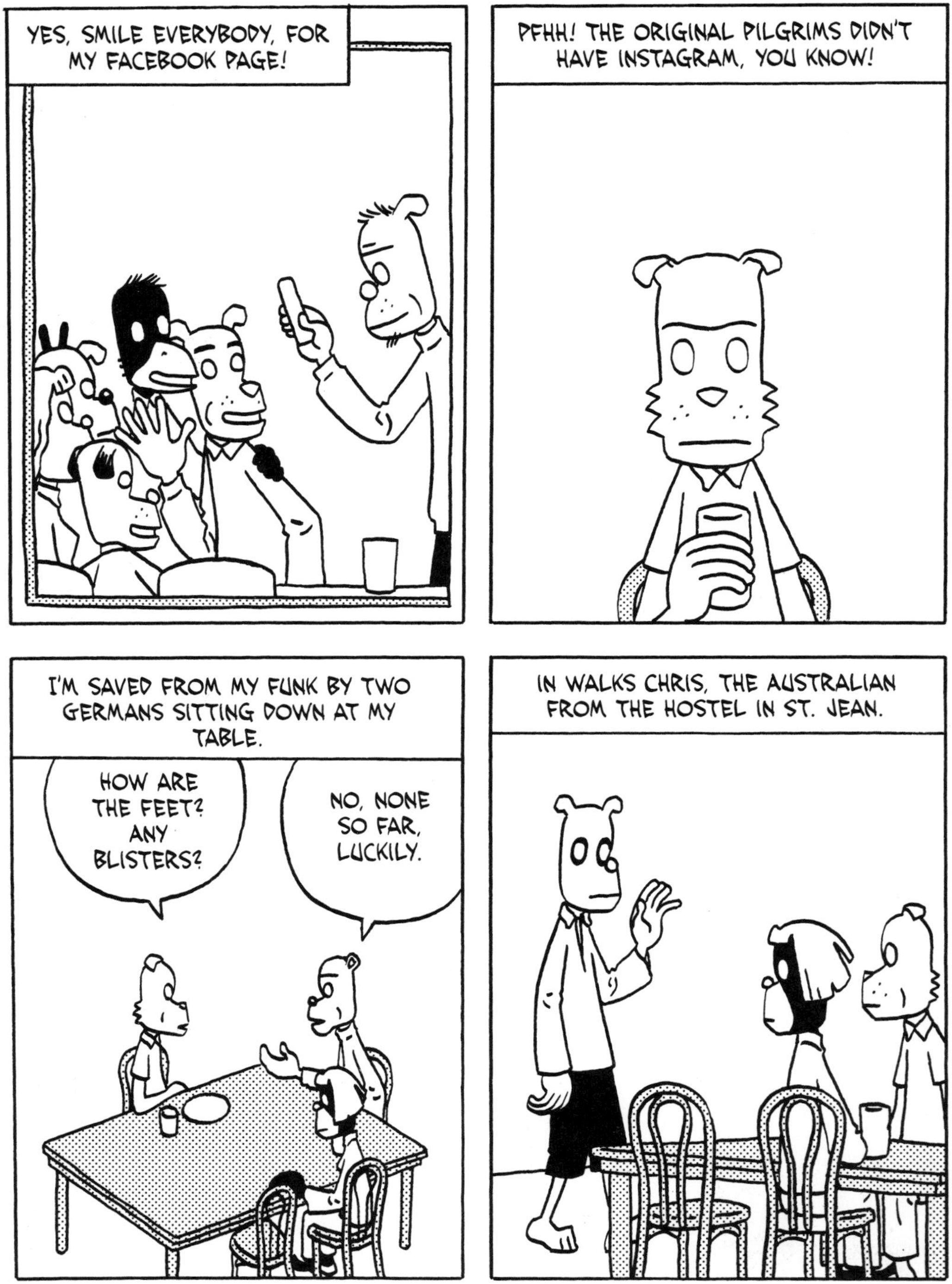
YES, SMILE EVERYBODY, FOR MY FACEBOOK PAGE!
PFHH! THE ORIGINAL PILGRIMS DIDN'T HAVE INSTAGRAM, YOU KNOW!
I'M SAVED FROM MY FUNK BY TWO GERMANS SITTING DOWN AT MY TABLE.
HOW ARE THE FEET? ANY BLISTERS?
NO, NONE SO FAR, LUCKILY.
IN WALKS CHRIS, THE AUSTRALIAN FROM THE HOSTEL IN ST. JEAN.

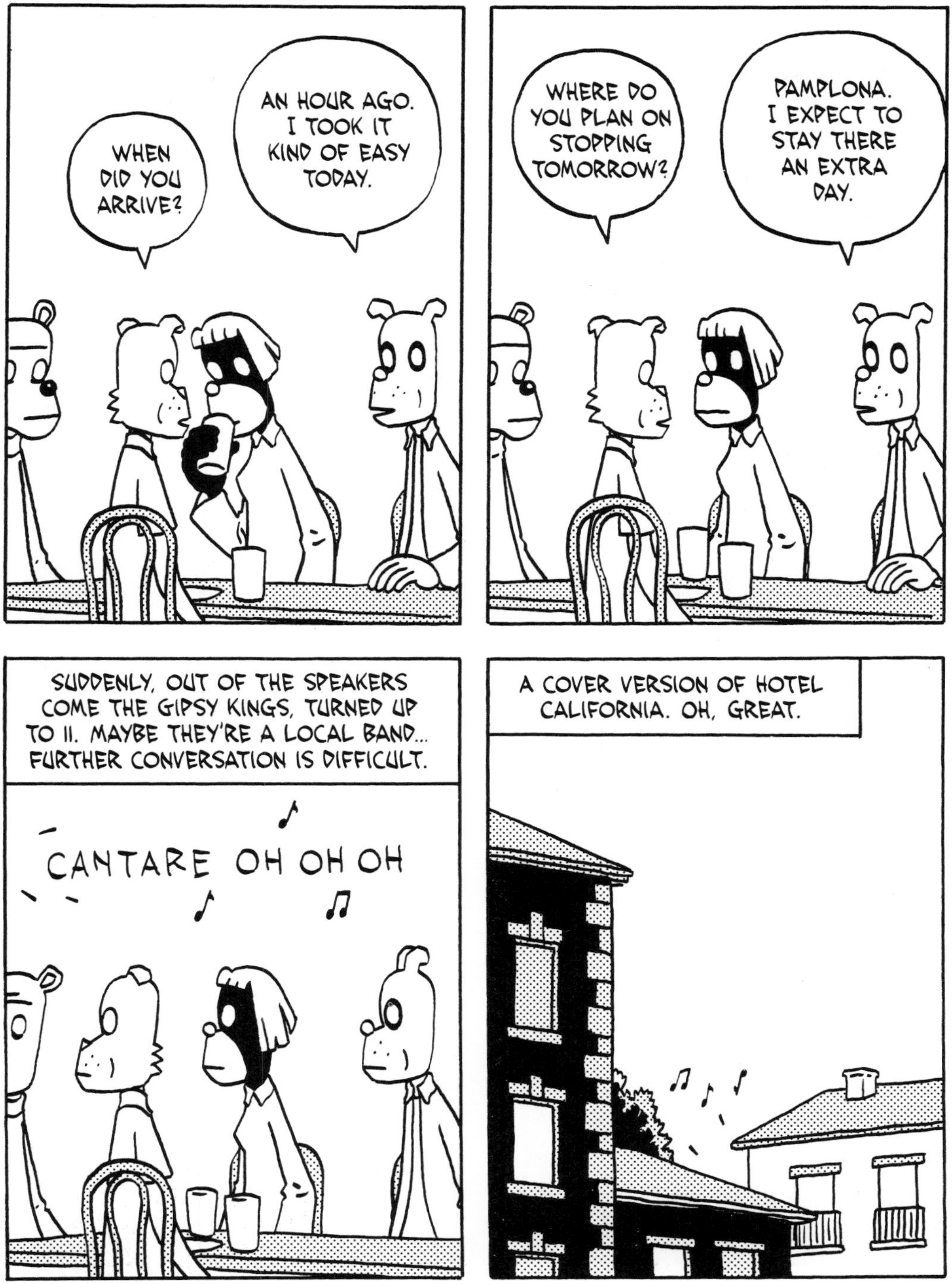
WHEN DID YOU ARRIVE?
AN HOUR AGO. I TOOK IT KIND OF EASY TODAY.
WHERE DO YOU PLAN ON STOPPING TOMORROW?
PAMPLONA. I EXPECT TO STAY THERE AN EXTRA DAY.
SUDDENLY, OUT OF THE SPEAKERS COME THE GIPSY KINGS, TURNED UP TO 11. MAYBE THEY'RE A LOCAL BAND... FURTHER CONVERSATION IS DIFFICULT.
CANTARE OH OH OH
A COVER VERSION OF HOTEL CALIFORNIA. OH, GREAT.

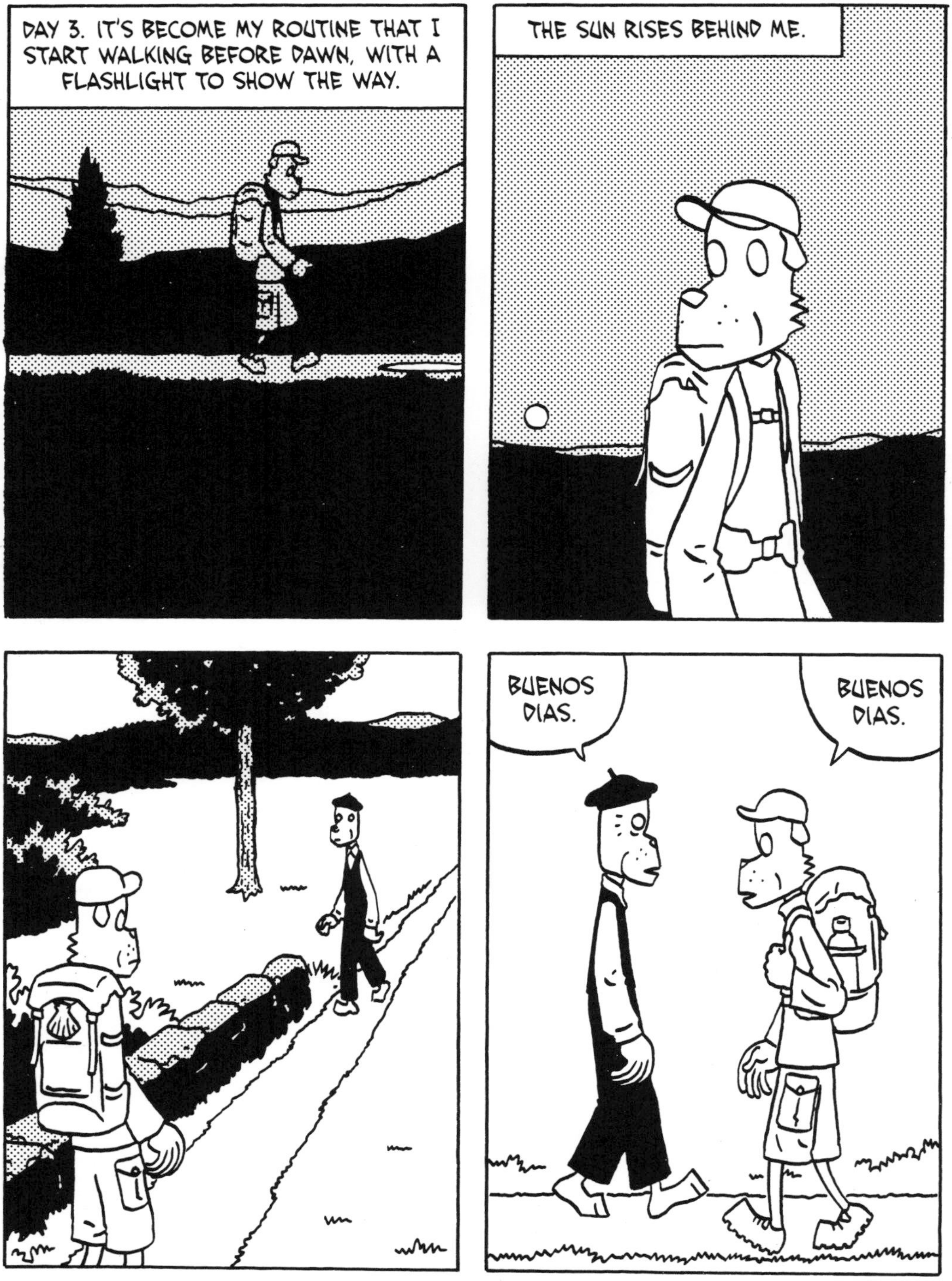
DAY 3. IT'S BECOME MY ROUTINE THAT I START WALKING BEFORE DAWN, WITH A FLASHLIGHT TO SHOW THE WAY.
THE SUN RISES BEHIND ME.
BUENOS DIAS.
BUENOS DIAS.

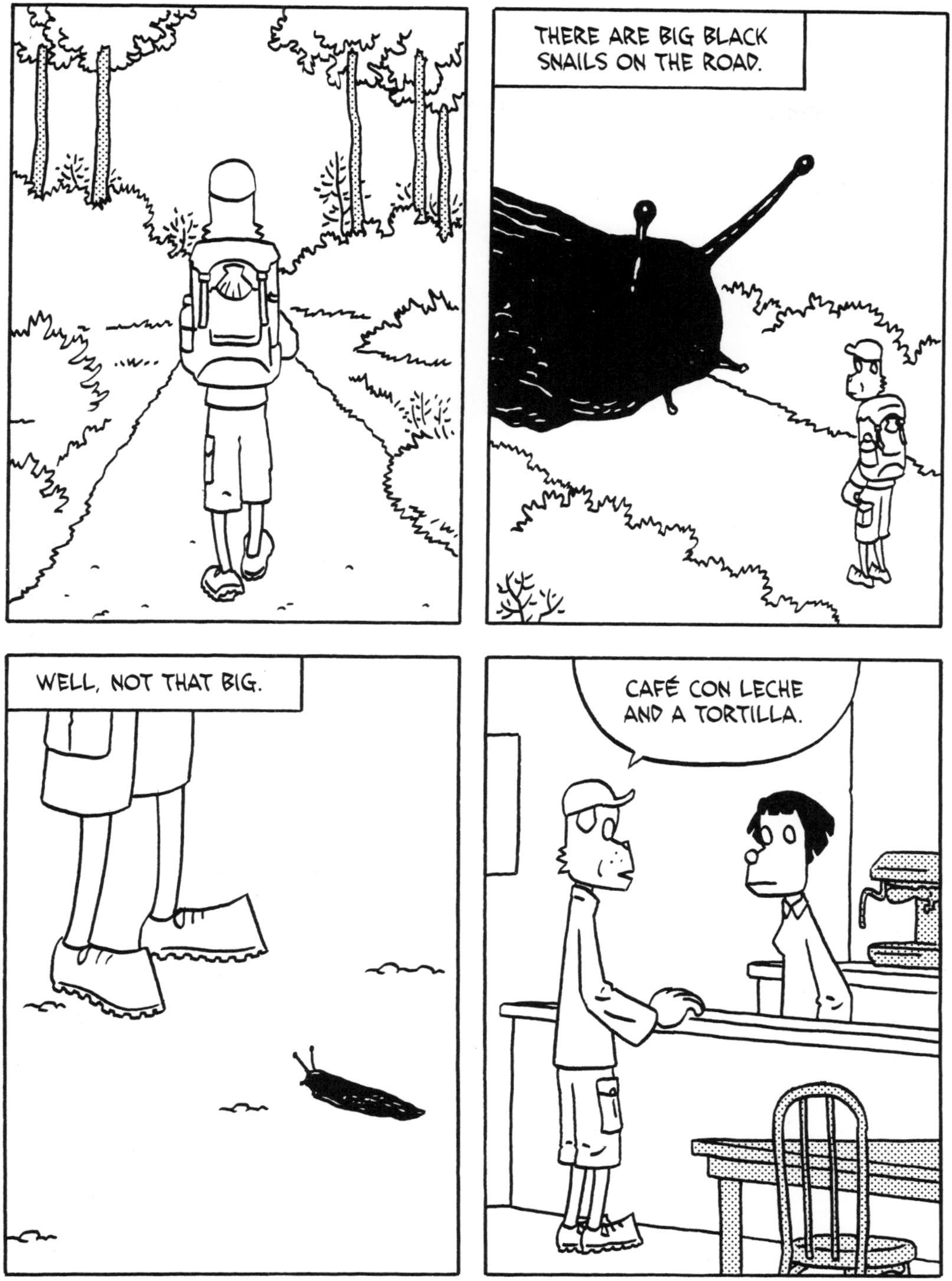
THERE ARE BIG BLACK SNAILS ON THE ROAD.
WELL, NOT THAT BIG.
CAFÉ CON LECHE AND A TORTILLA.

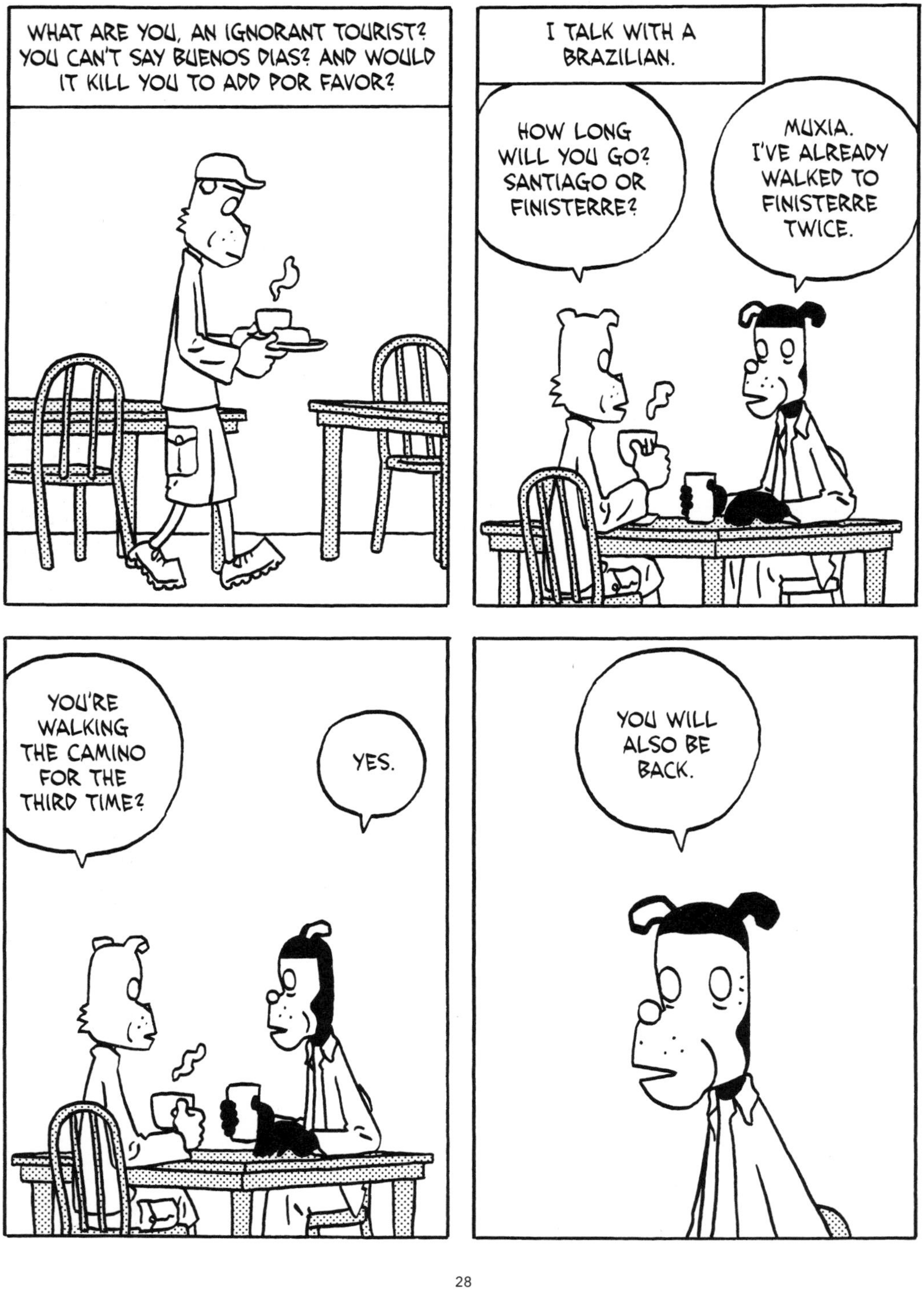
WHAT ARE YOU, AN IGNORANT TOURIST? YOU CAN'T SAY BUENOS DIAS? AND WOULD IT KILL YOU TO ADD POR FAVOR?
I TALK WITH A BRAZILIAN.
HOW LONG WILL YOU GO? SANTIAGO OR FINISTERRE?
MUXIA. I'VE ALREADY WALKED TO FINISTERRE TWICE.
YOU'RE WALKING THE CAMINO FOR THE THIRD TIME?
YES.
YOU WILL ALSO BE BACK.

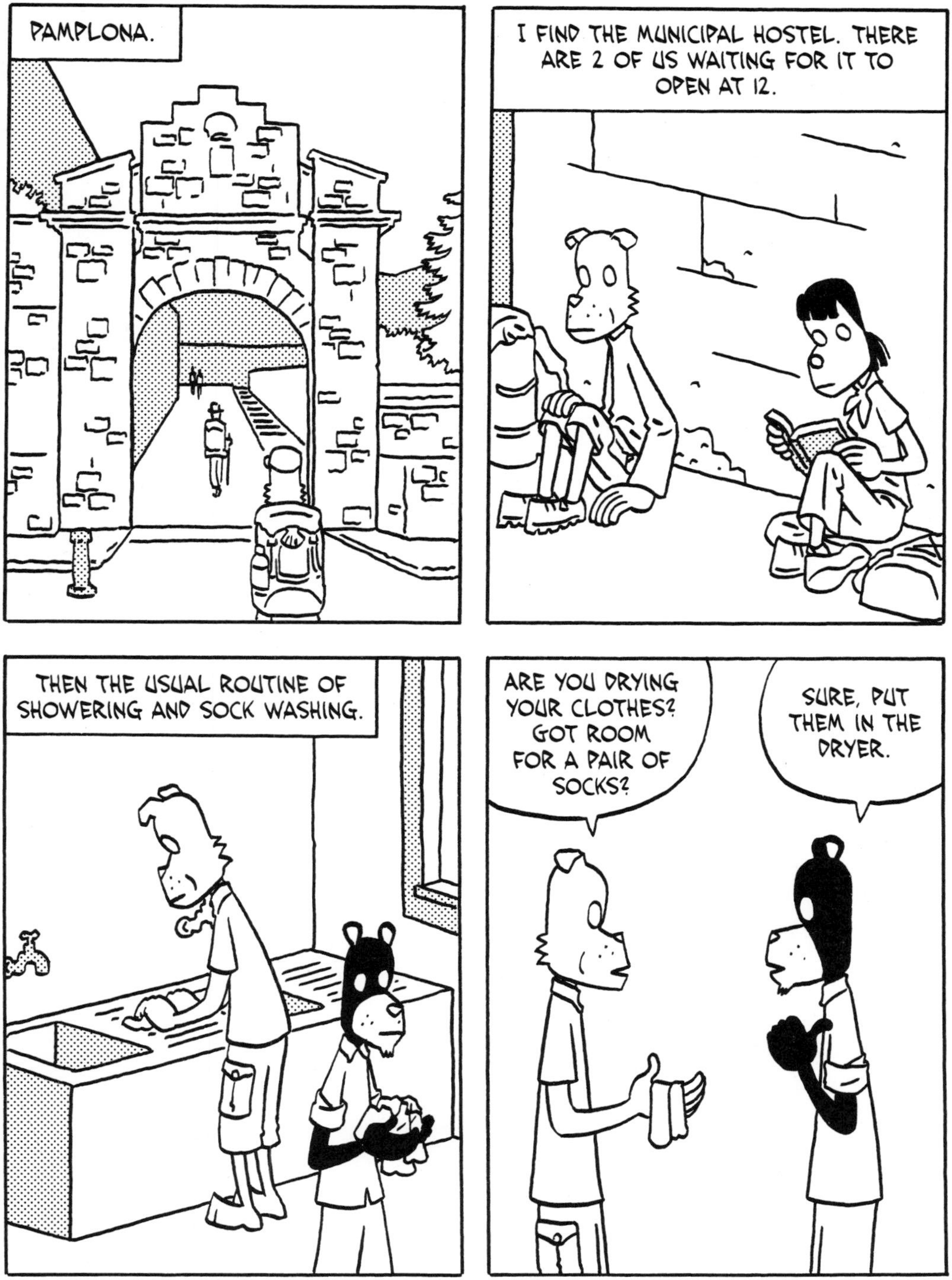
PAMPLONA.
I FIND THE MUNICIPAL HOSTEL. THERE ARE 2 OF US WAITING FOR IT TO OPEN AT 12.
THEN THE USUAL ROUTINE OF SHOWERING AND SOCK WASHING.
ARE YOU DRYING YOUR CLOTHES? GOT ROOM FOR A PAIR OF SOCKS?
SURE, PUT THEM IN THE DRYER.

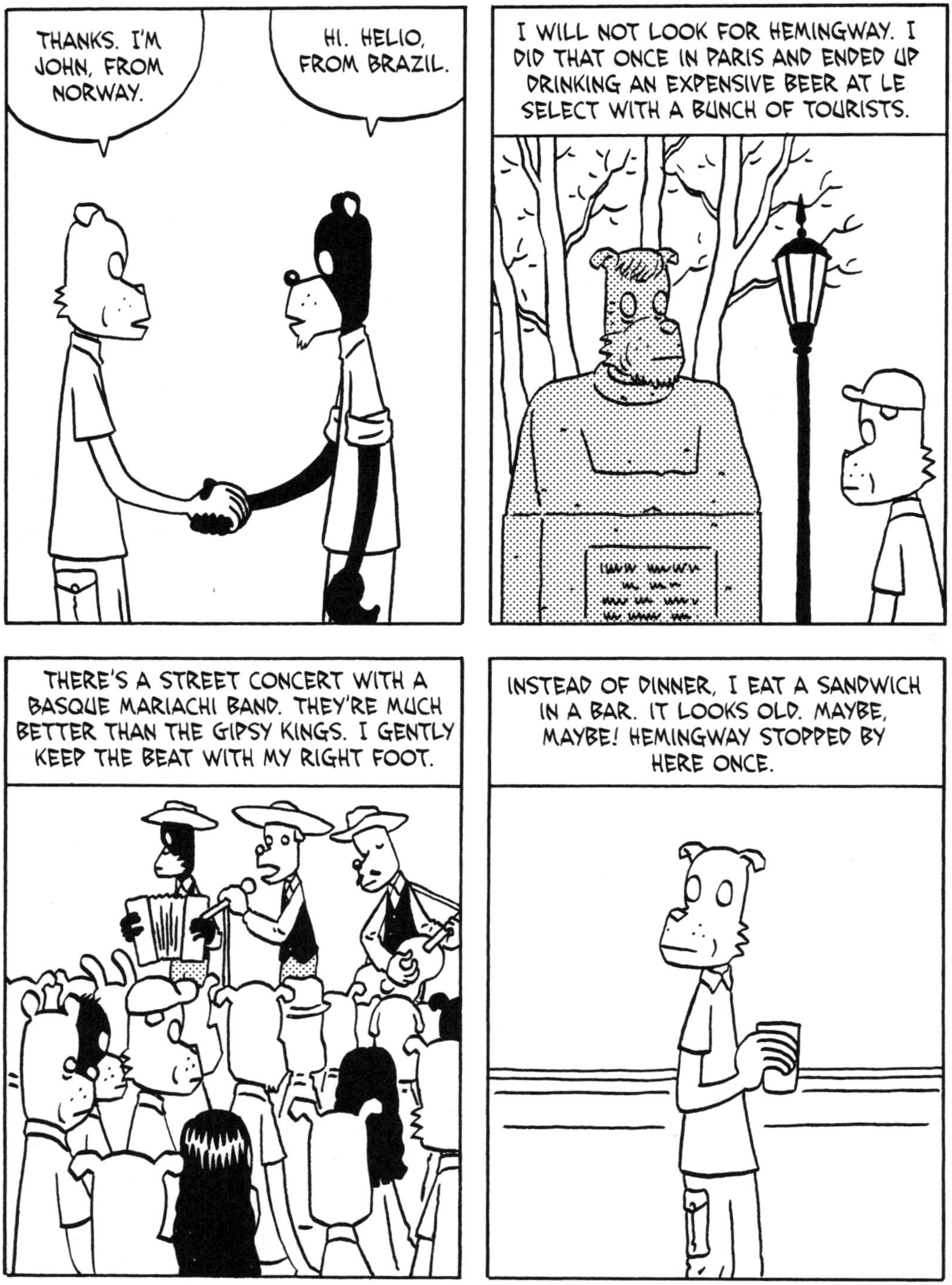
THANKS. I'M JOHN, FROM NORWAY.
HI. HELIO, FROM BRAZIL.
I WILL NOT LOOK FOR HEMINGWAY. I DID THAT ONCE IN PARIS AND ENDED UP DRINKING AN EXPENSIVE BEER AT LE SELECT WITH A BUNCH OF TOURISTS.
THERE'S A STREET CONCERT WITH A BASQUE MARIACHI BAND. THEY'RE MUCH BETTER THAN THE GIPSY KINGS. I GENTLY KEEP THE BEAT WITH MY RIGHT FOOT.
INSTEAD OF DINNER, I EAT A SANDWICH IN A BAR. IT LOOKS OLD. MAYBE, MAYBE! HEMINGWAY STOPPED BY HERE ONCE.

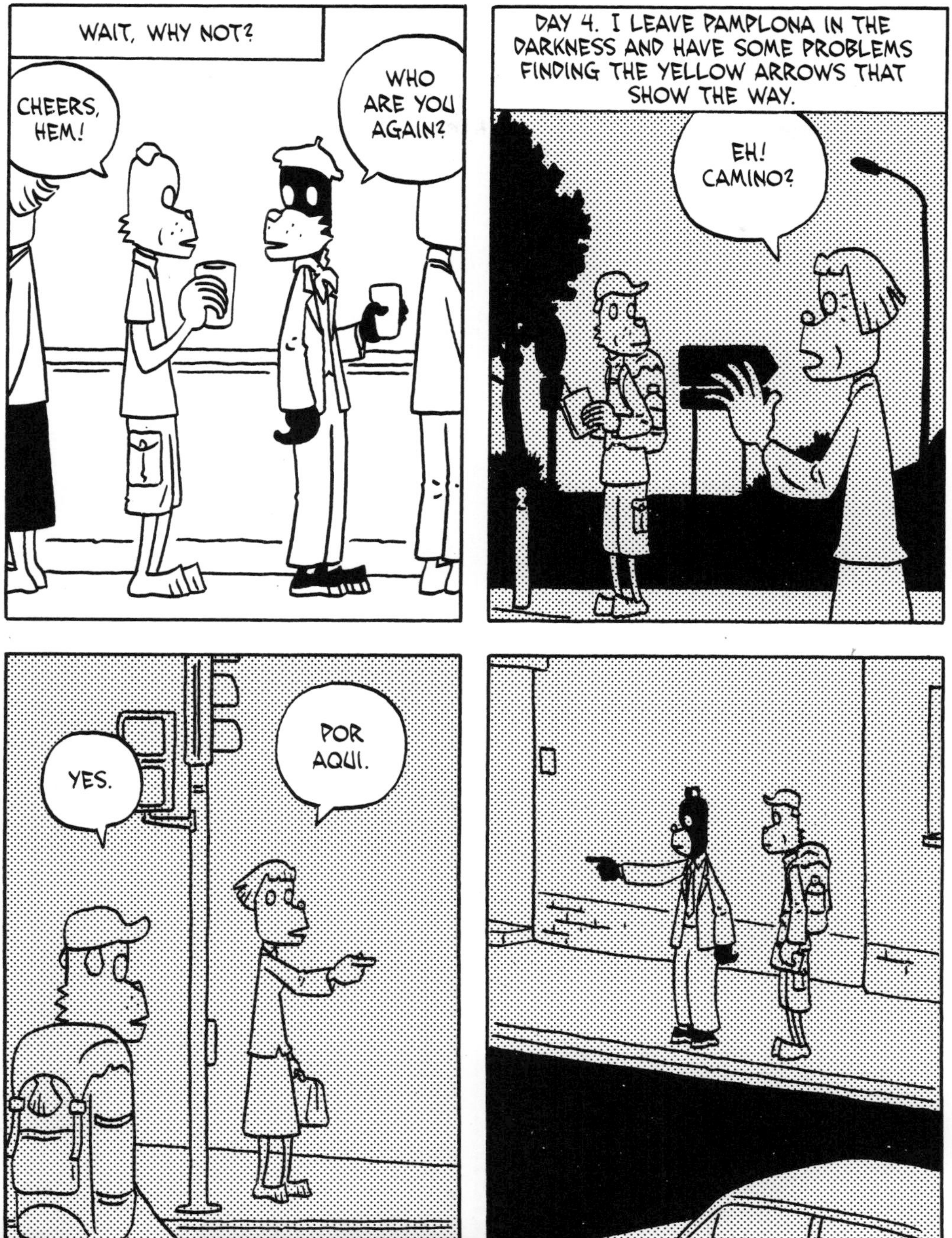
WAIT, WHY NOT?
CHEERS, HEM!
WHO ARE YOU AGAIN?
DAY 4. I LEAVE PAMPLONA IN THE DARKNESS AND HAVE SOME PROBLEMS FINDING THE YELLOW ARROWS THAT SHOW THE WAY.
EH! CAMINO?
YES.
POR AQUI.

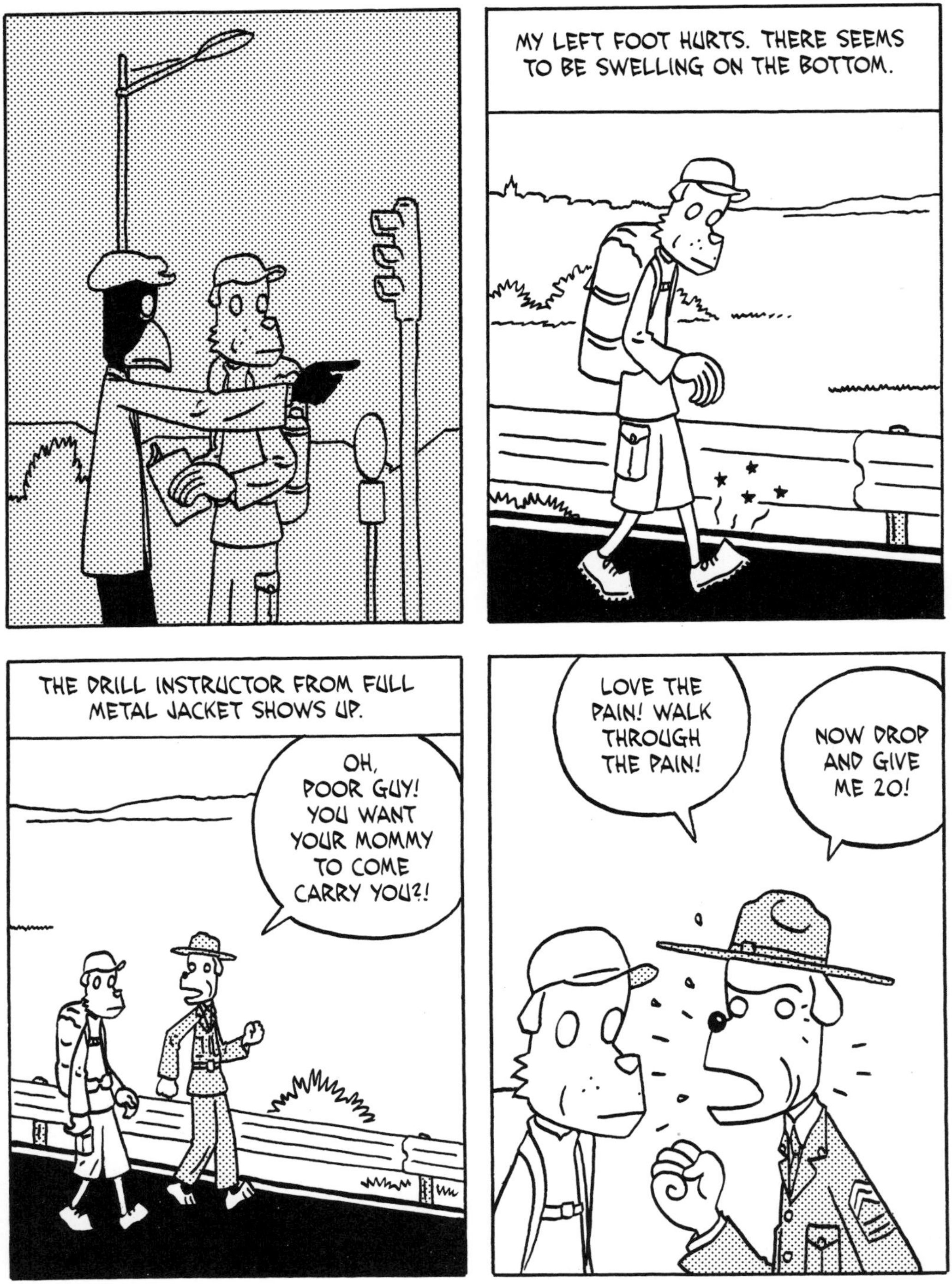
MY LEFT FOOT HURTS. THERE SEEMS TO BE SWELLING ON THE BOTTOM.
THE DRILL INSTRUCTOR FROM FULL METAL JACKET SHOWS UP.
OH, POOR GUY! YOU WANT YOUR MOMMY TO COME CARRY YOU?!
LOVE THE PAIN! WALK THROUGH THE PAIN!
NOW DROP AND GIVE ME 20!

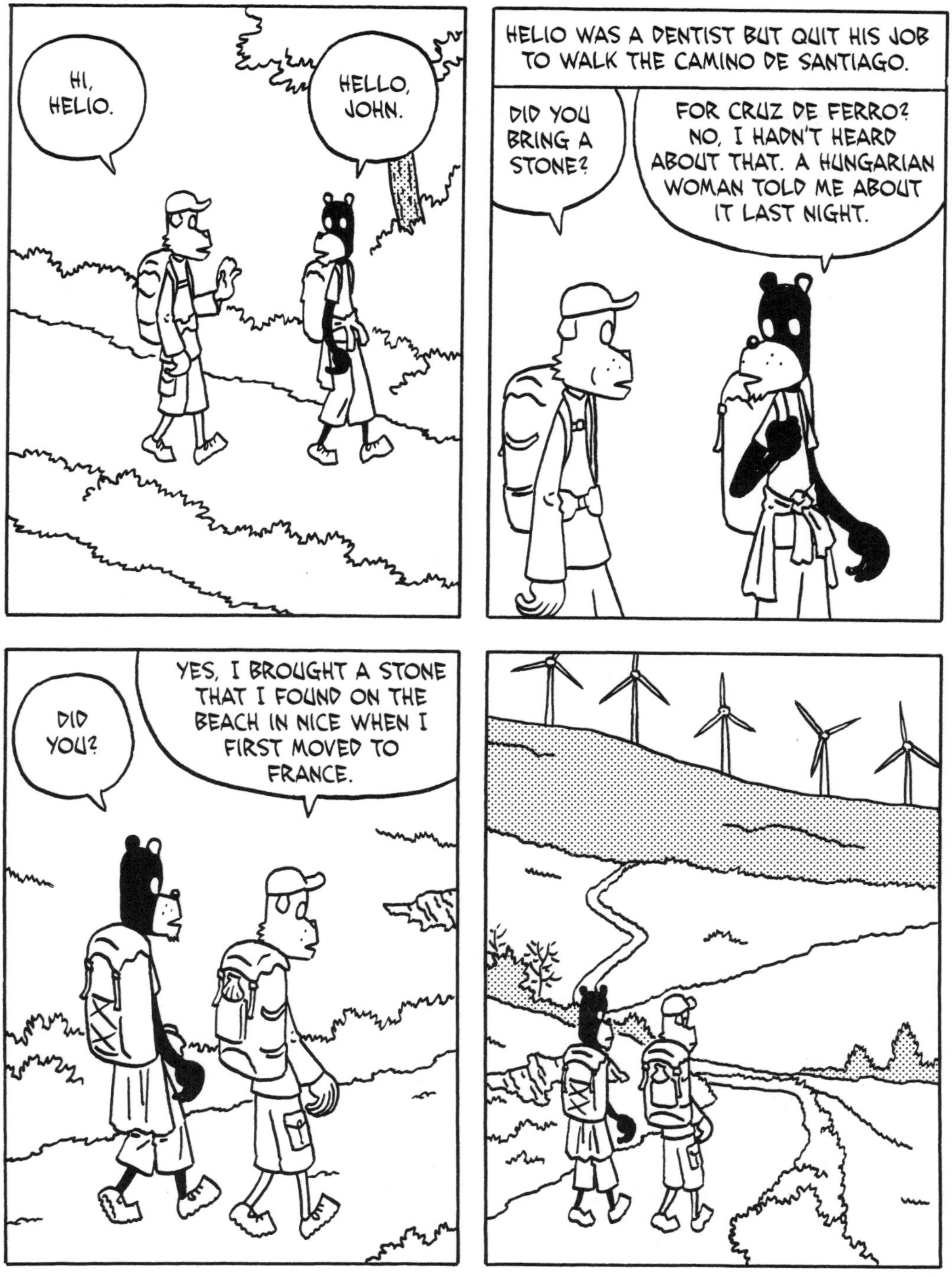

HI, HELIO.
HELLO, JOHN.
HELIO WAS A DENTIST BUT QUIT HIS JOB TO WALK THE CAMINO DE SANTIAGO.
DID YOU BRING A STONE?
FOR CRUZ DE FERRO? NO, I HADN'T HEARD ABOUT THAT. A HUNGARIAN WOMAN TOLD ME ABOUT IT LAST NIGHT.
DID YOU?
YES, I BROUGHT A STONE THAT I FOUND ON THE BEACH IN NICE WHEN I FIRST MOVED TO FRANCE.

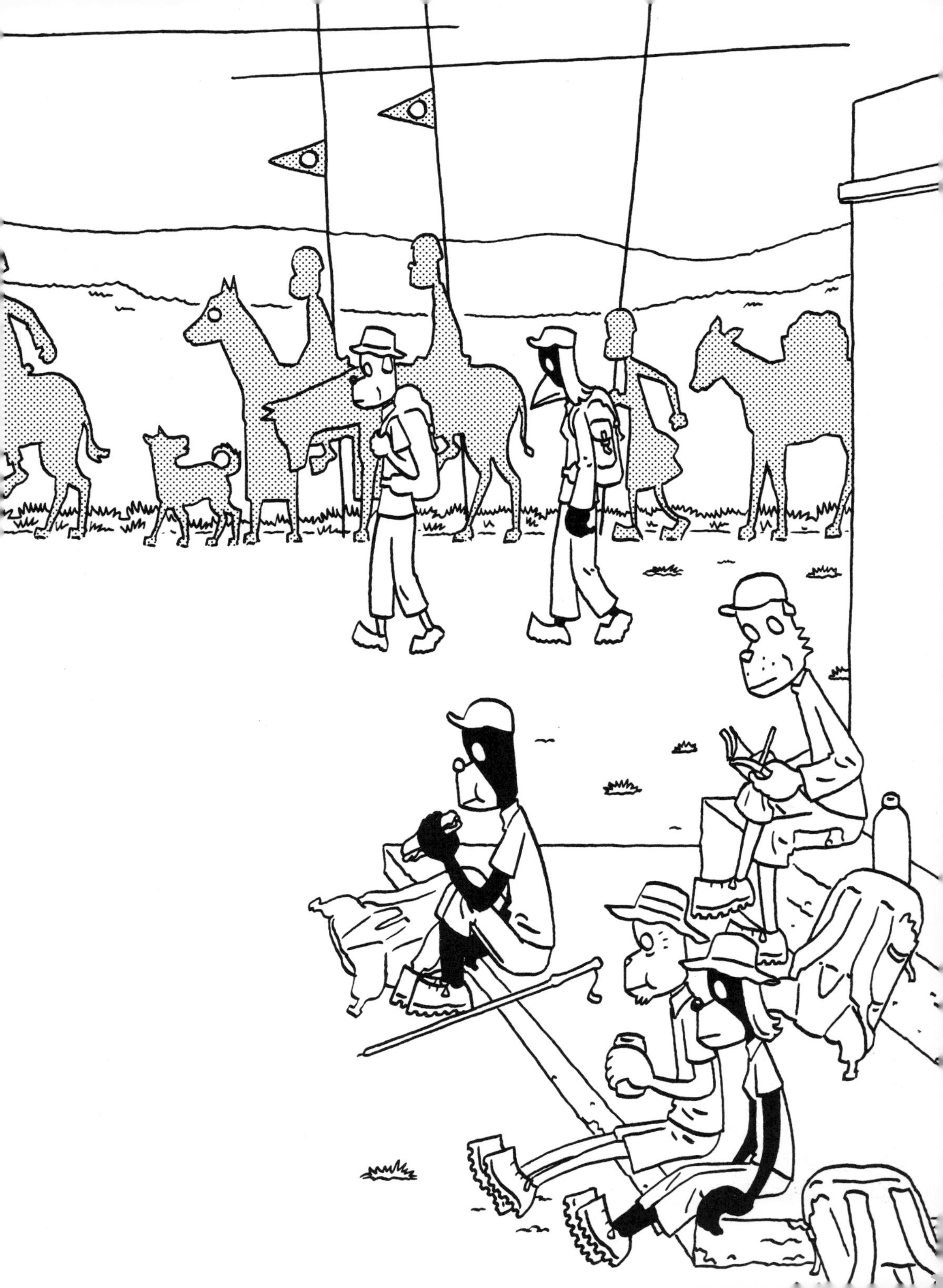

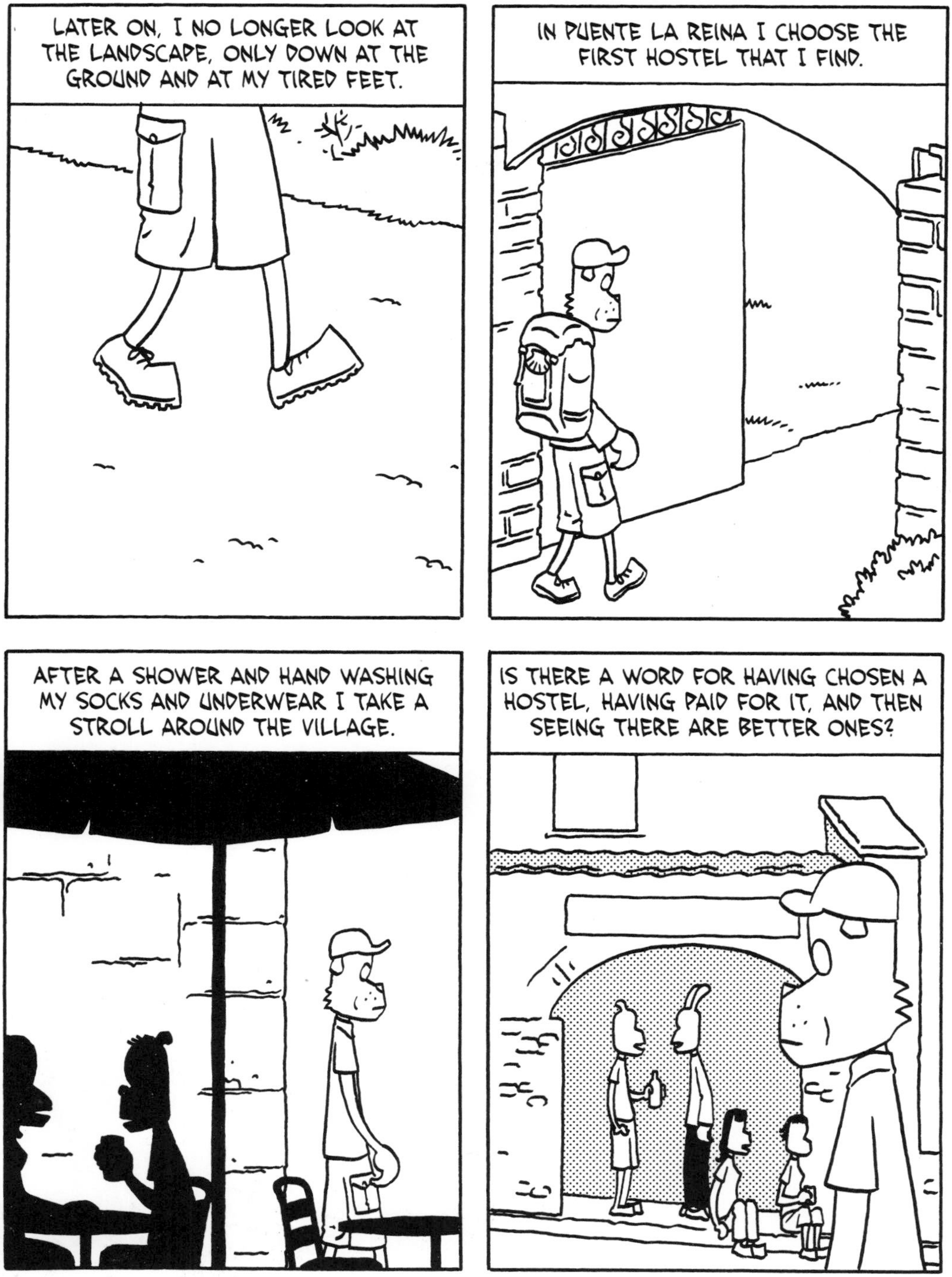
LATER ON, I NO LONGER LOOK AT THE LANDSCAPE, ONLY DOWN AT THE GROUND AND AT MY TIRED FEET.
IN PUENTE LA REINA I CHOOSE THE FIRST HOSTEL THAT I FIND.
AFTER A SHOWER AND HAND WASHING MY SOCKS AND UNDERWEAR I TAKE A STROLL AROUND THE VILLAGE.
IS THERE A WORD FOR HAVING CHOSEN A HOSTEL, HAVING PAID FOR IT, AND THEN SEEING THERE ARE BETTER ONES?

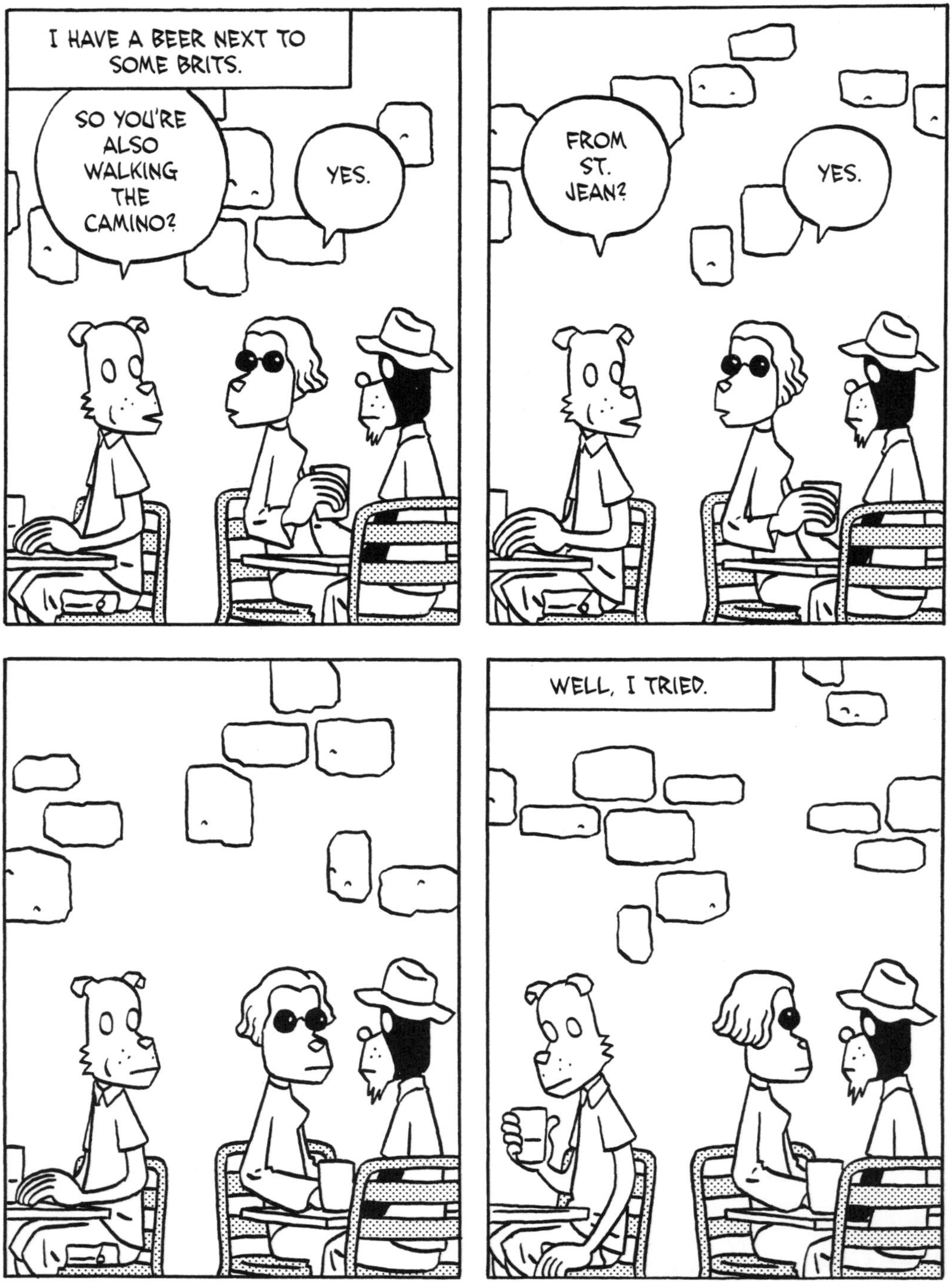
I HAVE A BEER NEXT TO SOME BRITS.
SO YOU'RE ALSO WALKING THE CAMINO?
YES.
FROM ST. JEAN?
YES.
WELL, I TRIED.

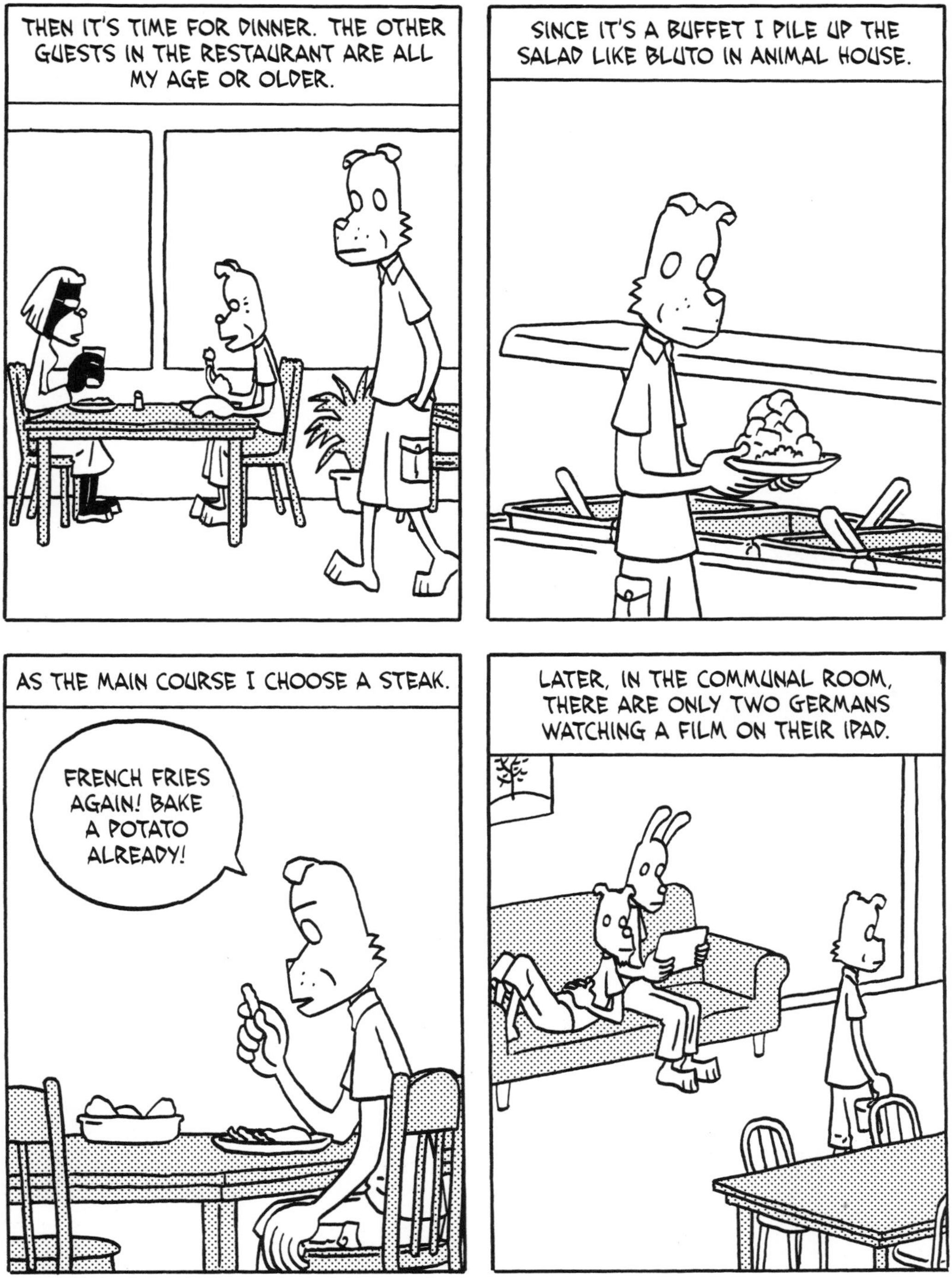
THEN IT'S TIME FOR DINNER. THE OTHER GUESTS IN THE RESTAURANT ARE ALL MY AGE OR OLDER.
SINCE IT'S A BUFFET I PILE UP THE SALAD LIKE BLUTO IN ANIMAL HOUSE.
AS THE MAIN COURSE I CHOOSE A STEAK.
FRENCH FRIES AGAIN! BAKE A POTATO ALREADY!
LATER, IN THE COMMUNAL ROOM, THERE ARE ONLY TWO GERMANS WATCHING A FILM ON THEIR IPAD.

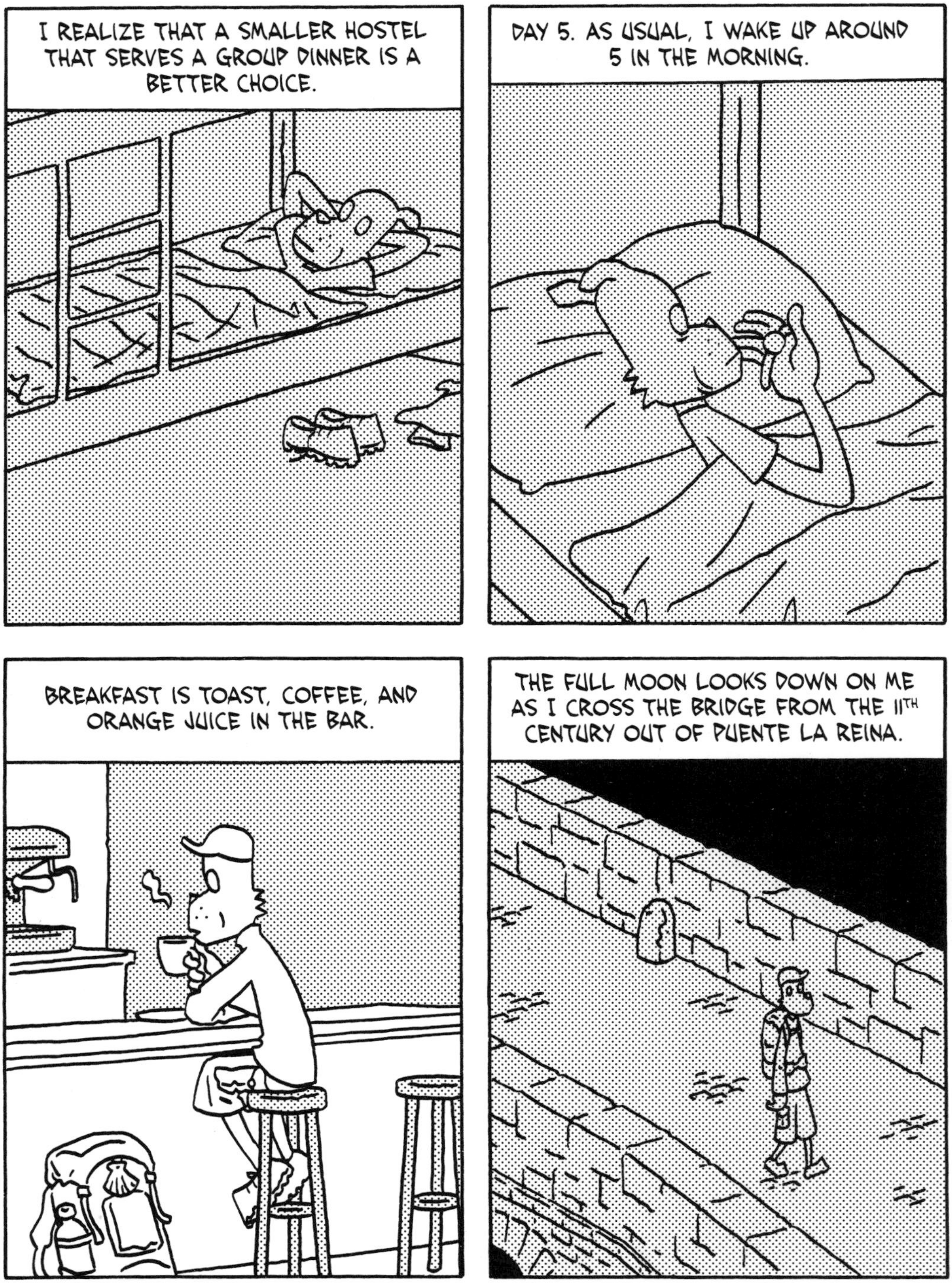
I REALIZE THAT A SMALLER HOSTEL THAT SERVES A GROUP DINNER IS A BETTER CHOICE.
DAY 5. AS USUAL, I WAKE UP AROUND 5 IN THE MORNING.
BREAKFAST IS TOAST, COFFEE, AND ORANGE JUICE IN THE BAR.
THE FULL MOON LOOKS DOWN ON ME AS I CROSS THE BRIDGE FROM THE 11TH CENTURY OUT OF PUENTE LA REINA.

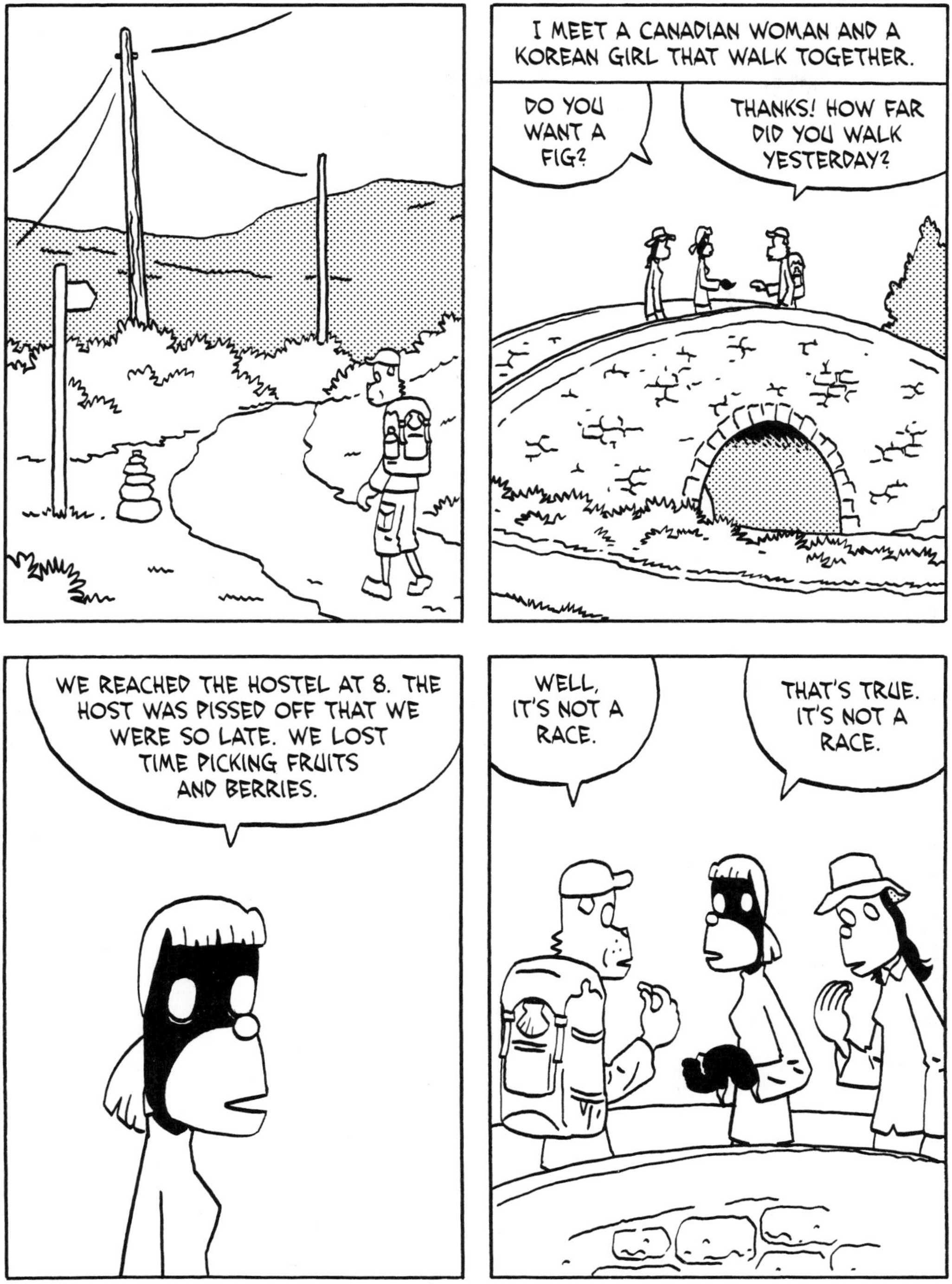
I MEET A CANADIAN WOMAN AND A KOREAN GIRL THAT WALK TOGETHER.
DO YOU WANT A FIG?
THANKS! HOW FAR DID YOU WALK YESTERDAY?
WE REACHED THE HOSTEL AT 8. THE HOST WAS PISSED OFF THAT WE WERE SO LATE. WE LOST TIME PICKING FRUITS AND BERRIES.
WELL, IT'S NOT A RACE.
THAT'S TRUE. IT'S NOT A RACE.

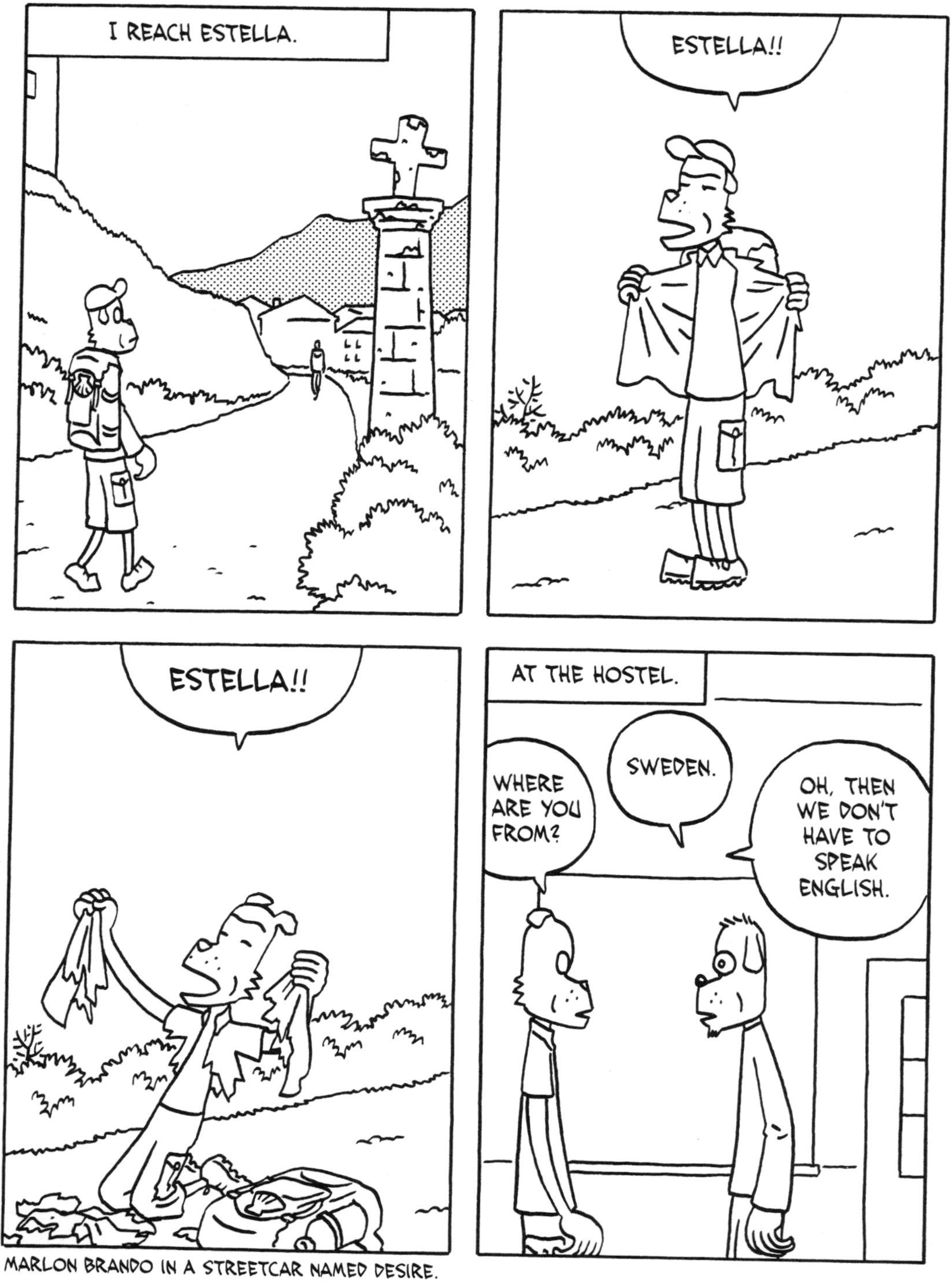
I REACH ESTELLA.
ESTELLA!!
ESTELLA!!
AT THE HOSTEL.
WHERE ARE YOU FROM?
SWEDEN.
OH, THEN WE DON'T HAVE TO SPEAK ENGLISH.

MARLON BRANDO IN A STREETCAR NAMED DESIRE.

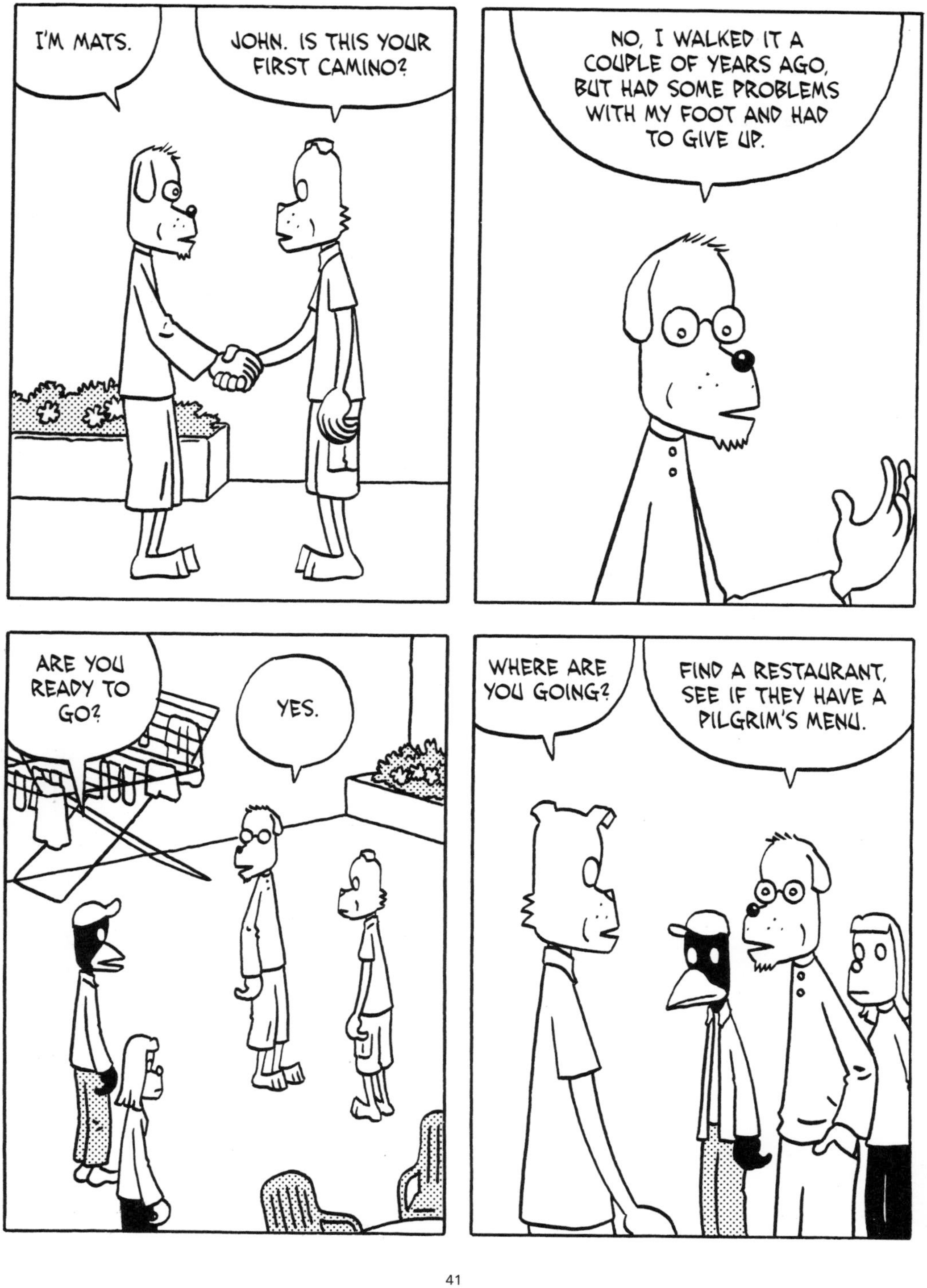
I'M MATS.
JOHN. IS THIS YOUR FIRST CAMINO?
NO, I WALKED IT A COUPLE OF YEARS AGO, BUT HAD SOME PROBLEMS WITH MY FOOT AND HAD TO GIVE UP.
ARE YOU READY TO GO?
YES.
WHERE ARE YOU GOING?
FIND A RESTAURANT, SEE IF THEY HAVE A PILGRIM'S MENU.

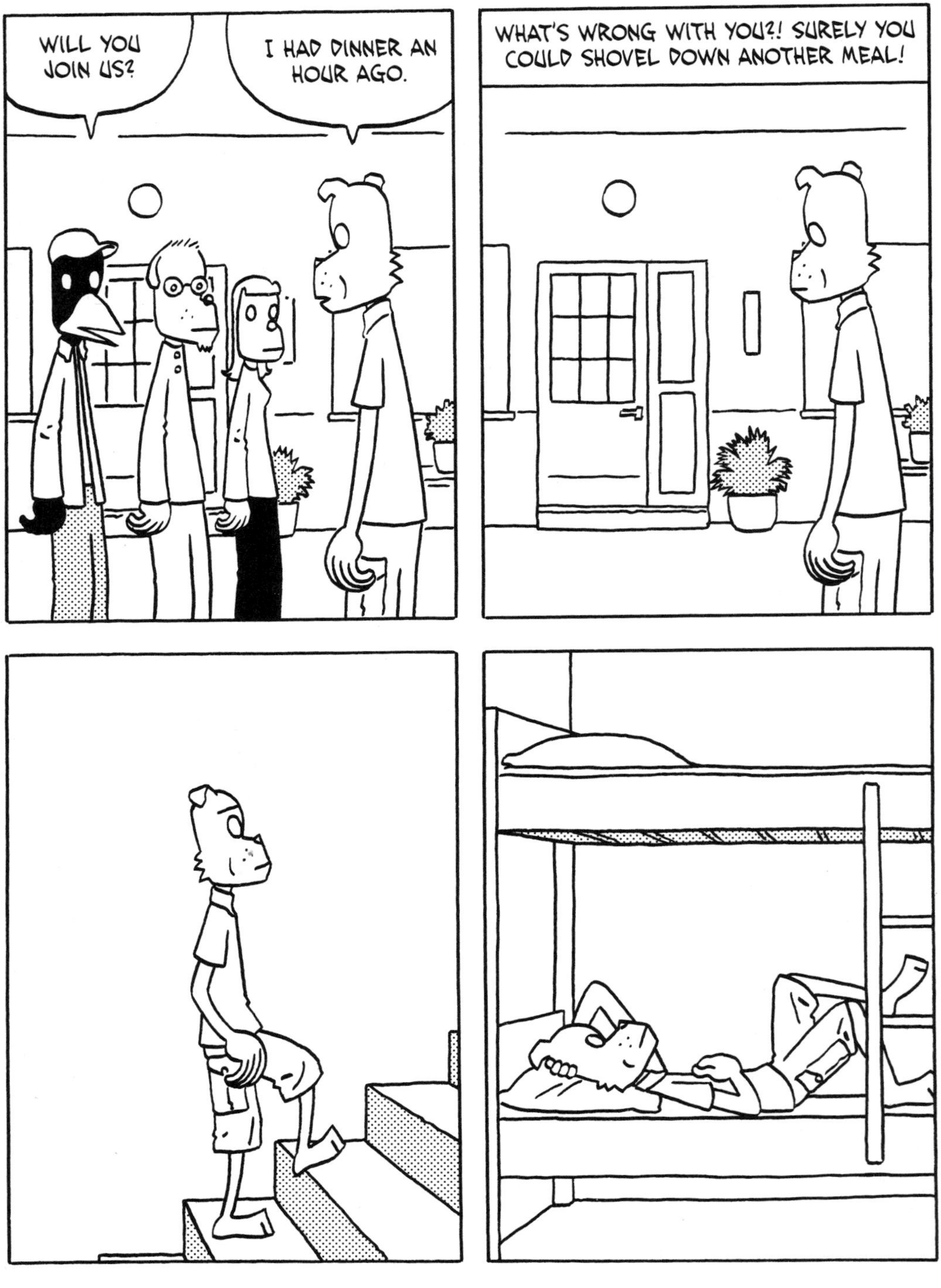
WILL YOU JOIN US?
I HAD DINNER AN HOUR AGO.
WHAT'S WRONG WITH YOU?! SURELY YOU COULD SHOVEL DOWN ANOTHER MEAL!

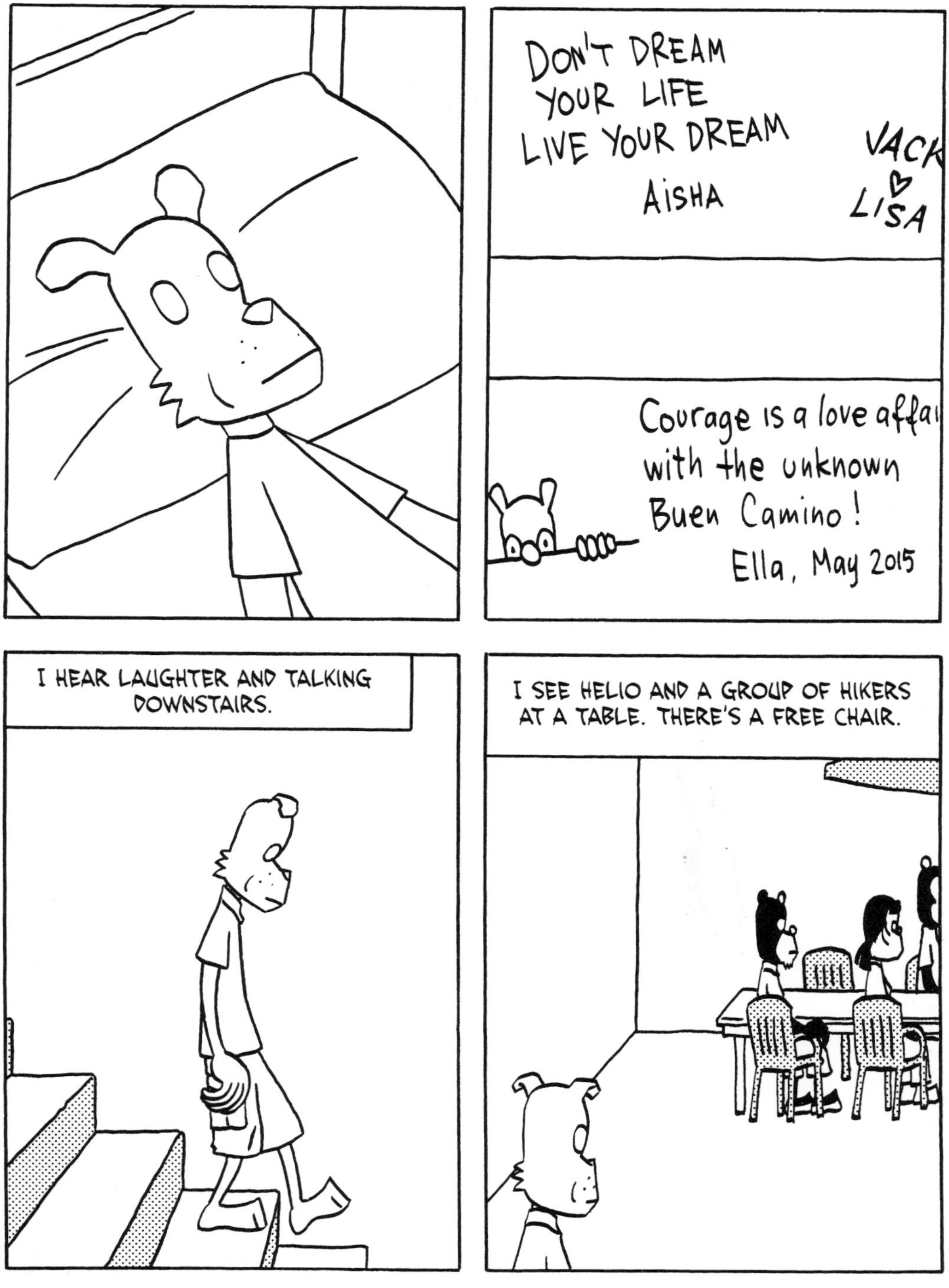

DON'T DREAM
YOUR LIFE
LIVE YOUR DREAM
AISHA
VACK ♡ LISA
Courage is a love affai
with the unknown
Buen Camino!
Ella, May 2015
I HEAR LAUGHTER AND TALKING DOWNSTAIRS.
I SEE HELIO AND A GROUP OF HIKERS AT A TABLE. THERE'S A FREE CHAIR.

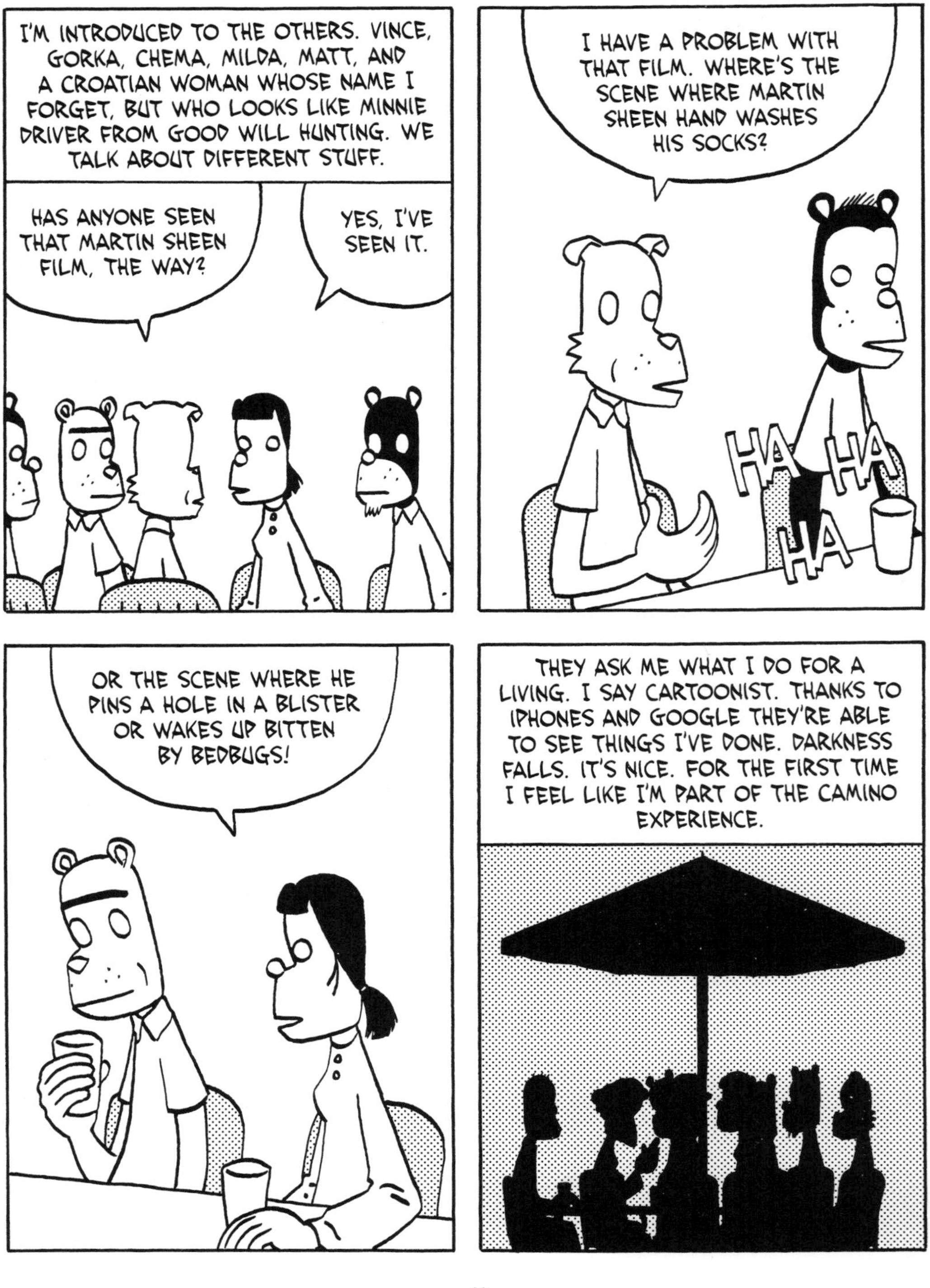
I'M INTRODUCED TO THE OTHERS. VINCE, GORKA, CHEMA, MILDA, MATT, AND A CROATIAN WOMAN WHOSE NAME I FORGET, BUT WHO LOOKS LIKE MINNIE DRIVER FROM GOOD WILL HUNTING. WE TALK ABOUT DIFFERENT STUFF.
HAS ANYONE SEEN THAT MARTIN SHEEN FILM, THE WAY?
YES, I'VE SEEN IT.
I HAVE A PROBLEM WITH THAT FILM. WHERE'S THE SCENE WHERE MARTIN SHEEN HAND WASHES HIS SOCKS?
HA HA HA
OR THE SCENE WHERE HE PINS A HOLE IN A BLISTER OR WAKES UP BITTEN BY BEDBUGS!
THEY ASK ME WHAT I DO FOR A LIVING. I SAY CARTOONIST. THANKS TO IPHONES AND GOOGLE THEY'RE ABLE TO SEE THINGS I'VE DONE. DARKNESS FALLS. IT'S NICE. FOR THE FIRST TIME I FEEL LIKE I'M PART OF THE CAMINO EXPERIENCE.

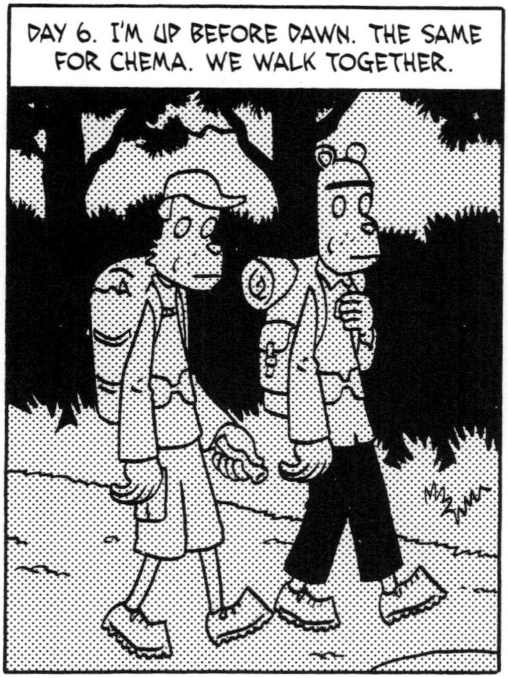
DAY 6. I'M UP BEFORE DAWN. THE SAME FOR CHEMA. WE WALK TOGETHER.

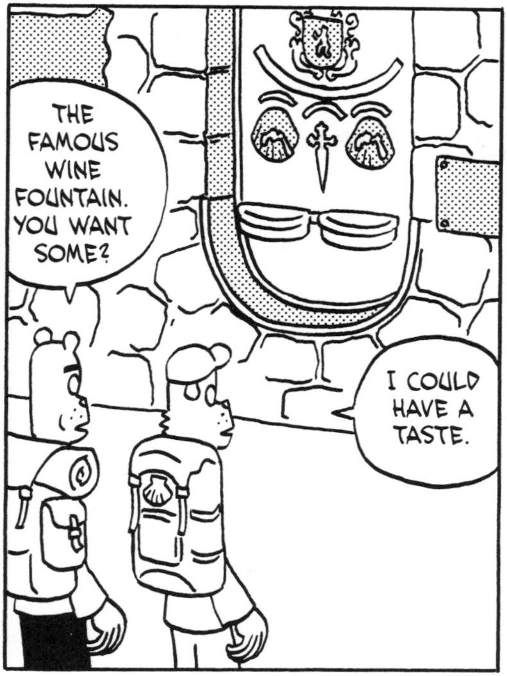
THE FAMOUS WINE FOUNTAIN. YOU WANT SOME?
I COULD HAVE A TASTE.

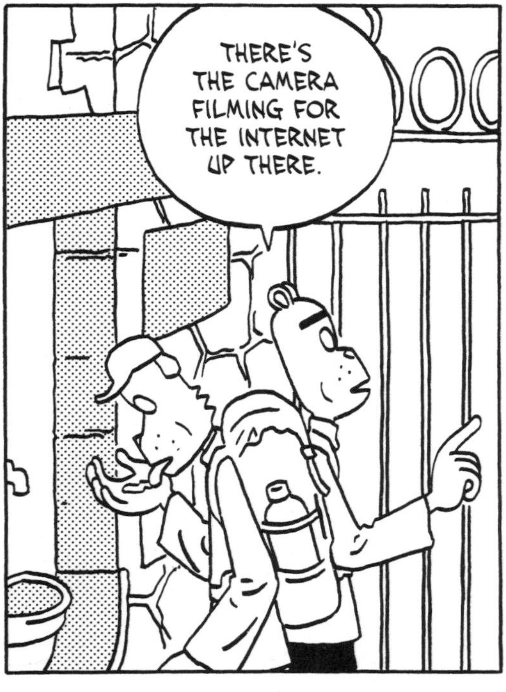
THERE'S THE CAMERA FILMING FOR THE INTERNET UP THERE.

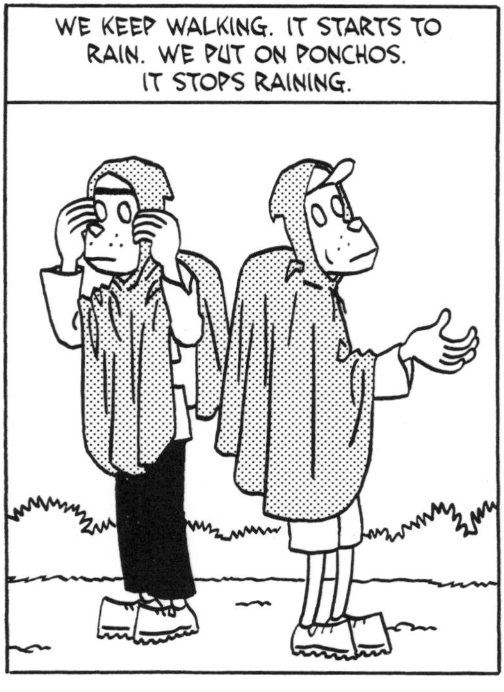
WE KEEP WALKING. IT STARTS TO RAIN. WE PUT ON PONCHOS. IT STOPS RAINING.

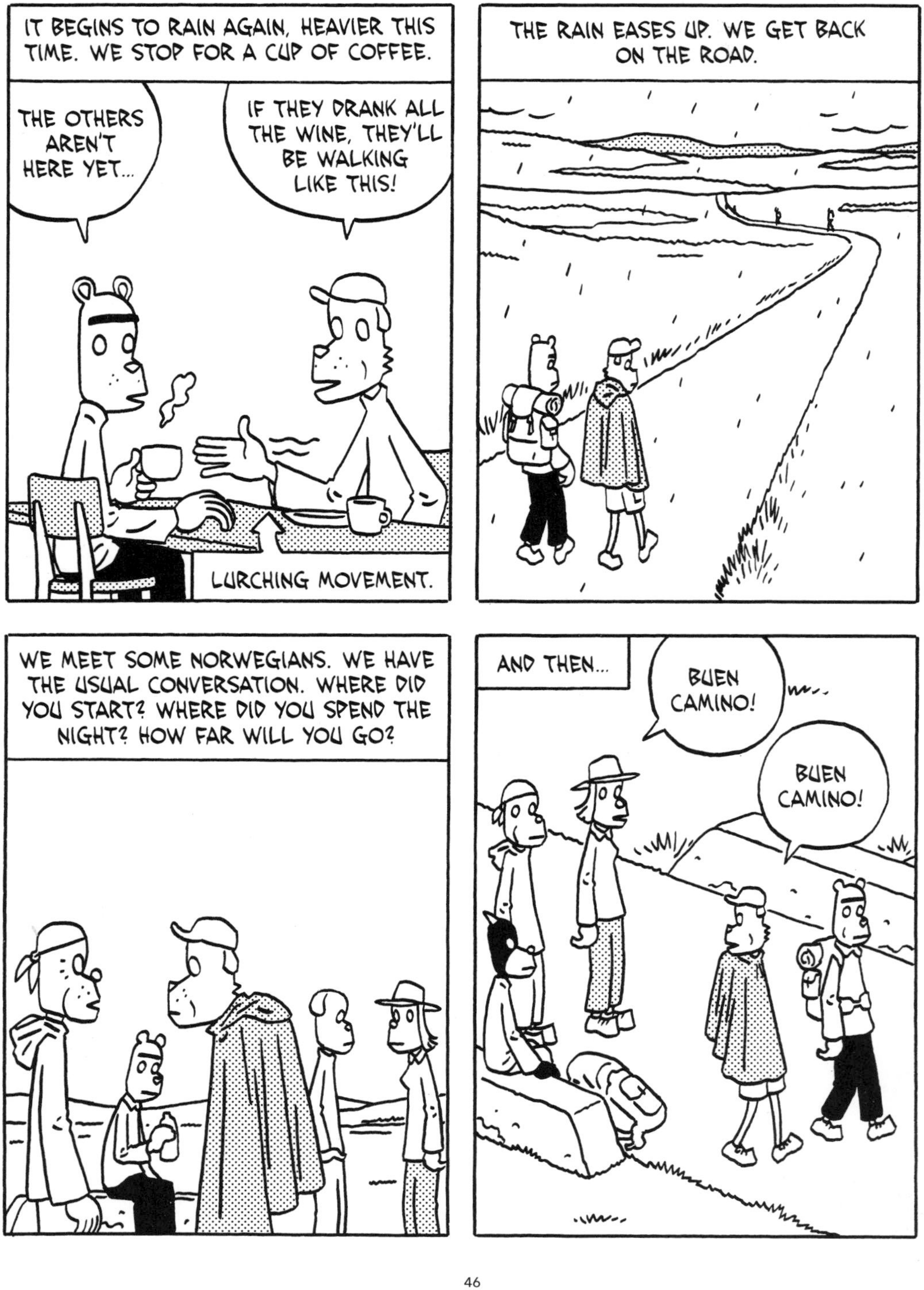
IT BEGINS TO RAIN AGAIN, HEAVIER THIS TIME. WE STOP FOR A CUP OF COFFEE.
THE OTHERS AREN'T HERE YET...
IF THEY DRANK ALL THE WINE, THEY'LL BE WALKING LIKE THIS!
LURCHING MOVEMENT.
THE RAIN EASES UP. WE GET BACK ON THE ROAD.
WE MEET SOME NORWEGIANS. WE HAVE THE USUAL CONVERSATION. WHERE DID YOU START? WHERE DID YOU SPEND THE NIGHT? HOW FAR WILL YOU GO?
AND THEN...
BUEN CAMINO!
BUEN CAMINO!

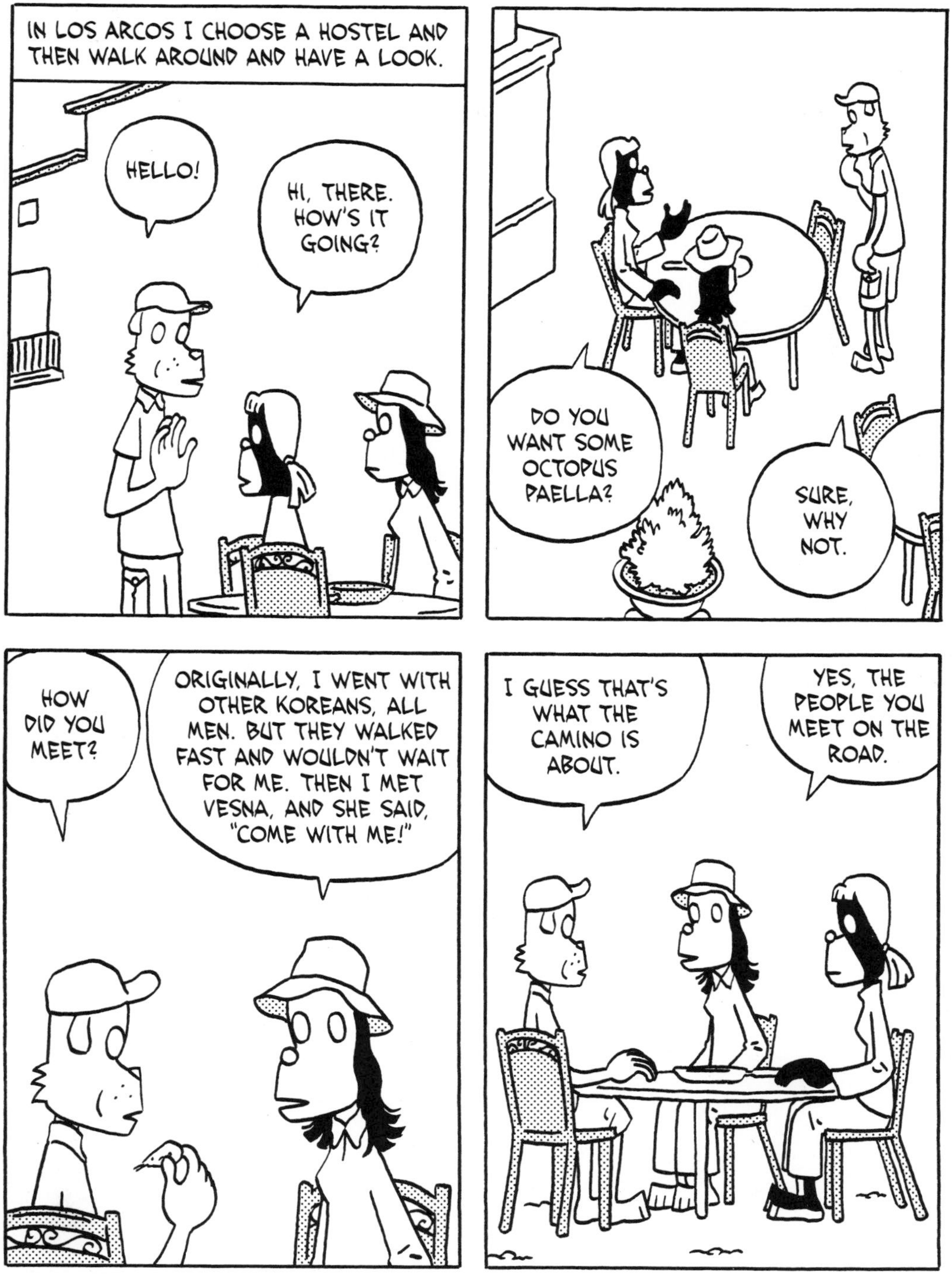
IN LOS ARCOS I CHOOSE A HOSTEL AND THEN WALK AROUND AND HAVE A LOOK.
HELLO!
HI, THERE. HOW'S IT GOING?
DO YOU WANT SOME OCTOPUS PAELLA?
SURE, WHY NOT.
HOW DID YOU MEET?
ORIGINALLY, I WENT WITH OTHER KOREANS, ALL MEN. BUT THEY WALKED FAST AND WOULDN'T WAIT FOR ME. THEN I MET VESNA, AND SHE SAID, "COME WITH ME!"
I GUESS THAT'S WHAT THE CAMINO IS ABOUT.
YES, THE PEOPLE YOU MEET ON THE ROAD.

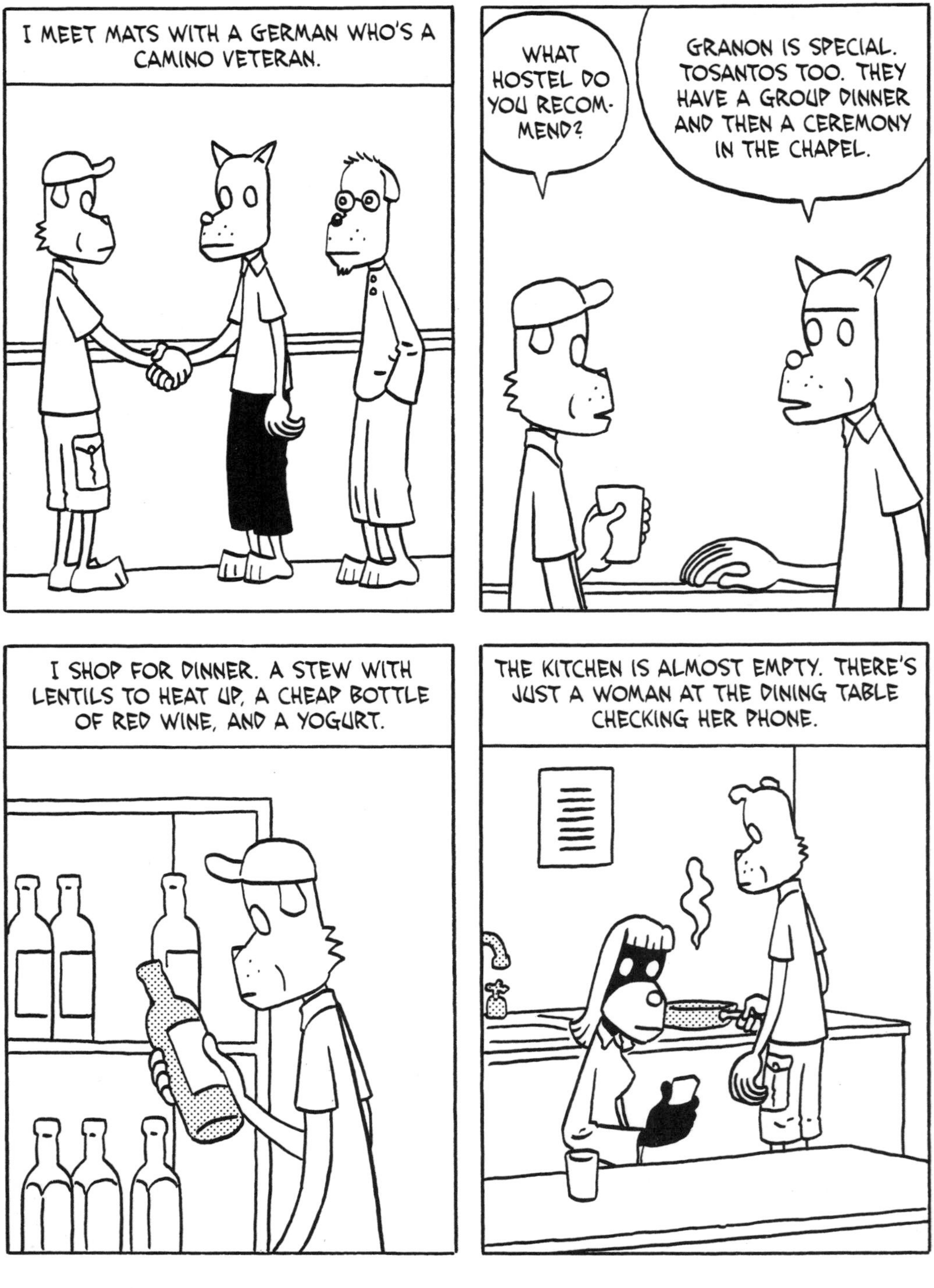
I MEET MATS WITH A GERMAN WHO'S A CAMINO VETERAN.
WHAT HOSTEL DO YOU RECOMMEND?
GRANON IS SPECIAL. TOSANTOS TOO. THEY HAVE A GROUP DINNER AND THEN A CEREMONY IN THE CHAPEL.
I SHOP FOR DINNER. A STEW WITH LENTILS TO HEAT UP, A CHEAP BOTTLE OF RED WINE, AND A YOGURT.
THE KITCHEN IS ALMOST EMPTY. THERE'S JUST A WOMAN AT THE DINING TABLE CHECKING HER PHONE.

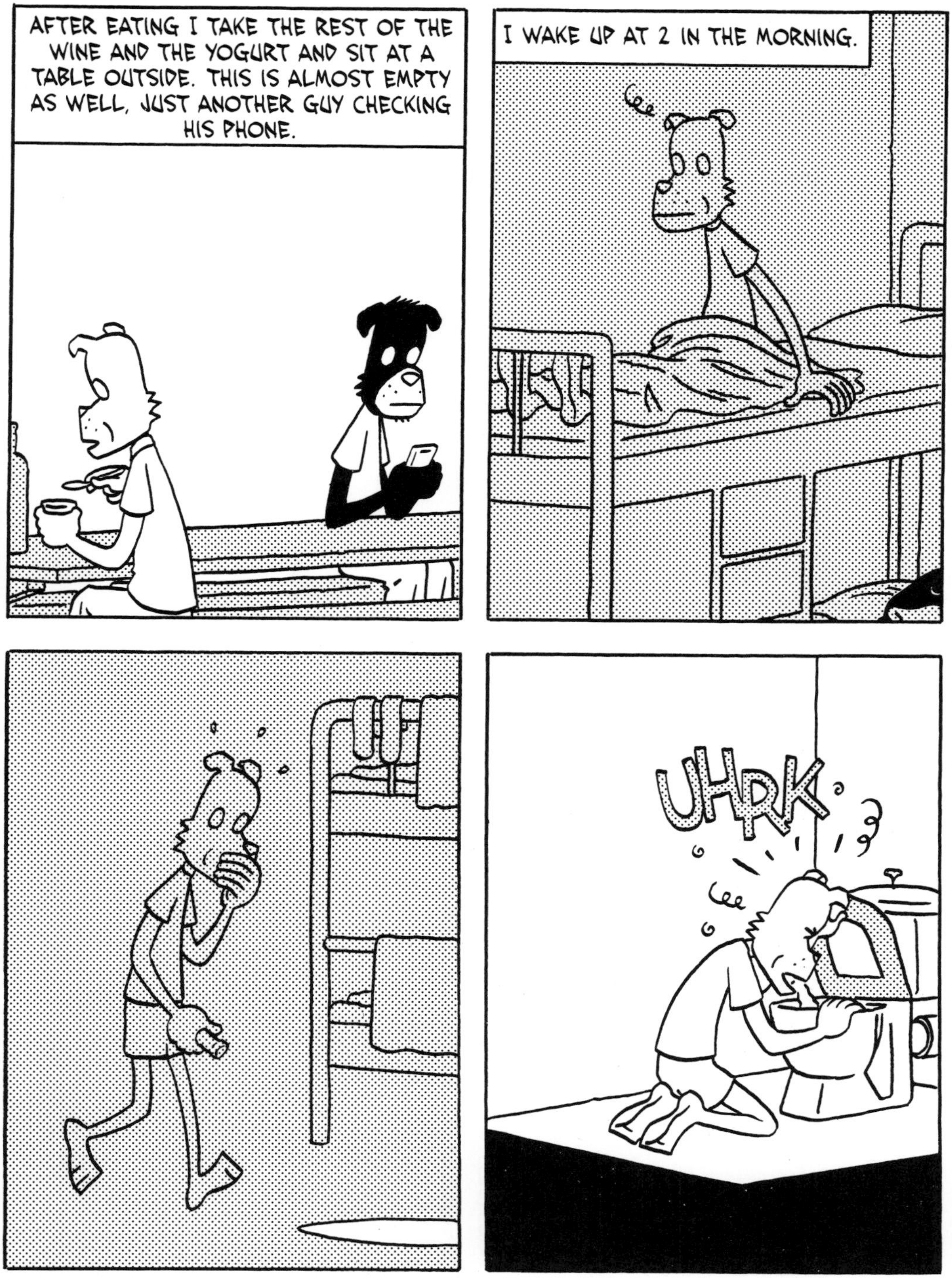
AFTER EATING I TAKE THE REST OF THE WINE AND THE YOGURT AND SIT AT A TABLE OUTSIDE. THIS IS ALMOST EMPTY AS WELL, JUST ANOTHER GUY CHECKING HIS PHONE.
I WAKE UP AT 2 IN THE MORNING.
UHRK

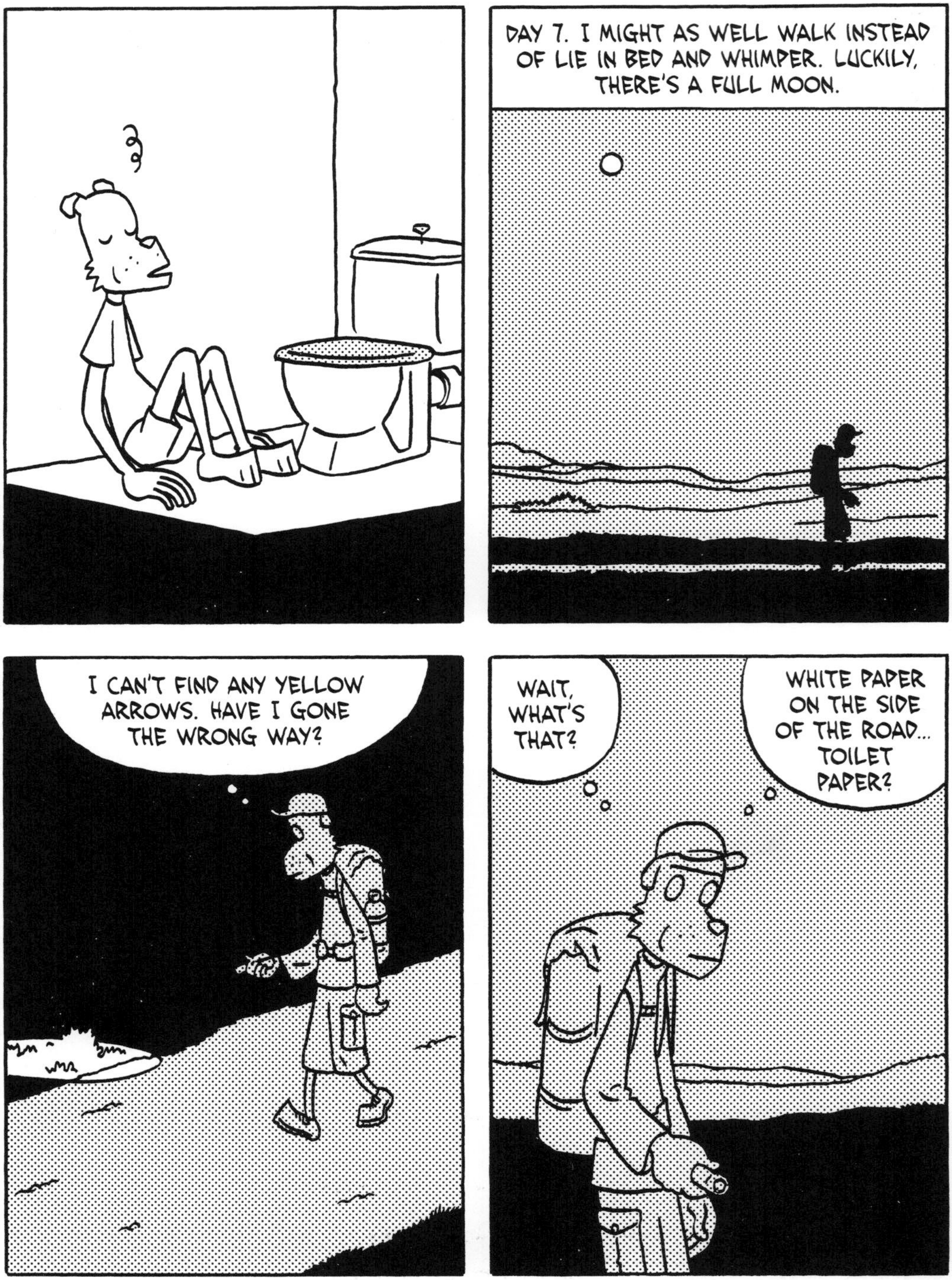
DAY 7. I MIGHT AS WELL WALK INSTEAD OF LIE IN BED AND WHIMPER. LUCKILY, THERE'S A FULL MOON.
I CAN'T FIND ANY YELLOW ARROWS. HAVE I GONE THE WRONG WAY?
WAIT, WHAT'S THAT?
WHITE PAPER ON THE SIDE OF THE ROAD... TOILET PAPER?

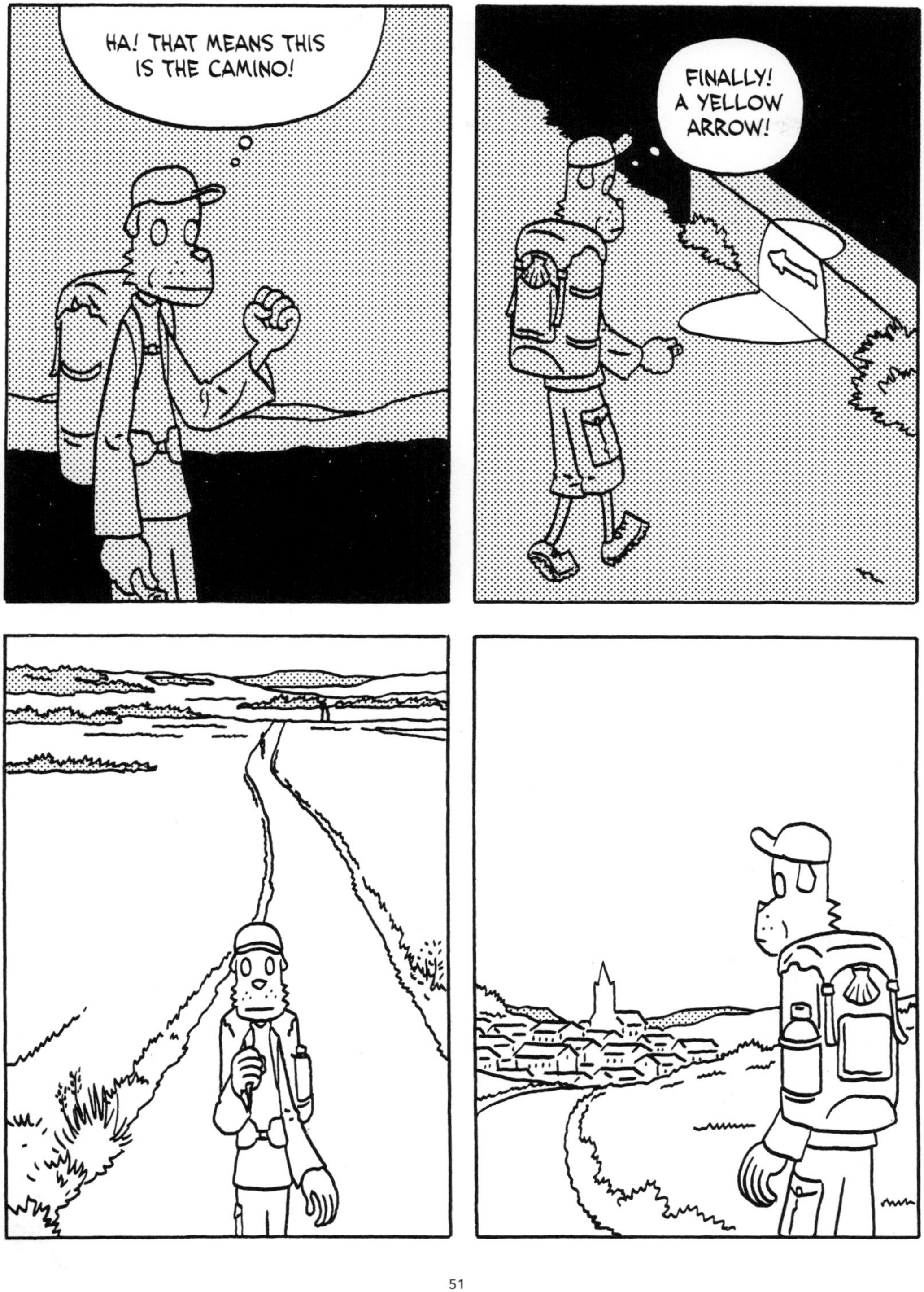
HA! THAT MEANS THIS IS THE CAMINO!
FINALLY! A YELLOW ARROW!

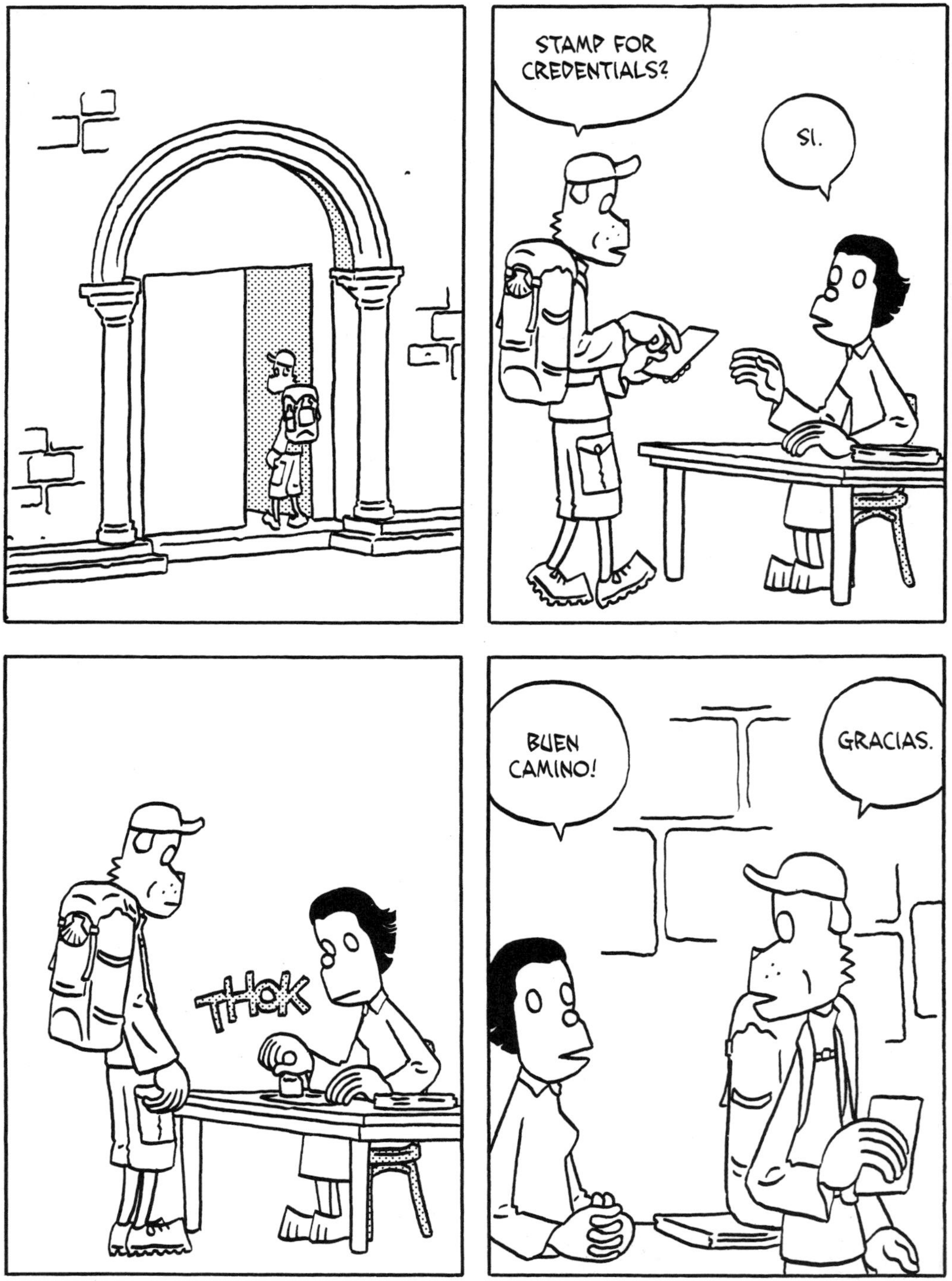
STAMP FOR CREDENTIALS?
SI.
THOK
BUEN CAMINO!
GRACIAS.

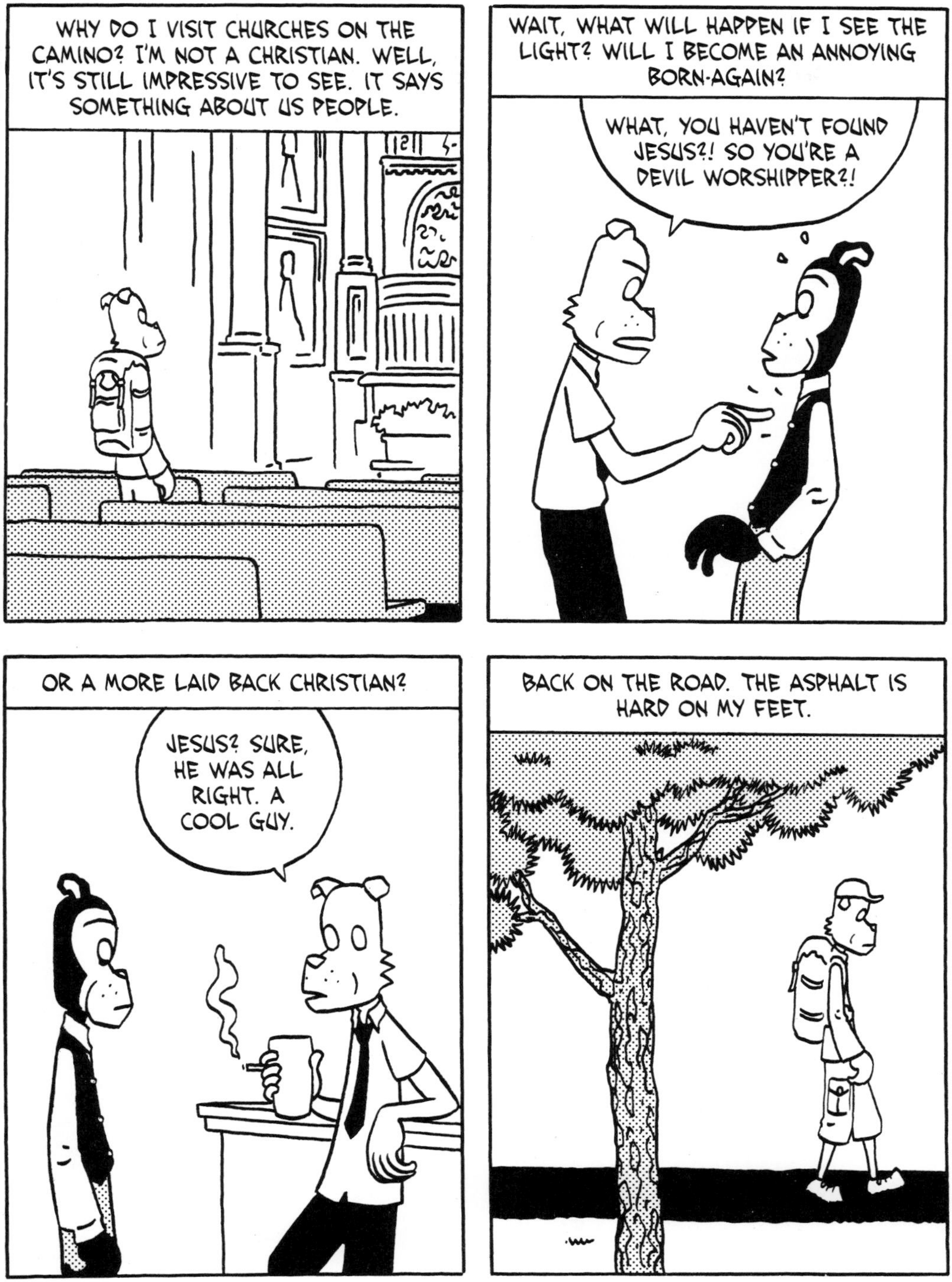
WHY DO I VISIT CHURCHES ON THE CAMINO? I'M NOT A CHRISTIAN. WELL, IT'S STILL IMPRESSIVE TO SEE. IT SAYS SOMETHING ABOUT US PEOPLE.
WAIT, WHAT WILL HAPPEN IF I SEE THE LIGHT? WILL I BECOME AN ANNOYING BORN-AGAIN?
WHAT, YOU HAVEN'T FOUND JESUS?! SO YOU'RE A DEVIL WORSHIPPER?!
OR A MORE LAID BACK CHRISTIAN?
JESUS? SURE, HE WAS ALL RIGHT. A COOL GUY.
BACK ON THE ROAD. THE ASPHALT IS HARD ON MY FEET.

FINALLY, LOGRONO!

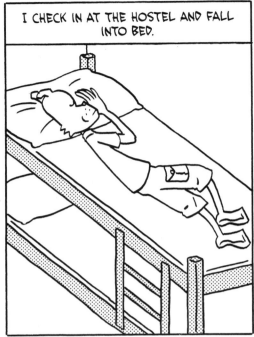

I CHECK IN AT THE HOSTEL AND FALL INTO BED.

ARE YOU OKAY?

YES, I'M JUST TIRED.

YOU'VE BEEN LYING THERE FOR A LONG TIME.

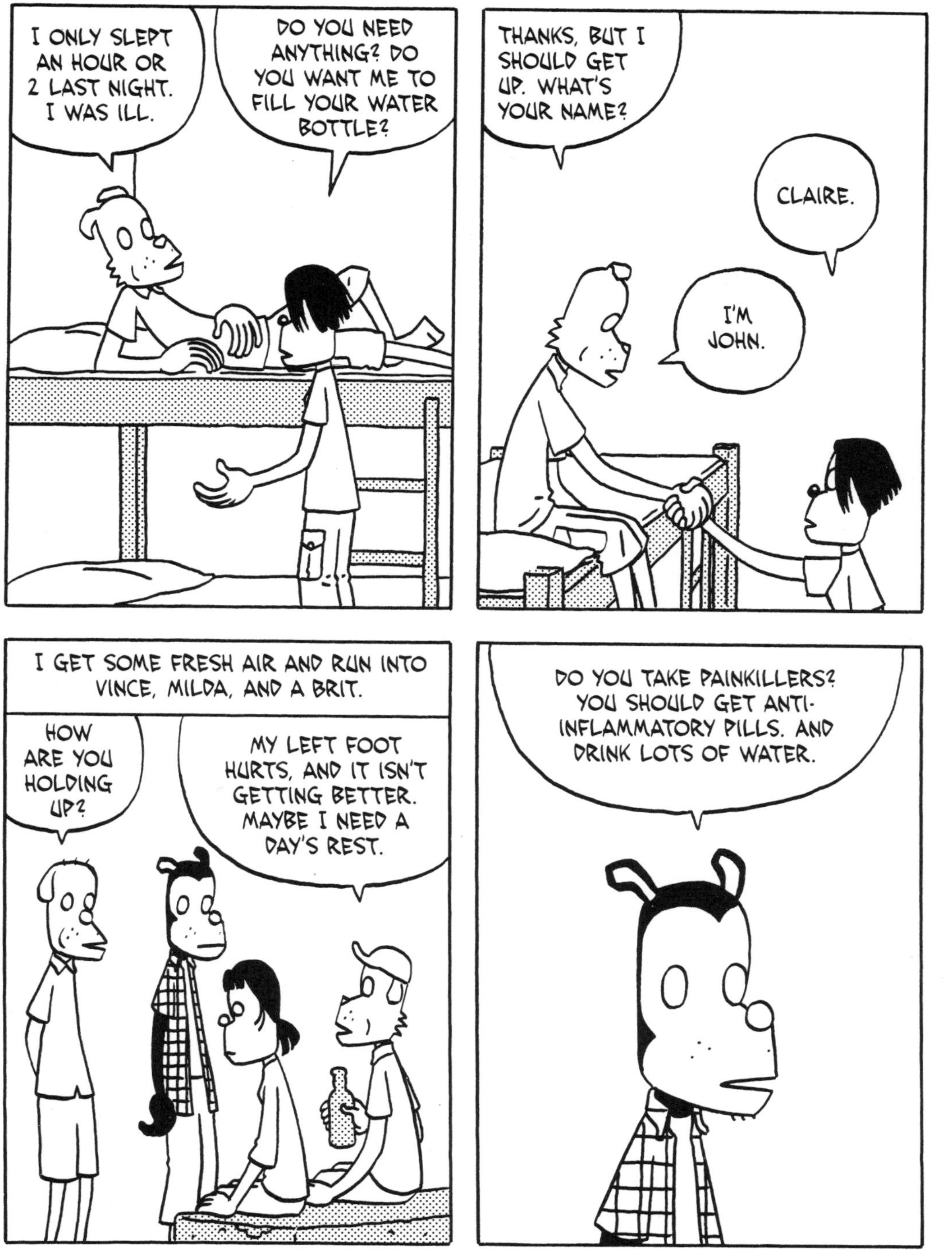
I ONLY SLEPT AN HOUR OR 2 LAST NIGHT. I WAS ILL.
DO YOU NEED ANYTHING? DO YOU WANT ME TO FILL YOUR WATER BOTTLE?
THANKS, BUT I SHOULD GET UP. WHAT'S YOUR NAME?
CLAIRE.
I'M JOHN.
I GET SOME FRESH AIR AND RUN INTO VINCE, MILDA, AND A BRIT.
HOW ARE YOU HOLDING UP?
MY LEFT FOOT HURTS, AND IT ISN'T GETTING BETTER. MAYBE I NEED A DAY'S REST.
DO YOU TAKE PAINKILLERS? YOU SHOULD GET ANTI-INFLAMMATORY PILLS. AND DRINK LOTS OF WATER.

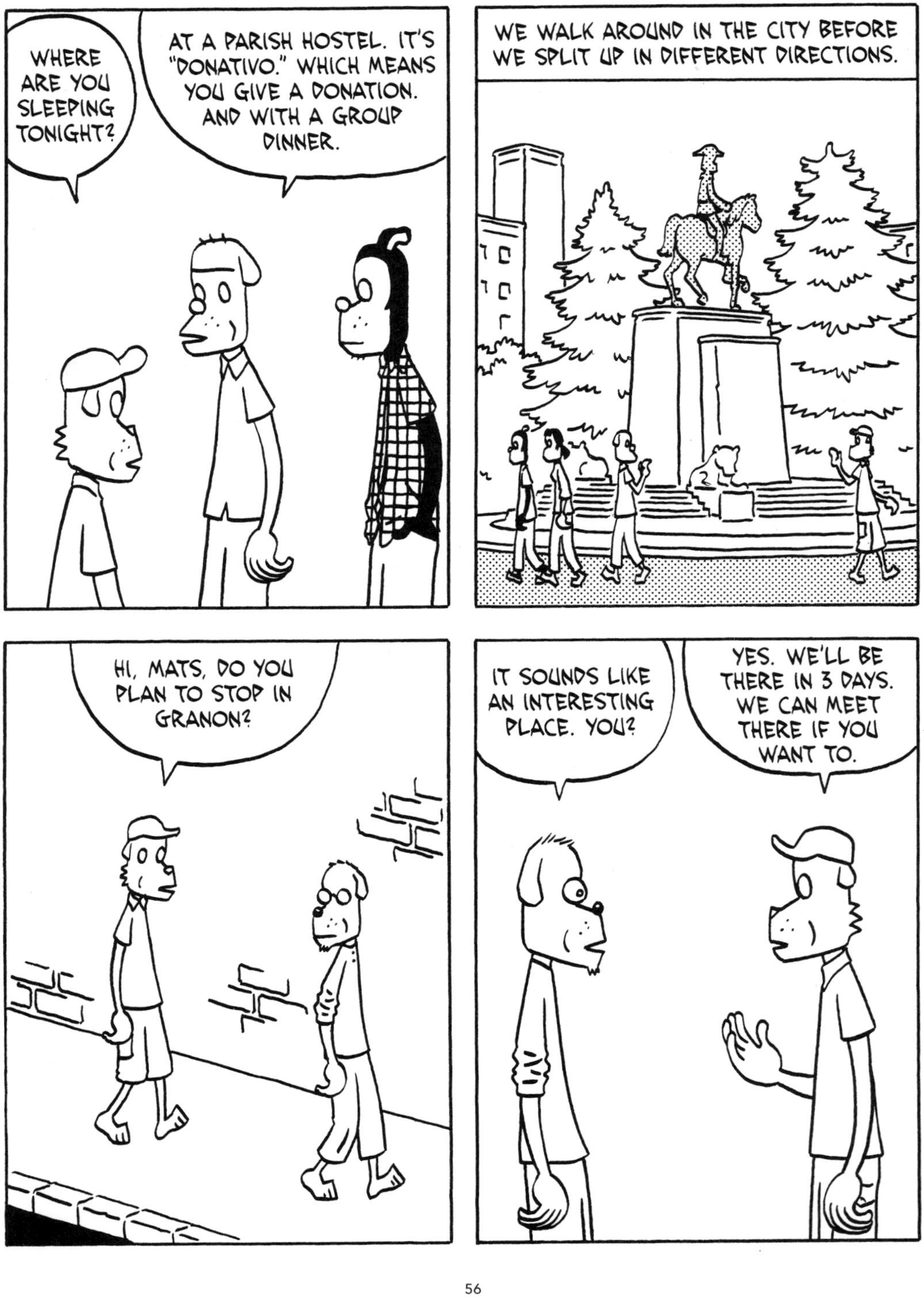
WHERE ARE YOU SLEEPING TONIGHT?
AT A PARISH HOSTEL. IT'S "DONATIVO." WHICH MEANS YOU GIVE A DONATION. AND WITH A GROUP DINNER.
WE WALK AROUND IN THE CITY BEFORE WE SPLIT UP IN DIFFERENT DIRECTIONS.
HI, MATS, DO YOU PLAN TO STOP IN GRANON?
IT SOUNDS LIKE AN INTERESTING PLACE. YOU?
YES. WE'LL BE THERE IN 3 DAYS. WE CAN MEET THERE IF YOU WANT TO.

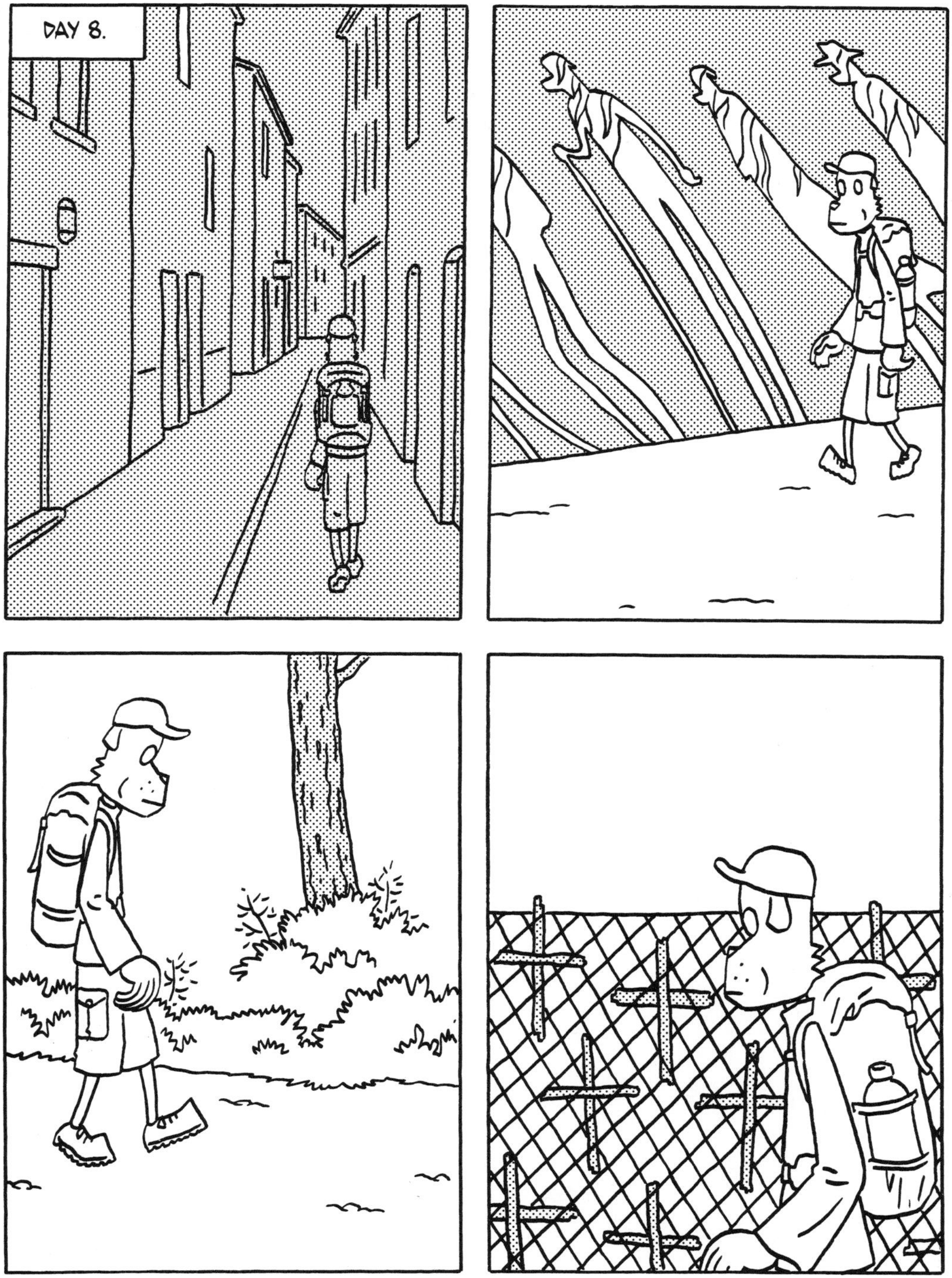
DAY 8.

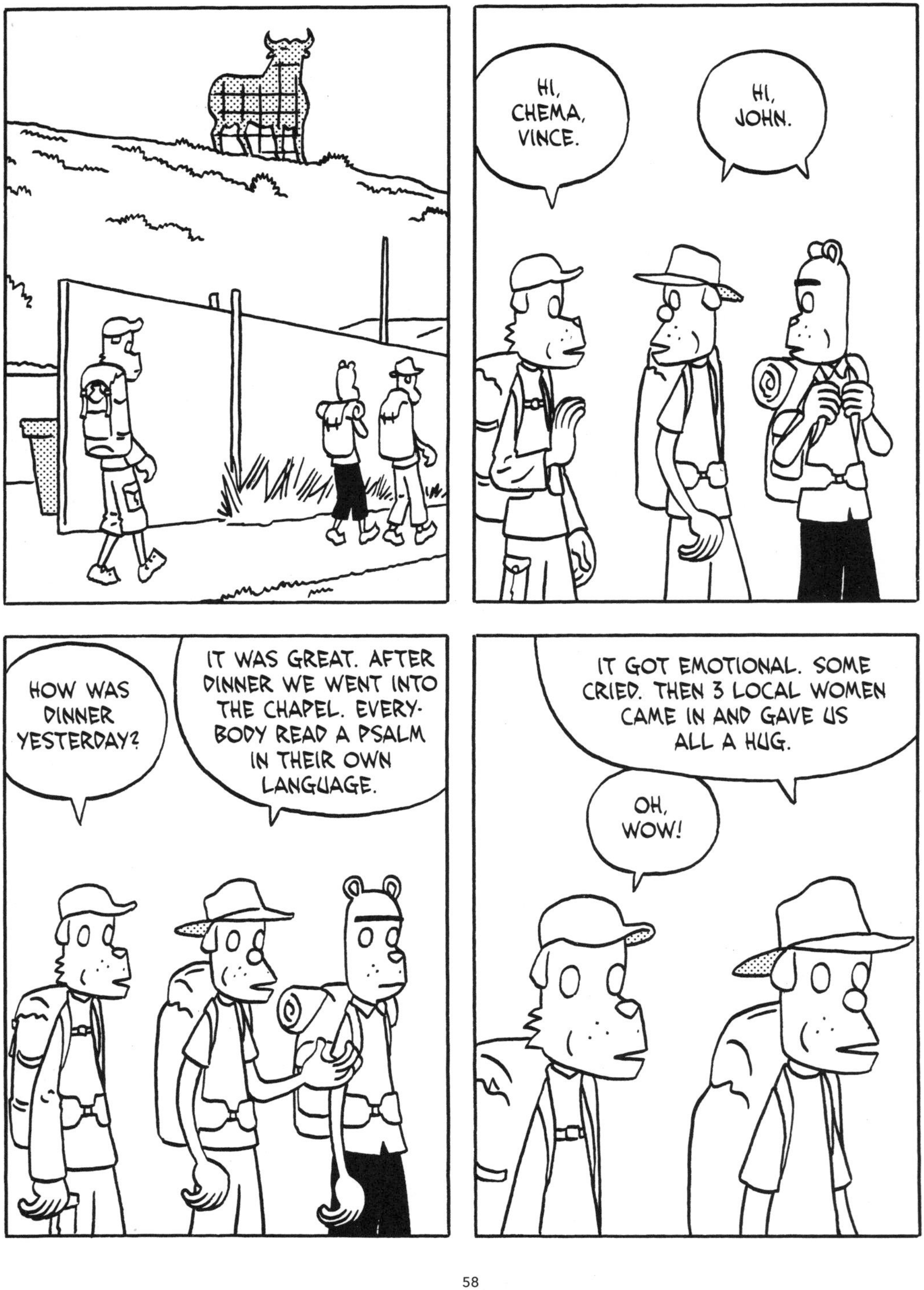
HI, CHEMA, VINCE.
HI, JOHN.
HOW WAS DINNER YESTERDAY?
IT WAS GREAT. AFTER DINNER WE WENT INTO THE CHAPEL. EVERY-BODY READ A PSALM IN THEIR OWN LANGUAGE.
IT GOT EMOTIONAL. SOME CRIED. THEN 3 LOCAL WOMEN CAME IN AND GAVE US ALL A HUG.
OH, WOW!

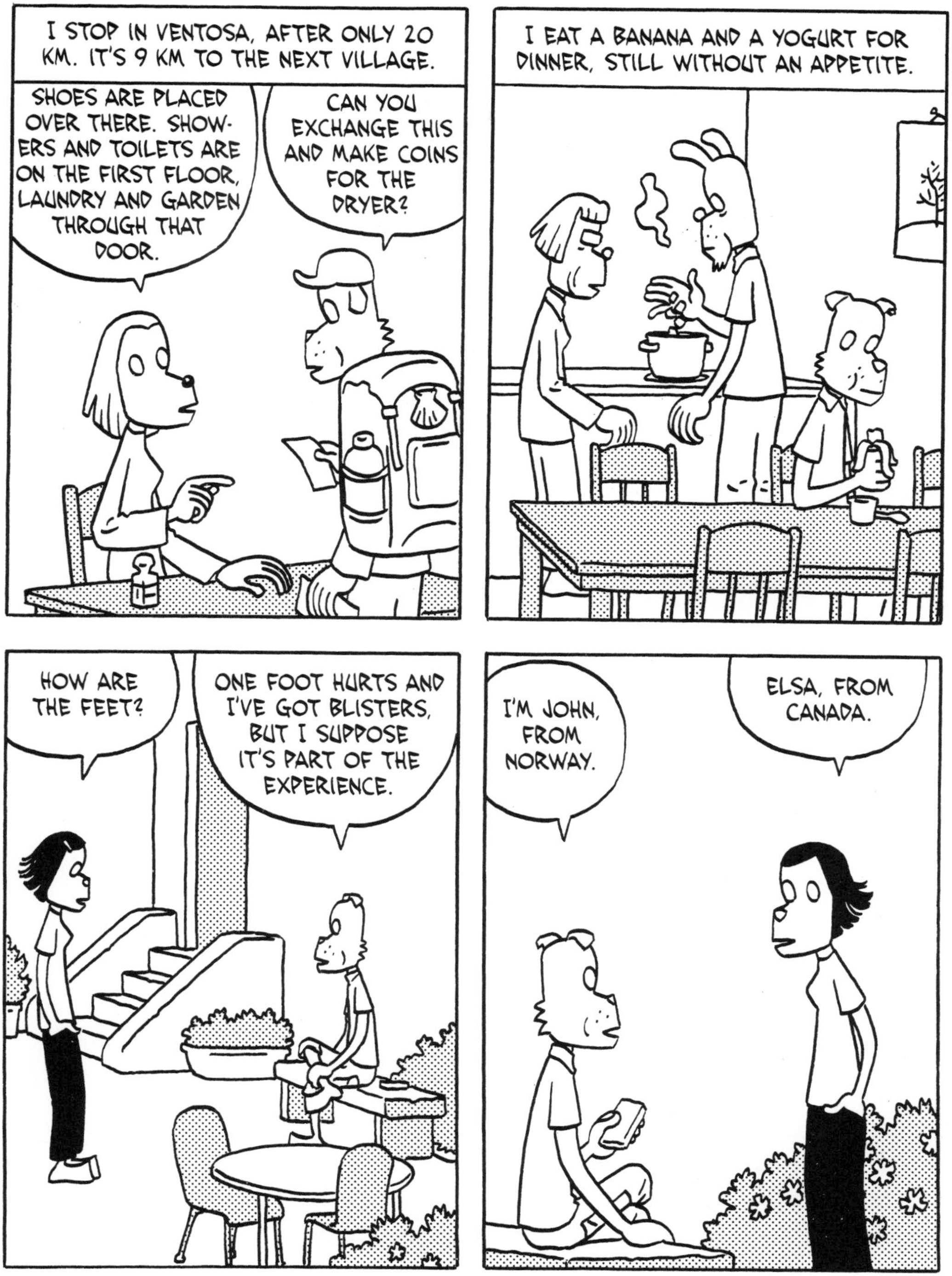
I STOP IN VENTOSA, AFTER ONLY 20 KM. IT'S 9 KM TO THE NEXT VILLAGE.
SHOES ARE PLACED OVER THERE. SHOWERS AND TOILETS ARE ON THE FIRST FLOOR, LAUNDRY AND GARDEN THROUGH THAT DOOR.
CAN YOU EXCHANGE THIS AND MAKE COINS FOR THE DRYER?
I EAT A BANANA AND A YOGURT FOR DINNER, STILL WITHOUT AN APPETITE.
HOW ARE THE FEET?
ONE FOOT HURTS AND I'VE GOT BLISTERS, BUT I SUPPOSE IT'S PART OF THE EXPERIENCE.
I'M JOHN, FROM NORWAY.
ELSA, FROM CANADA.

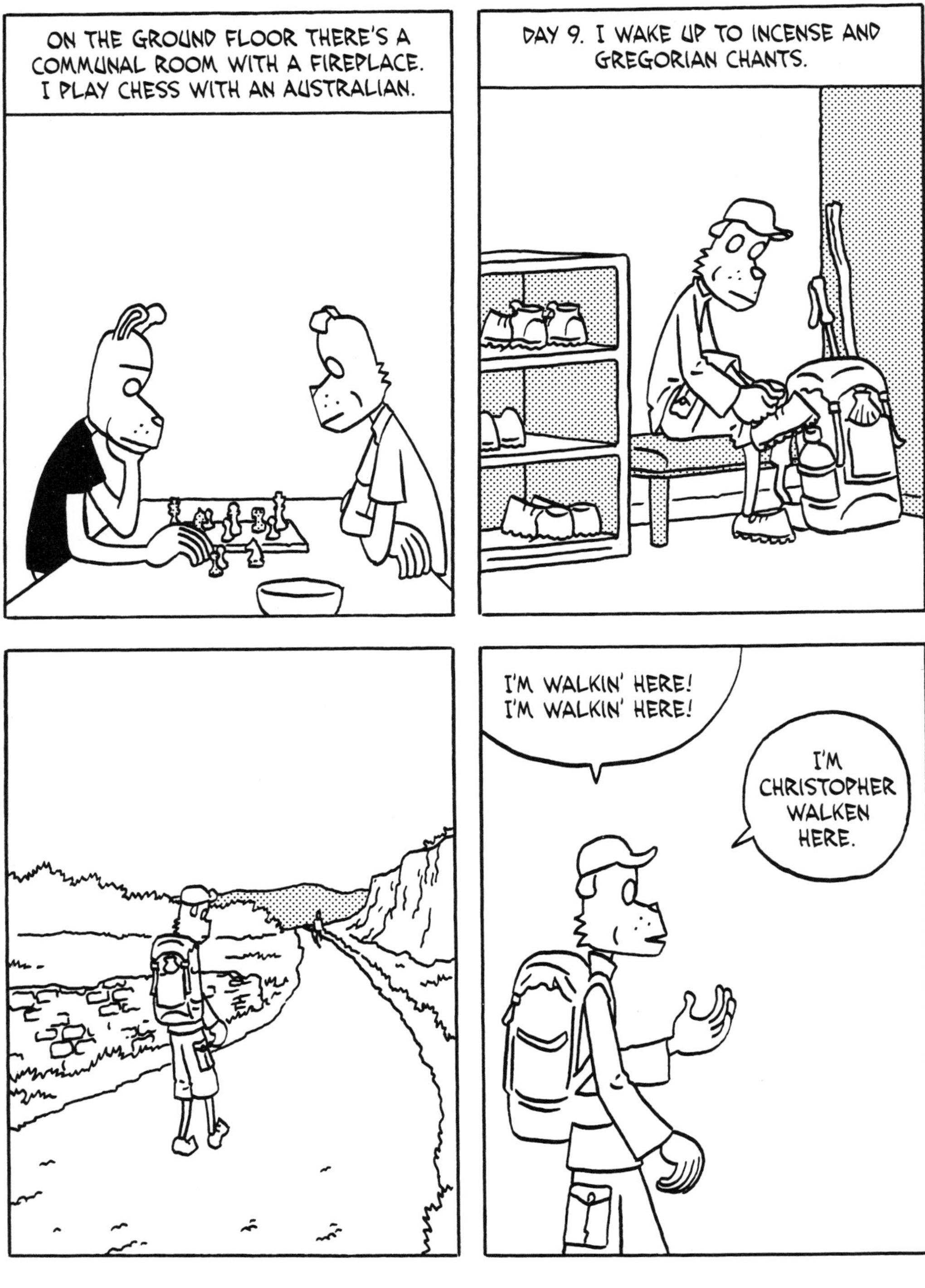
ON THE GROUND FLOOR THERE'S A COMMUNAL ROOM WITH A FIREPLACE. I PLAY CHESS WITH AN AUSTRALIAN.
DAY 9. I WAKE UP TO INCENSE AND GREGORIAN CHANTS.
I'M WALKIN' HERE! I'M WALKIN' HERE!
I'M CHRISTOPHER WALKEN HERE.

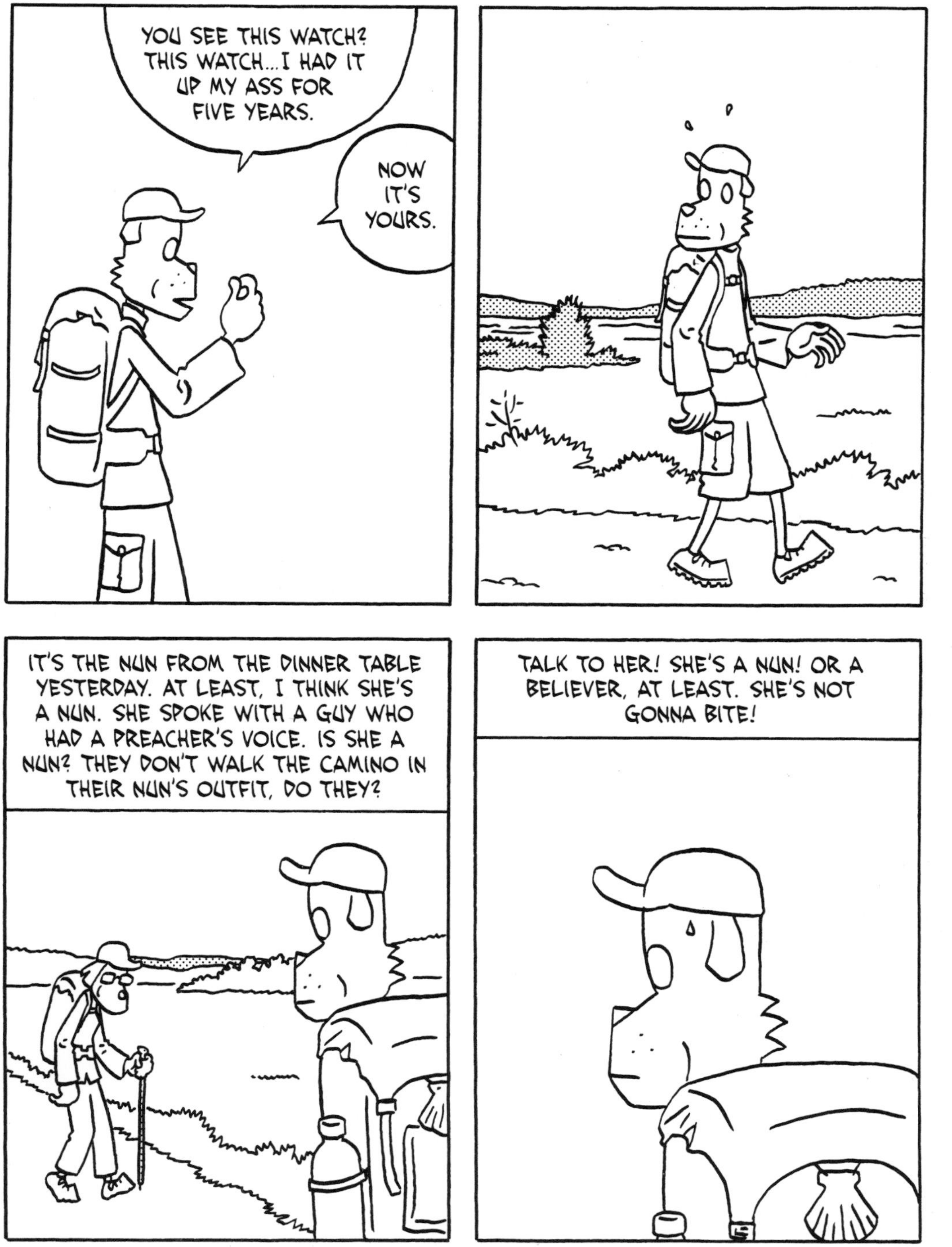
YOU SEE THIS WATCH? THIS WATCH...I HAD IT UP MY ASS FOR FIVE YEARS.
NOW IT'S YOURS.
IT'S THE NUN FROM THE DINNER TABLE YESTERDAY. AT LEAST, I THINK SHE'S A NUN. SHE SPOKE WITH A GUY WHO HAD A PREACHER'S VOICE. IS SHE A NUN? THEY DON'T WALK THE CAMINO IN THEIR NUN'S OUTFIT, DO THEY?
TALK TO HER! SHE'S A NUN! OR A BELIEVER, AT LEAST. SHE'S NOT GONNA BITE!

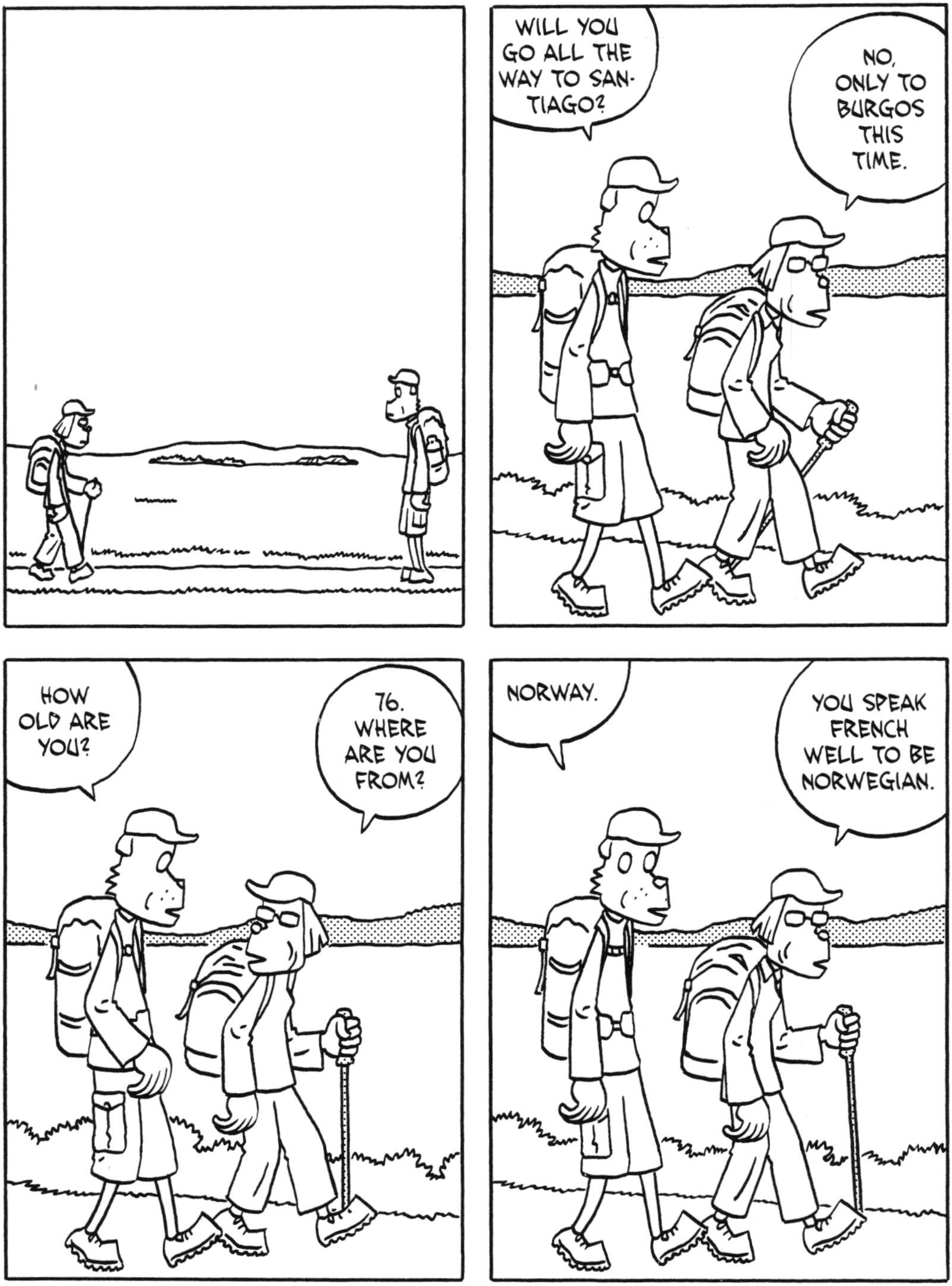
WILL YOU GO ALL THE WAY TO SAN-TIAGO?
NO, ONLY TO BURGOS THIS TIME.
HOW OLD ARE YOU?
76. WHERE ARE YOU FROM?
NORWAY.
YOU SPEAK FRENCH WELL TO BE NORWEGIAN.

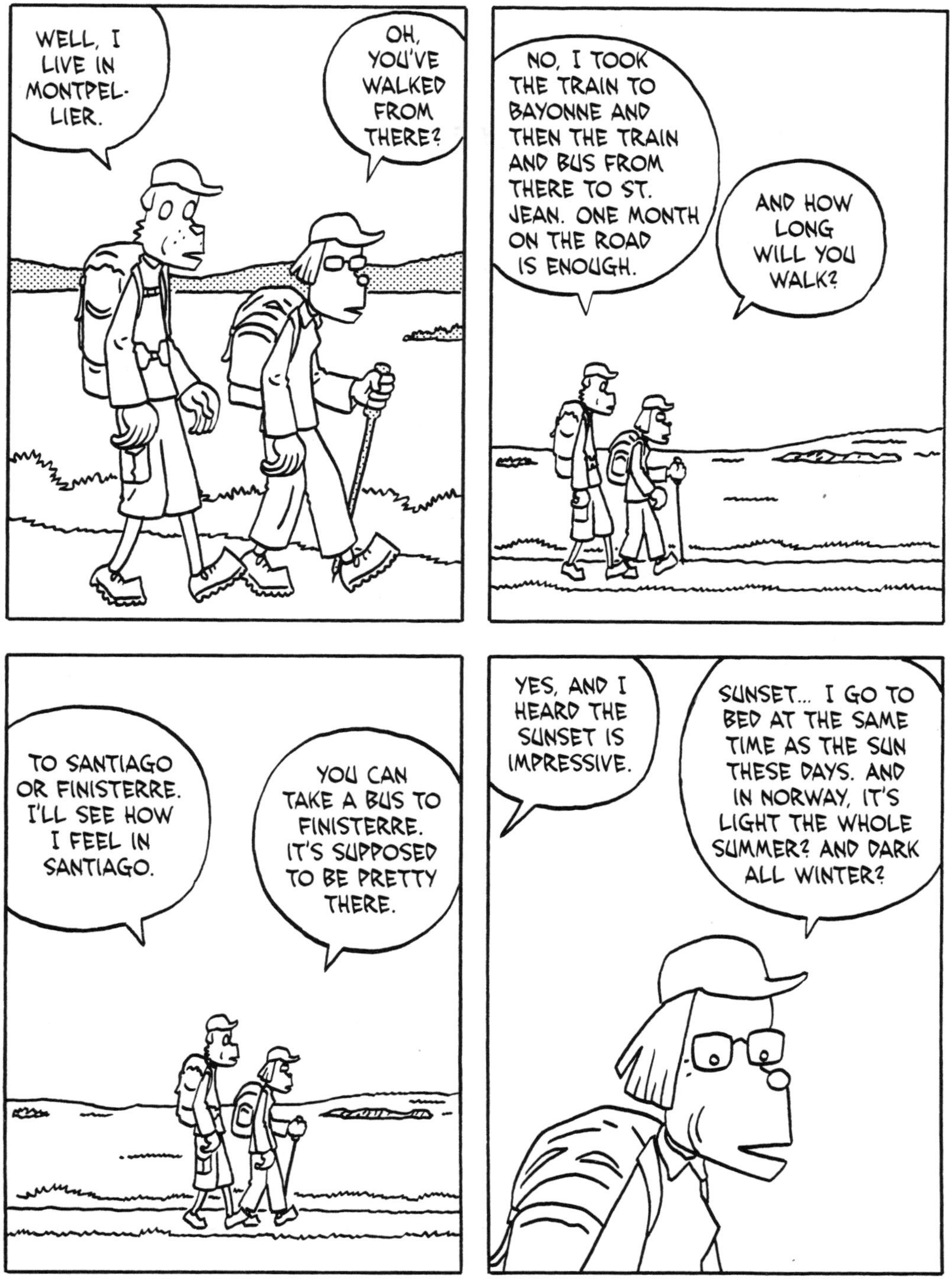
WELL, I LIVE IN MONTPEL-LIER.
OH, YOU'VE WALKED FROM THERE?
NO, I TOOK THE TRAIN TO BAYONNE AND THEN THE TRAIN AND BUS FROM THERE TO ST. JEAN. ONE MONTH ON THE ROAD IS ENOUGH.
AND HOW LONG WILL YOU WALK?
TO SANTIAGO OR FINISTERRE. I'LL SEE HOW I FEEL IN SANTIAGO.
YOU CAN TAKE A BUS TO FINISTERRE. IT'S SUPPOSED TO BE PRETTY THERE.
YES, AND I HEARD THE SUNSET IS IMPRESSIVE.
SUNSET... I GO TO BED AT THE SAME TIME AS THE SUN THESE DAYS. AND IN NORWAY, IT'S LIGHT THE WHOLE SUMMER? AND DARK ALL WINTER?

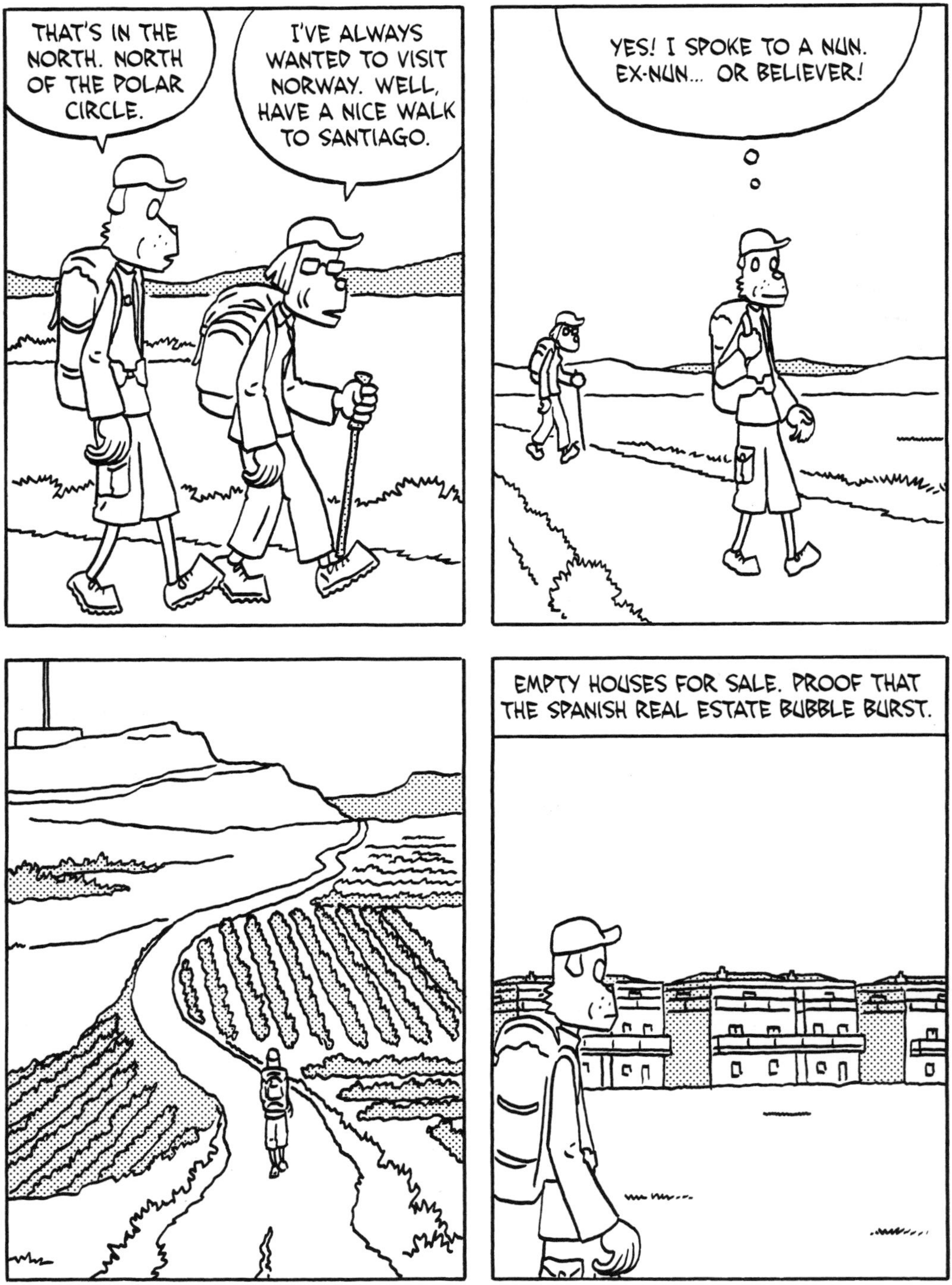
THAT'S IN THE NORTH. NORTH OF THE POLAR CIRCLE.
I'VE ALWAYS WANTED TO VISIT NORWAY. WELL, HAVE A NICE WALK TO SANTIAGO.
YES! I SPOKE TO A NUN. EX-NUN... OR BELIEVER!
EMPTY HOUSES FOR SALE. PROOF THAT THE SPANISH REAL ESTATE BUBBLE BURST.

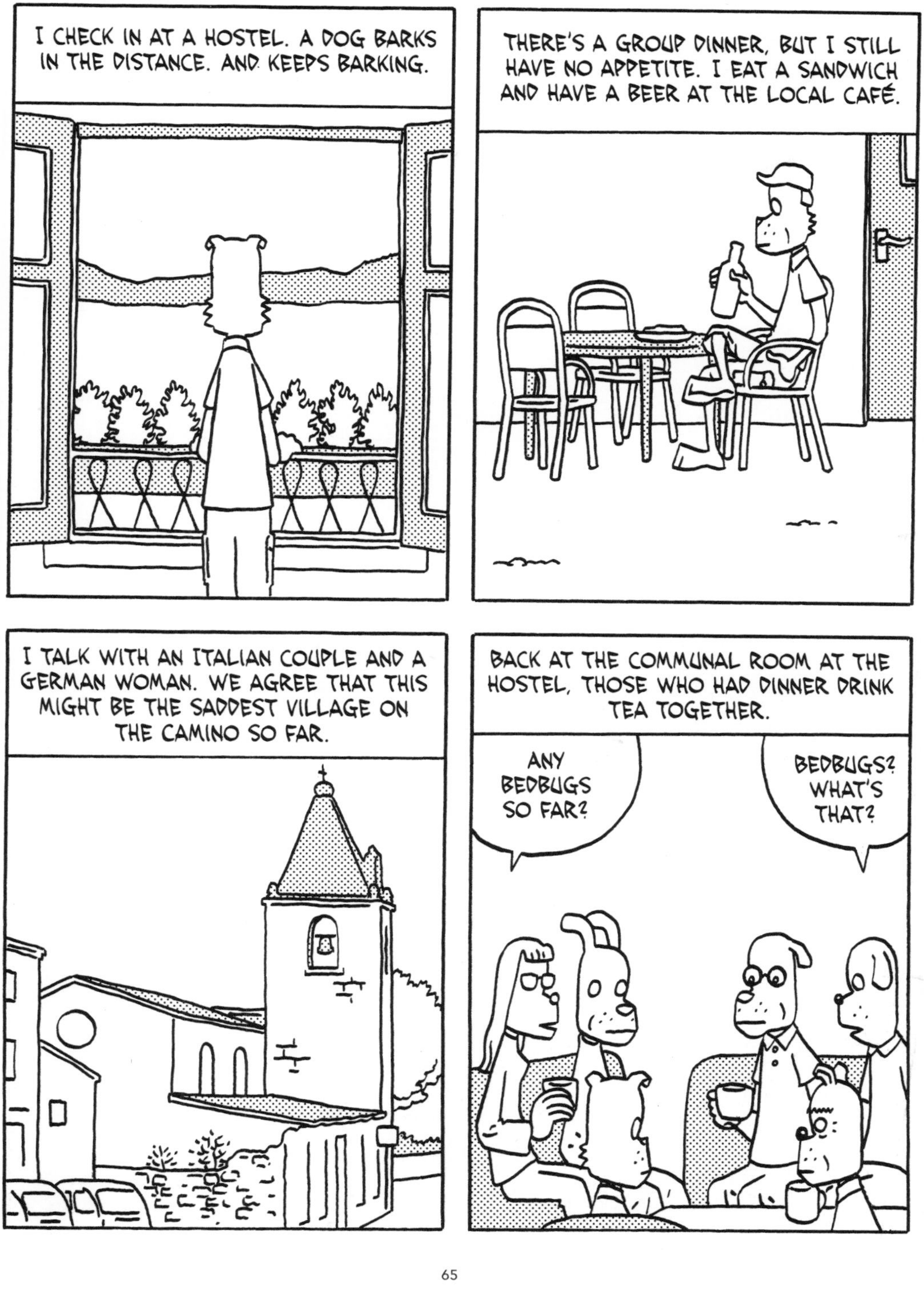
I CHECK IN AT A HOSTEL. A DOG BARKS IN THE DISTANCE. AND KEEPS BARKING.
THERE'S A GROUP DINNER, BUT I STILL HAVE NO APPETITE. I EAT A SANDWICH AND HAVE A BEER AT THE LOCAL CAFÉ.
I TALK WITH AN ITALIAN COUPLE AND A GERMAN WOMAN. WE AGREE THAT THIS MIGHT BE THE SADDEST VILLAGE ON THE CAMINO SO FAR.
BACK AT THE COMMUNAL ROOM AT THE HOSTEL, THOSE WHO HAD DINNER DRINK TEA TOGETHER.
ANY BEDBUGS SO FAR?
BEDBUGS? WHAT'S THAT?

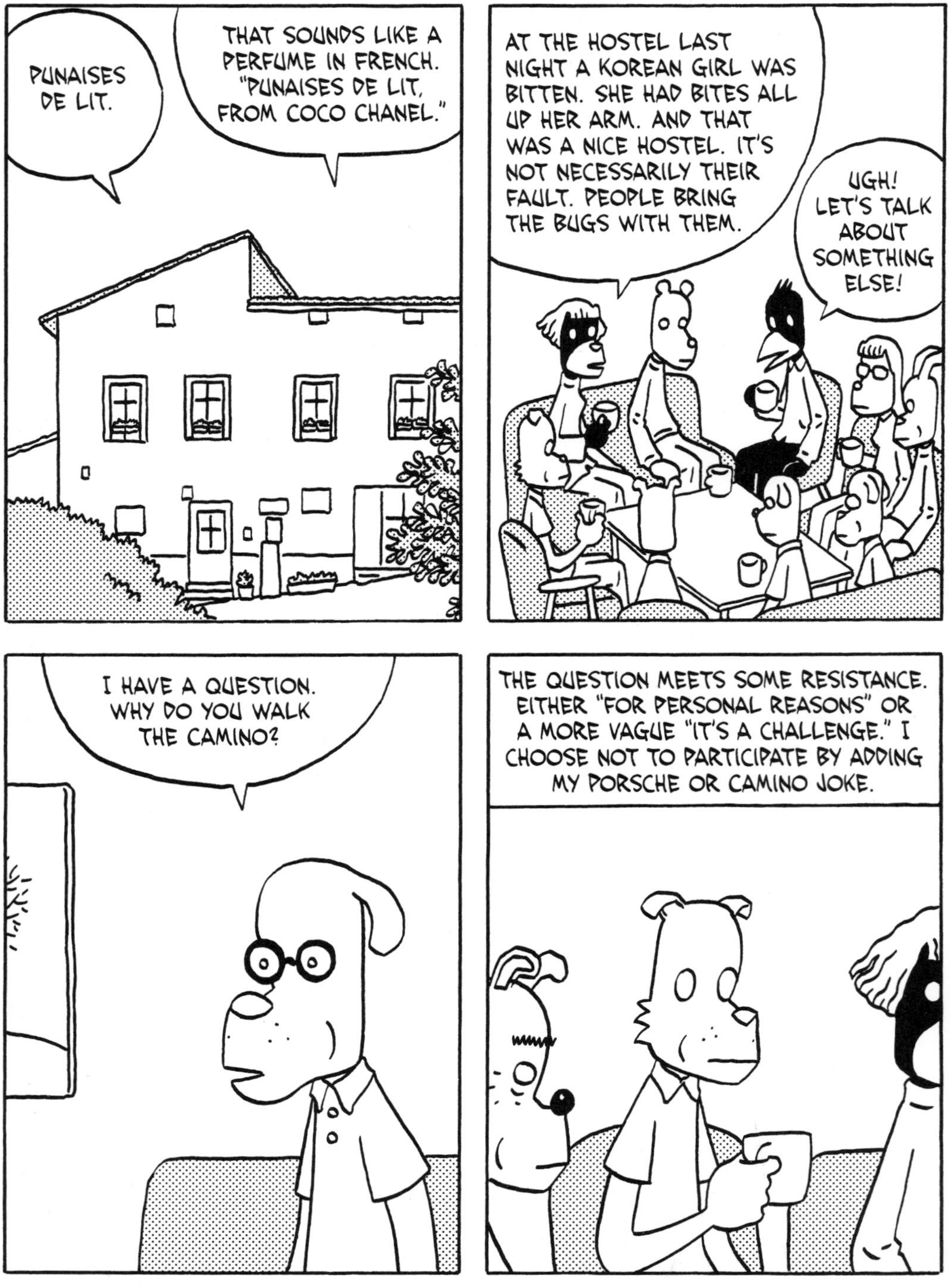
PUNAISES DE LIT.
THAT SOUNDS LIKE A PERFUME IN FRENCH. "PUNAISES DE LIT, FROM COCO CHANEL."
AT THE HOSTEL LAST NIGHT A KOREAN GIRL WAS BITTEN. SHE HAD BITES ALL UP HER ARM. AND THAT WAS A NICE HOSTEL. IT'S NOT NECESSARILY THEIR FAULT. PEOPLE BRING THE BUGS WITH THEM.
UGH! LET'S TALK ABOUT SOMETHING ELSE!
I HAVE A QUESTION. WHY DO YOU WALK THE CAMINO?
THE QUESTION MEETS SOME RESISTANCE. EITHER "FOR PERSONAL REASONS" OR A MORE VAGUE "IT'S A CHALLENGE." I CHOOSE NOT TO PARTICIPATE BY ADDING MY PORSCHE OR CAMINO JOKE.

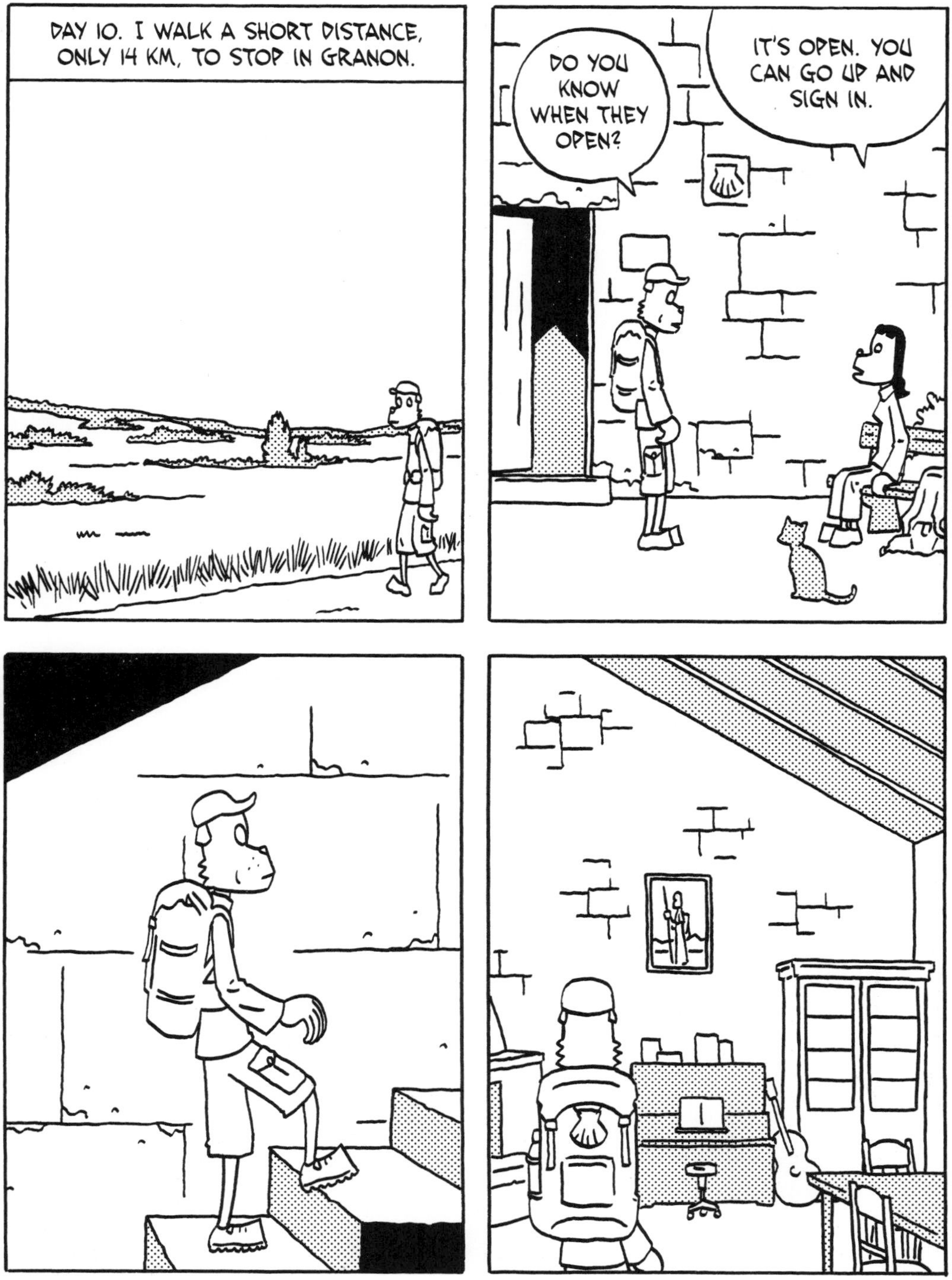
DAY 10. I WALK A SHORT DISTANCE, ONLY 14 KM, TO STOP IN GRANON.
DO YOU KNOW WHEN THEY OPEN?
IT'S OPEN. YOU CAN GO UP AND SIGN IN.

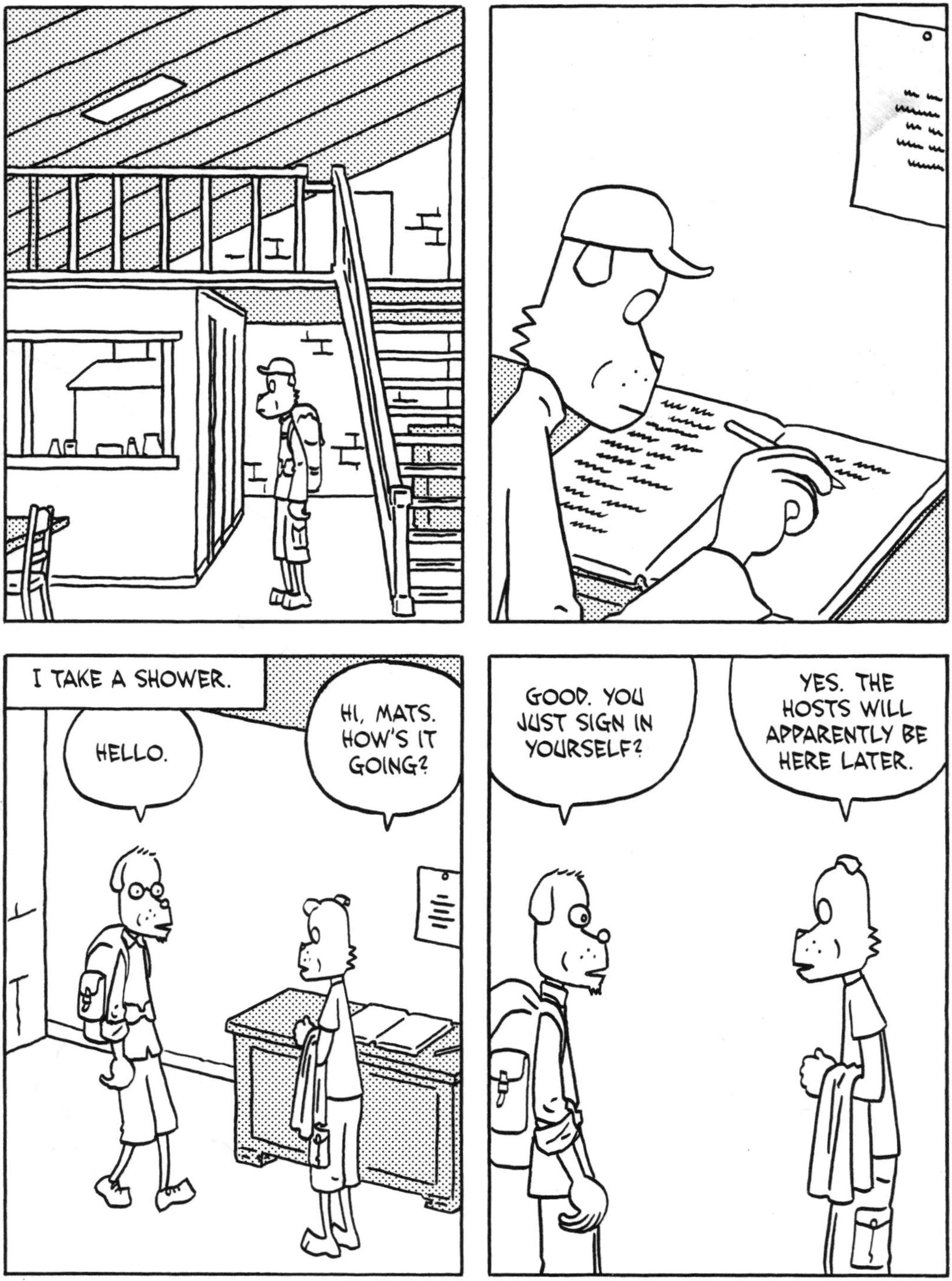
I TAKE A SHOWER.
HELLO.
HI, MATS. HOW'S IT GOING?
GOOD. YOU JUST SIGN IN YOURSELF?
YES. THE HOSTS WILL APPARENTLY BE HERE LATER.

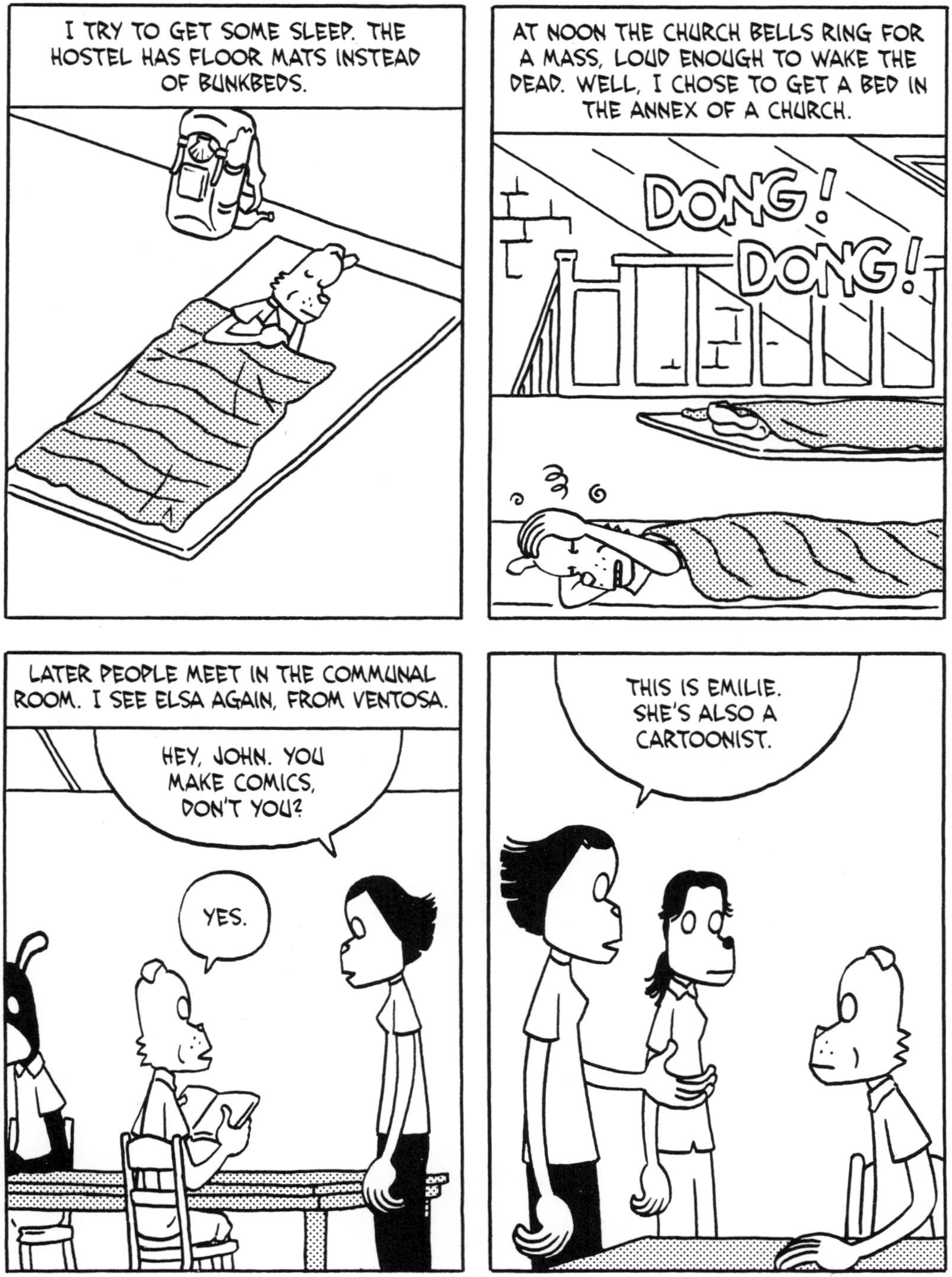
I TRY TO GET SOME SLEEP. THE HOSTEL HAS FLOOR MATS INSTEAD OF BUNKBEDS.
AT NOON THE CHURCH BELLS RING FOR A MASS, LOUD ENOUGH TO WAKE THE DEAD. WELL, I CHOSE TO GET A BED IN THE ANNEX OF A CHURCH.
DONG!
DONG!
LATER PEOPLE MEET IN THE COMMUNAL ROOM. I SEE ELSA AGAIN, FROM VENTOSA.
HEY, JOHN. YOU MAKE COMICS, DON'T YOU?
YES.
THIS IS EMILIE. SHE'S ALSO A CARTOONIST.

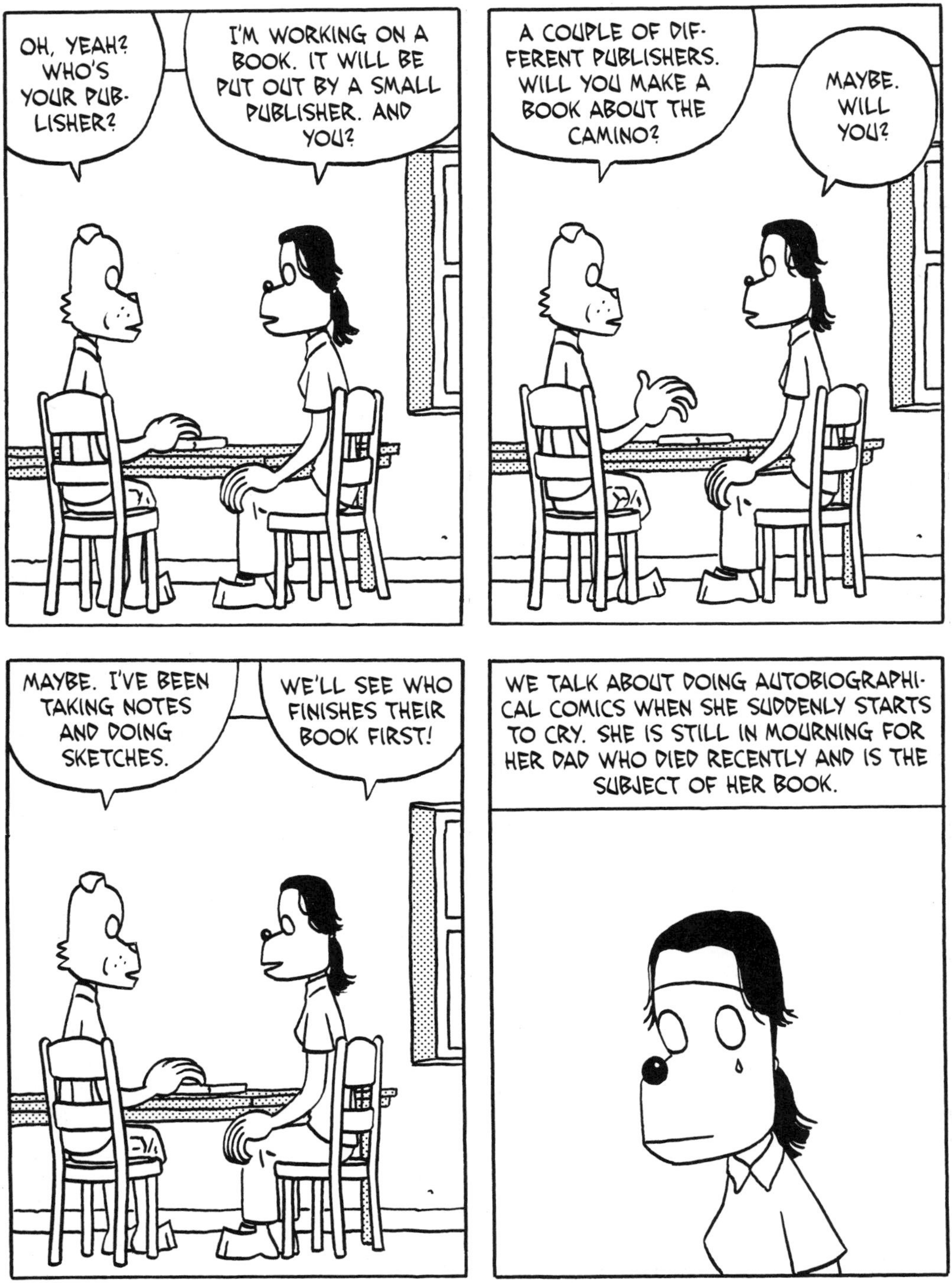
OH, YEAH? WHO'S YOUR PUB-LISHER?
I'M WORKING ON A BOOK. IT WILL BE PUT OUT BY A SMALL PUBLISHER. AND YOU?
A COUPLE OF DIF-FERENT PUBLISHERS. WILL YOU MAKE A BOOK ABOUT THE CAMINO?
MAYBE. WILL YOU?
MAYBE. I'VE BEEN TAKING NOTES AND DOING SKETCHES.
WE'LL SEE WHO FINISHES THEIR BOOK FIRST!
WE TALK ABOUT DOING AUTOBIOGRAPHI-CAL COMICS WHEN SHE SUDDENLY STARTS TO CRY. SHE IS STILL IN MOURNING FOR HER DAD WHO DIED RECENTLY AND IS THE SUBJECT OF HER BOOK.

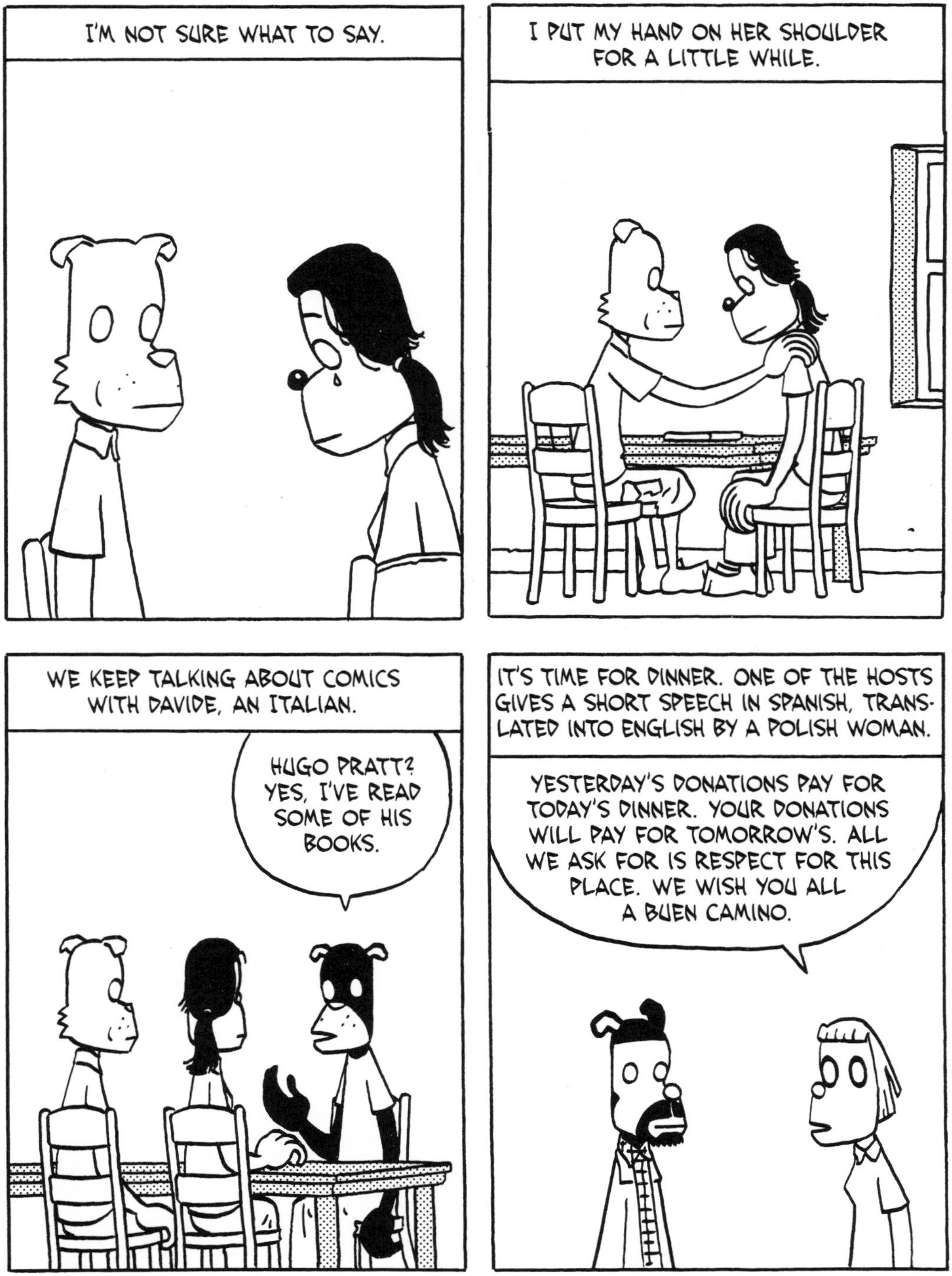

I'M NOT SURE WHAT TO SAY.
I PUT MY HAND ON HER SHOULDER FOR A LITTLE WHILE.
WE KEEP TALKING ABOUT COMICS WITH DAVIDE, AN ITALIAN.
HUGO PRATT? YES, I'VE READ SOME OF HIS BOOKS.
IT'S TIME FOR DINNER. ONE OF THE HOSTS GIVES A SHORT SPEECH IN SPANISH, TRANSLATED INTO ENGLISH BY A POLISH WOMAN.
YESTERDAY'S DONATIONS PAY FOR TODAY'S DINNER. YOUR DONATIONS WILL PAY FOR TOMORROW'S. ALL WE ASK FOR IS RESPECT FOR THIS PLACE. WE WISH YOU ALL A BUEN CAMINO.

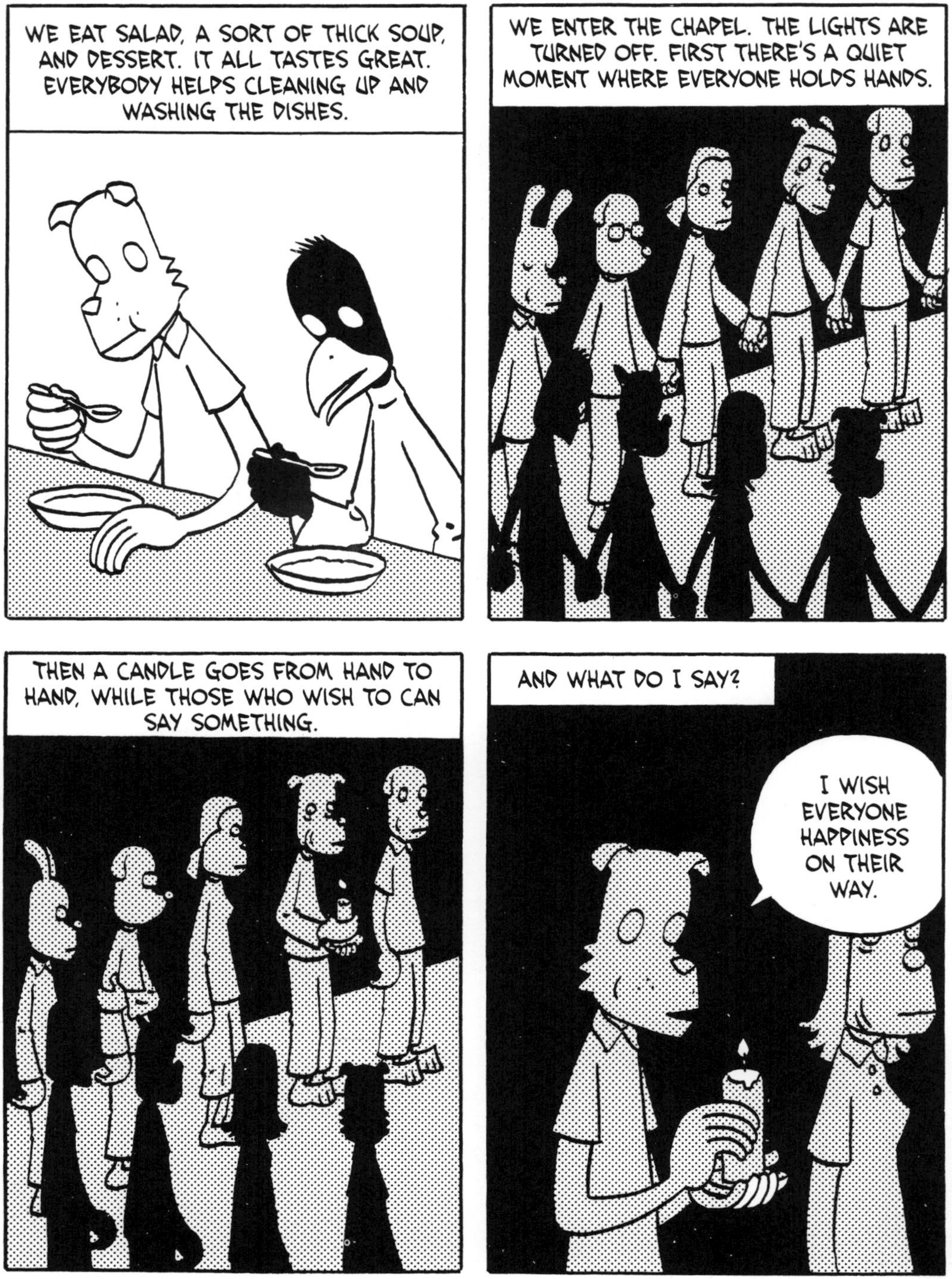
WE EAT SALAD, A SORT OF THICK SOUP, AND DESSERT. IT ALL TASTES GREAT. EVERYBODY HELPS CLEANING UP AND WASHING THE DISHES.
WE ENTER THE CHAPEL. THE LIGHTS ARE TURNED OFF. FIRST THERE'S A QUIET MOMENT WHERE EVERYONE HOLDS HANDS.
THEN A CANDLE GOES FROM HAND TO HAND, WHILE THOSE WHO WISH TO CAN SAY SOMETHING.
AND WHAT DO I SAY?
I WISH EVERYONE HAPPINESS ON THEIR WAY.

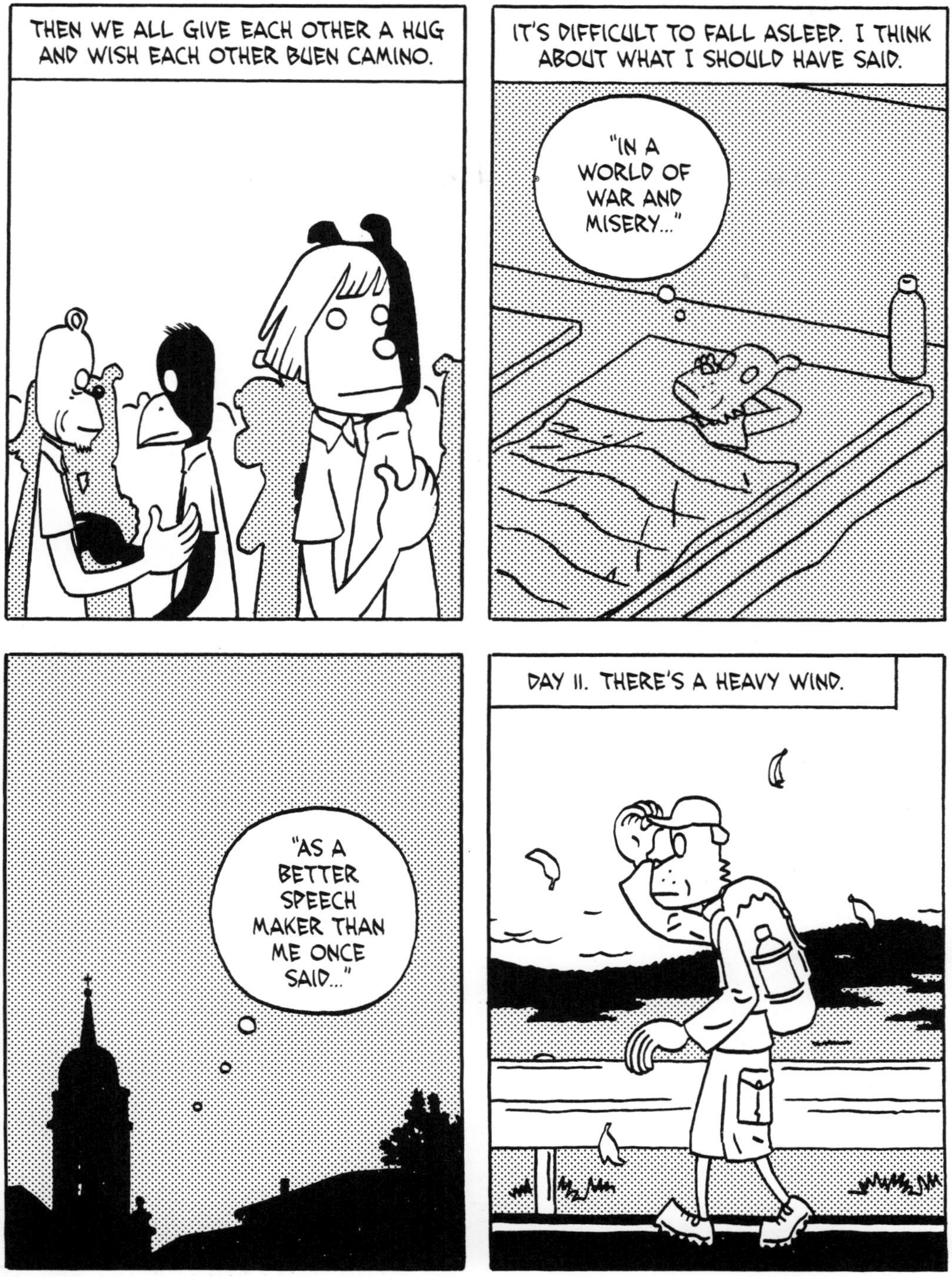
THEN WE ALL GIVE EACH OTHER A HUG AND WISH EACH OTHER BUEN CAMINO.
IT'S DIFFICULT TO FALL ASLEEP. I THINK ABOUT WHAT I SHOULD HAVE SAID.
"IN A WORLD OF WAR AND MISERY..."
"AS A BETTER SPEECH MAKER THAN ME ONCE SAID..."
DAY 11. THERE'S A HEAVY WIND.

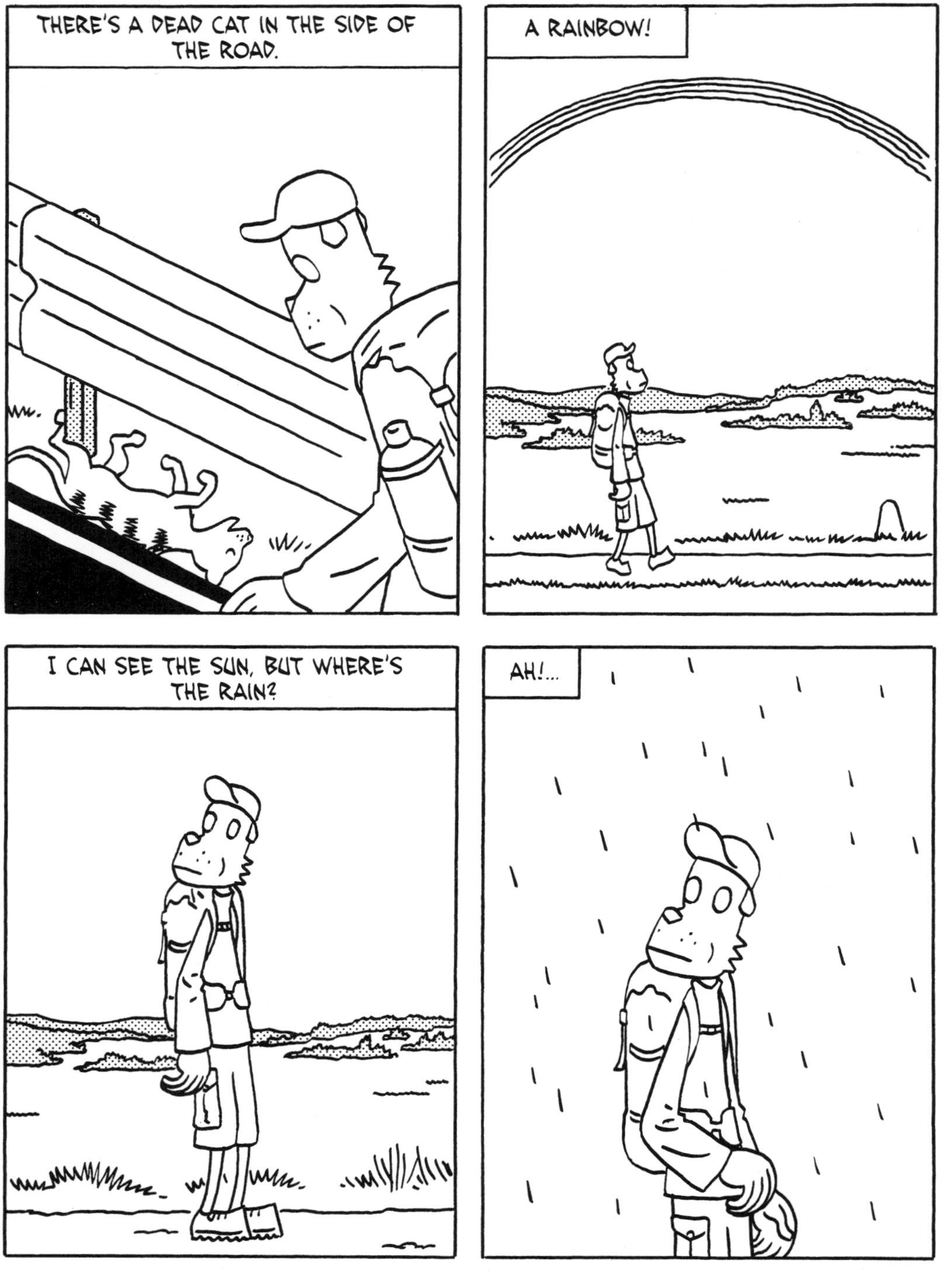
THERE'S A DEAD CAT IN THE SIDE OF THE ROAD.
A RAINBOW!
I CAN SEE THE SUN, BUT WHERE'S THE RAIN?
AH!...

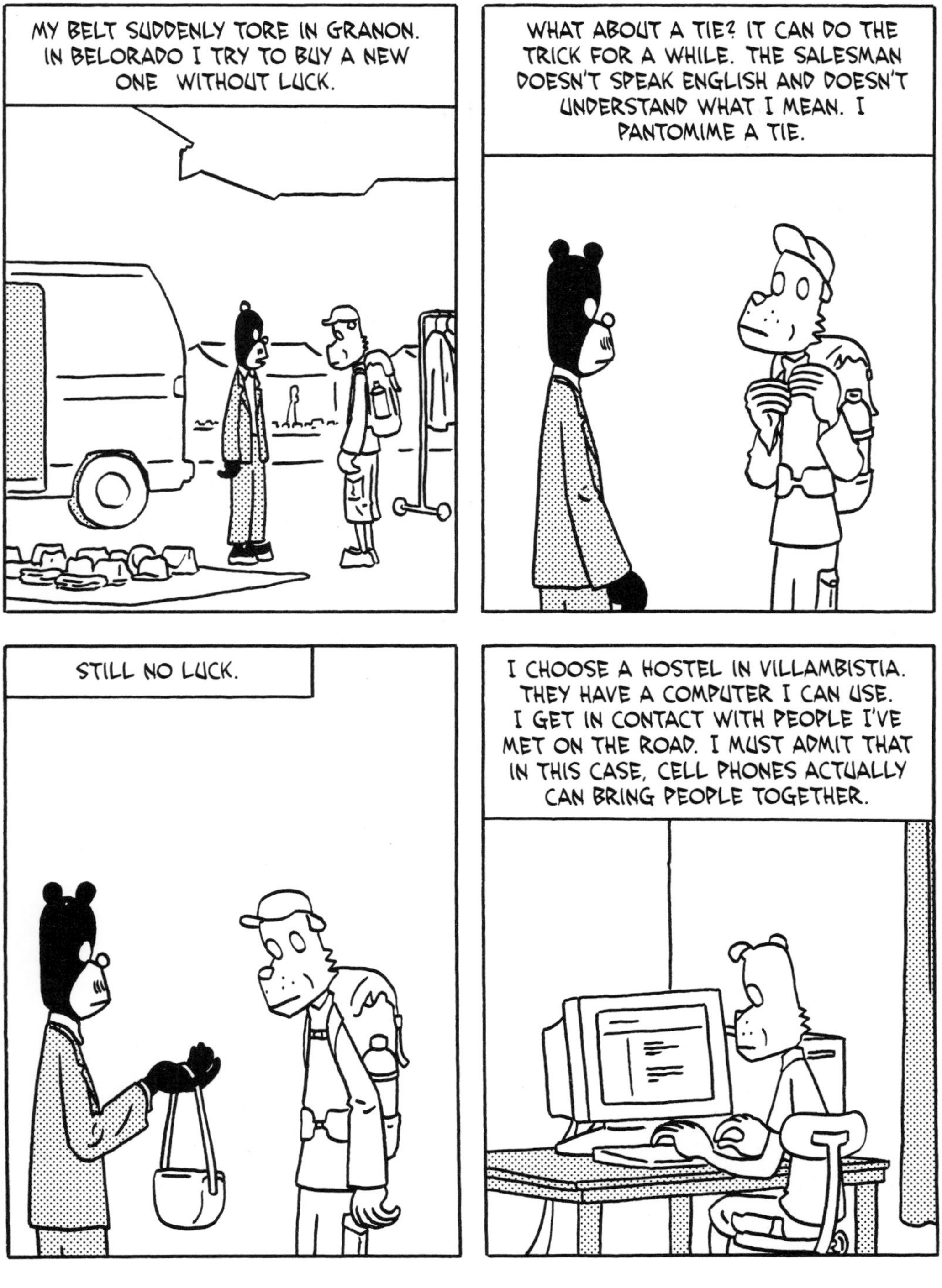
MY BELT SUDDENLY TORE IN GRANON. IN BELORADO I TRY TO BUY A NEW ONE WITHOUT LUCK.
WHAT ABOUT A TIE? IT CAN DO THE TRICK FOR A WHILE. THE SALESMAN DOESN'T SPEAK ENGLISH AND DOESN'T UNDERSTAND WHAT I MEAN. I PANTOMIME A TIE.
STILL NO LUCK.
I CHOOSE A HOSTEL IN VILLAMBISTIA. THEY HAVE A COMPUTER I CAN USE. I GET IN CONTACT WITH PEOPLE I'VE MET ON THE ROAD. I MUST ADMIT THAT IN THIS CASE, CELL PHONES ACTUALLY CAN BRING PEOPLE TOGETHER.

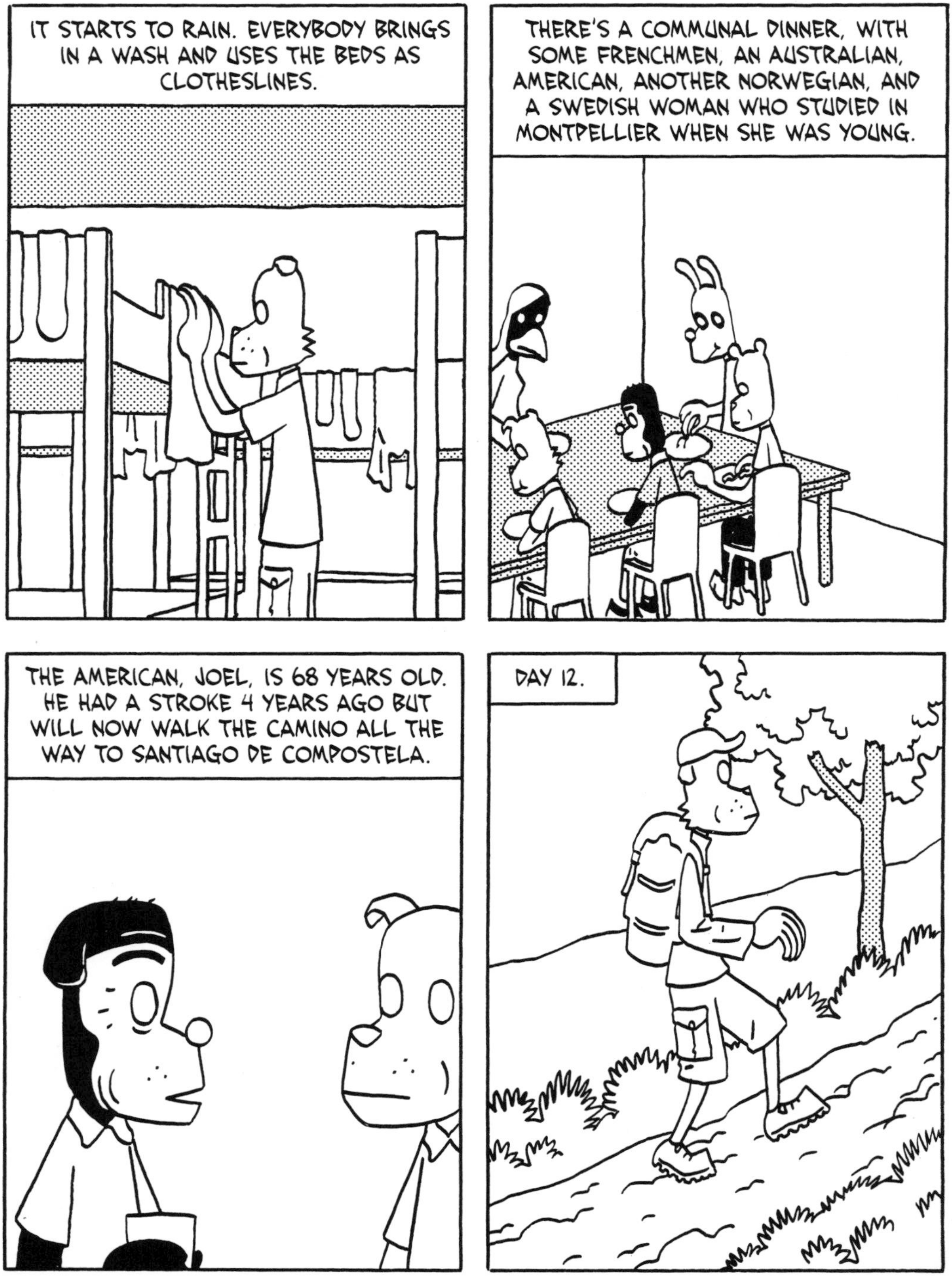
IT STARTS TO RAIN. EVERYBODY BRINGS IN A WASH AND USES THE BEDS AS CLOTHESLINES.
THERE'S A COMMUNAL DINNER, WITH SOME FRENCHMEN, AN AUSTRALIAN, AMERICAN, ANOTHER NORWEGIAN, AND A SWEDISH WOMAN WHO STUDIED IN MONTPELLIER WHEN SHE WAS YOUNG.
THE AMERICAN, JOEL, IS 68 YEARS OLD. HE HAD A STROKE 4 YEARS AGO BUT WILL NOW WALK THE CAMINO ALL THE WAY TO SANTIAGO DE COMPOSTELA.
DAY 12.

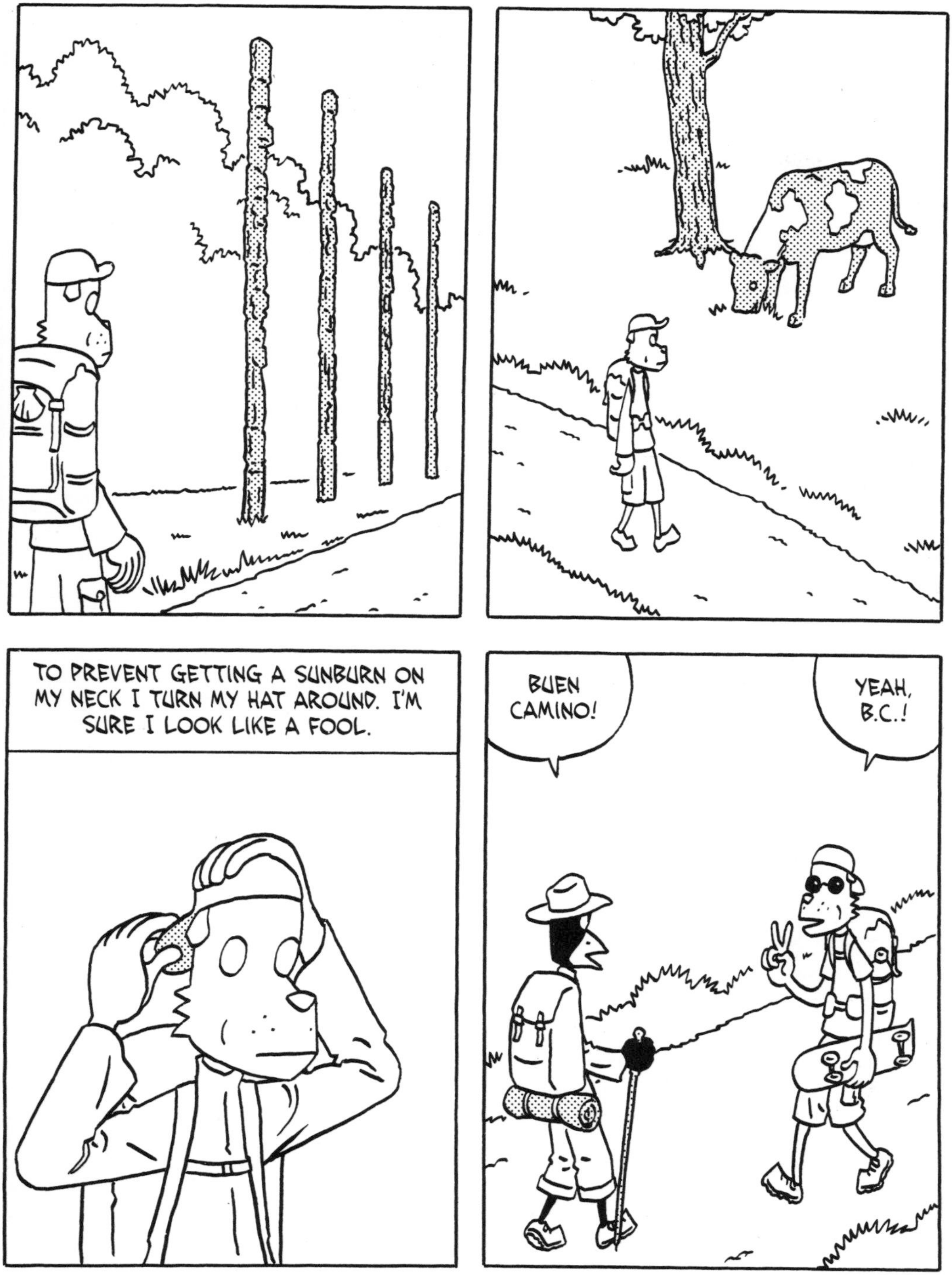
TO PREVENT GETTING A SUNBURN ON MY NECK I TURN MY HAT AROUND. I'M SURE I LOOK LIKE A FOOL.
BUEN CAMINO!
YEAH, B.C..!

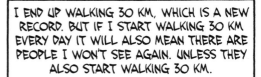

I END UP WALKING 30 KM, WHICH IS A NEW RECORD. BUT IF I START WALKING 30 KM EVERY DAY IT WILL ALSO MEAN THERE ARE PEOPLE I WON'T SEE AGAIN. UNLESS THEY ALSO START WALKING 30 KM.

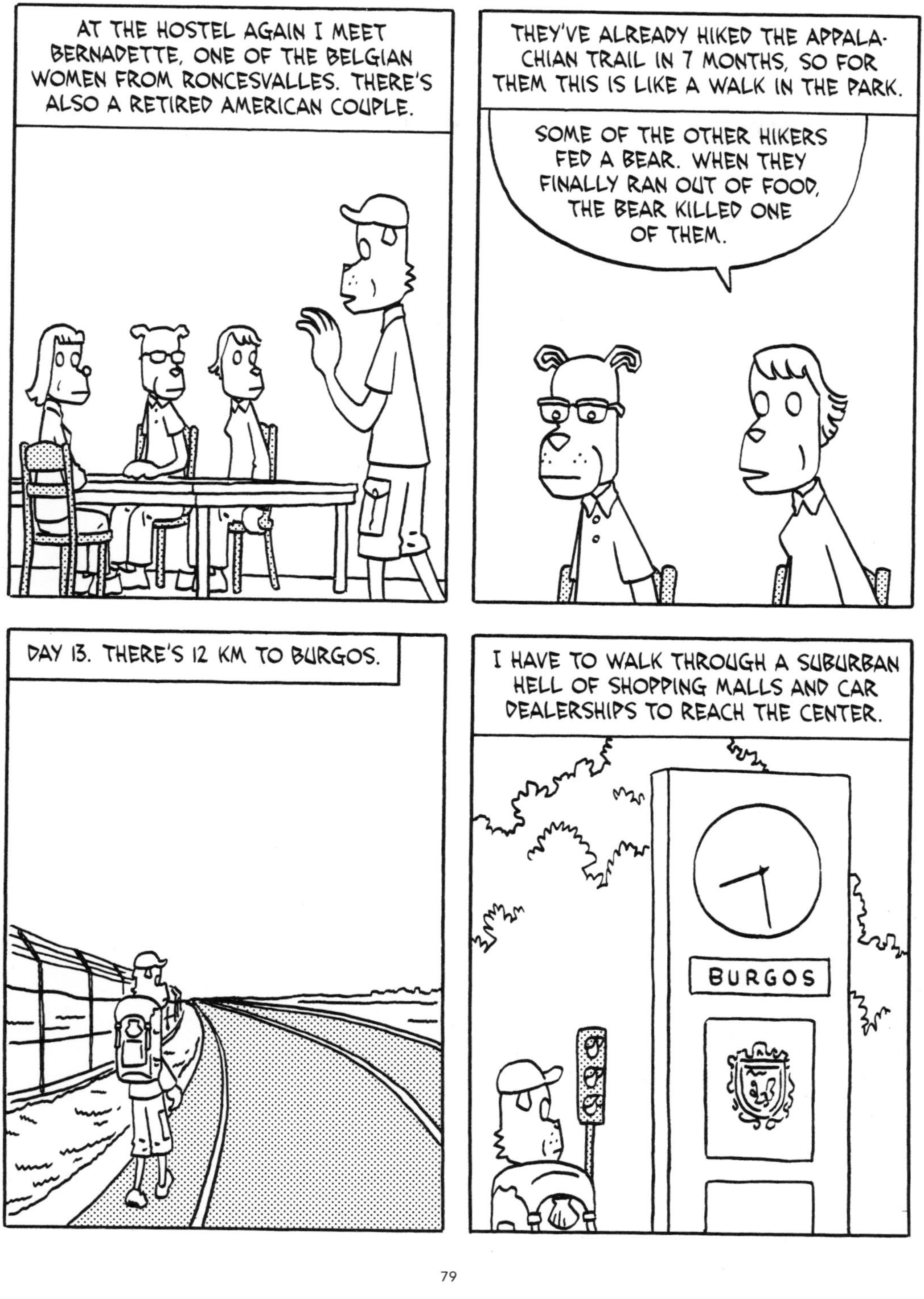
AT THE HOSTEL AGAIN I MEET BERNADETTE, ONE OF THE BELGIAN WOMEN FROM RONCESVALLES. THERE'S ALSO A RETIRED AMERICAN COUPLE.
THEY'VE ALREADY HIKED THE APPALACHIAN TRAIL IN 7 MONTHS, SO FOR THEM THIS IS LIKE A WALK IN THE PARK.
SOME OF THE OTHER HIKERS FED A BEAR. WHEN THEY FINALLY RAN OUT OF FOOD, THE BEAR KILLED ONE OF THEM.
DAY 13. THERE'S 12 KM TO BURGOS.
I HAVE TO WALK THROUGH A SUBURBAN HELL OF SHOPPING MALLS AND CAR DEALERSHIPS TO REACH THE CENTER.
BURGOS

I MEET LAUREANO, MY SPANISH PUBLISHER, FOR TAPAS AND CATHEDRAL VISITING...

...AND FINALLY MANAGE TO BUY A NEW BELT BEFORE I GET BACK ON THE ROAD.

I ONLY HAVE A BIT OF WATER LEFT IN MY BOTTLE FOR THE LAST 8 KM OF TODAY'S MARCH. I ASSUMED THAT WOULD BE ENOUGH. BUT! WHAT IF I GOT LOST AND THEN BREAK MY FOOT?! THIS IS DAY 13! DON'T FEED THE BEAR!!

I REACH HORMILLOS DEL CAMINO WITHOUT ANY ACCIDENTS AND CHOOSE A HOSTEL. THERE ARE NO PEOPLE I KNOW.

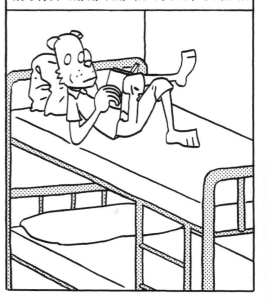

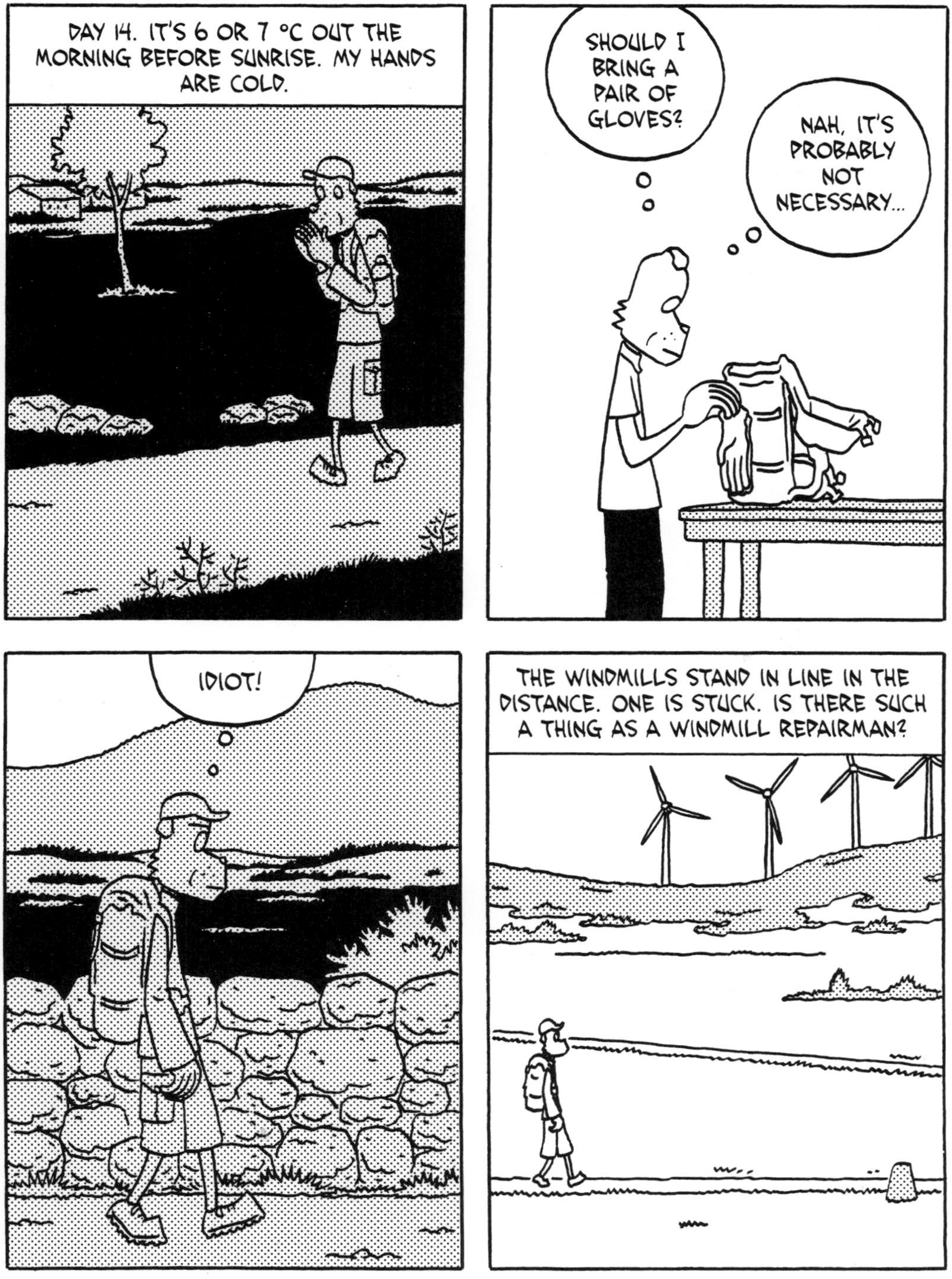
DAY 14. IT'S 6 OR 7 °C OUT THE MORNING BEFORE SUNRISE. MY HANDS ARE COLD.
SHOULD I BRING A PAIR OF GLOVES?
NAH, IT'S PROBABLY NOT NECESSARY...
IDIOT!
THE WINDMILLS STAND IN LINE IN THE DISTANCE. ONE IS STUCK. IS THERE SUCH A THING AS A WINDMILL REPAIRMAN?

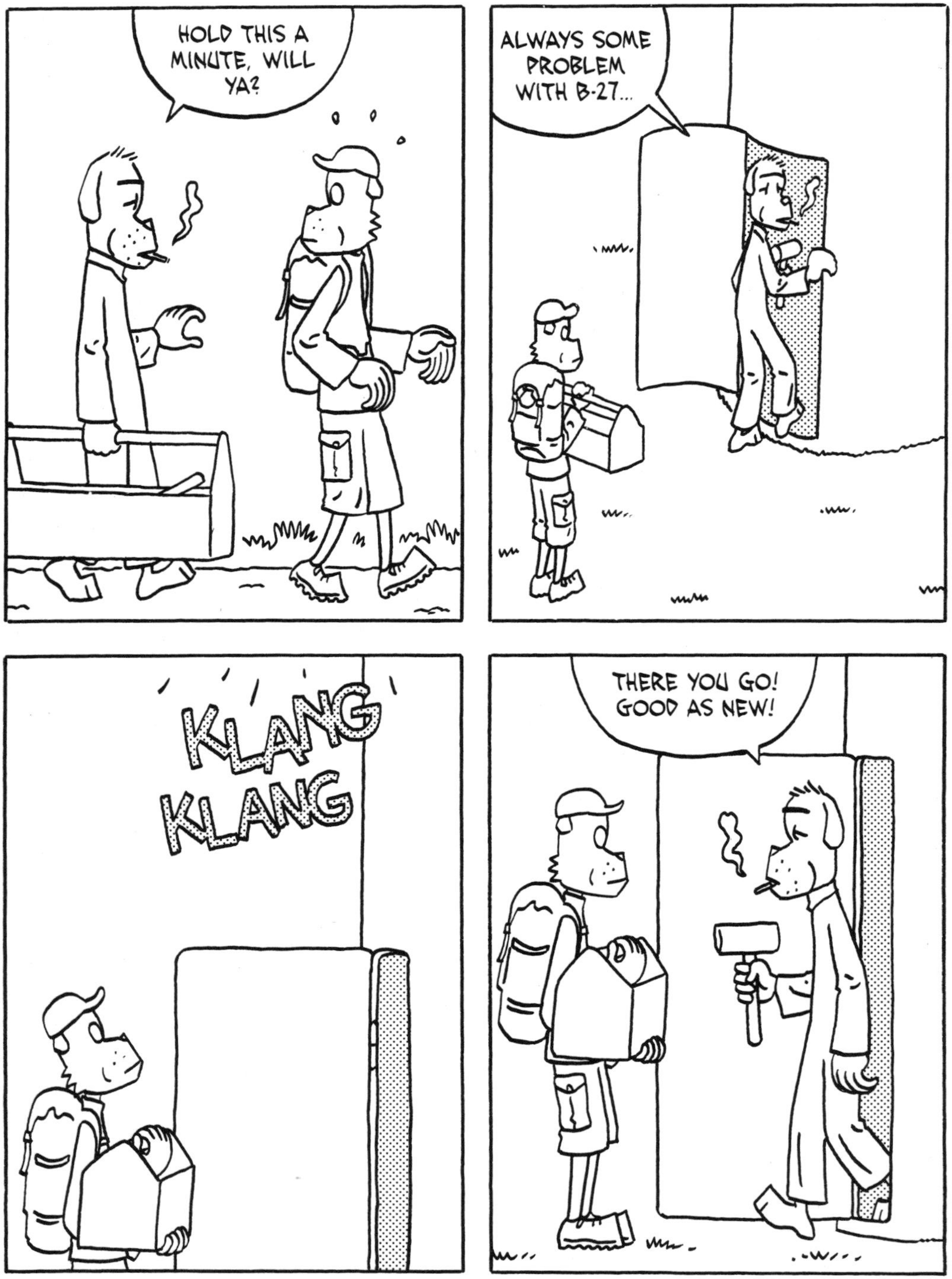
HOLD THIS A MINUTE, WILL YA?
ALWAYS SOME PROBLEM WITH B-27...
KLANG KLANG
THERE YOU GO! GOOD AS NEW!

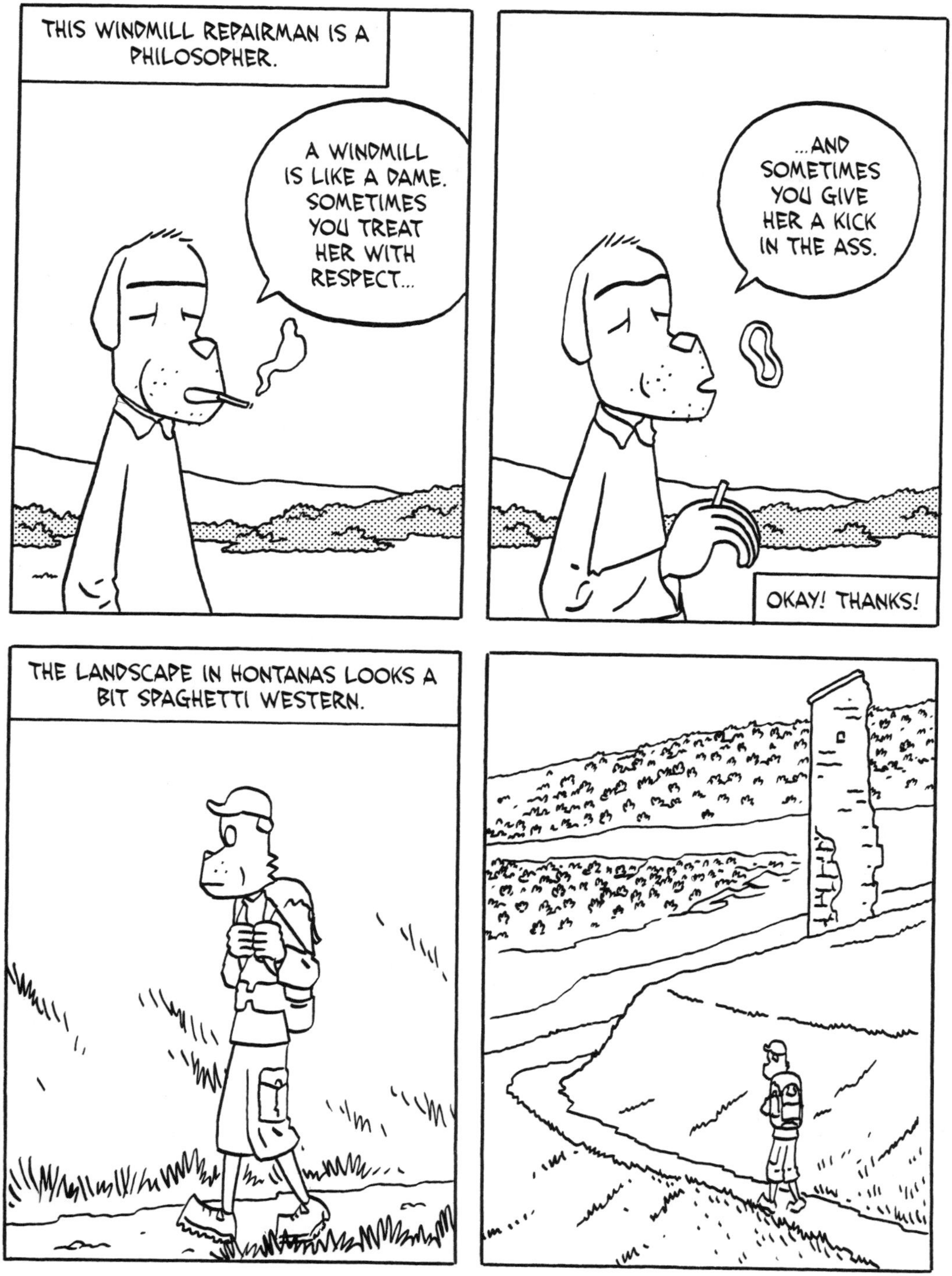
THIS WINDMILL REPAIRMAN IS A PHILOSOPHER.
A WINDMILL IS LIKE A DAME. SOMETIMES YOU TREAT HER WITH RESPECT...
...AND SOMETIMES YOU GIVE HER A KICK IN THE ASS.
OKAY! THANKS!
THE LANDSCAPE IN HONTANAS LOOKS A BIT SPAGHETTI WESTERN.

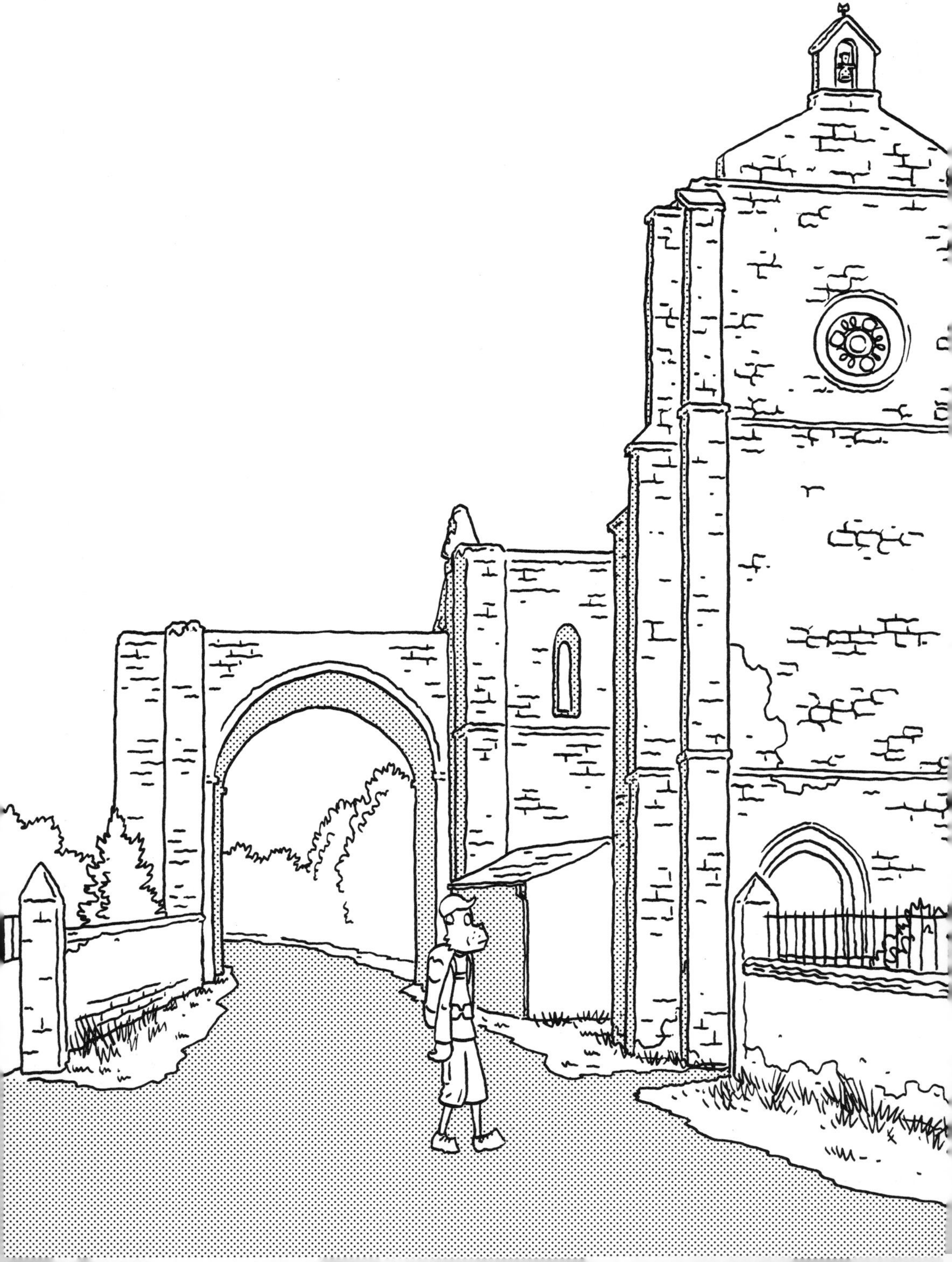

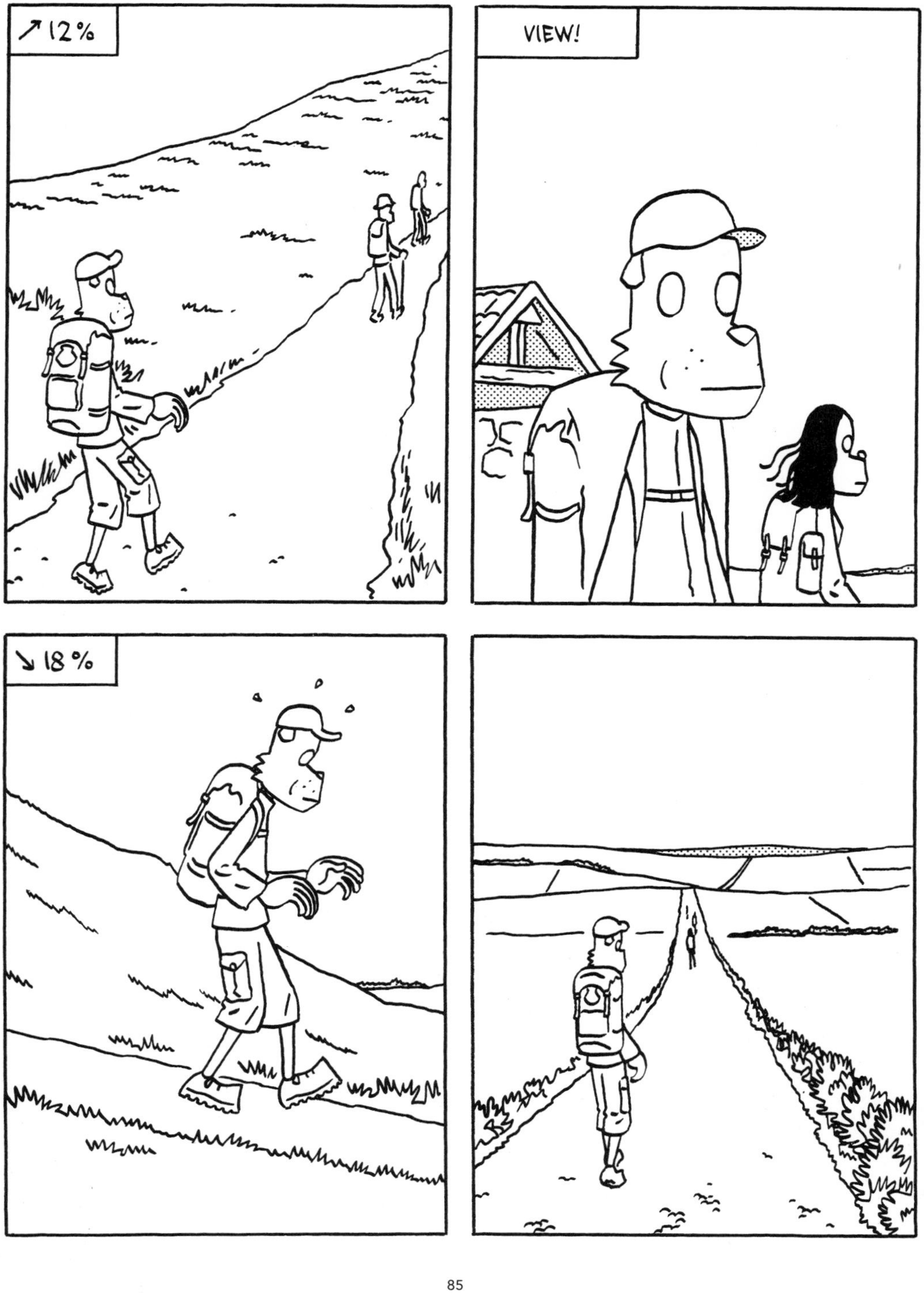
↗ 12%
VIEW!
↘ 18%

TODAY'S MARCH IS 30 KM. I CHOOSE A HOSTEL IN ITERO DE LA VEGA.

I'M TIRED.

THAT'S A NICE CHURCH. I COULD GO OVER AND DO A SKETCH.

THERE'S A GROUP DINNER, WITH TWO SWEDISH WOMEN, ULRIKA AND LISA, TWO FRENCHMEN, AND AN AMERICAN NAMED PIERRE.

DID YOU BRING A STONE?

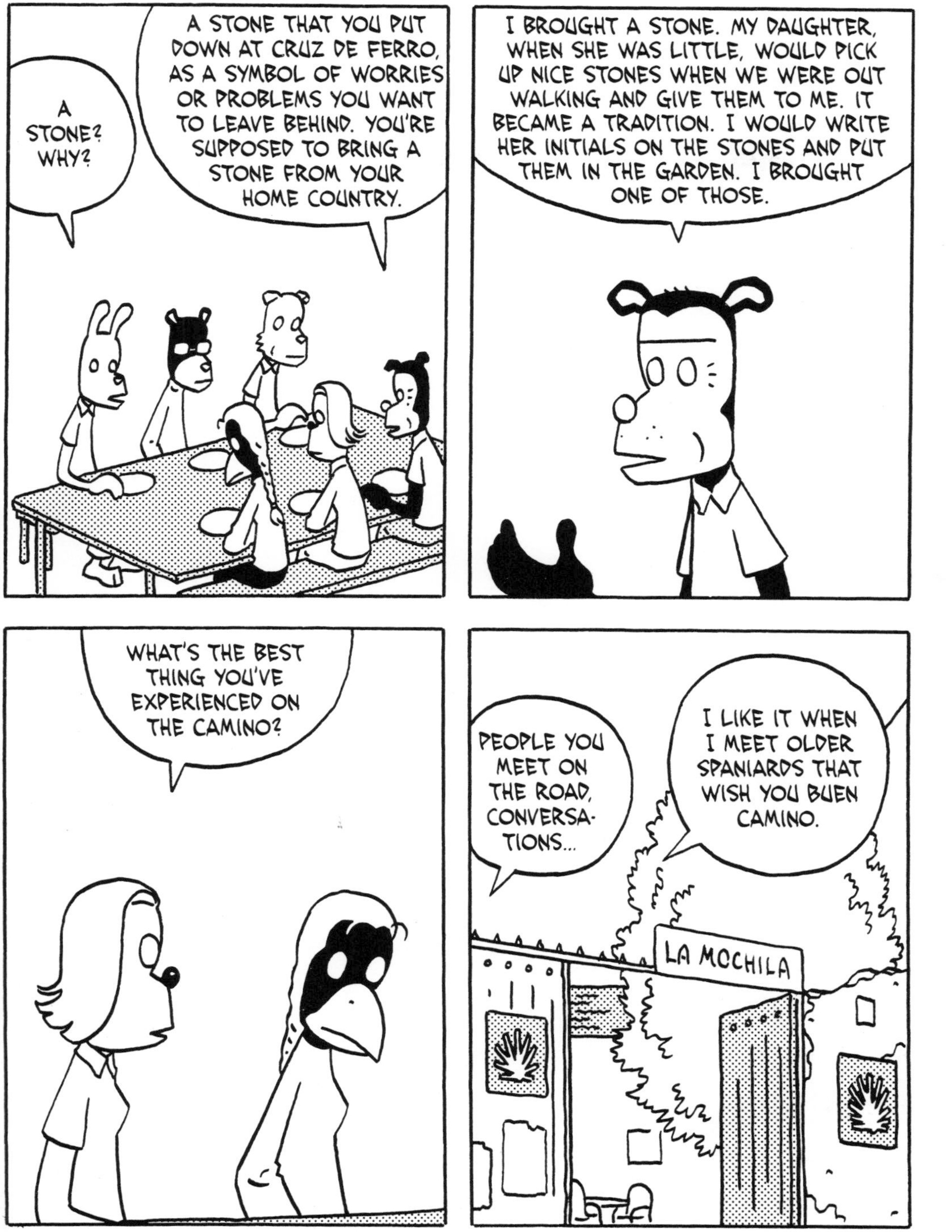
A STONE? WHY?
A STONE THAT YOU PUT DOWN AT CRUZ DE FERRO, AS A SYMBOL OF WORRIES OR PROBLEMS YOU WANT TO LEAVE BEHIND. YOU'RE SUPPOSED TO BRING A STONE FROM YOUR HOME COUNTRY.
I BROUGHT A STONE. MY DAUGHTER, WHEN SHE WAS LITTLE, WOULD PICK UP NICE STONES WHEN WE WERE OUT WALKING AND GIVE THEM TO ME. IT BECAME A TRADITION. I WOULD WRITE HER INITIALS ON THE STONES AND PUT THEM IN THE GARDEN. I BROUGHT ONE OF THOSE.
WHAT'S THE BEST THING YOU'VE EXPERIENCED ON THE CAMINO?
PEOPLE YOU MEET ON THE ROAD, CONVERSA-TIONS...
I LIKE IT WHEN I MEET OLDER SPANIARDS THAT WISH YOU BUEN CAMINO.
LA MOCHILA

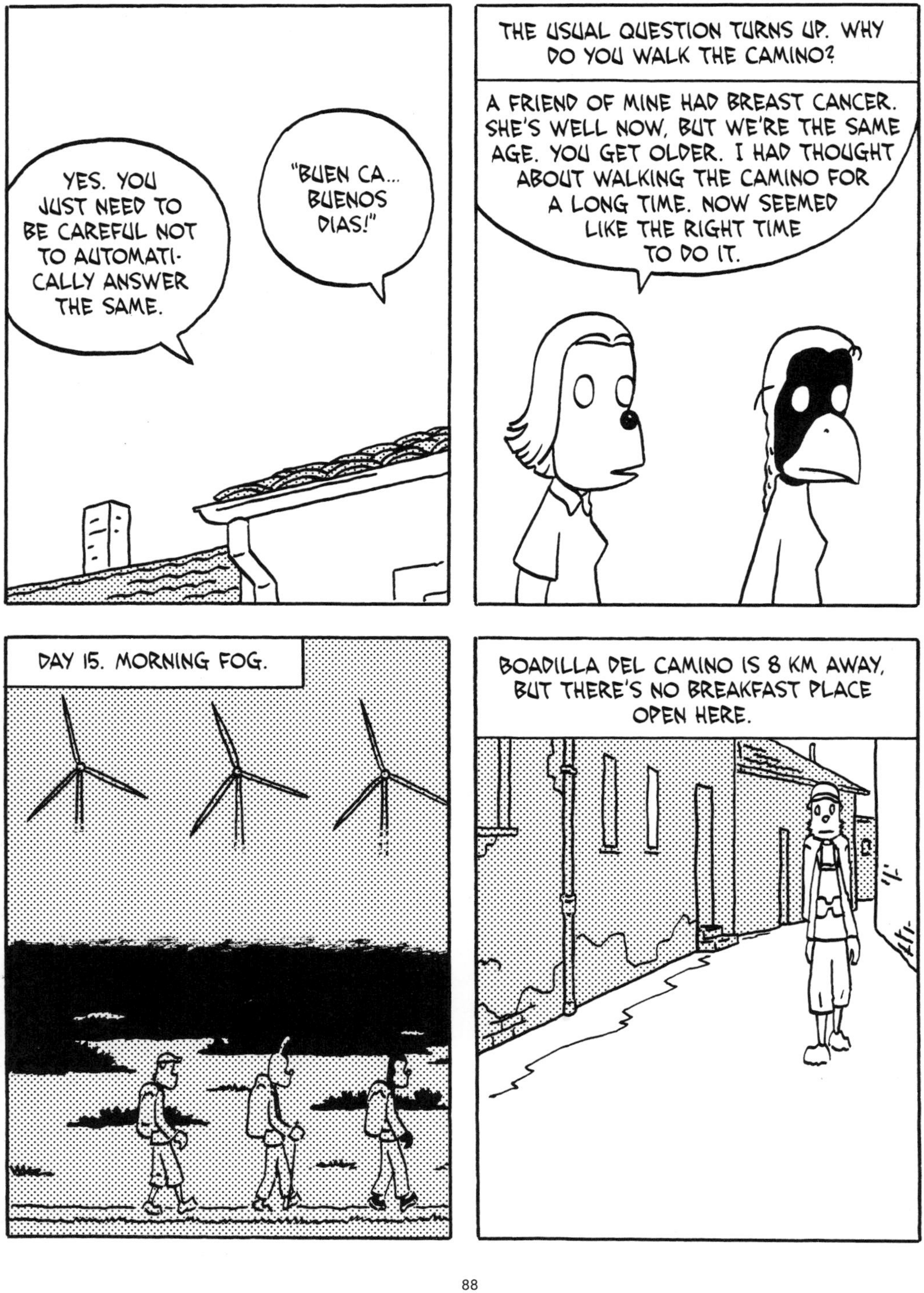
YES. YOU JUST NEED TO BE CAREFUL NOT TO AUTOMATICALLY ANSWER THE SAME.
"BUEN CA... BUENOS DIAS!"
THE USUAL QUESTION TURNS UP. WHY DO YOU WALK THE CAMINO?
A FRIEND OF MINE HAD BREAST CANCER. SHE'S WELL NOW, BUT WE'RE THE SAME AGE. YOU GET OLDER. I HAD THOUGHT ABOUT WALKING THE CAMINO FOR A LONG TIME. NOW SEEMED LIKE THE RIGHT TIME TO DO IT.
DAY 15. MORNING FOG.
BOADILLA DEL CAMINO IS 8 KM AWAY, BUT THERE'S NO BREAKFAST PLACE OPEN HERE.

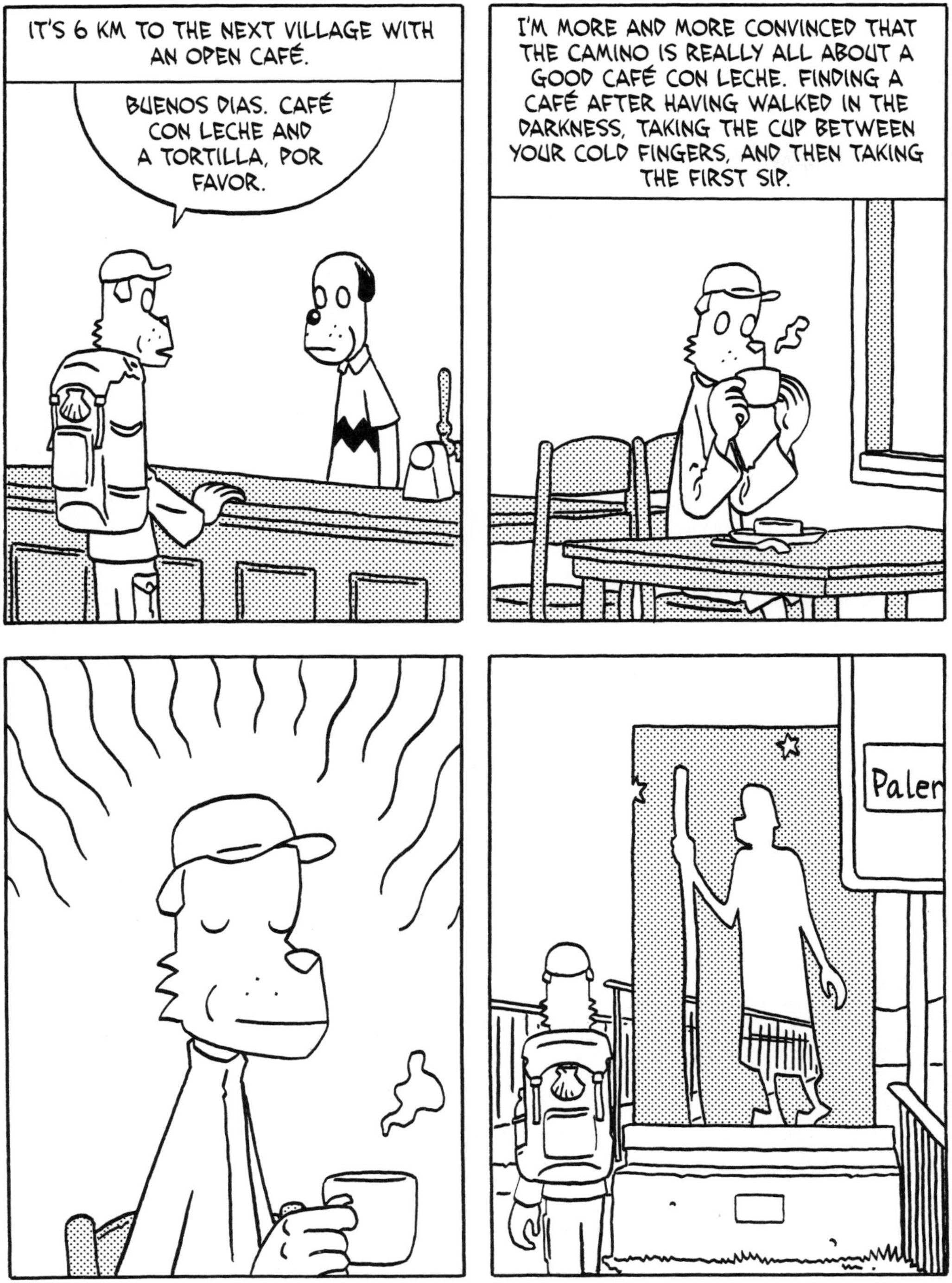
IT'S 6 KM TO THE NEXT VILLAGE WITH AN OPEN CAFÉ.
BUENOS DIAS. CAFÉ CON LECHE AND A TORTILLA, POR FAVOR.
I'M MORE AND MORE CONVINCED THAT THE CAMINO IS REALLY ALL ABOUT A GOOD CAFÉ CON LECHE. FINDING A CAFÉ AFTER HAVING WALKED IN THE DARKNESS, TAKING THE CUP BETWEEN YOUR COLD FINGERS, AND THEN TAKING THE FIRST SIP.
Paler

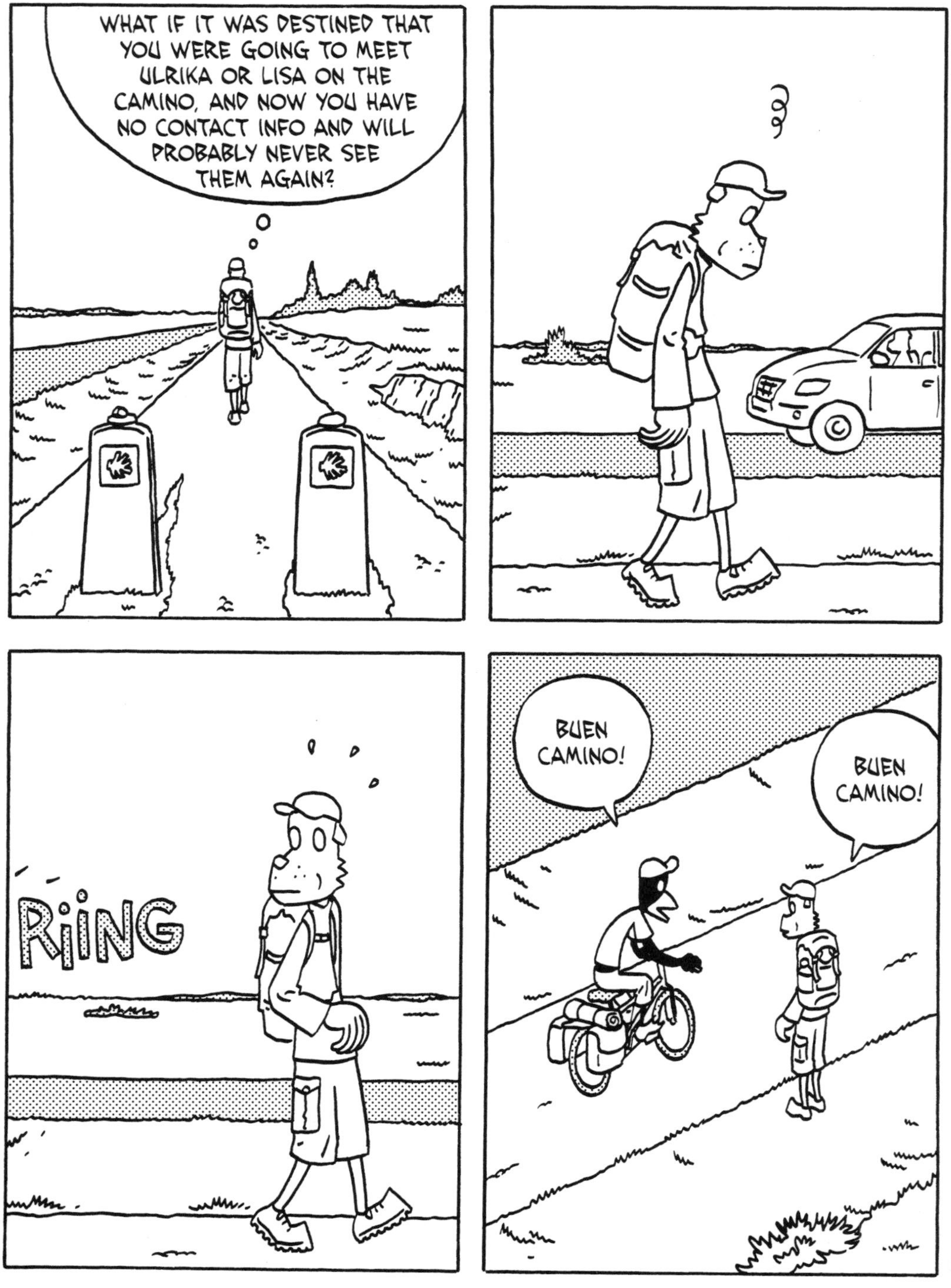
WHAT IF IT WAS DESTINED THAT YOU WERE GOING TO MEET ULRIKA OR LISA ON THE CAMINO, AND NOW YOU HAVE NO CONTACT INFO AND WILL PROBABLY NEVER SEE THEM AGAIN?
RING
BUEN CAMINO!
BUEN CAMINO!

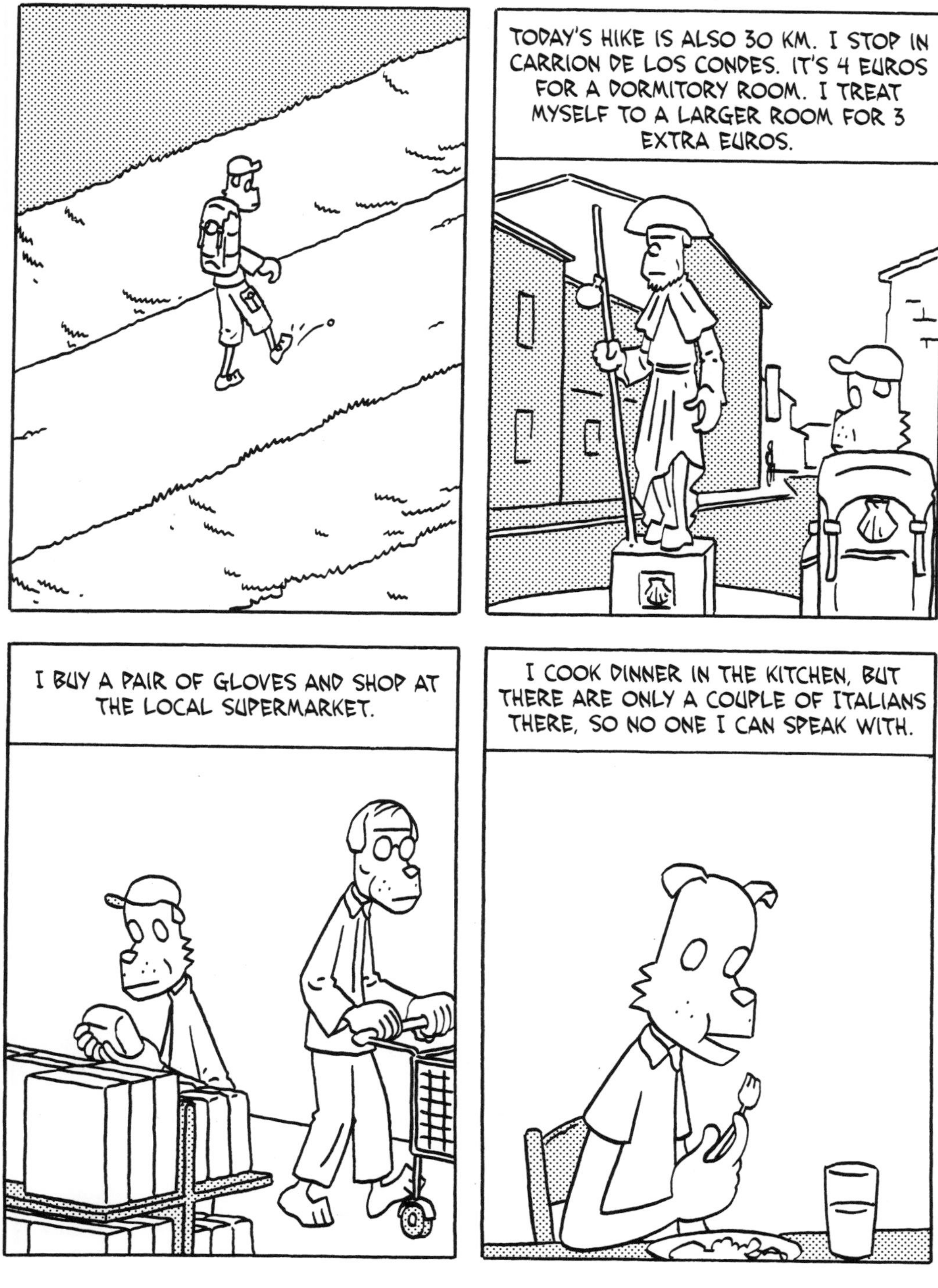
TODAY'S HIKE IS ALSO 30 KM. I STOP IN CARRION DE LOS CONDES. IT'S 4 EUROS FOR A DORMITORY ROOM. I TREAT MYSELF TO A LARGER ROOM FOR 3 EXTRA EUROS.
I BUY A PAIR OF GLOVES AND SHOP AT THE LOCAL SUPERMARKET.
I COOK DINNER IN THE KITCHEN, BUT THERE ARE ONLY A COUPLE OF ITALIANS THERE, SO NO ONE I CAN SPEAK WITH.

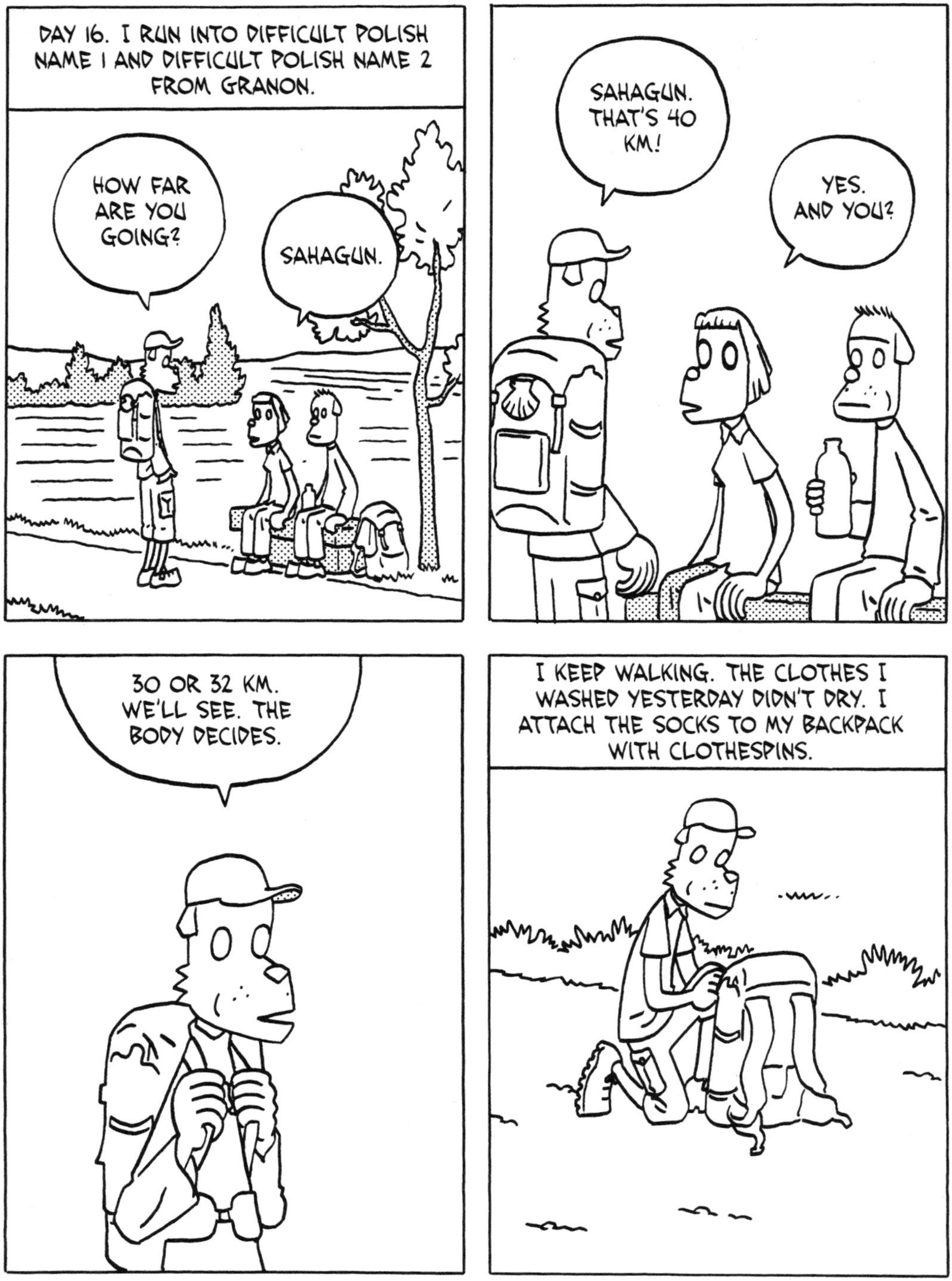
DAY 16. I RUN INTO DIFFICULT POLISH NAME 1 AND DIFFICULT POLISH NAME 2 FROM GRANON.
HOW FAR ARE YOU GOING?
SAHAGUN.
SAHAGUN. THAT'S 40 KM!
YES. AND YOU?
30 OR 32 KM. WE'LL SEE. THE BODY DECIDES.
I KEEP WALKING. THE CLOTHES I WASHED YESTERDAY DIDN'T DRY. I ATTACH THE SOCKS TO MY BACKPACK WITH CLOTHESPINS.

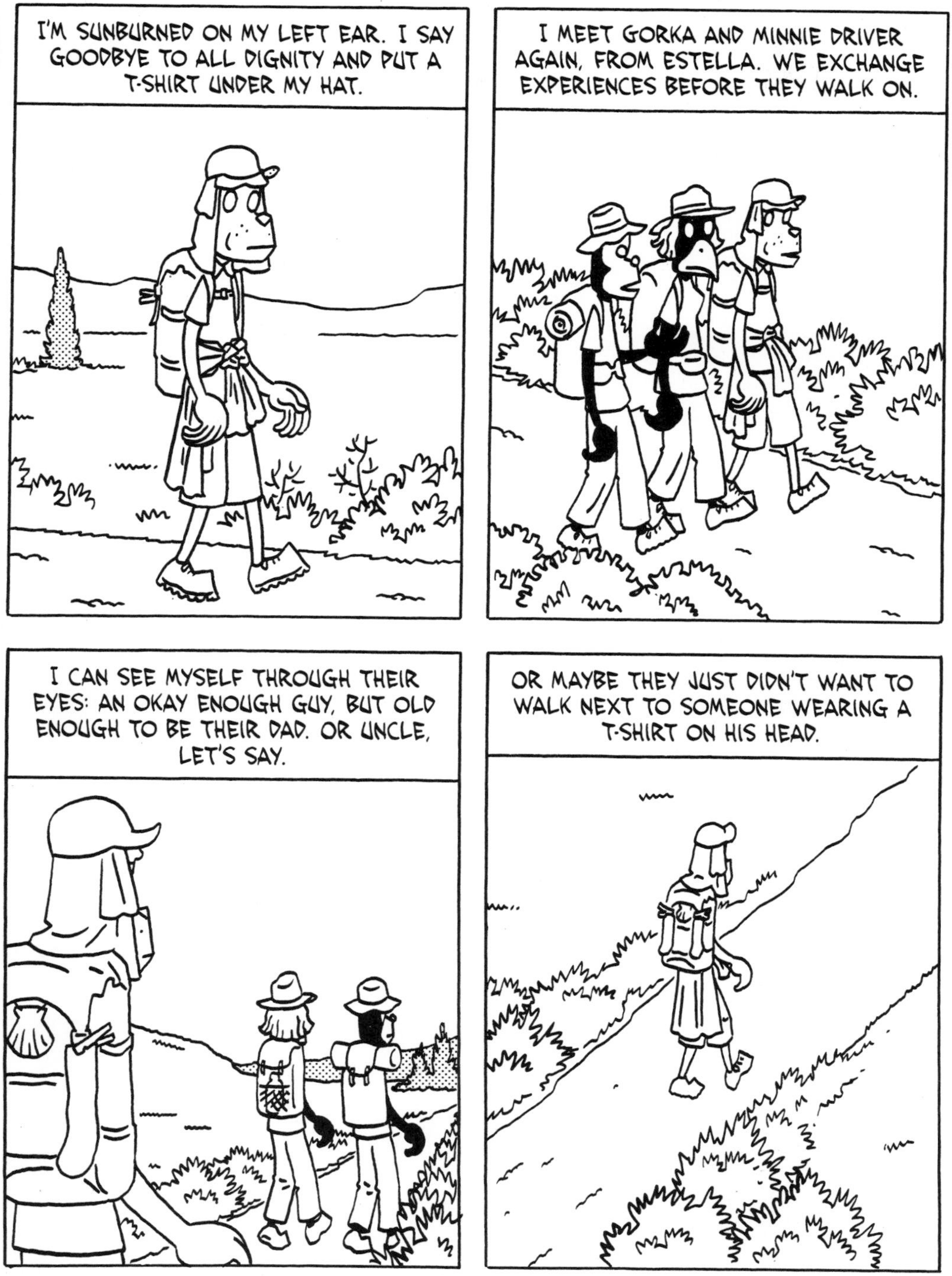
I'M SUNBURNED ON MY LEFT EAR. I SAY GOODBYE TO ALL DIGNITY AND PUT A T-SHIRT UNDER MY HAT.
I MEET GORKA AND MINNIE DRIVER AGAIN, FROM ESTELLA. WE EXCHANGE EXPERIENCES BEFORE THEY WALK ON.
I CAN SEE MYSELF THROUGH THEIR EYES: AN OKAY ENOUGH GUY, BUT OLD ENOUGH TO BE THEIR DAD. OR UNCLE, LET'S SAY.
OR MAYBE THEY JUST DIDN'T WANT TO WALK NEXT TO SOMEONE WEARING A T-SHIRT ON HIS HEAD.

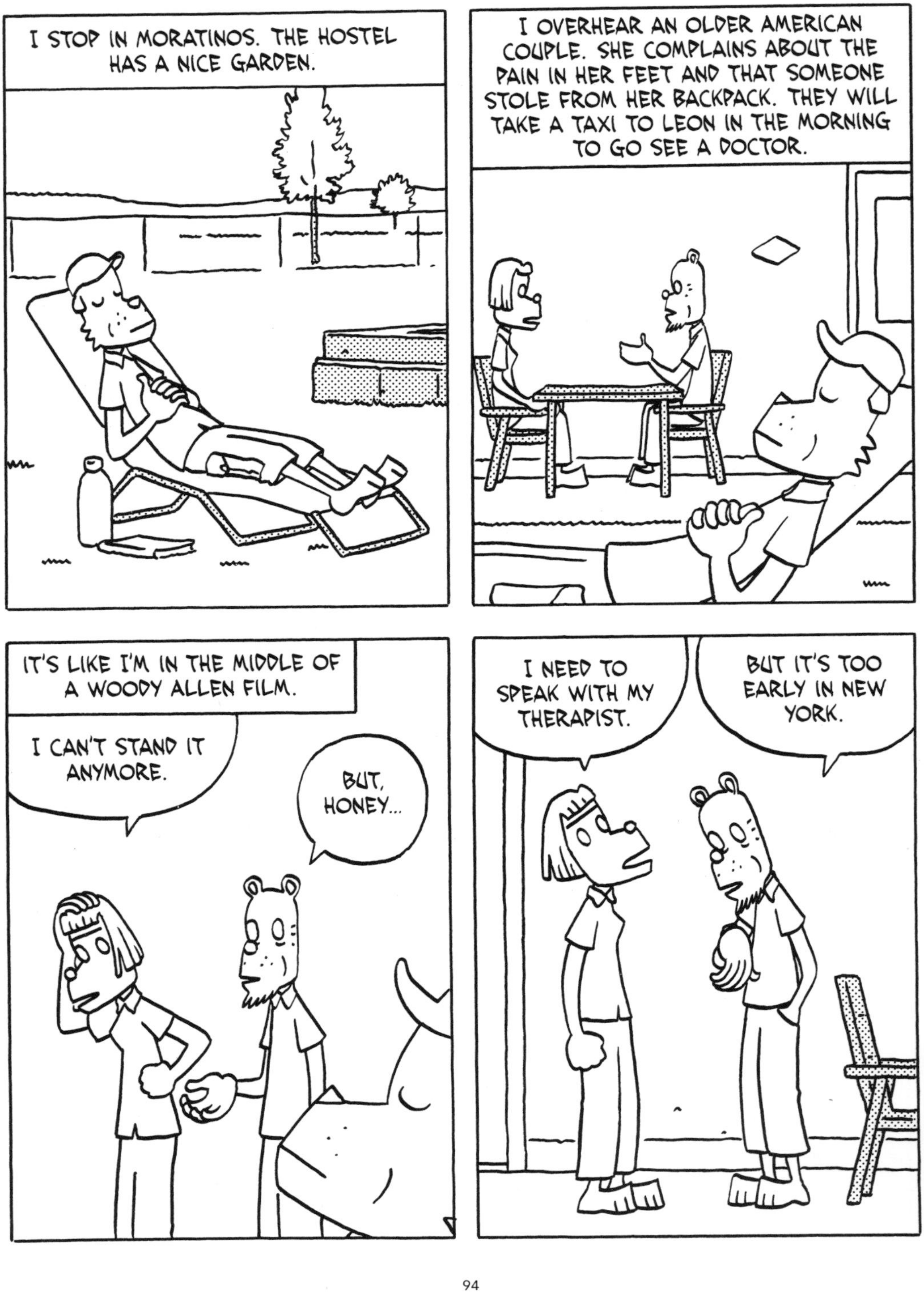
I STOP IN MORATINOS. THE HOSTEL HAS A NICE GARDEN.
I OVERHEAR AN OLDER AMERICAN COUPLE. SHE COMPLAINS ABOUT THE PAIN IN HER FEET AND THAT SOMEONE STOLE FROM HER BACKPACK. THEY WILL TAKE A TAXI TO LEON IN THE MORNING TO GO SEE A DOCTOR.
IT'S LIKE I'M IN THE MIDDLE OF A WOODY ALLEN FILM.
I CAN'T STAND IT ANYMORE.
BUT, HONEY...
I NEED TO SPEAK WITH MY THERAPIST.
BUT IT'S TOO EARLY IN NEW YORK.

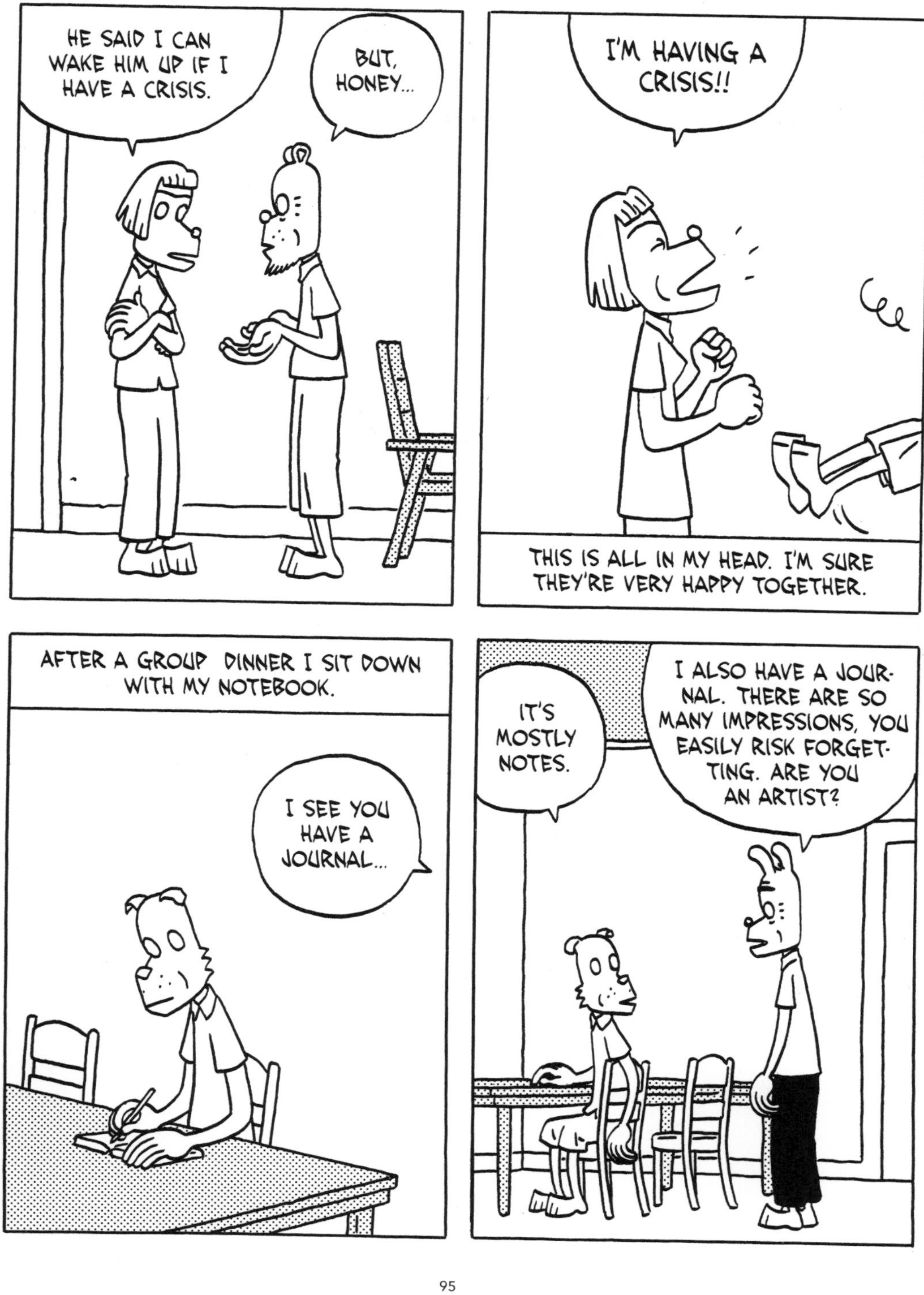
HE SAID I CAN WAKE HIM UP IF I HAVE A CRISIS.
BUT, HONEY...
I'M HAVING A CRISIS!!
THIS IS ALL IN MY HEAD. I'M SURE THEY'RE VERY HAPPY TOGETHER.
AFTER A GROUP DINNER I SIT DOWN WITH MY NOTEBOOK.
I SEE YOU HAVE A JOURNAL...
IT'S MOSTLY NOTES.
I ALSO HAVE A JOUR-NAL. THERE ARE SO MANY IMPRESSIONS, YOU EASILY RISK FORGET-TING. ARE YOU AN ARTIST?

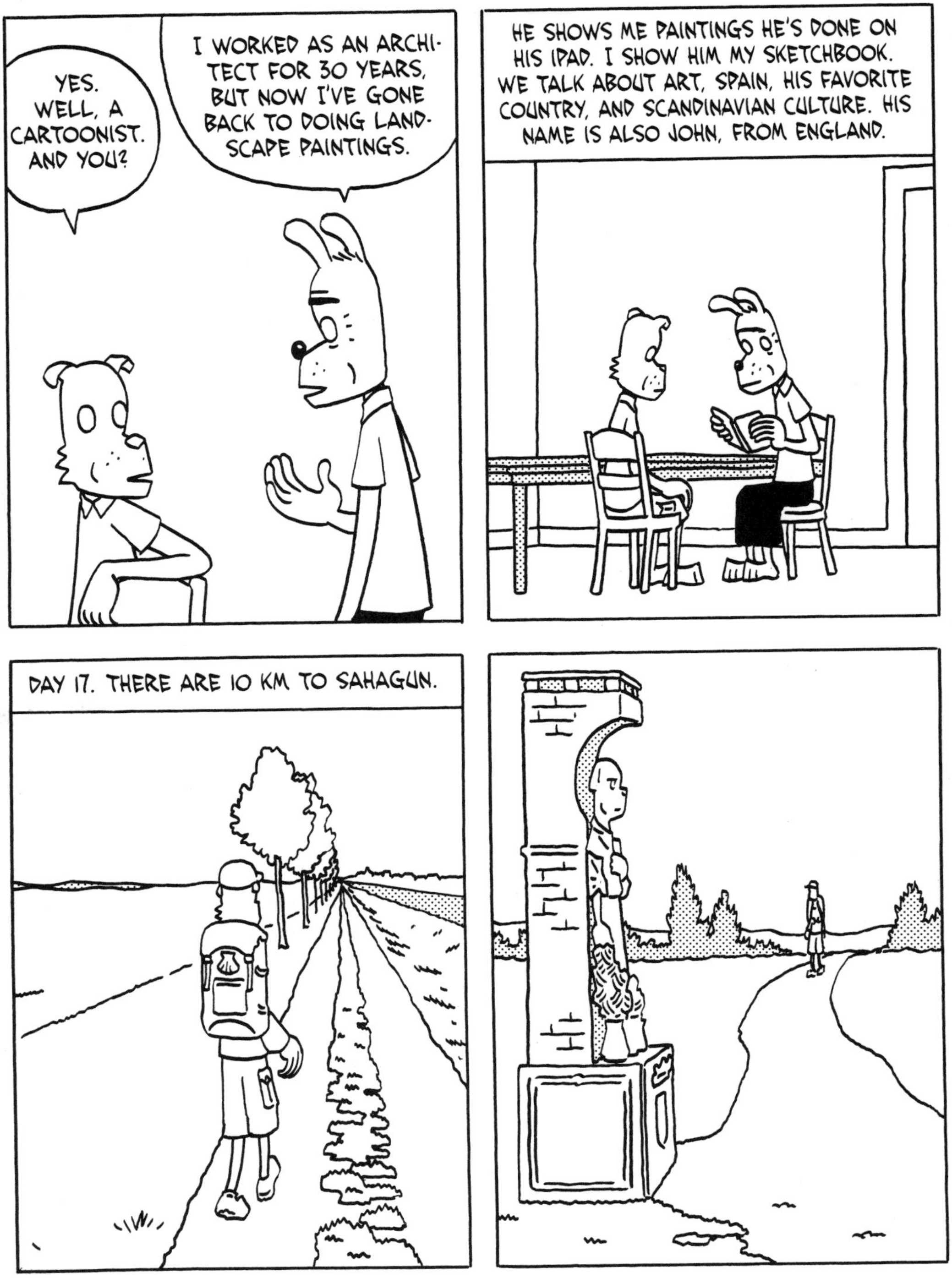
YES. WELL, A CARTOONIST. AND YOU?
I WORKED AS AN ARCHITECT FOR 30 YEARS, BUT NOW I'VE GONE BACK TO DOING LANDSCAPE PAINTINGS.
HE SHOWS ME PAINTINGS HE'S DONE ON HIS IPAD. I SHOW HIM MY SKETCHBOOK. WE TALK ABOUT ART, SPAIN, HIS FAVORITE COUNTRY, AND SCANDINAVIAN CULTURE. HIS NAME IS ALSO JOHN, FROM ENGLAND.
DAY 17. THERE ARE 10 KM TO SAHAGUN.

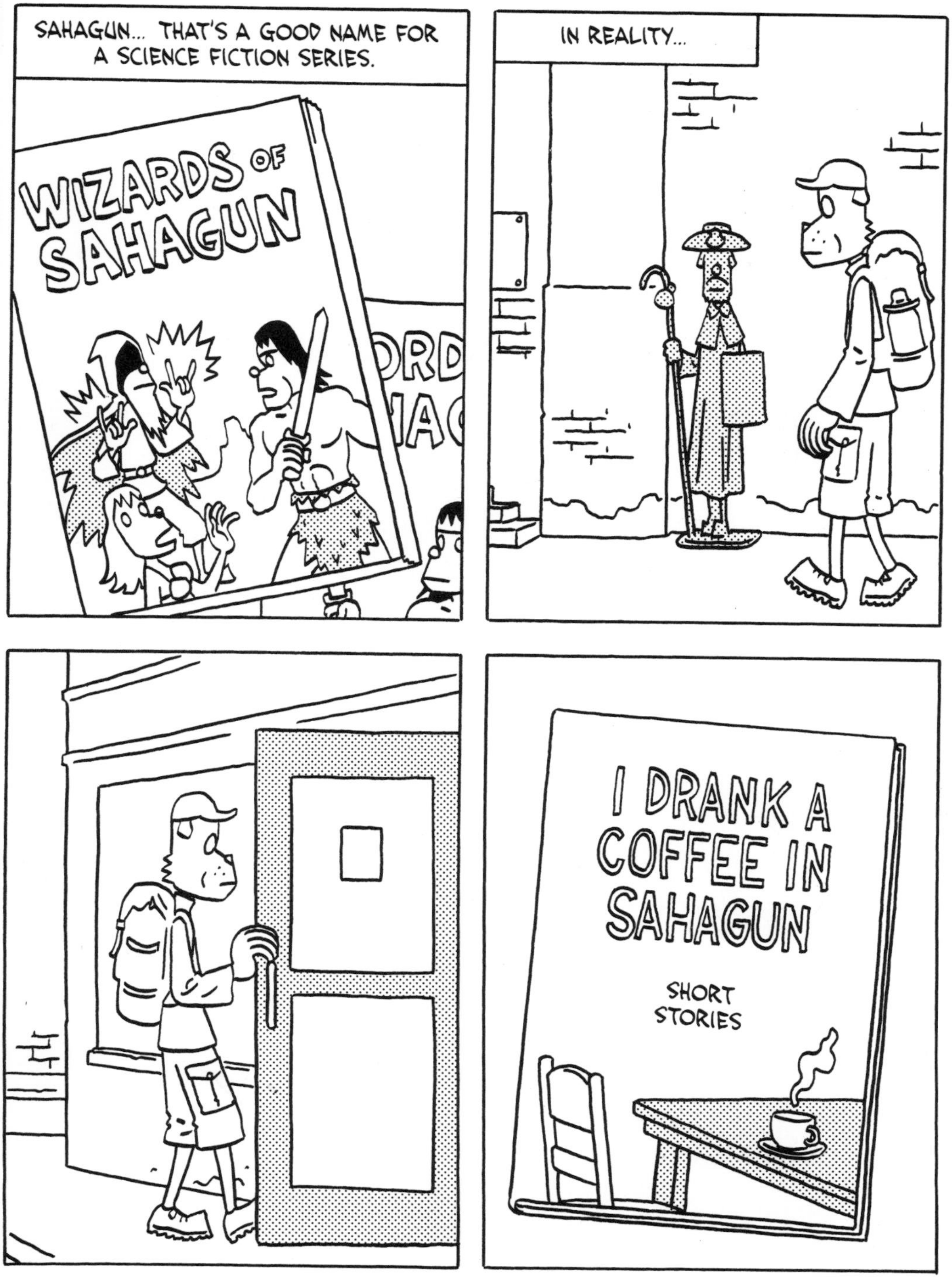
SAHAGUN... THAT'S A GOOD NAME FOR A SCIENCE FICTION SERIES.
WIZARDS OF SAHAGUN
IN REALITY...
I DRANK A COFFEE IN SAHAGUN
SHORT STORIES

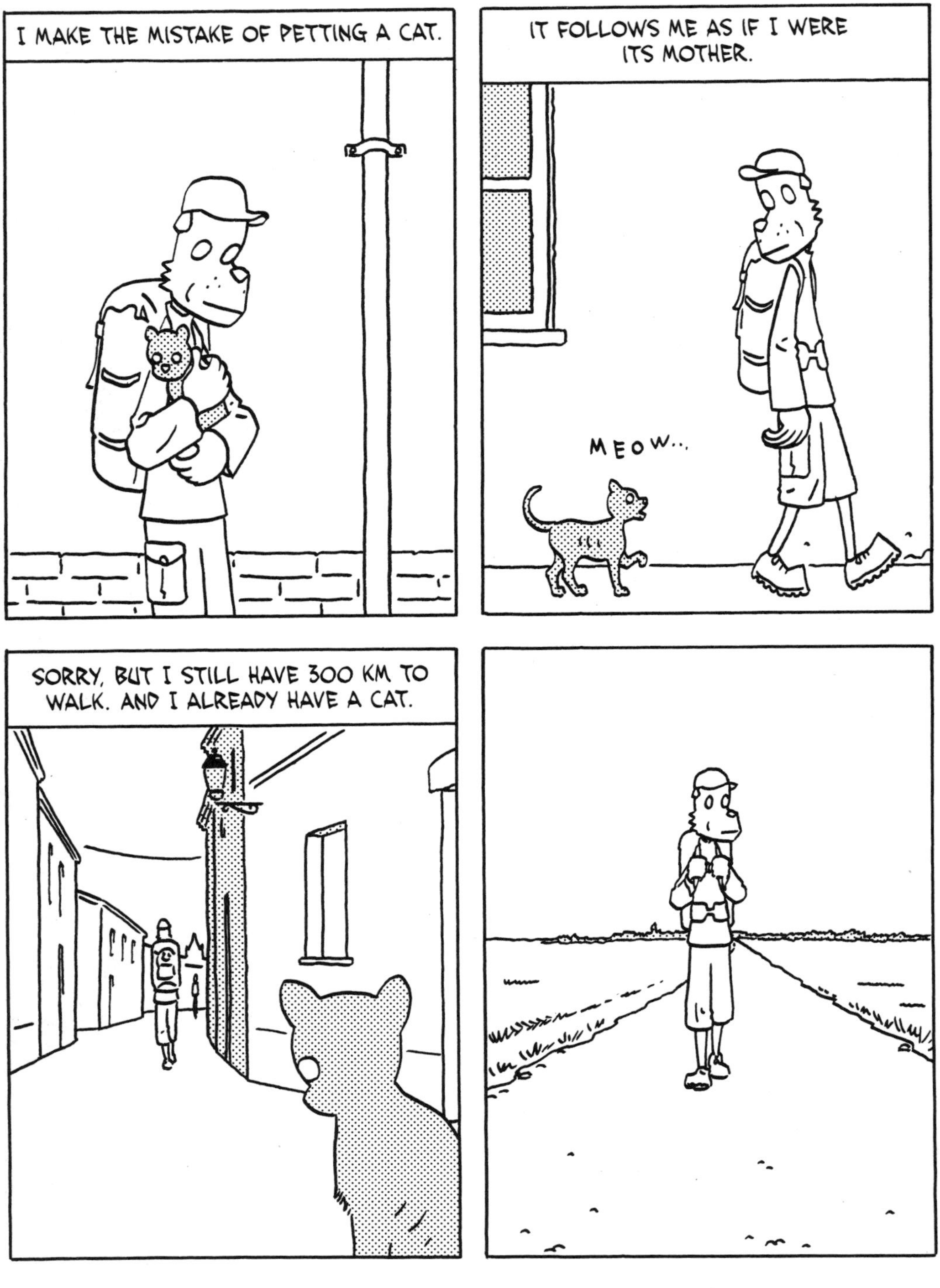
I MAKE THE MISTAKE OF PETTING A CAT.
IT FOLLOWS ME AS IF I WERE ITS MOTHER.
MEOW...
SORRY, BUT I STILL HAVE 300 KM TO WALK. AND I ALREADY HAVE A CAT.

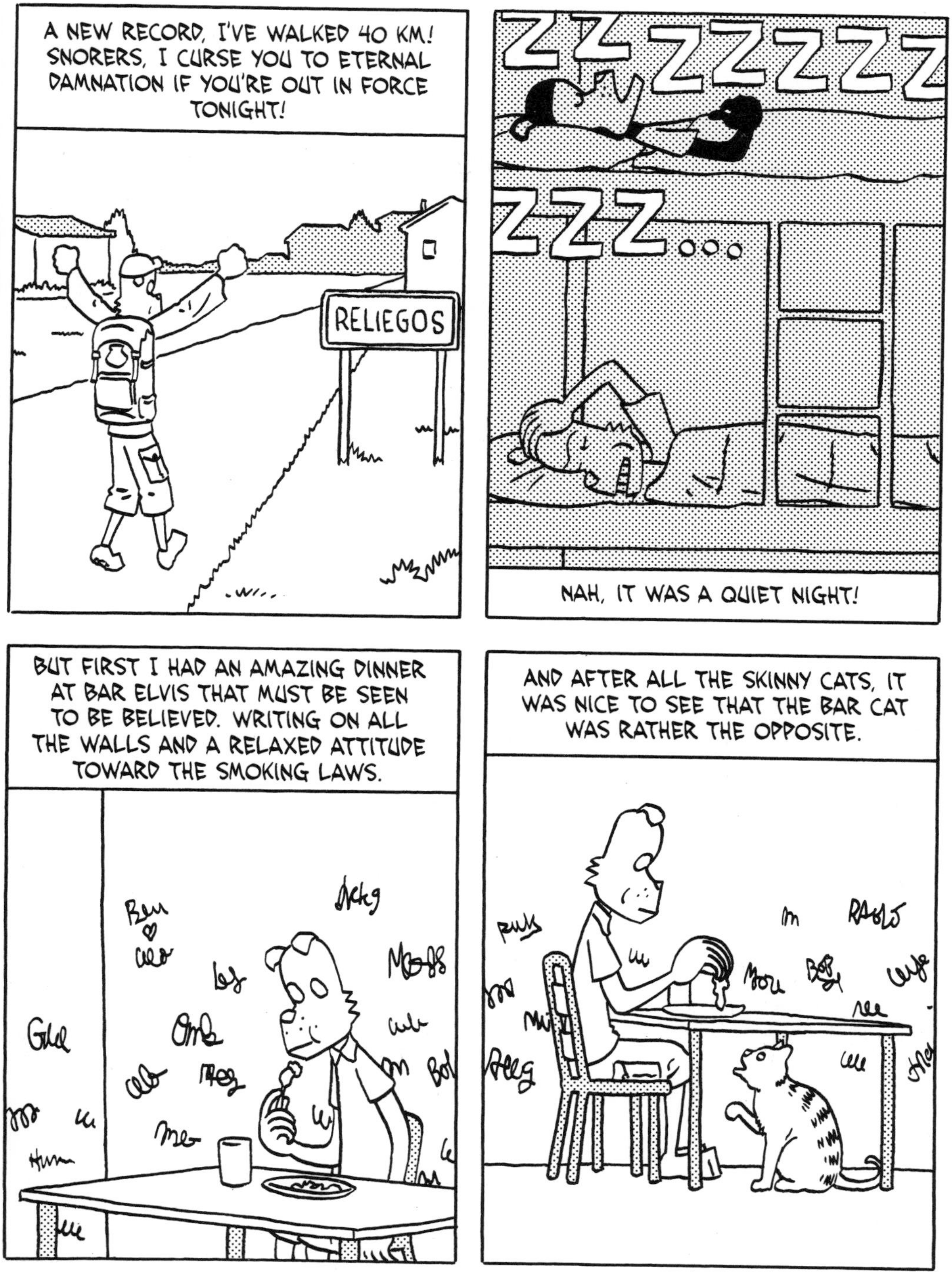
A NEW RECORD, I'VE WALKED 40 KM! SNORERS, I CURSE YOU TO ETERNAL DAMNATION IF YOU'RE OUT IN FORCE TONIGHT!
RELIEGOS
ZZZZZZZZ
ZZZ...
NAH, IT WAS A QUIET NIGHT!
BUT FIRST I HAD AN AMAZING DINNER AT BAR ELVIS THAT MUST BE SEEN TO BE BELIEVED. WRITING ON ALL THE WALLS AND A RELAXED ATTITUDE TOWARD THE SMOKING LAWS.
AND AFTER ALL THE SKINNY CATS, IT WAS NICE TO SEE THAT THE BAR CAT WAS RATHER THE OPPOSITE.

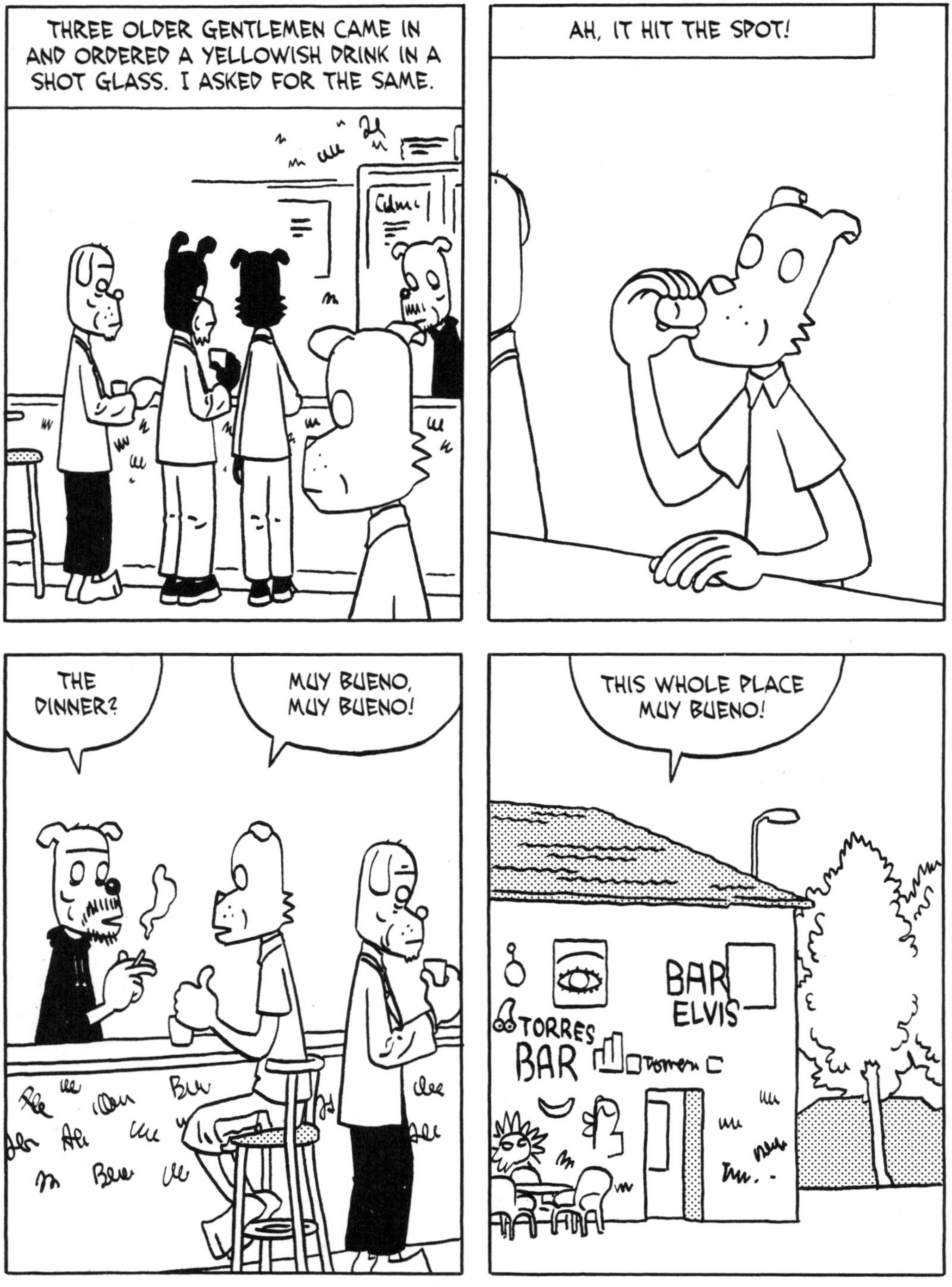
THREE OLDER GENTLEMEN CAME IN AND ORDERED A YELLOWISH DRINK IN A SHOT GLASS. I ASKED FOR THE SAME.
AH, IT HIT THE SPOT!
THE DINNER?
MUY BUENO, MUY BUENO!
THIS WHOLE PLACE MUY BUENO!
BAR
ELVIS
TORRES
BAR

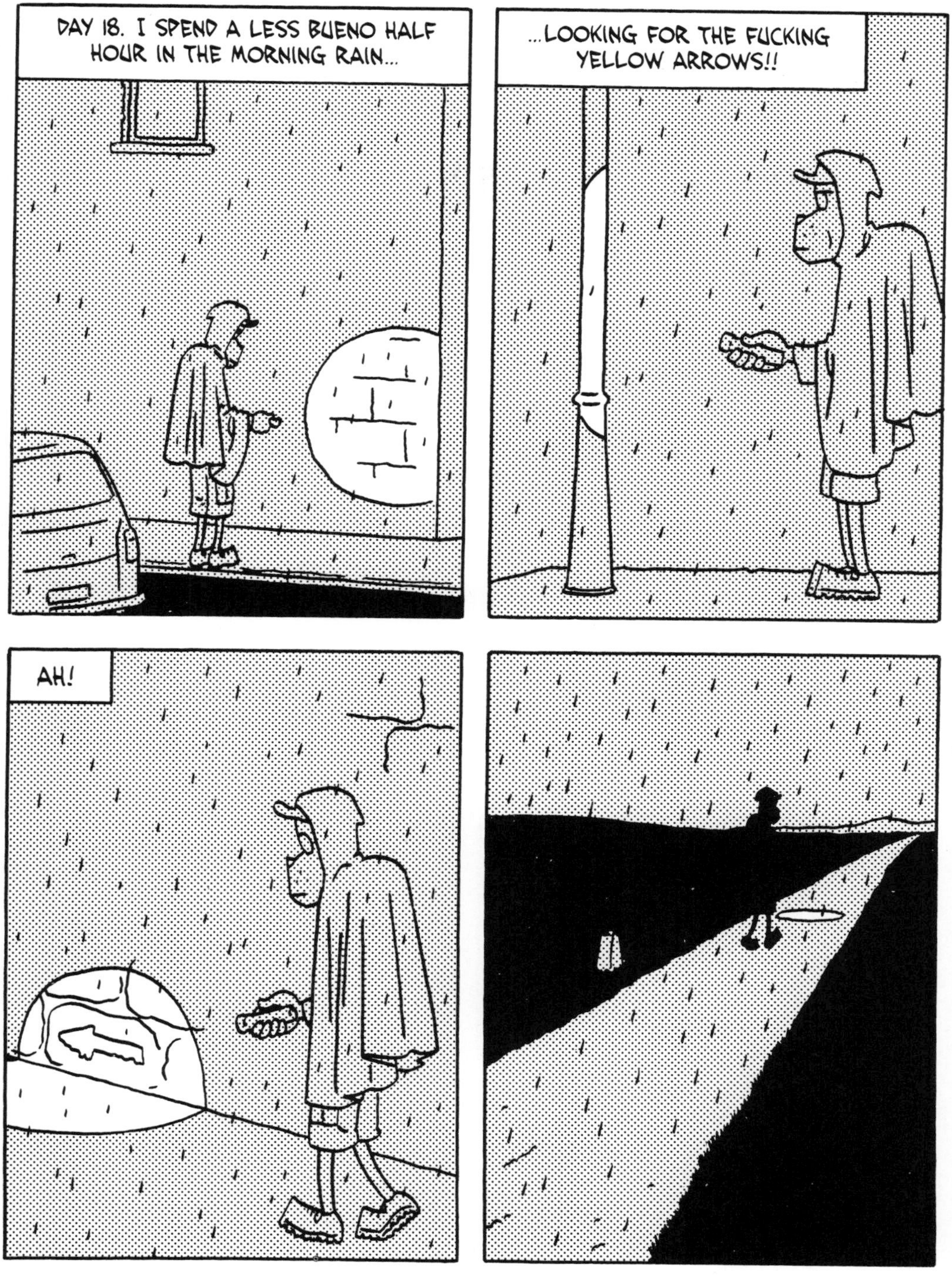
DAY 18. I SPEND A LESS BUENO HALF HOUR IN THE MORNING RAIN...
...LOOKING FOR THE FUCKING YELLOW ARROWS!!
AH!

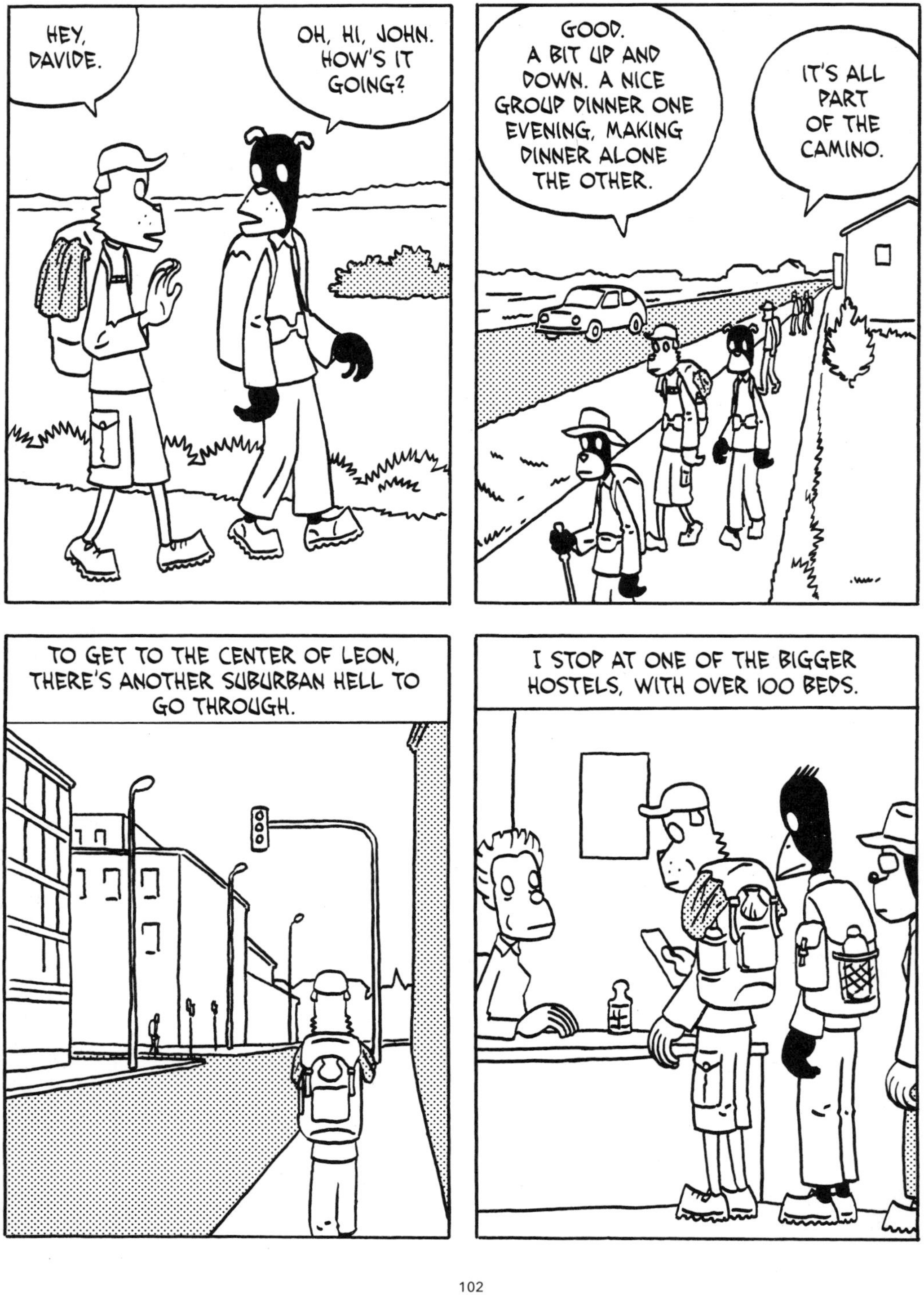
HEY, DAVIDE.
OH, HI, JOHN. HOW'S IT GOING?
GOOD. A BIT UP AND DOWN. A NICE GROUP DINNER ONE EVENING, MAKING DINNER ALONE THE OTHER.
IT'S ALL PART OF THE CAMINO.
TO GET TO THE CENTER OF LEON, THERE'S ANOTHER SUBURBAN HELL TO GO THROUGH.
I STOP AT ONE OF THE BIGGER HOSTELS, WITH OVER 100 BEDS.

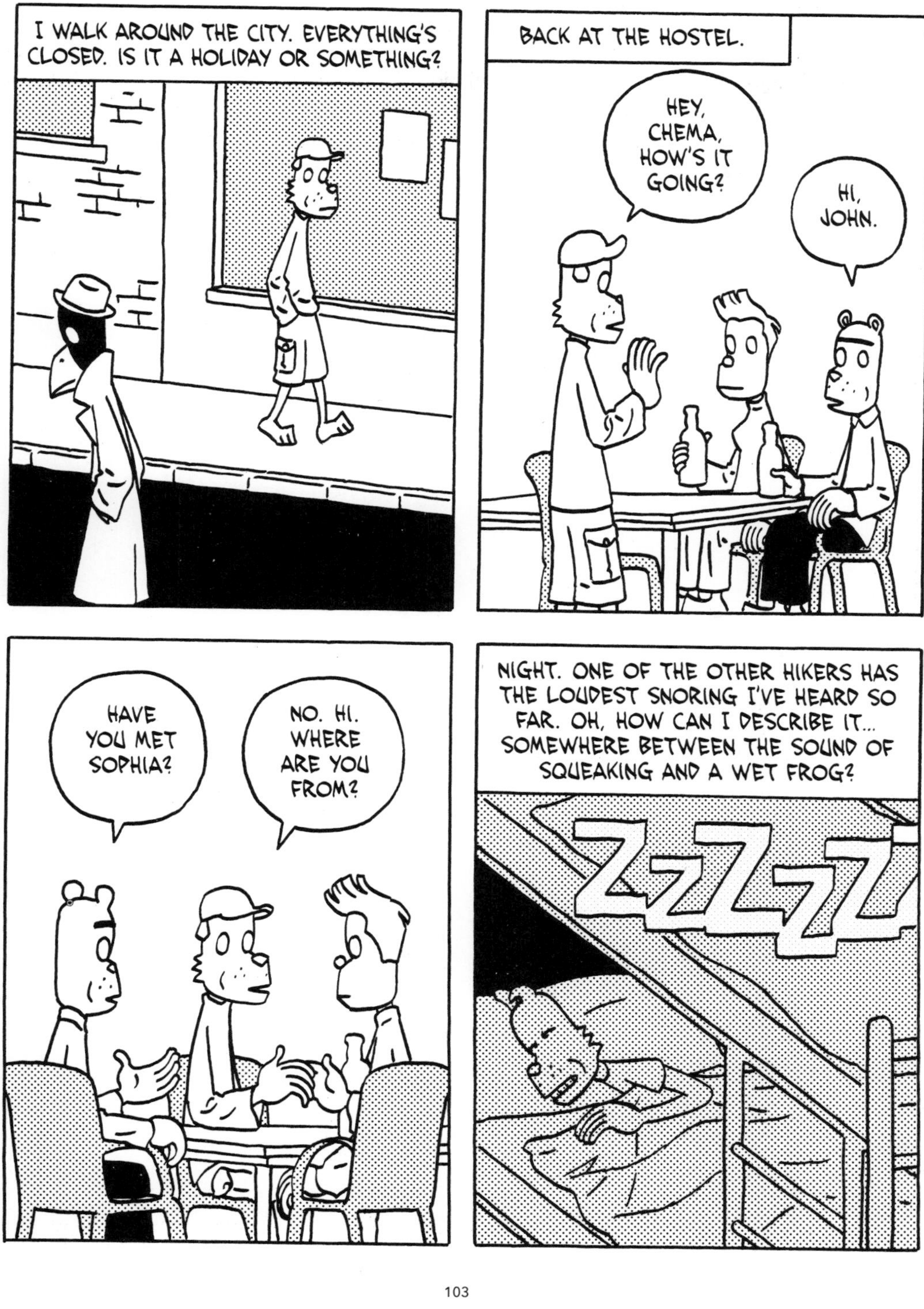

I WALK AROUND THE CITY. EVERYTHING'S CLOSED. IS IT A HOLIDAY OR SOMETHING?
BACK AT THE HOSTEL.
HEY, CHEMA, HOW'S IT GOING?
HI, JOHN.
HAVE YOU MET SOPHIA?
NO. HI. WHERE ARE YOU FROM?
NIGHT. ONE OF THE OTHER HIKERS HAS THE LOUDEST SNORING I'VE HEARD SO FAR. OH, HOW CAN I DESCRIBE IT... SOMEWHERE BETWEEN THE SOUND OF SQUEAKING AND A WET FROG?
ZZZZZ

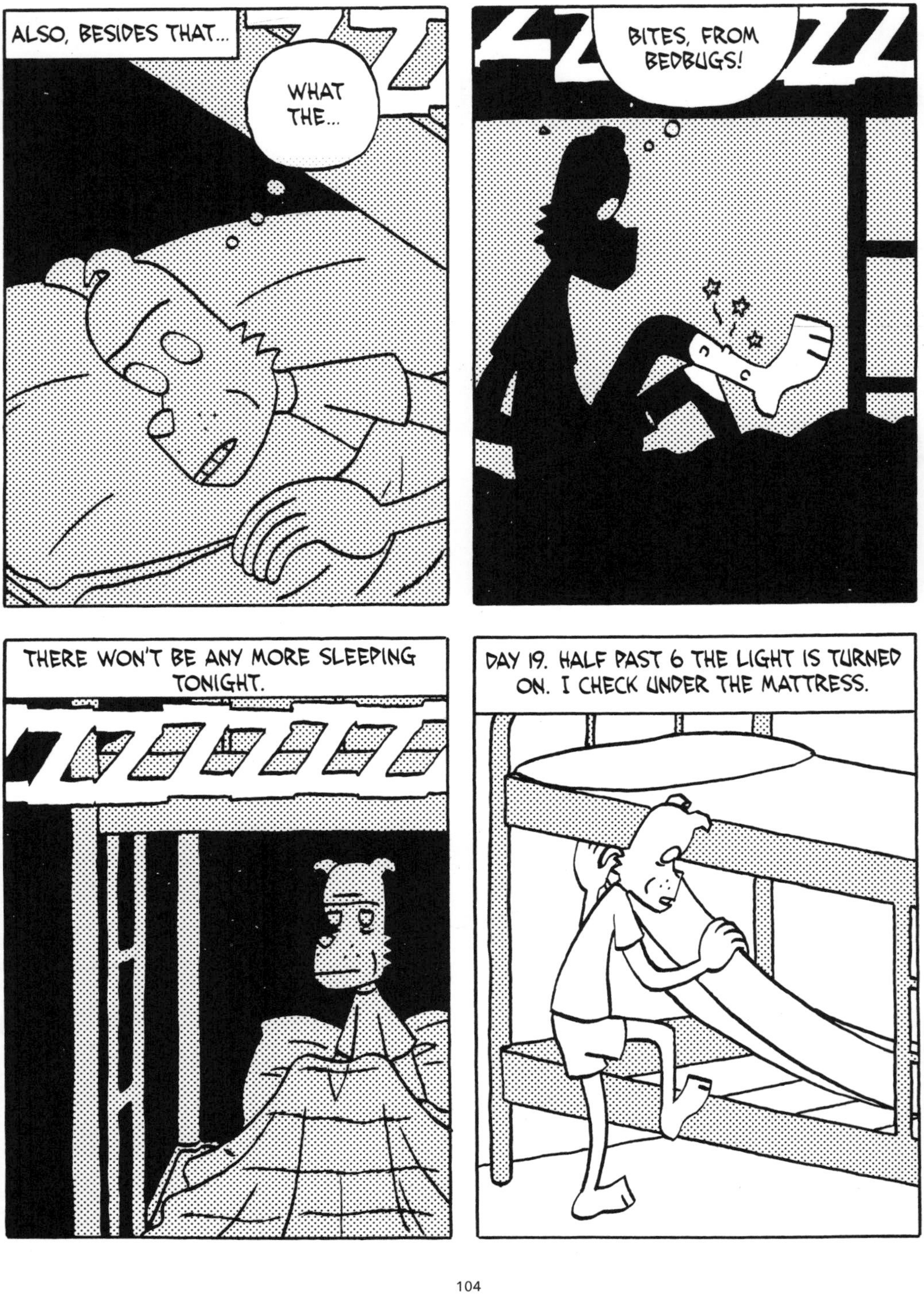
ALSO, BESIDES THAT...
WHAT THE...
BITES, FROM BEDBUGS!
THERE WON'T BE ANY MORE SLEEPING TONIGHT.
DAY 19. HALF PAST 6 THE LIGHT IS TURNED ON. I CHECK UNDER THE MATTRESS.

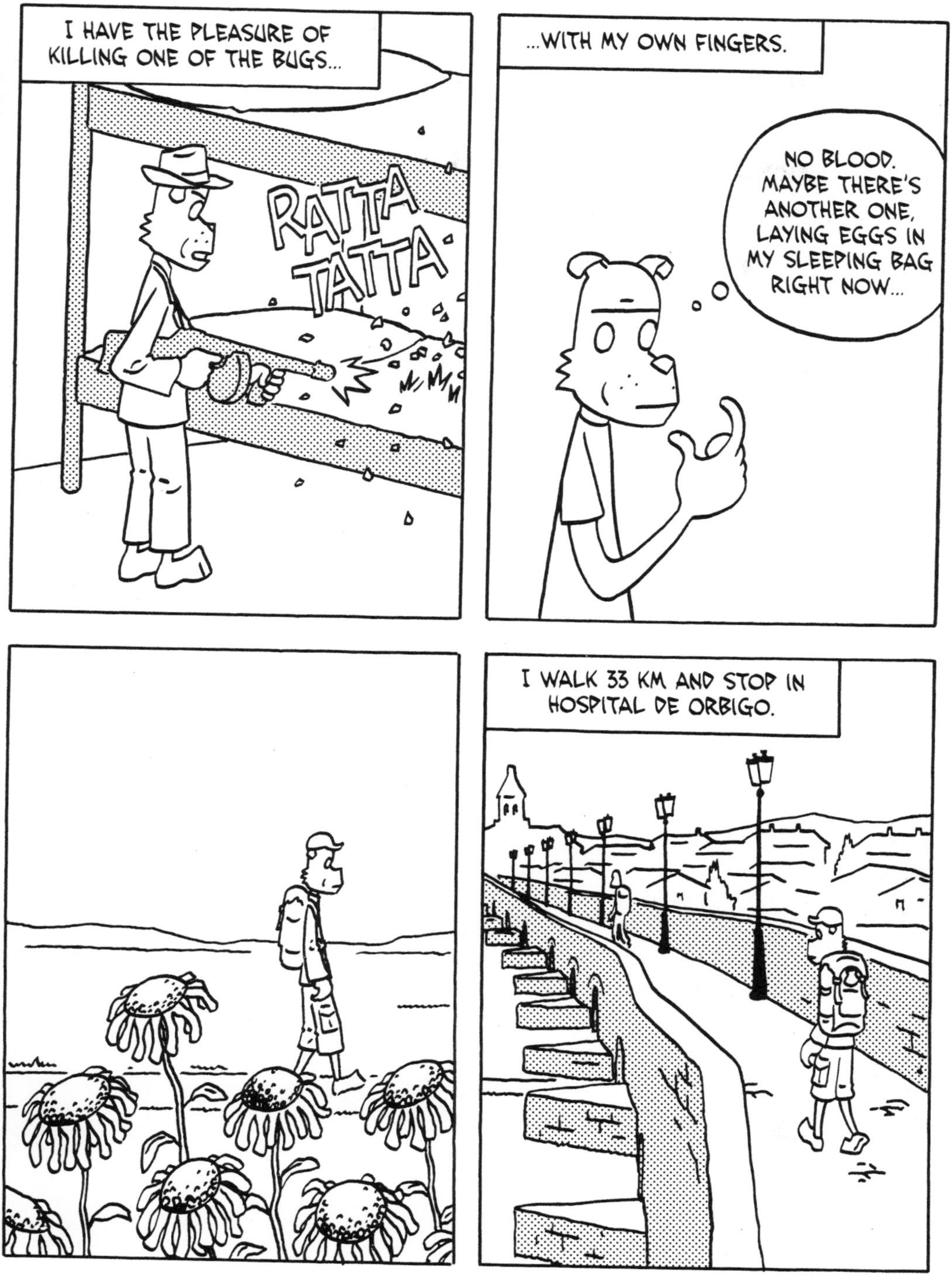
I HAVE THE PLEASURE OF KILLING ONE OF THE BUGS...
RATTA TATTA
...WITH MY OWN FINGERS.
NO BLOOD. MAYBE THERE'S ANOTHER ONE, LAYING EGGS IN MY SLEEPING BAG RIGHT NOW...
I WALK 33 KM AND STOP IN HOSPITAL DE ORBIGO.

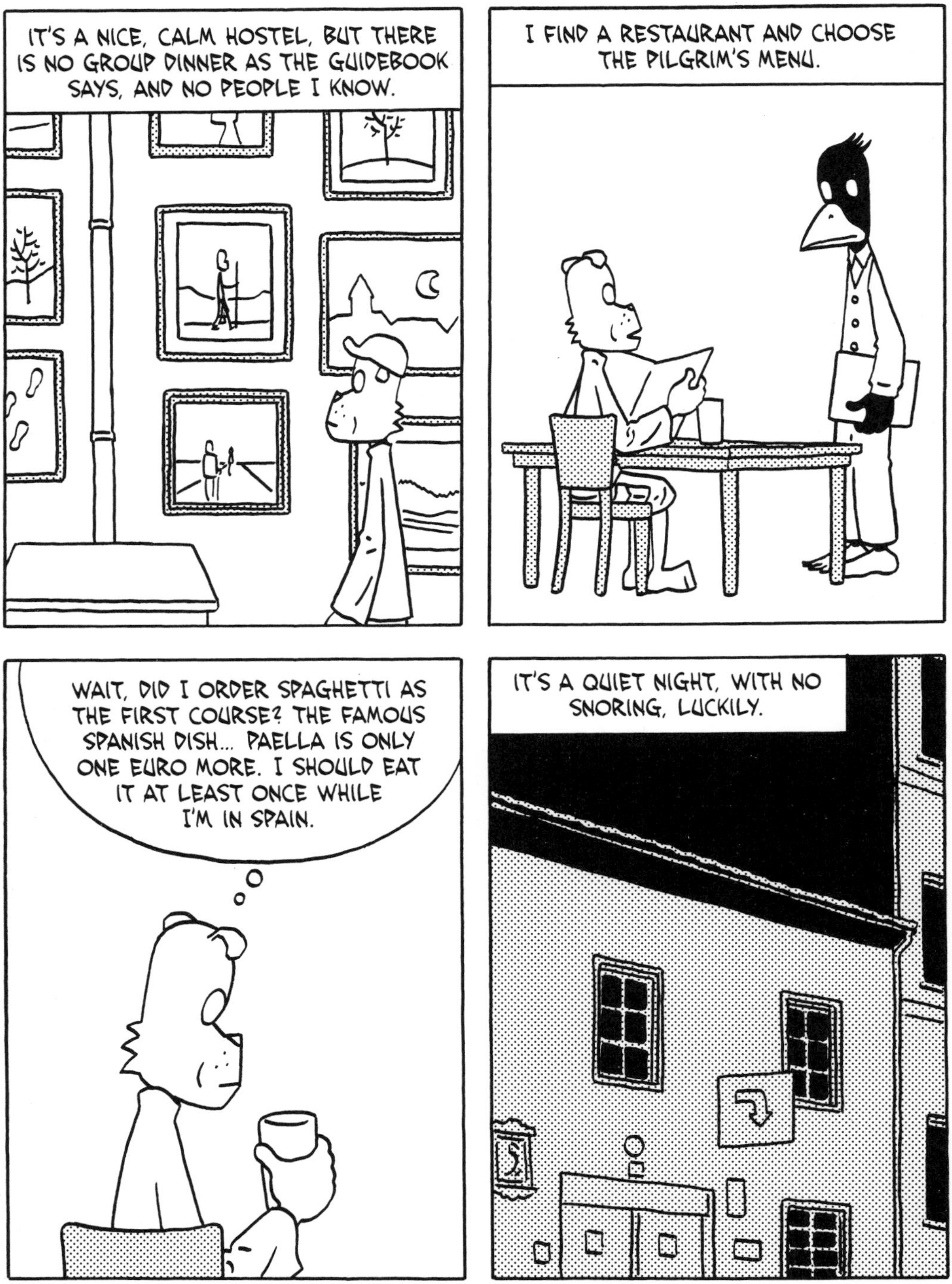
IT'S A NICE, CALM HOSTEL, BUT THERE IS NO GROUP DINNER AS THE GUIDEBOOK SAYS, AND NO PEOPLE I KNOW.
I FIND A RESTAURANT AND CHOOSE THE PILGRIM'S MENU.
WAIT, DID I ORDER SPAGHETTI AS THE FIRST COURSE? THE FAMOUS SPANISH DISH... PAELLA IS ONLY ONE EURO MORE. I SHOULD EAT IT AT LEAST ONCE WHILE I'M IN SPAIN.
IT'S A QUIET NIGHT, WITH NO SNORING, LUCKILY.

DAY 20. I'M GETTING PRETTY GOOD AT PACKING MY SLEEPING BAG IN THE DARK.

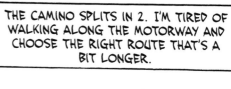

THE CAMINO SPLITS IN 2. I'M TIRED OF WALKING ALONG THE MOTORWAY AND CHOOSE THE RIGHT ROUTE THAT'S A BIT LONGER.

HI, SERVE YOURSELF. WHERE ARE YOU FROM?

NORWAY.

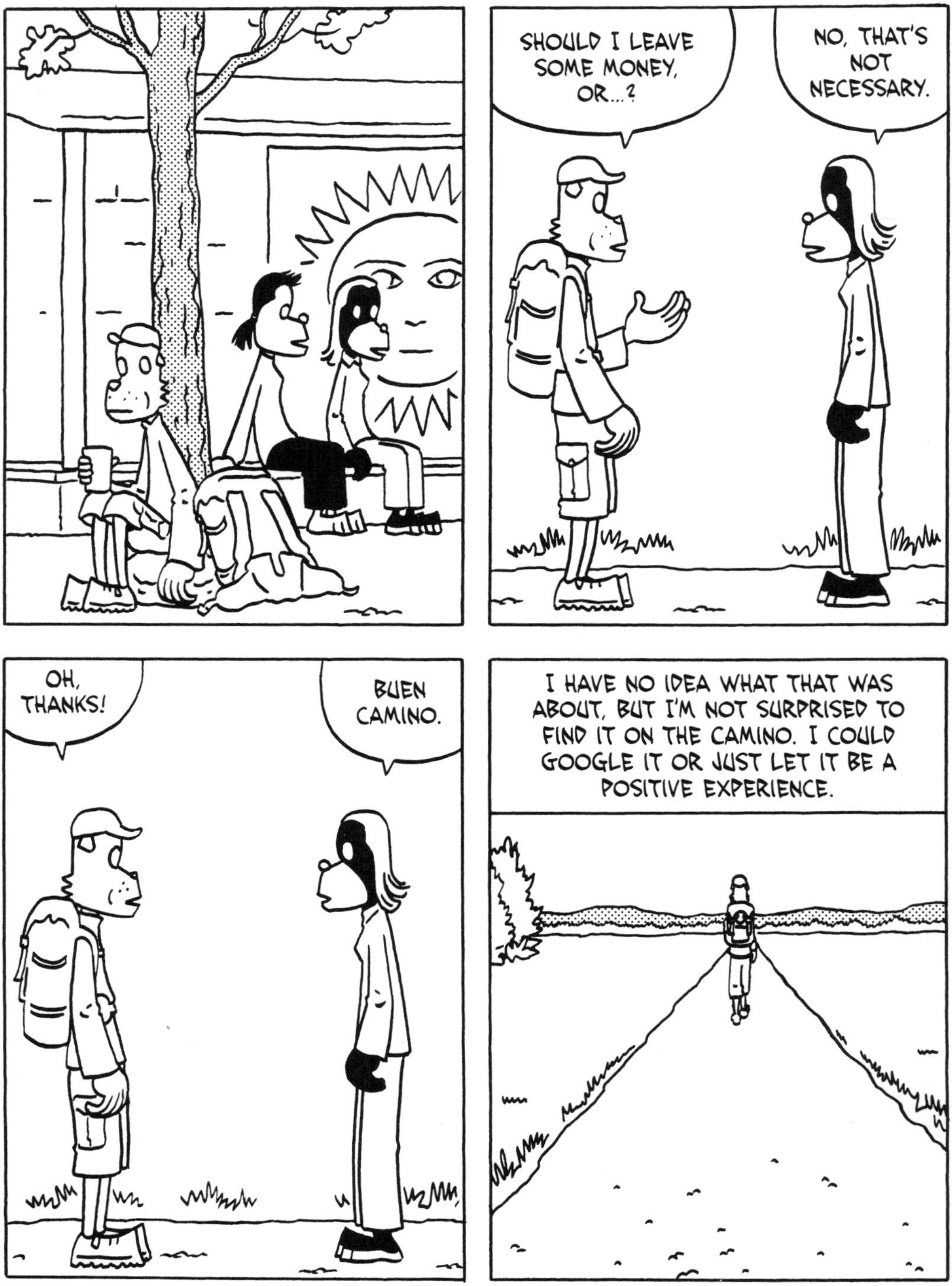

SHOULD I LEAVE SOME MONEY, OR...?
NO, THAT'S NOT NECESSARY.
OH, THANKS!
BUEN CAMINO.
I HAVE NO IDEA WHAT THAT WAS ABOUT, BUT I'M NOT SURPRISED TO FIND IT ON THE CAMINO. I COULD GOOGLE IT OR JUST LET IT BE A POSITIVE EXPERIENCE.

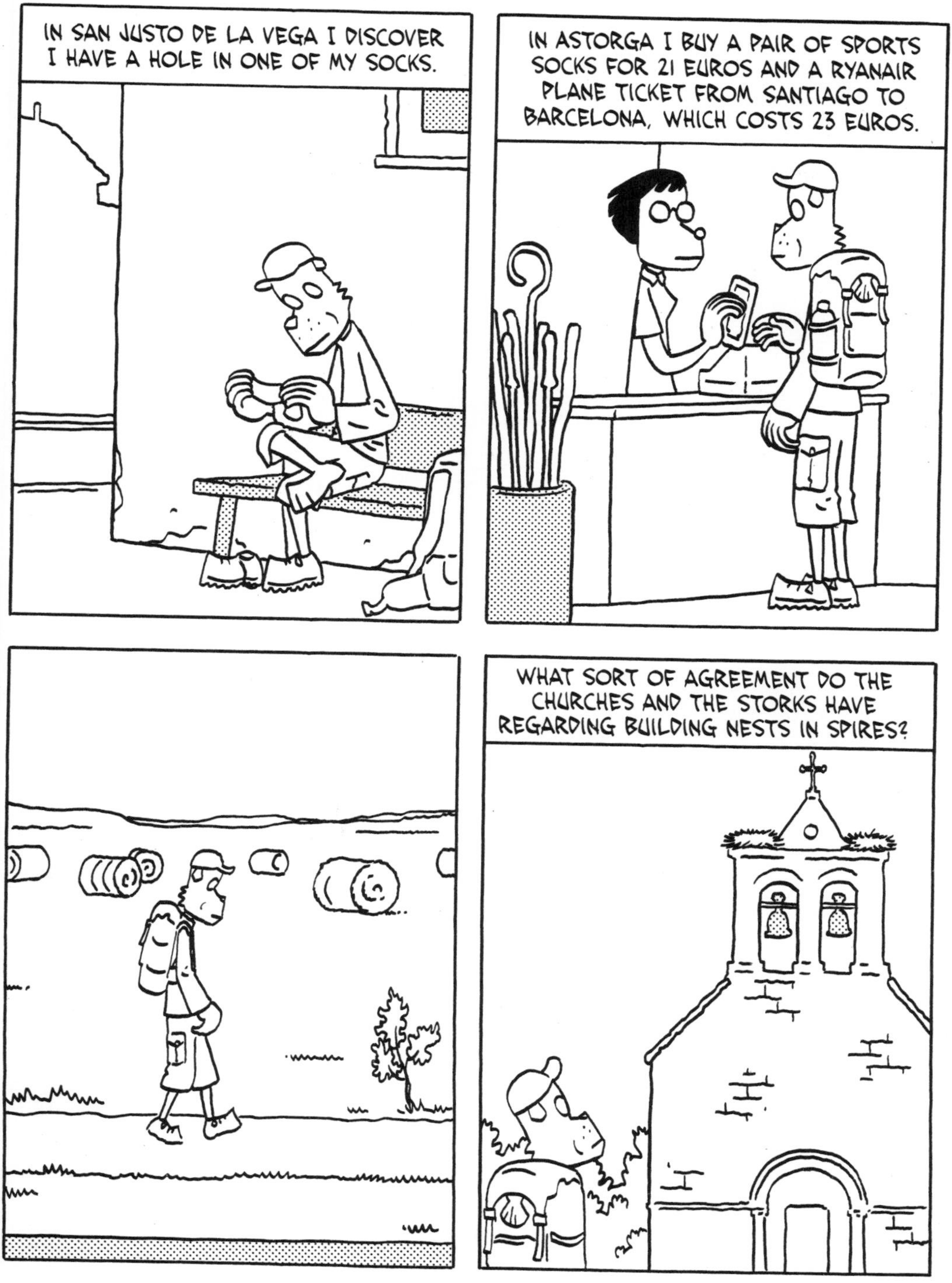
IN SAN JUSTO DE LA VEGA I DISCOVER I HAVE A HOLE IN ONE OF MY SOCKS.
IN ASTORGA I BUY A PAIR OF SPORTS SOCKS FOR 21 EUROS AND A RYANAIR PLANE TICKET FROM SANTIAGO TO BARCELONA, WHICH COSTS 23 EUROS.
WHAT SORT OF AGREEMENT DO THE CHURCHES AND THE STORKS HAVE REGARDING BUILDING NESTS IN SPIRES?

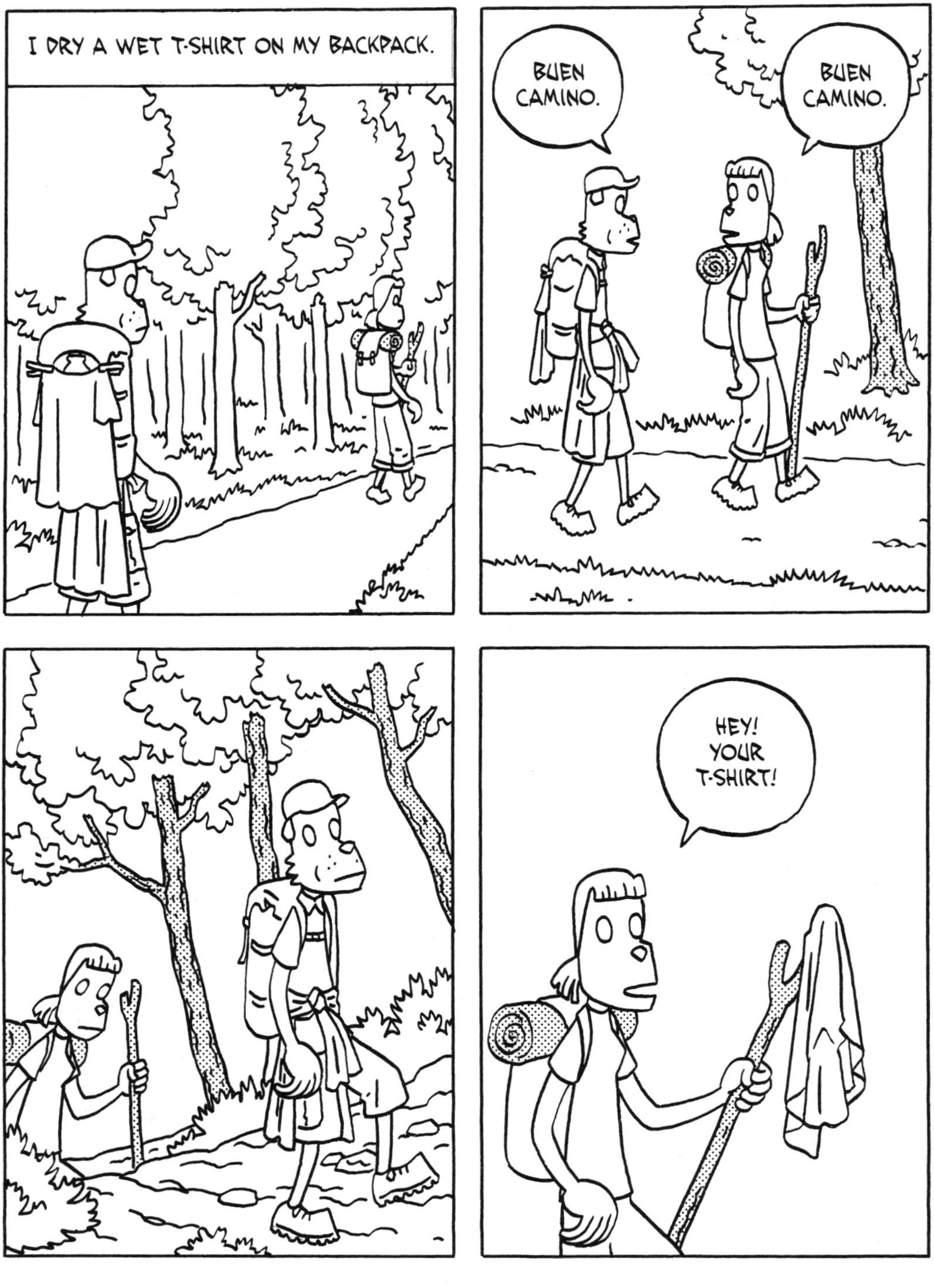
I DRY A WET T-SHIRT ON MY BACKPACK.
BUEN CAMINO.
BUEN CAMINO.
HEY! YOUR T-SHIRT!

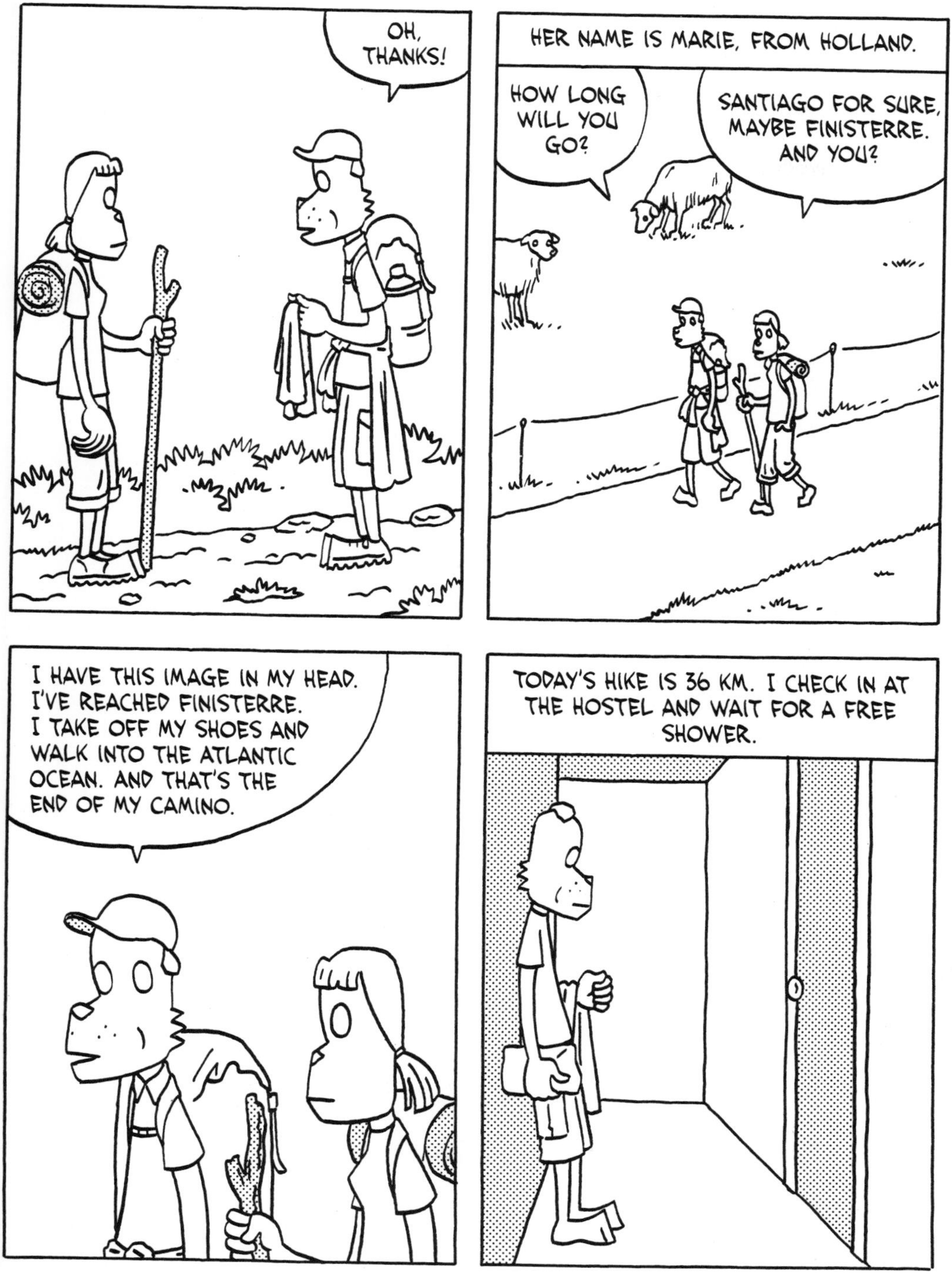
OH, THANKS!
HER NAME IS MARIE, FROM HOLLAND.
HOW LONG WILL YOU GO?
SANTIAGO FOR SURE, MAYBE FINISTERRE. AND YOU?
I HAVE THIS IMAGE IN MY HEAD. I'VE REACHED FINISTERRE. I TAKE OFF MY SHOES AND WALK INTO THE ATLANTIC OCEAN. AND THAT'S THE END OF MY CAMINO.
TODAY'S HIKE IS 36 KM. I CHECK IN AT THE HOSTEL AND WAIT FOR A FREE SHOWER.

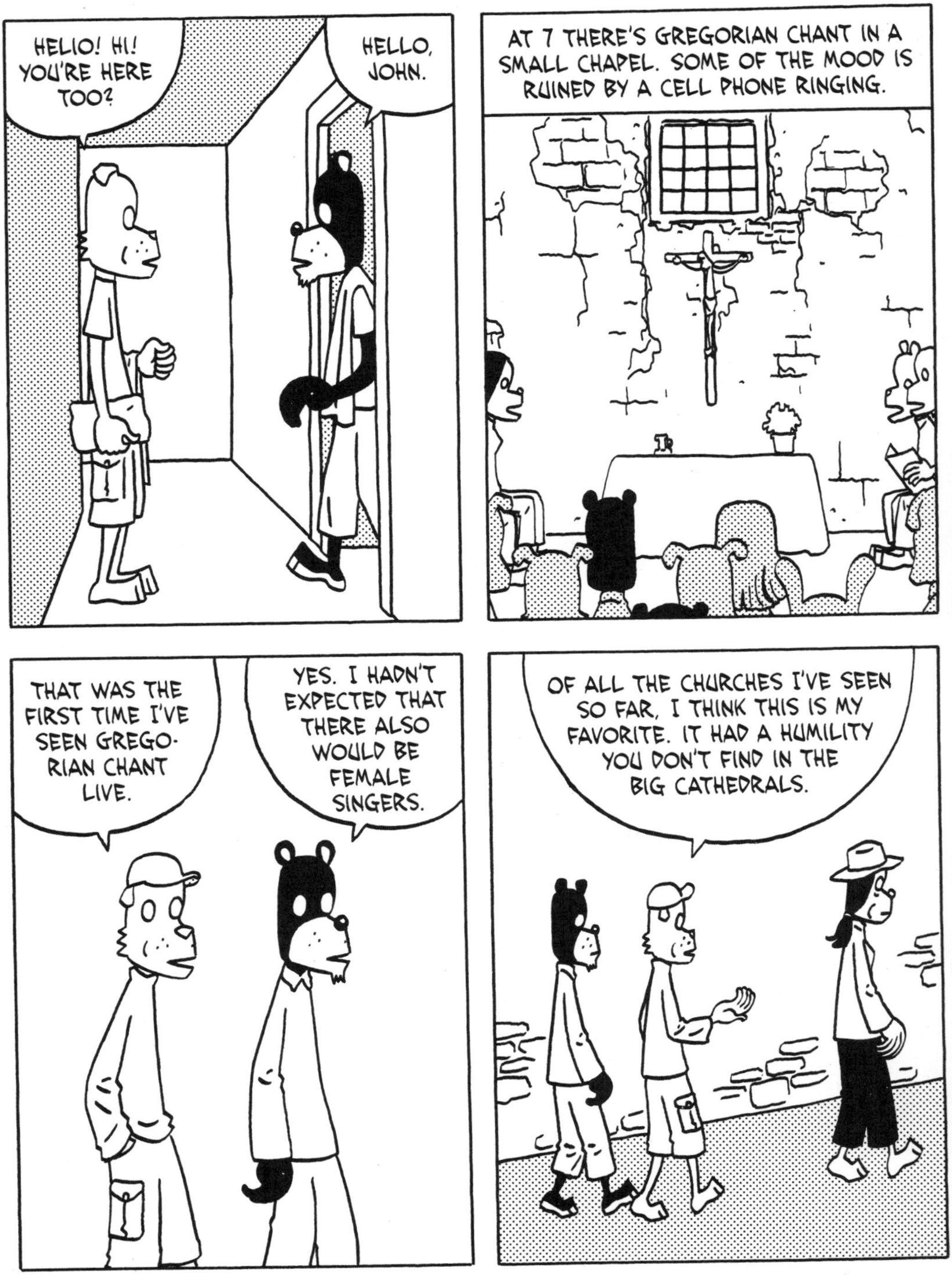

HELIO! HI! YOU'RE HERE TOO?
HELLO, JOHN.
AT 7 THERE'S GREGORIAN CHANT IN A SMALL CHAPEL. SOME OF THE MOOD IS RUINED BY A CELL PHONE RINGING.
THAT WAS THE FIRST TIME I'VE SEEN GREGO-RIAN CHANT LIVE.
YES. I HADN'T EXPECTED THAT THERE ALSO WOULD BE FEMALE SINGERS.
OF ALL THE CHURCHES I'VE SEEN SO FAR, I THINK THIS IS MY FAVORITE. IT HAD A HUMILITY YOU DON'T FIND IN THE BIG CATHEDRALS.

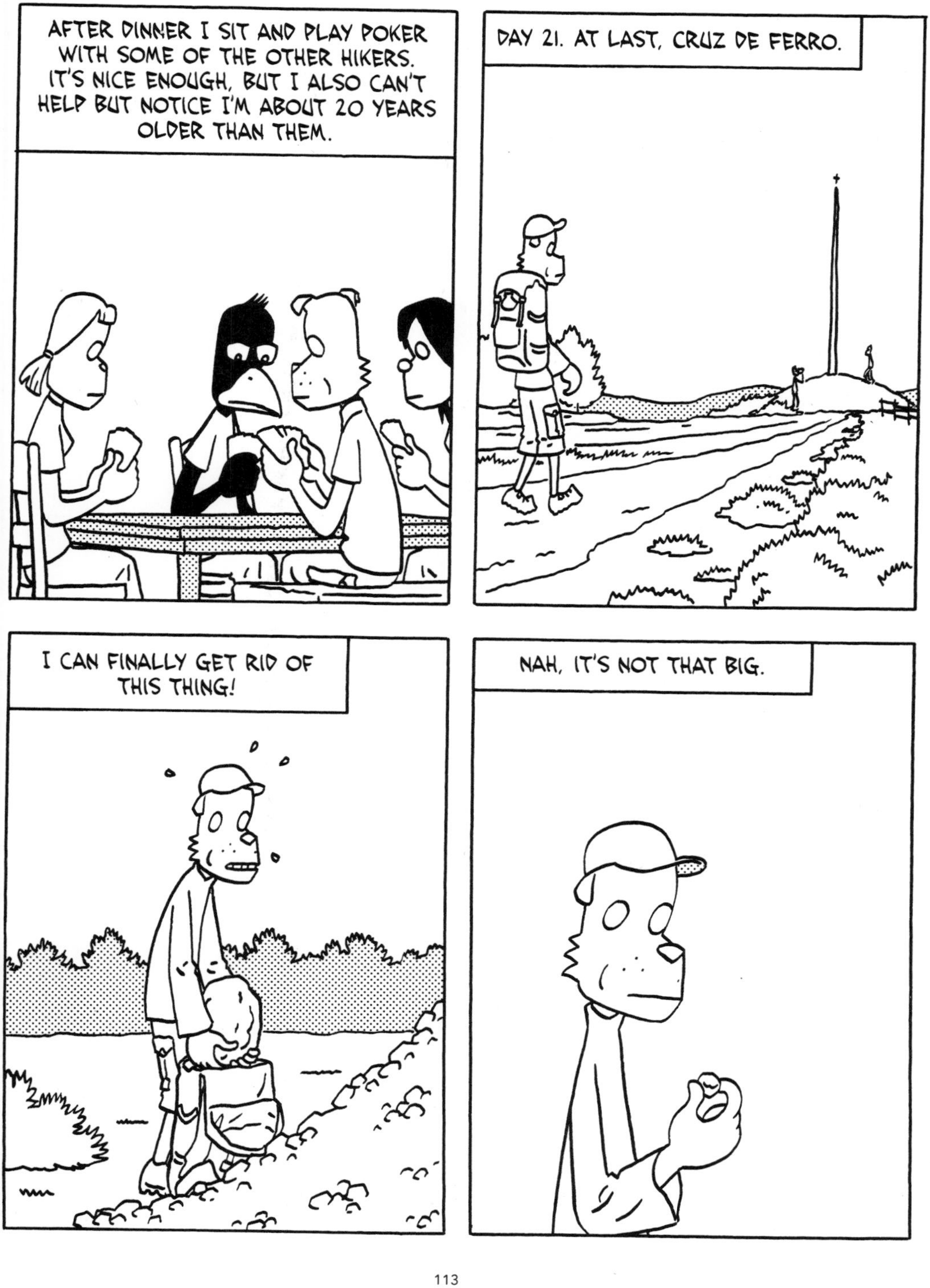
AFTER DINNER I SIT AND PLAY POKER WITH SOME OF THE OTHER HIKERS. IT'S NICE ENOUGH, BUT I ALSO CAN'T HELP BUT NOTICE I'M ABOUT 20 YEARS OLDER THAN THEM.
DAY 21. AT LAST, CRUZ DE FERRO.
I CAN FINALLY GET RID OF THIS THING!
NAH, IT'S NOT THAT BIG.

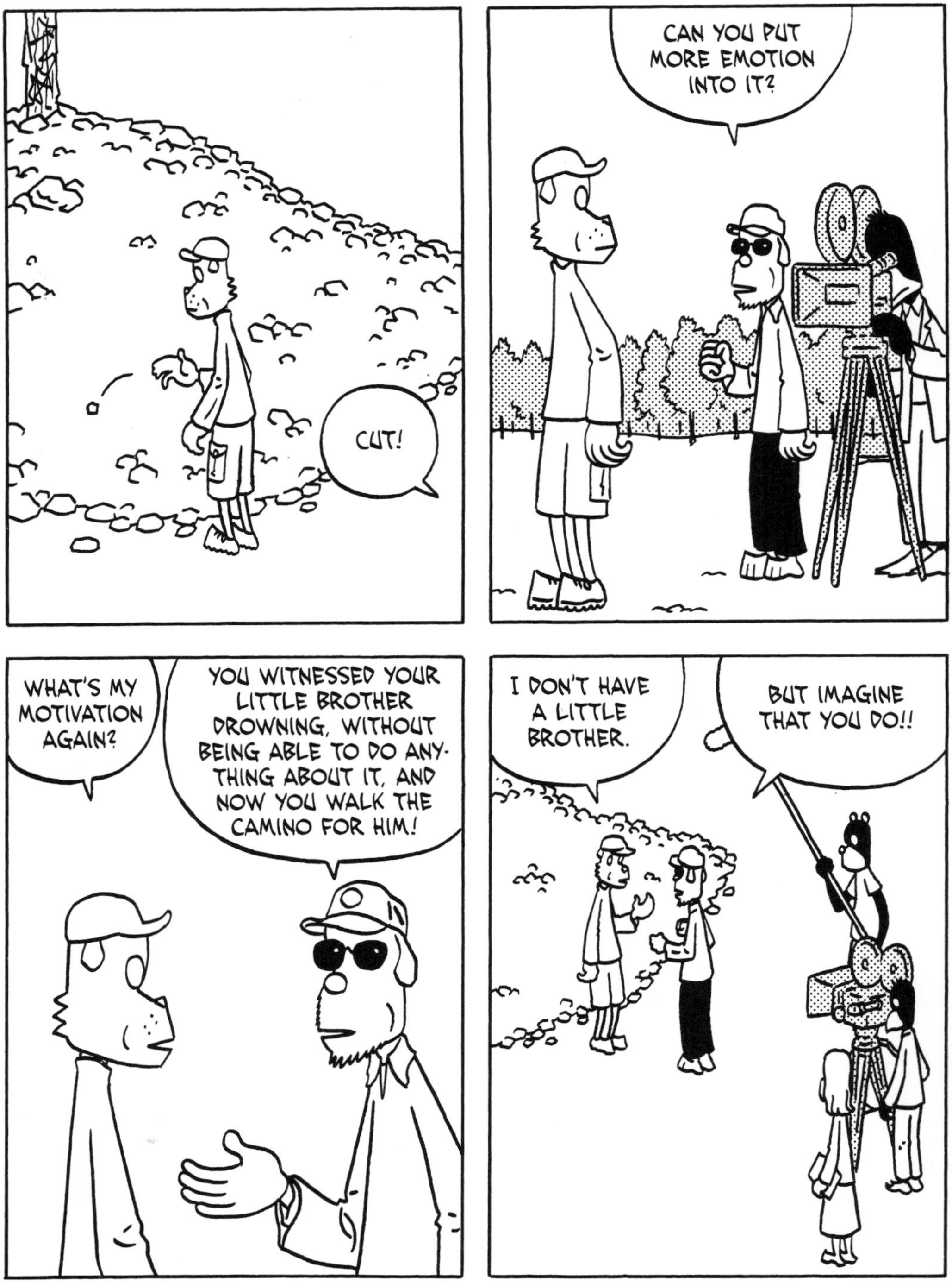
CUT!
CAN YOU PUT MORE EMOTION INTO IT?
WHAT'S MY MOTIVATION AGAIN?
YOU WITNESSED YOUR LITTLE BROTHER DROWNING, WITHOUT BEING ABLE TO DO ANYTHING ABOUT IT, AND NOW YOU WALK THE CAMINO FOR HIM!
I DON'T HAVE A LITTLE BROTHER.
BUT IMAGINE THAT YOU DO!!

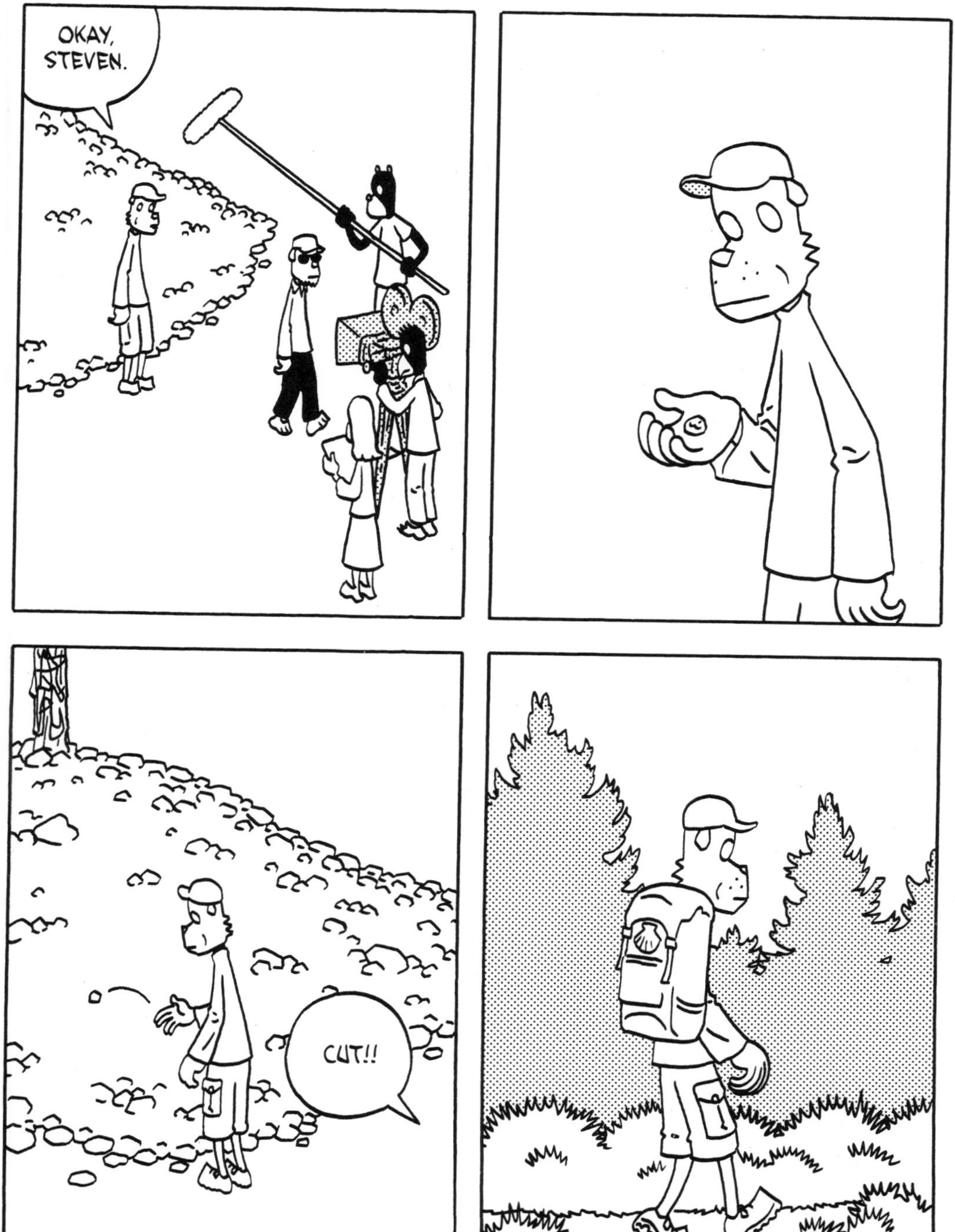
OKAY, STEVEN.
CUT!!

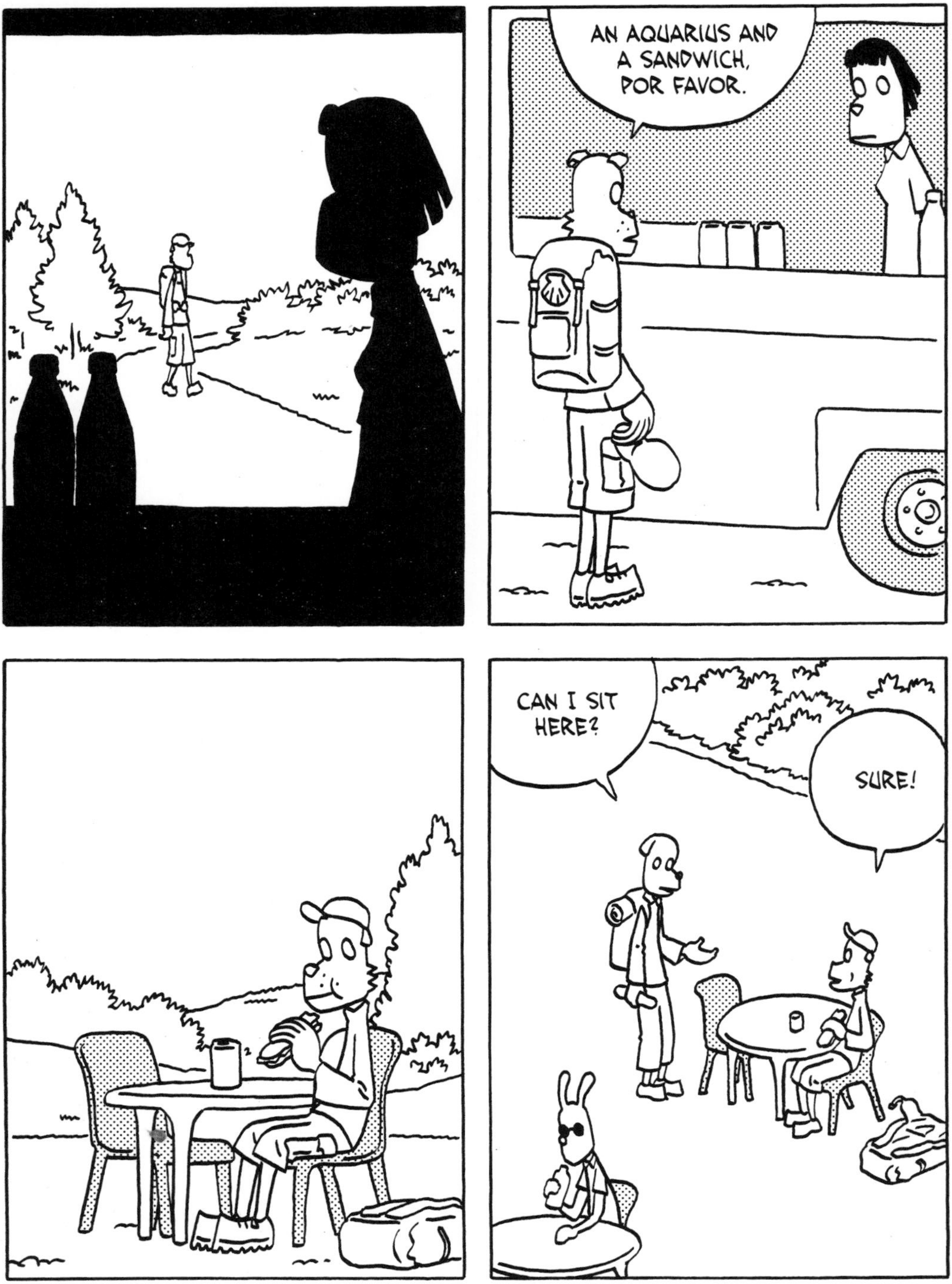
AN AQUARIUS AND A SANDWICH, POR FAVOR.
CAN I SIT HERE?
SURE!

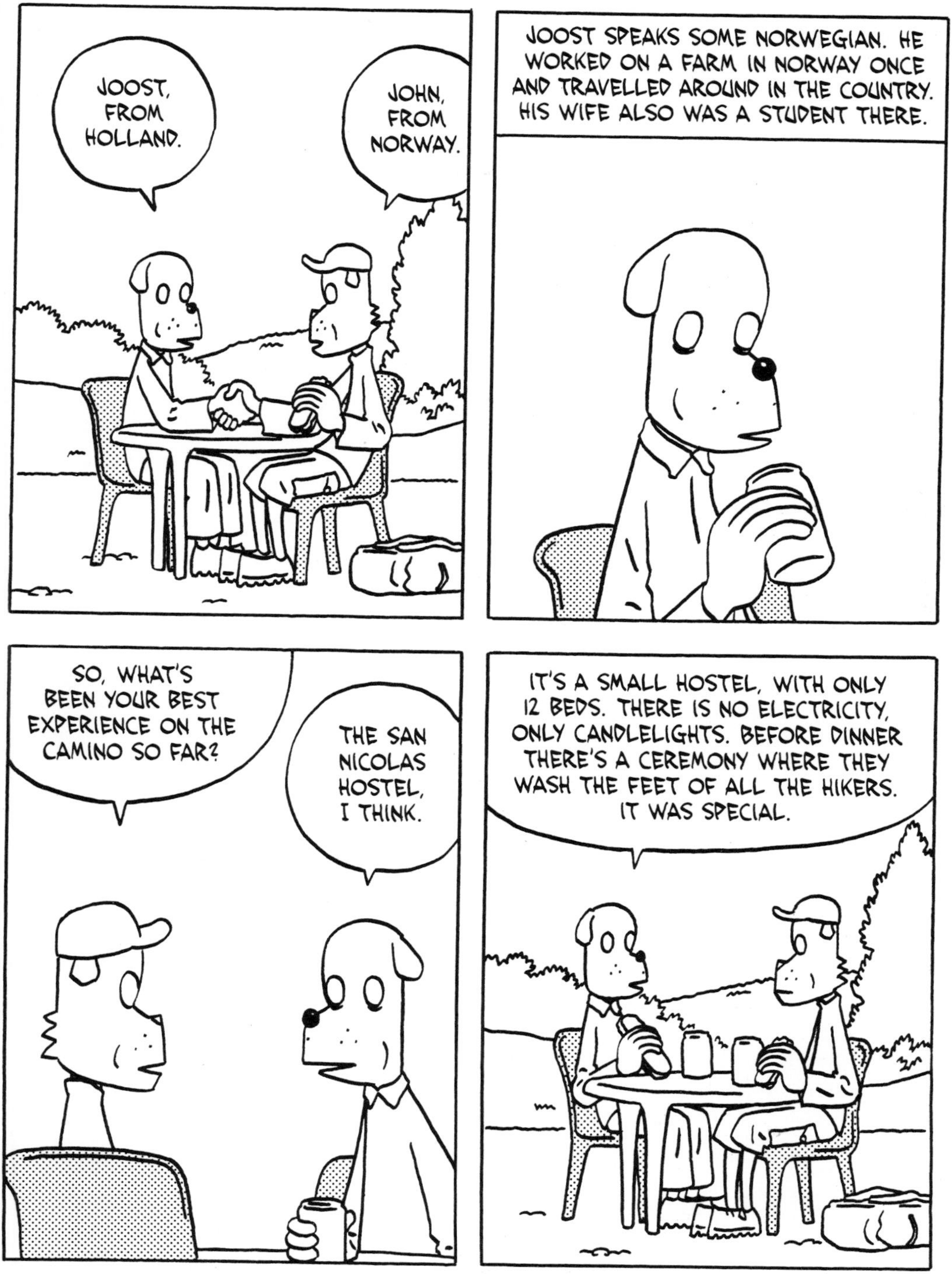
JOOST, FROM HOLLAND.
JOHN, FROM NORWAY.
JOOST SPEAKS SOME NORWEGIAN. HE WORKED ON A FARM IN NORWAY ONCE AND TRAVELLED AROUND IN THE COUNTRY. HIS WIFE ALSO WAS A STUDENT THERE.
SO, WHAT'S BEEN YOUR BEST EXPERIENCE ON THE CAMINO SO FAR?
THE SAN NICOLAS HOSTEL, I THINK.
IT'S A SMALL HOSTEL, WITH ONLY 12 BEDS. THERE IS NO ELECTRICITY, ONLY CANDLELIGHTS. BEFORE DINNER THERE'S A CEREMONY WHERE THEY WASH THE FEET OF ALL THE HIKERS. IT WAS SPECIAL.

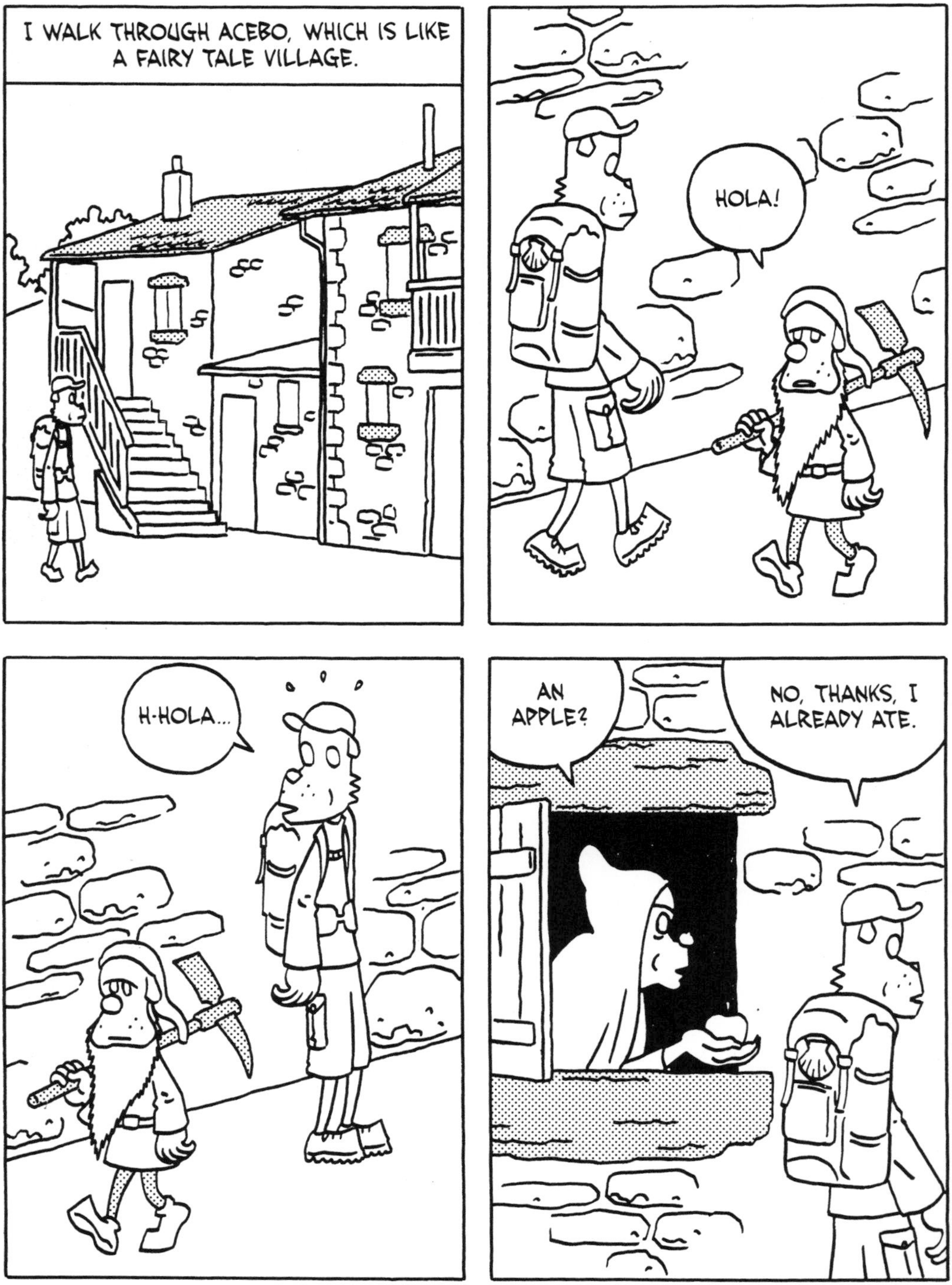
I WALK THROUGH ACEBO, WHICH IS LIKE A FAIRY TALE VILLAGE.
HOLA!
H-HOLA...
AN APPLE?
NO, THANKS, I ALREADY ATE.

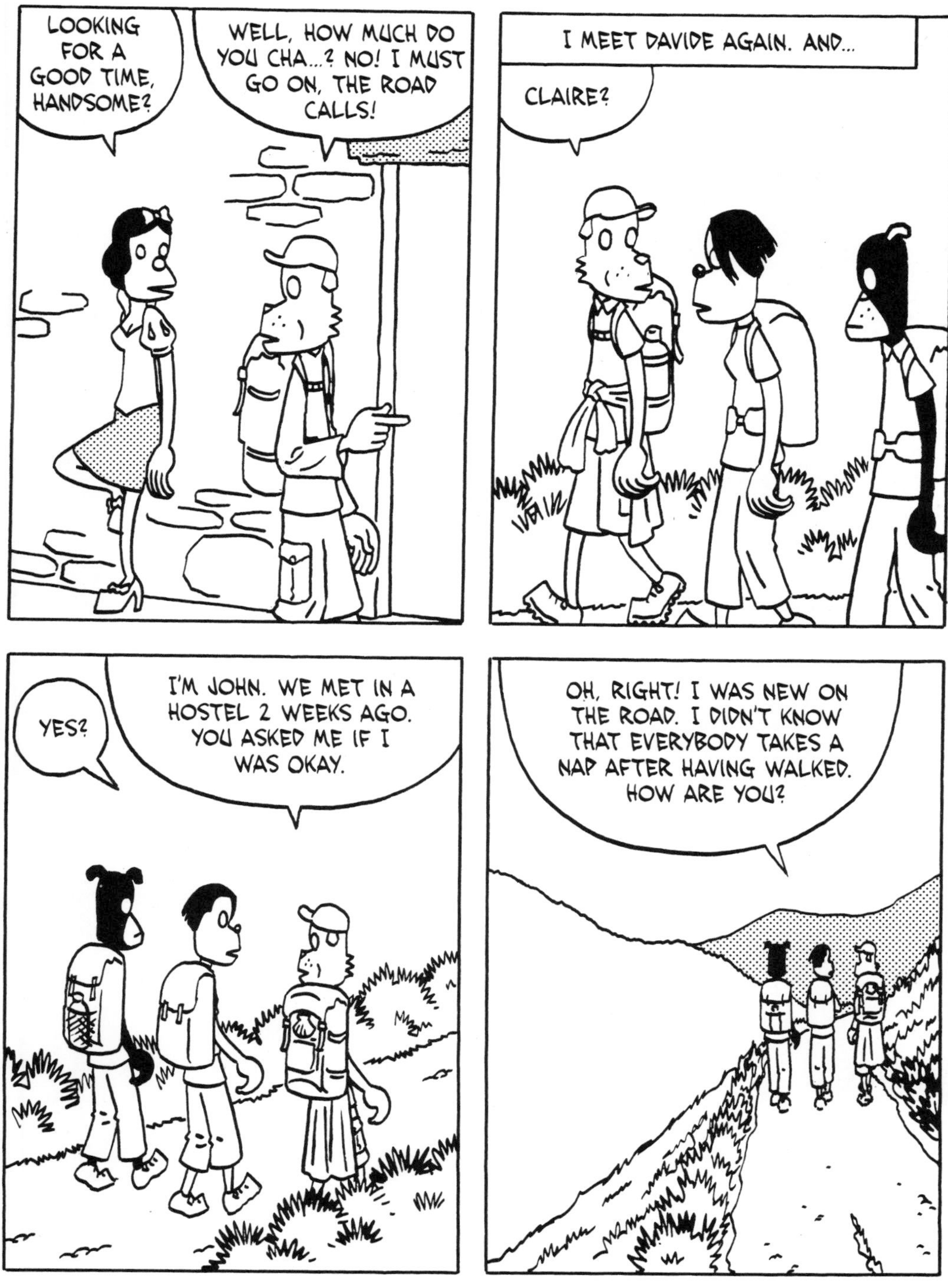
LOOKING FOR A GOOD TIME, HANDSOME?
WELL, HOW MUCH DO YOU CHA...? NO! I MUST GO ON, THE ROAD CALLS!
I MEET DAVIDE AGAIN. AND...
CLAIRE?
YES?
I'M JOHN. WE MET IN A HOSTEL 2 WEEKS AGO. YOU ASKED ME IF I WAS OKAY.
OH, RIGHT! I WAS NEW ON THE ROAD. I DIDN'T KNOW THAT EVERYBODY TAKES A NAP AFTER HAVING WALKED. HOW ARE YOU?

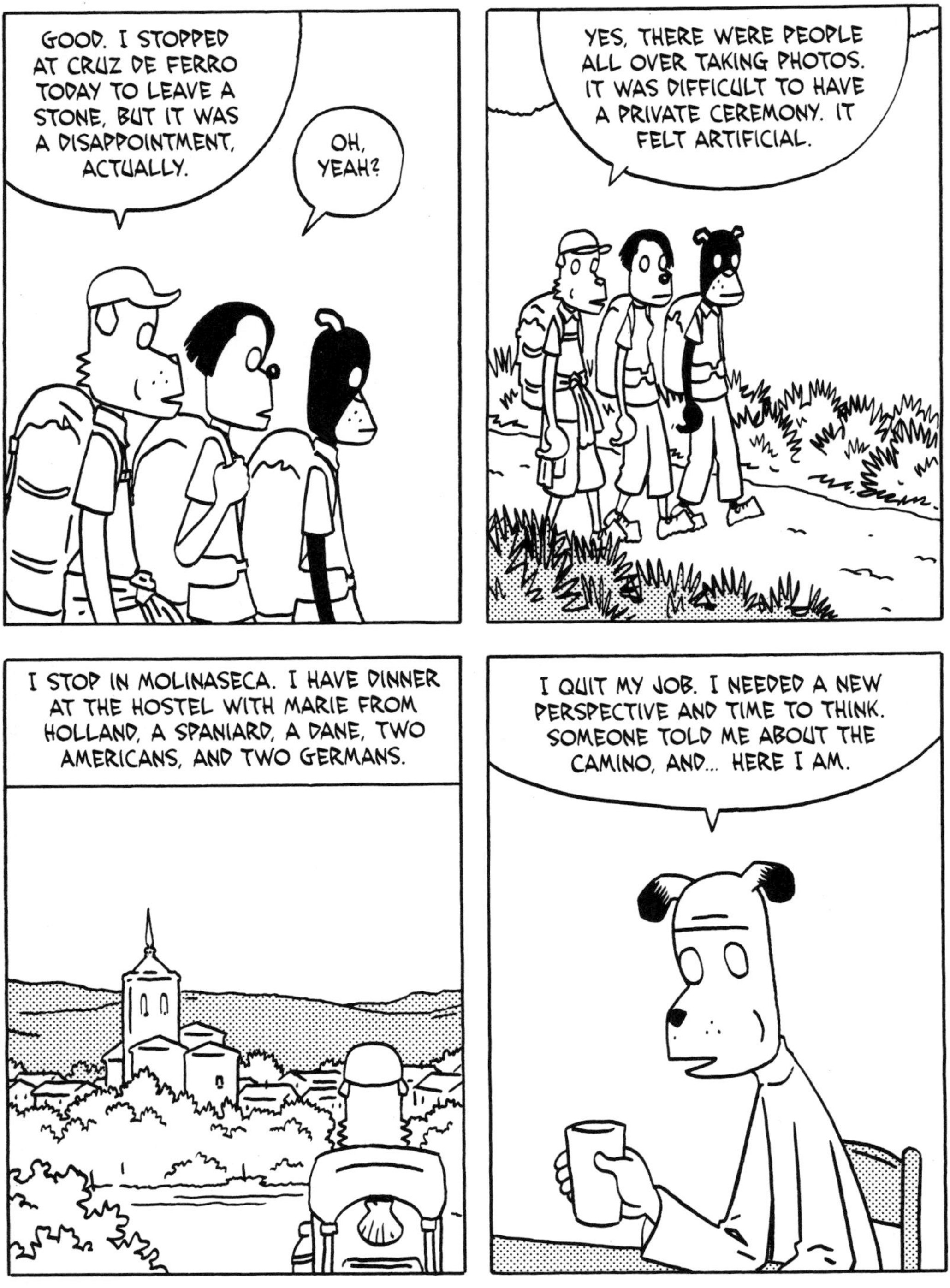
GOOD. I STOPPED AT CRUZ DE FERRO TODAY TO LEAVE A STONE, BUT IT WAS A DISAPPOINTMENT, ACTUALLY.
OH, YEAH?
YES, THERE WERE PEOPLE ALL OVER TAKING PHOTOS. IT WAS DIFFICULT TO HAVE A PRIVATE CEREMONY. IT FELT ARTIFICIAL.
I STOP IN MOLINASECA. I HAVE DINNER AT THE HOSTEL WITH MARIE FROM HOLLAND, A SPANIARD, A DANE, TWO AMERICANS, AND TWO GERMANS.
I QUIT MY JOB. I NEEDED A NEW PERSPECTIVE AND TIME TO THINK. SOMEONE TOLD ME ABOUT THE CAMINO, AND... HERE I AM.

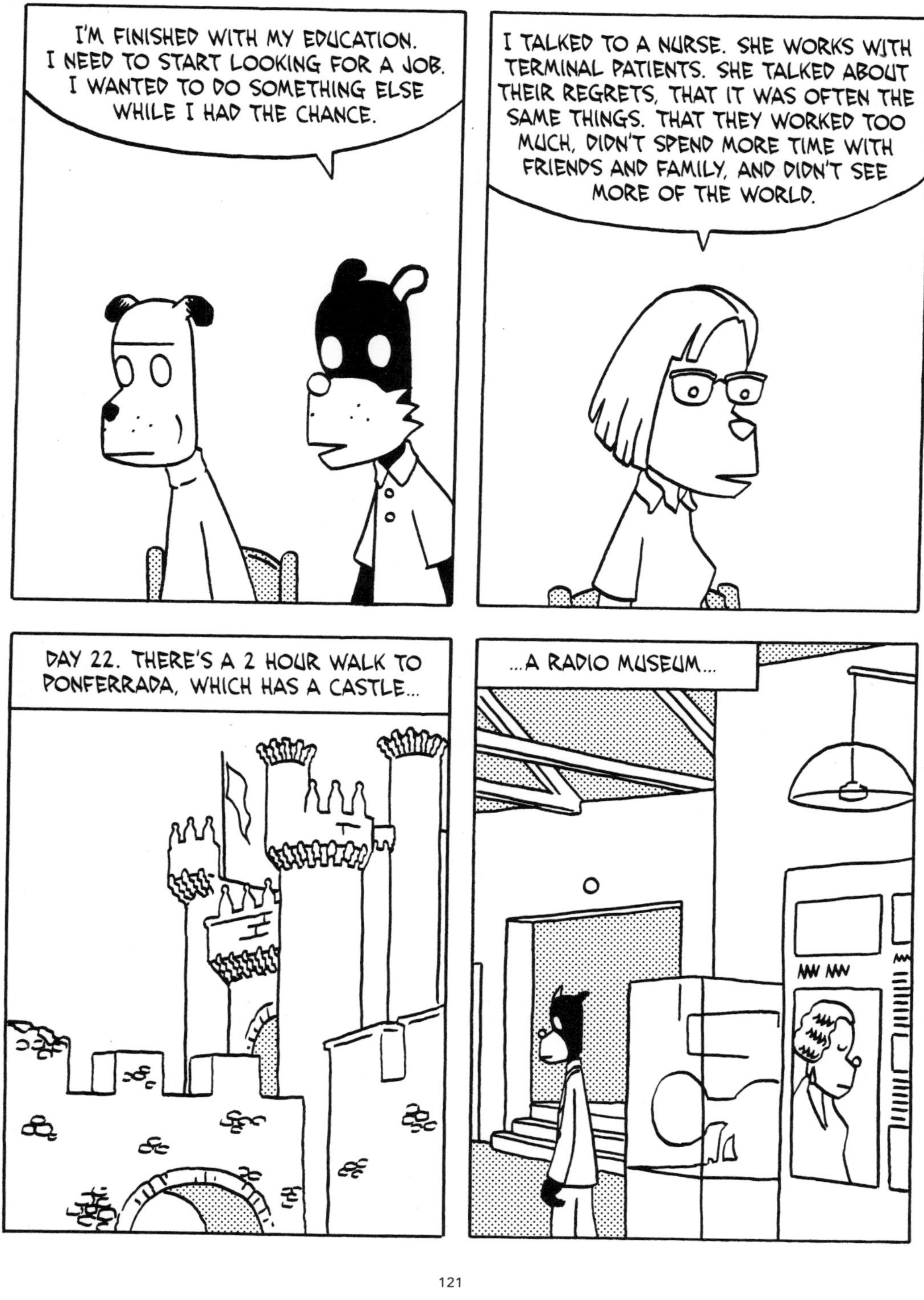
I'M FINISHED WITH MY EDUCATION. I NEED TO START LOOKING FOR A JOB. I WANTED TO DO SOMETHING ELSE WHILE I HAD THE CHANCE.
I TALKED TO A NURSE. SHE WORKS WITH TERMINAL PATIENTS. SHE TALKED ABOUT THEIR REGRETS, THAT IT WAS OFTEN THE SAME THINGS. THAT THEY WORKED TOO MUCH, DIDN'T SPEND MORE TIME WITH FRIENDS AND FAMILY, AND DIDN'T SEE MORE OF THE WORLD.
DAY 22. THERE'S A 2 HOUR WALK TO PONFERRADA, WHICH HAS A CASTLE...
...A RADIO MUSEUM...

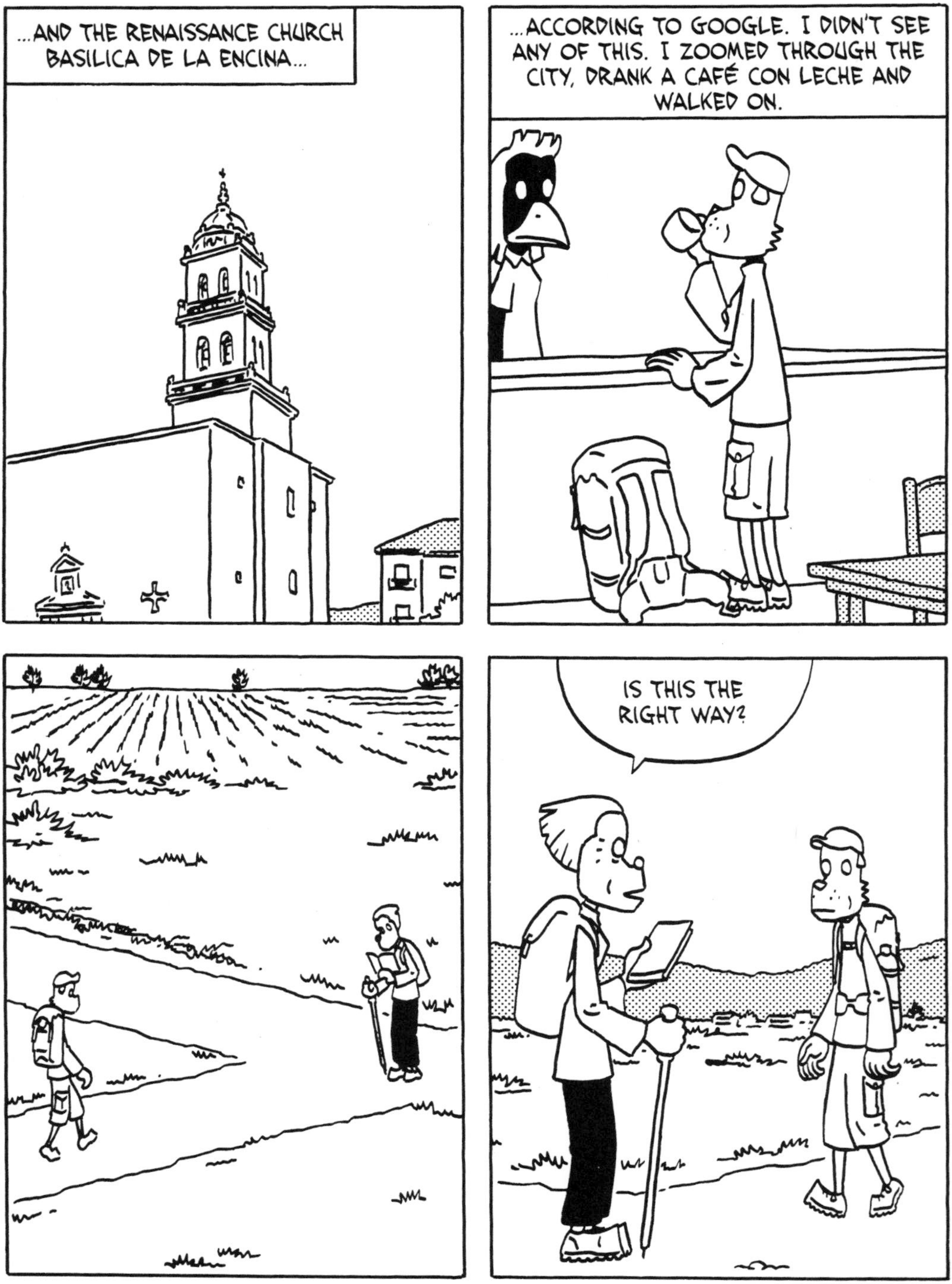
...AND THE RENAISSANCE CHURCH BASILICA DE LA ENCINA...
...ACCORDING TO GOOGLE. I DIDN'T SEE ANY OF THIS. I ZOOMED THROUGH THE CITY, DRANK A CAFÉ CON LECHE AND WALKED ON.
IS THIS THE RIGHT WAY?

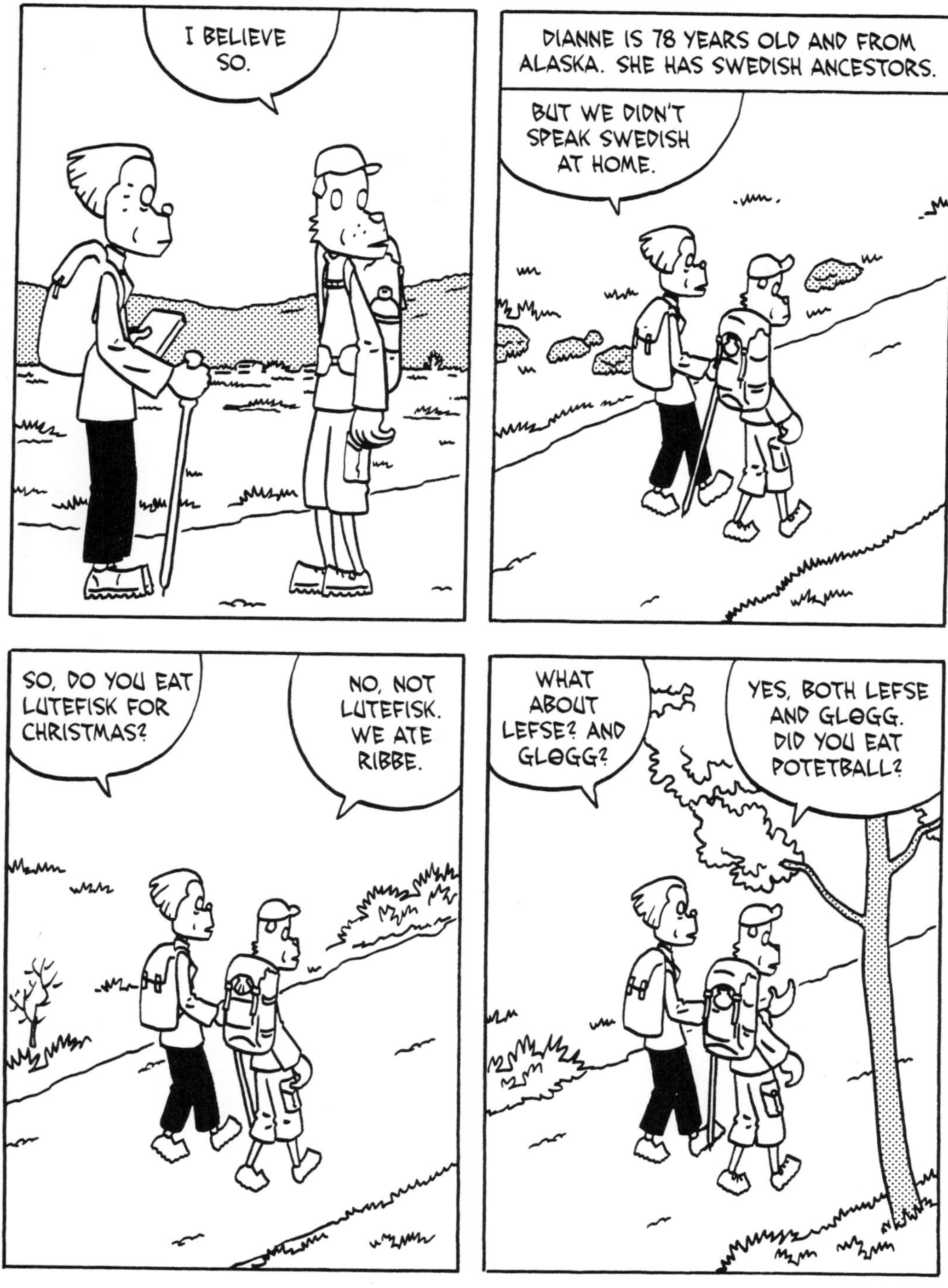
I BELIEVE SO.
DIANNE IS 78 YEARS OLD AND FROM ALASKA. SHE HAS SWEDISH ANCESTORS.
BUT WE DIDN'T SPEAK SWEDISH AT HOME.
SO, DO YOU EAT LUTEFISK FOR CHRISTMAS?
NO, NOT LUTEFISK. WE ATE RIBBE.
WHAT ABOUT LEFSE? AND GLØGG?
YES, BOTH LEFSE AND GLØGG. DID YOU EAT POTETBALL?

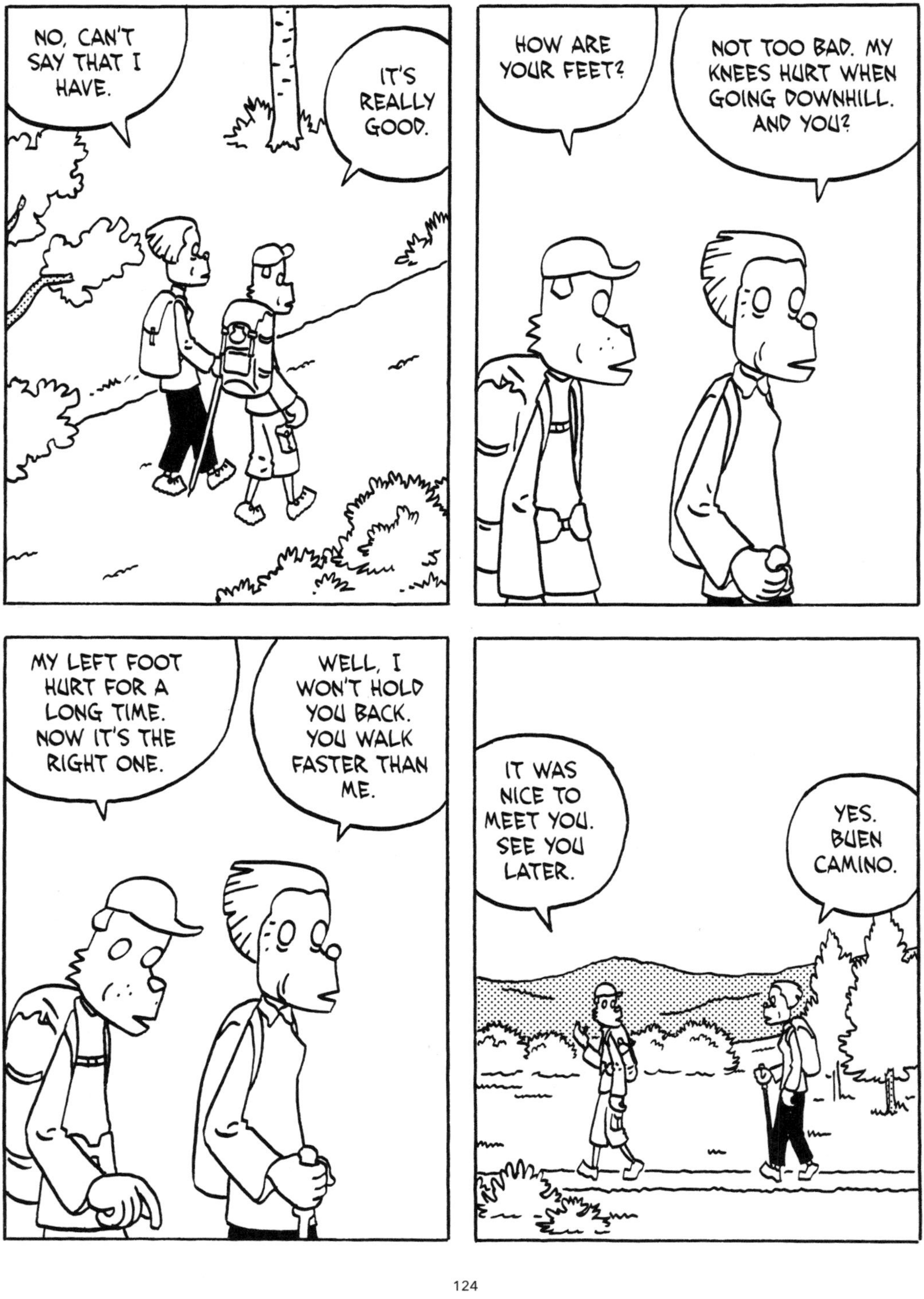
NO, CAN'T SAY THAT I HAVE.
IT'S REALLY GOOD.
HOW ARE YOUR FEET?
NOT TOO BAD. MY KNEES HURT WHEN GOING DOWNHILL. AND YOU?
MY LEFT FOOT HURT FOR A LONG TIME. NOW IT'S THE RIGHT ONE.
WELL, I WON'T HOLD YOU BACK. YOU WALK FASTER THAN ME.
IT WAS NICE TO MEET YOU. SEE YOU LATER.
YES. BUEN CAMINO.

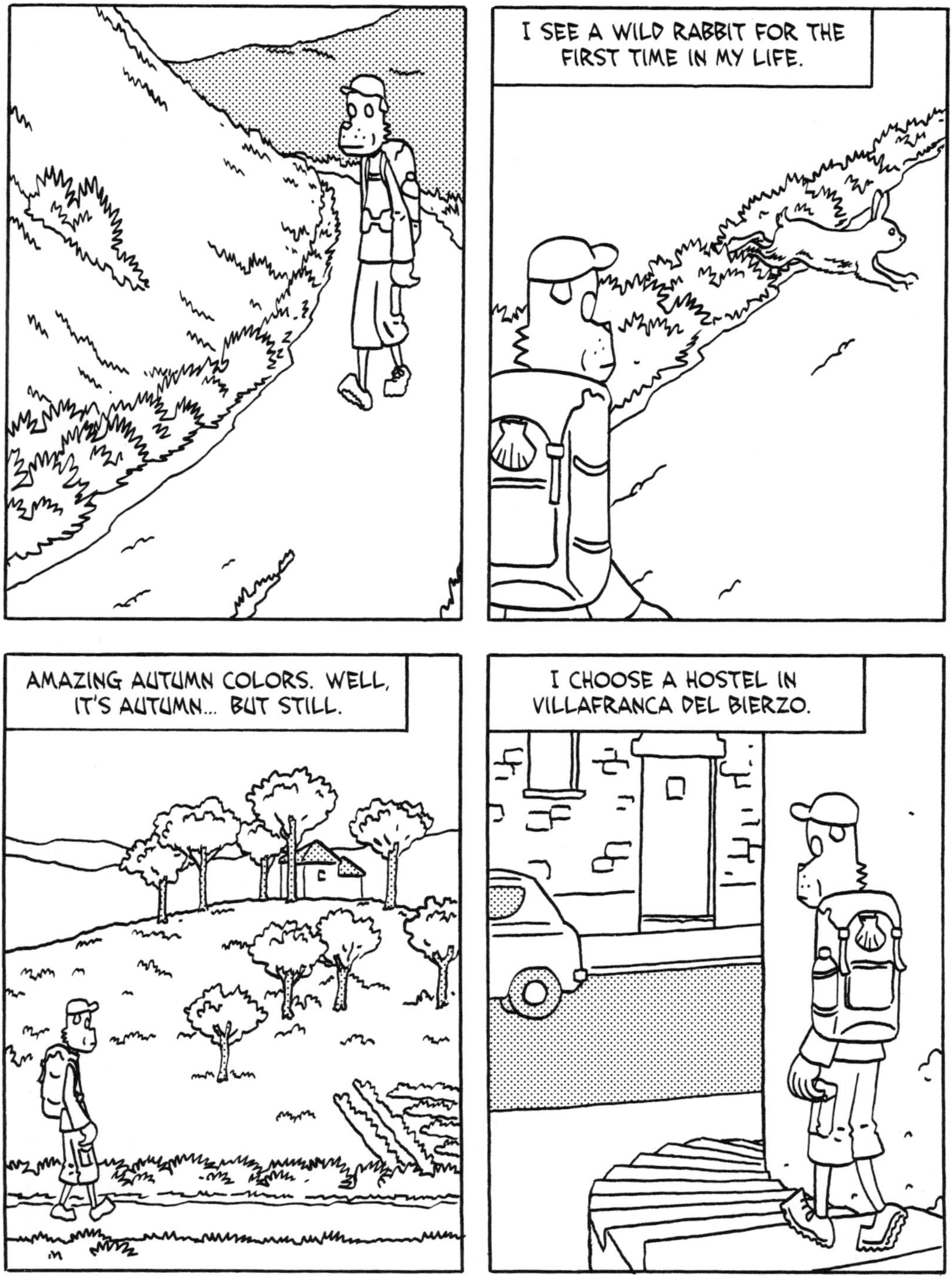
I SEE A WILD RABBIT FOR THE FIRST TIME IN MY LIFE.
AMAZING AUTUMN COLORS. WELL, IT'S AUTUMN... BUT STILL.
I CHOOSE A HOSTEL IN VILLAFRANCA DEL BIERZO.

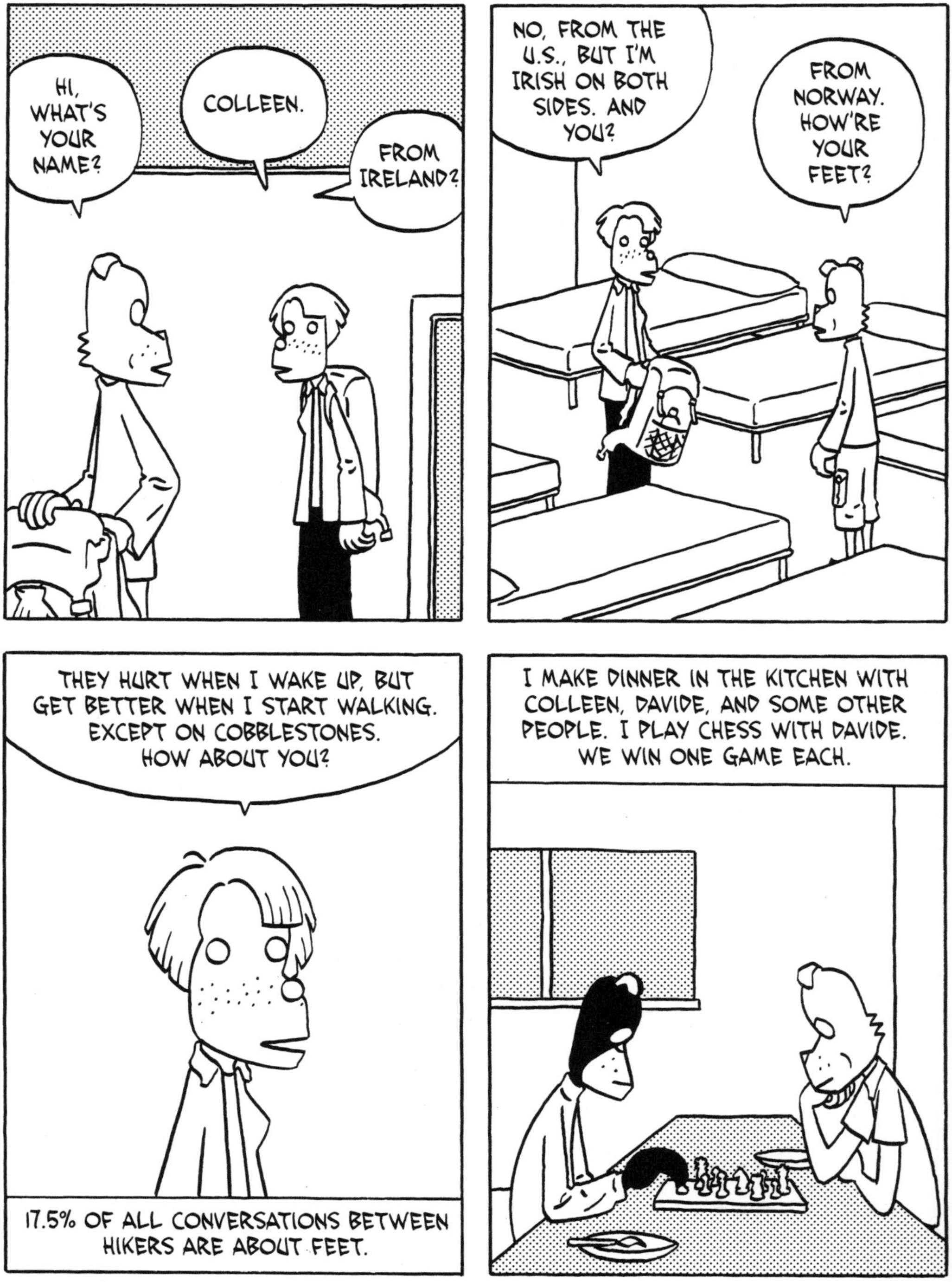

HI, WHAT'S YOUR NAME?
COLLEEN.
FROM IRELAND?
NO, FROM THE U.S., BUT I'M IRISH ON BOTH SIDES. AND YOU?
FROM NORWAY. HOW'RE YOUR FEET?
THEY HURT WHEN I WAKE UP, BUT GET BETTER WHEN I START WALKING. EXCEPT ON COBBLESTONES. HOW ABOUT YOU?
17.5% OF ALL CONVERSATIONS BETWEEN HIKERS ARE ABOUT FEET.
I MAKE DINNER IN THE KITCHEN WITH COLLEEN, DAVIDE, AND SOME OTHER PEOPLE. I PLAY CHESS WITH DAVIDE. WE WIN ONE GAME EACH.

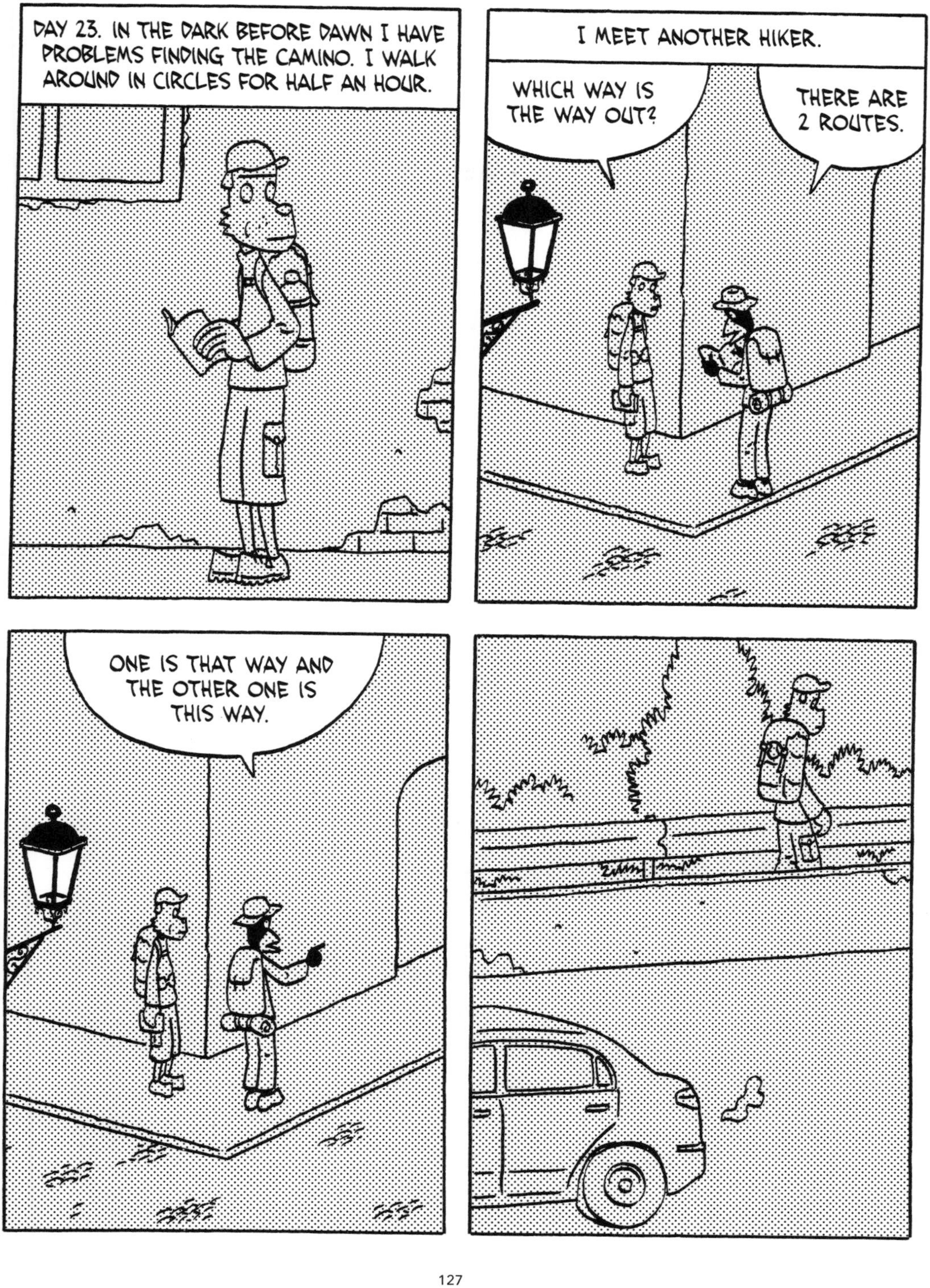
DAY 23. IN THE DARK BEFORE DAWN I HAVE PROBLEMS FINDING THE CAMINO. I WALK AROUND IN CIRCLES FOR HALF AN HOUR.
I MEET ANOTHER HIKER.
WHICH WAY IS THE WAY OUT?
THERE ARE 2 ROUTES.
ONE IS THAT WAY AND THE OTHER ONE IS THIS WAY.

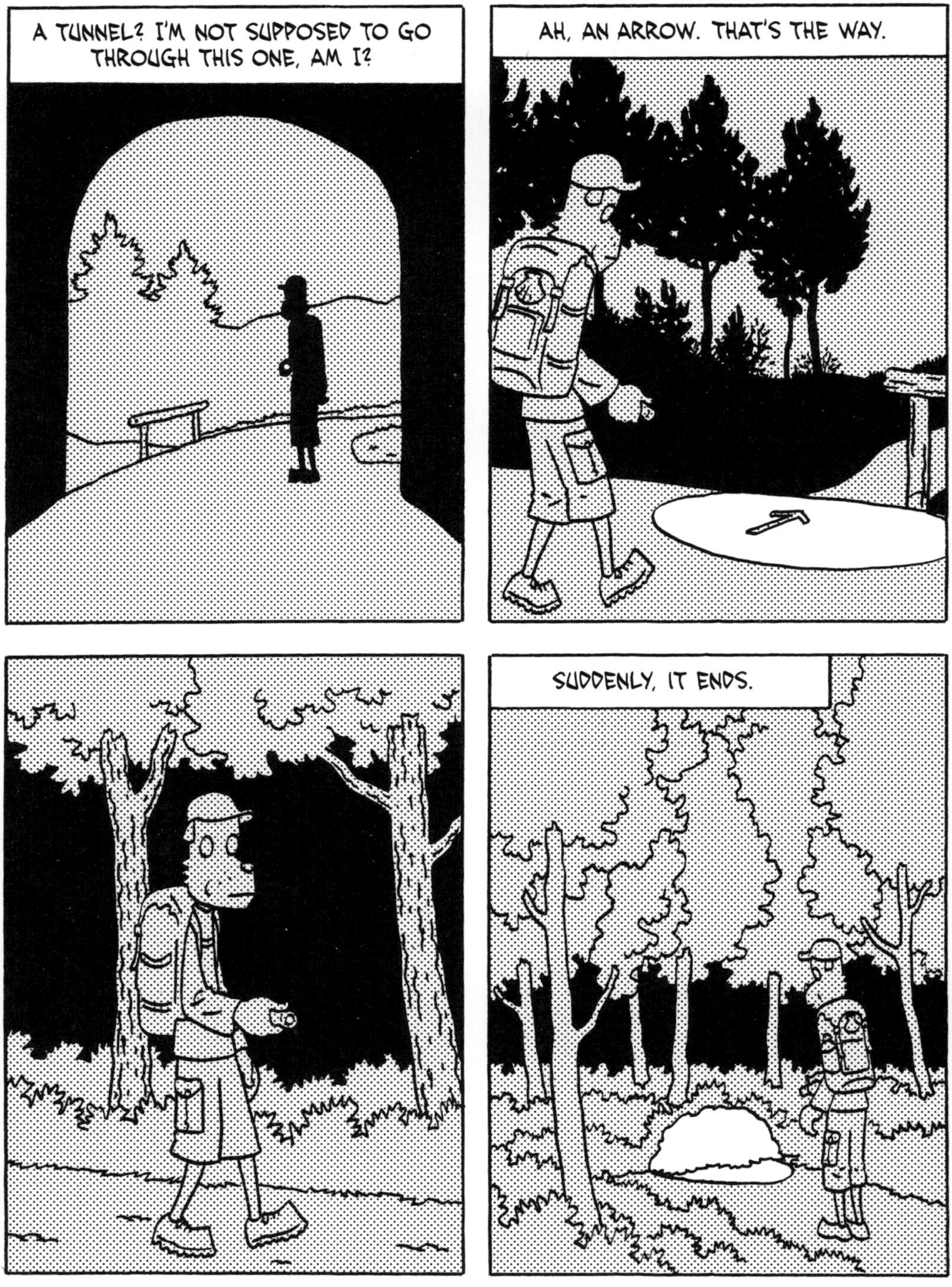
A TUNNEL? I'M NOT SUPPOSED TO GO THROUGH THIS ONE, AM I?
AH, AN ARROW. THAT'S THE WAY.
SUDDENLY, IT ENDS.

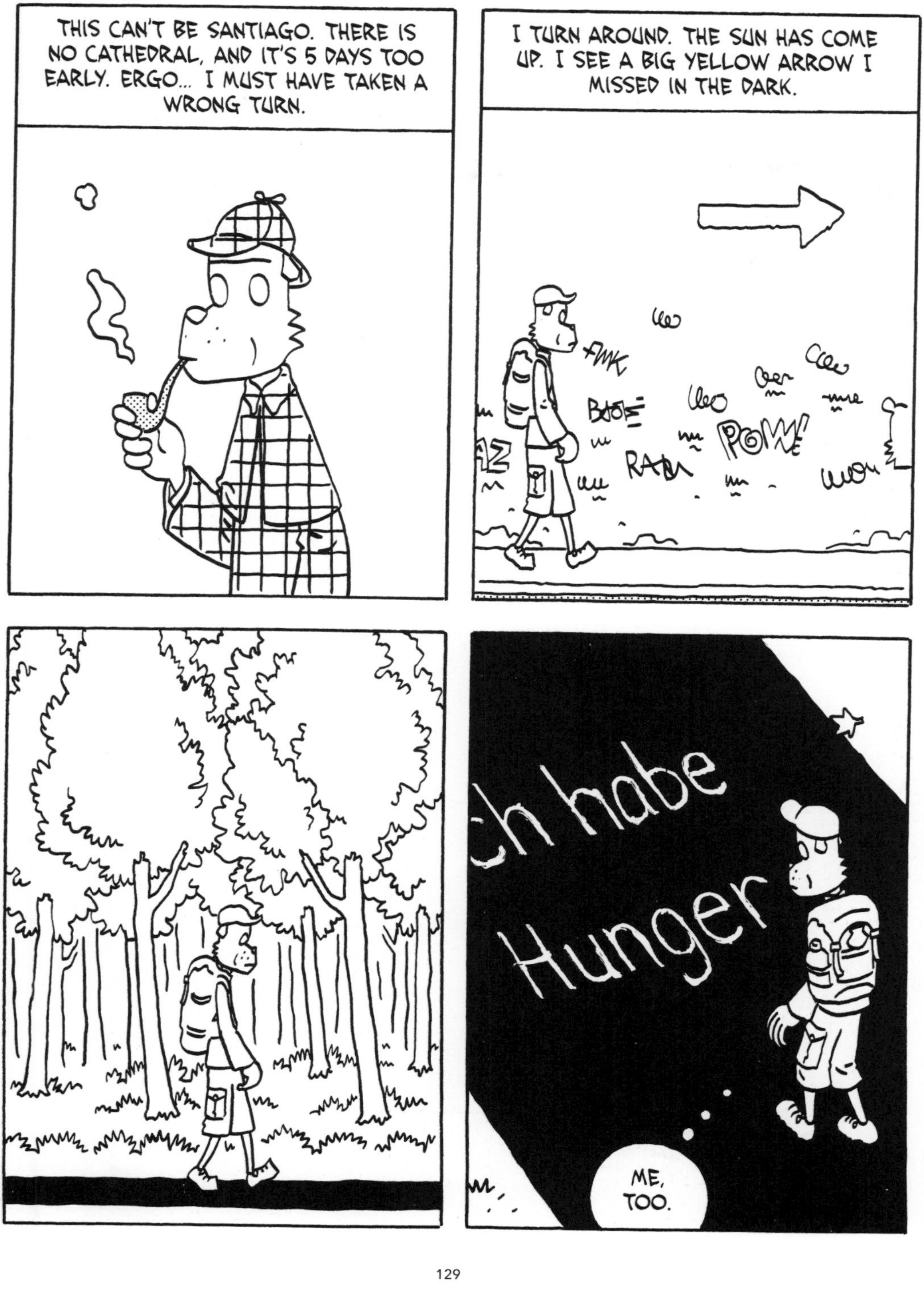
THIS CAN'T BE SANTIAGO. THERE IS NO CATHEDRAL, AND IT'S 5 DAYS TOO EARLY. ERGO... I MUST HAVE TAKEN A WRONG TURN.
I TURN AROUND. THE SUN HAS COME UP. I SEE A BIG YELLOW ARROW I MISSED IN THE DARK.
POW!
ch habe Hunger
ME, TOO.

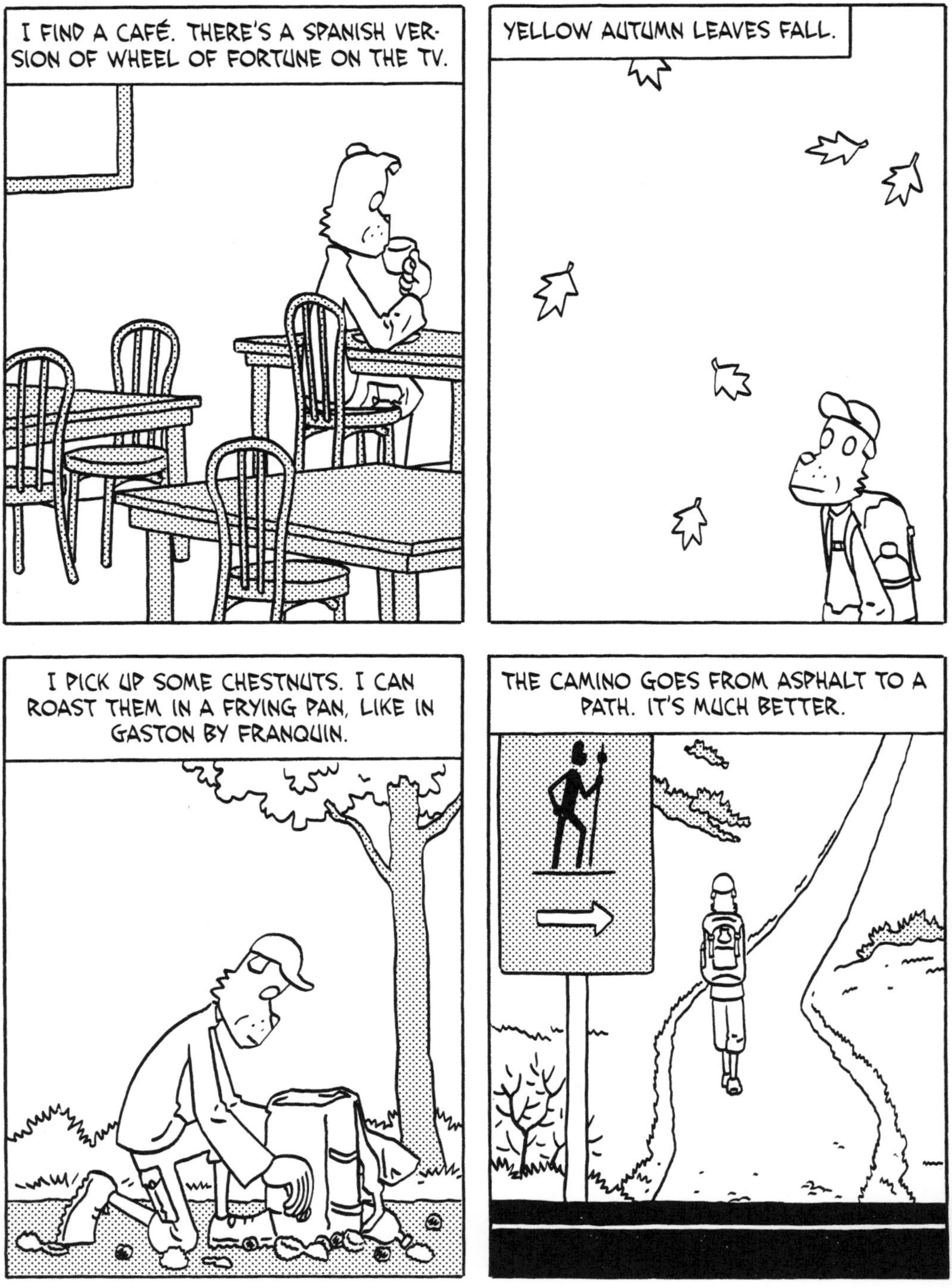
I FIND A CAFÉ. THERE'S A SPANISH VERSION OF WHEEL OF FORTUNE ON THE TV.
YELLOW AUTUMN LEAVES FALL.
I PICK UP SOME CHESTNUTS. I CAN ROAST THEM IN A FRYING PAN, LIKE IN GASTON BY FRANQUIN.
THE CAMINO GOES FROM ASPHALT TO A PATH. IT'S MUCH BETTER.

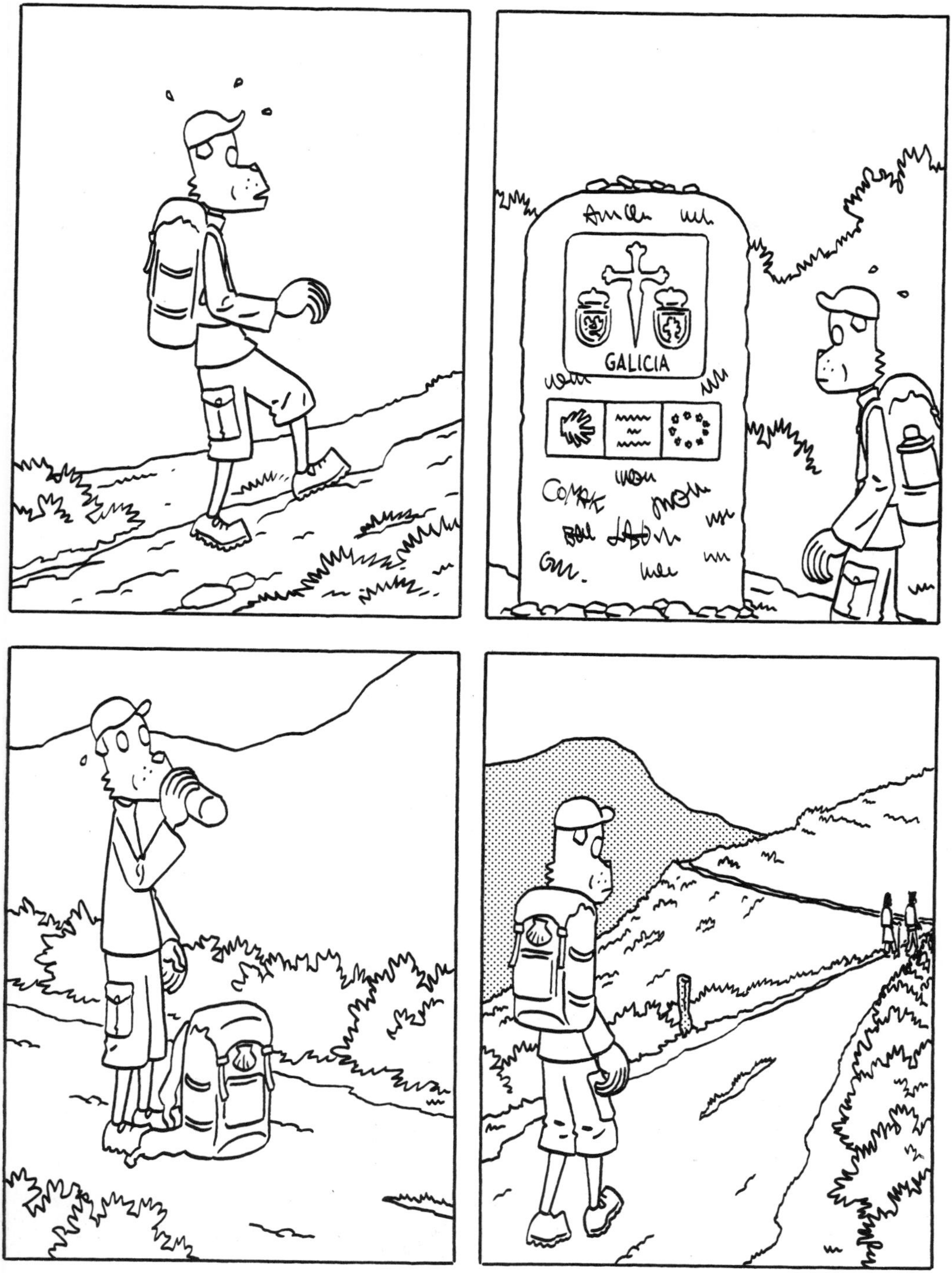
GALICIA

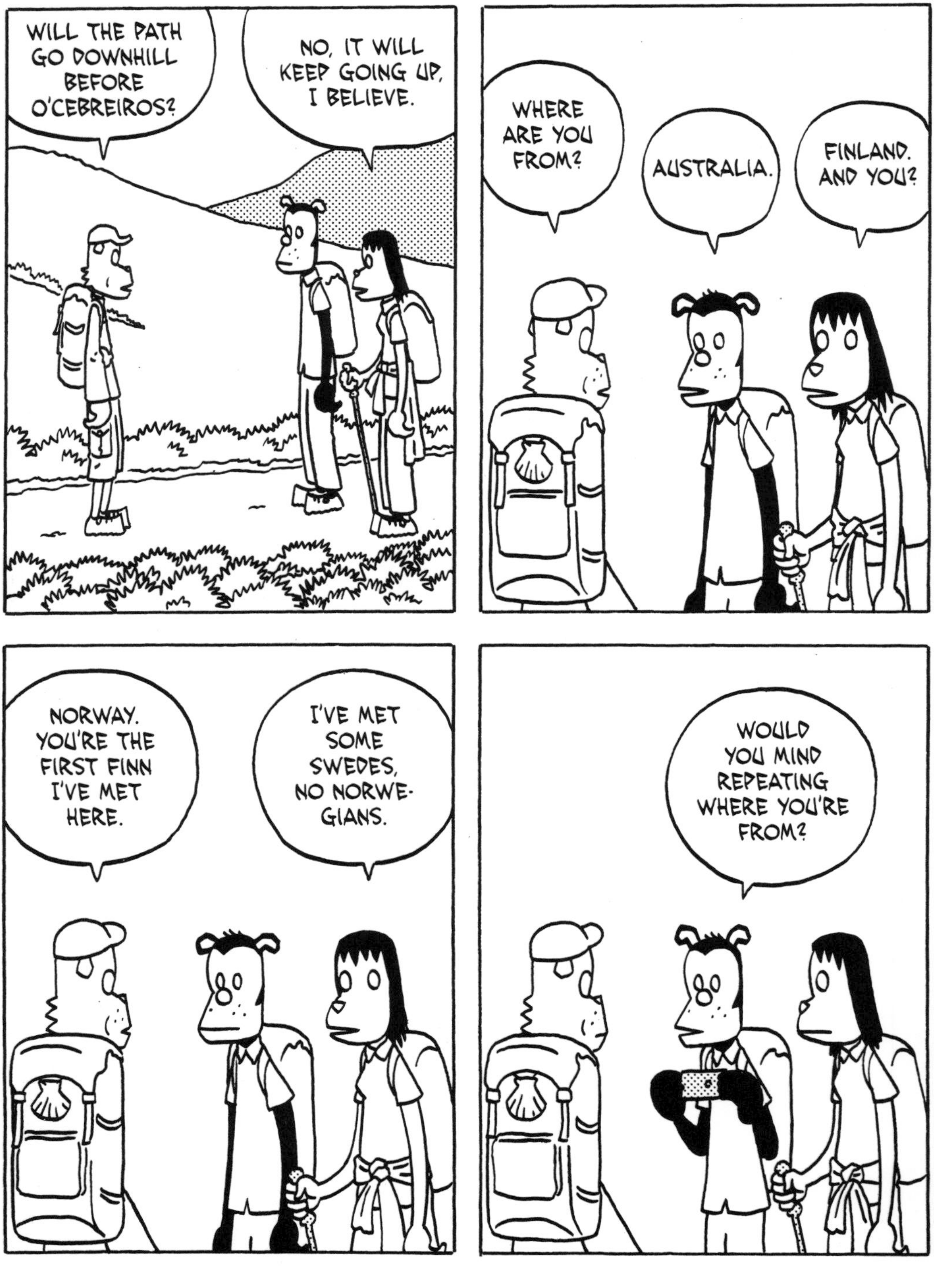

WILL THE PATH GO DOWNHILL BEFORE O'CEBREIROS?
NO, IT WILL KEEP GOING UP, I BELIEVE.
WHERE ARE YOU FROM?
AUSTRALIA.
FINLAND. AND YOU?
NORWAY. YOU'RE THE FIRST FINN I'VE MET HERE.
I'VE MET SOME SWEDES, NO NORWE-GIANS.
WOULD YOU MIND REPEATING WHERE YOU'RE FROM?

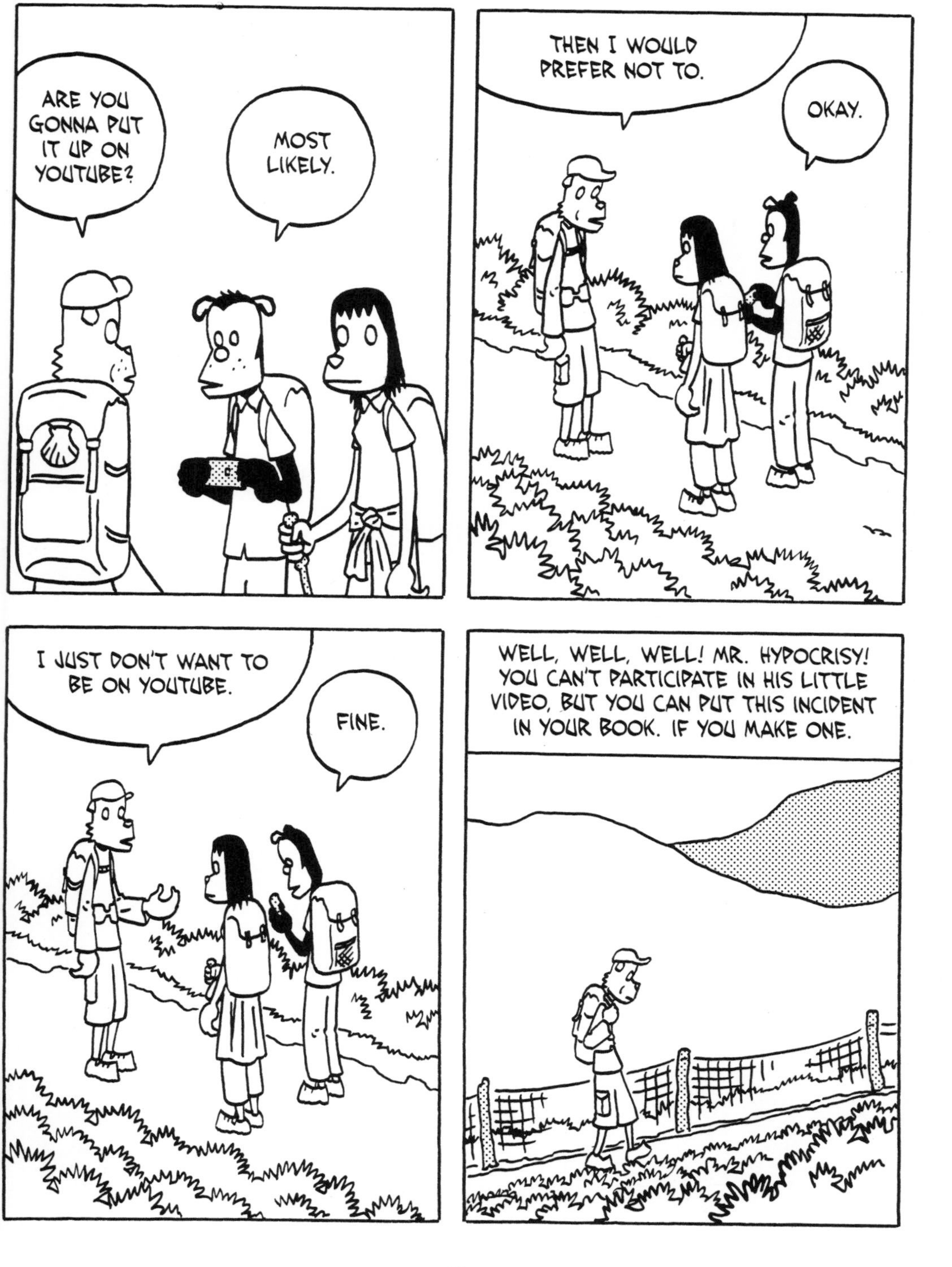
ARE YOU GONNA PUT IT UP ON YOUTUBE?
MOST LIKELY.
THEN I WOULD PREFER NOT TO.
OKAY.
I JUST DON'T WANT TO BE ON YOUTUBE.
FINE.
WELL, WELL, WELL! MR. HYPOCRISY! YOU CAN'T PARTICIPATE IN HIS LITTLE VIDEO, BUT YOU CAN PUT THIS INCIDENT IN YOUR BOOK. IF YOU MAKE ONE.

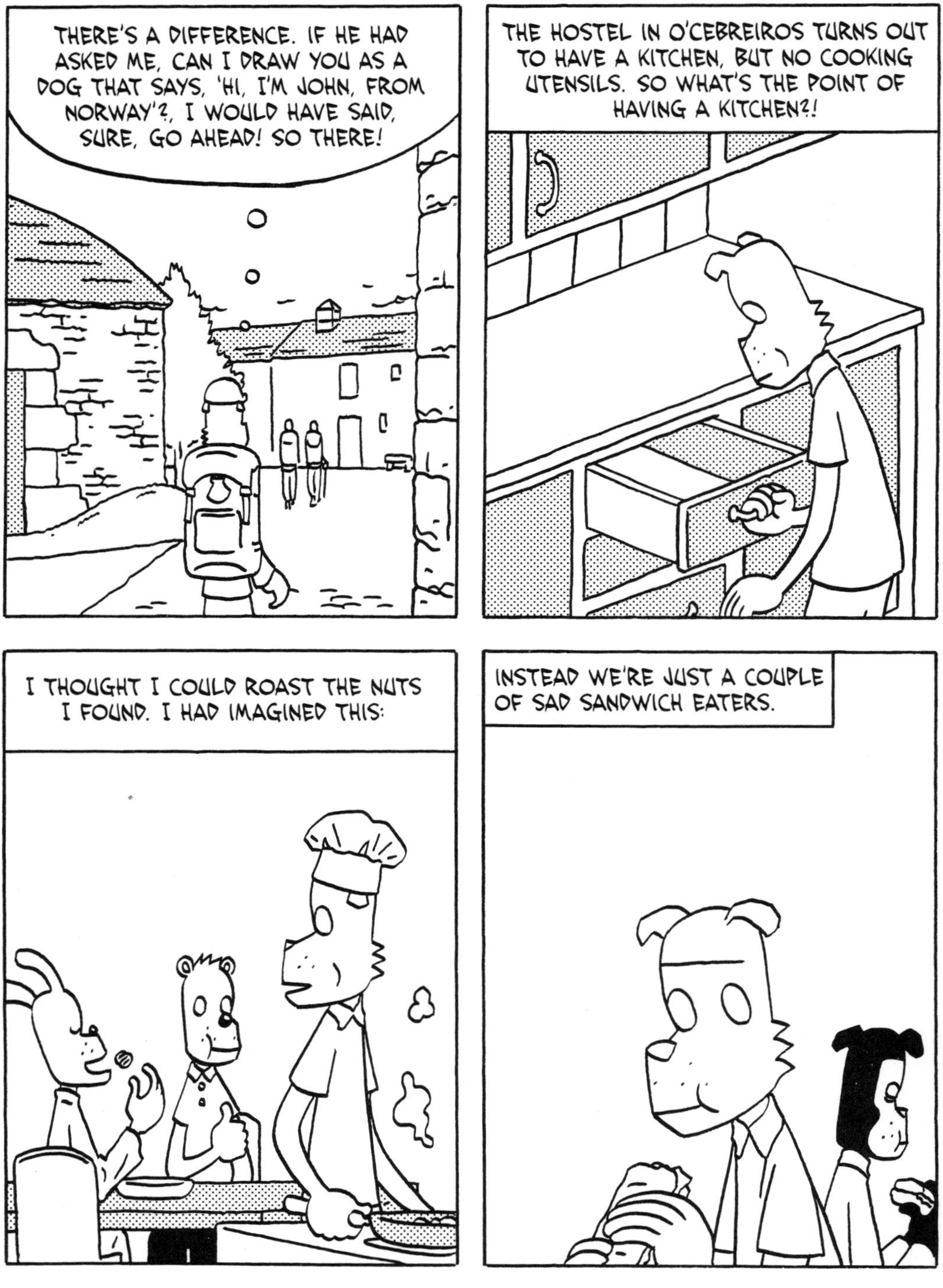
THERE'S A DIFFERENCE. IF HE HAD ASKED ME, CAN I DRAW YOU AS A DOG THAT SAYS, 'HI, I'M JOHN, FROM NORWAY'?, I WOULD HAVE SAID, SURE, GO AHEAD! SO THERE!
THE HOSTEL IN O'CEBREIROS TURNS OUT TO HAVE A KITCHEN, BUT NO COOKING UTENSILS. SO WHAT'S THE POINT OF HAVING A KITCHEN?!
I THOUGHT I COULD ROAST THE NUTS I FOUND. I HAD IMAGINED THIS:
INSTEAD WE'RE JUST A COUPLE OF SAD SANDWICH EATERS.

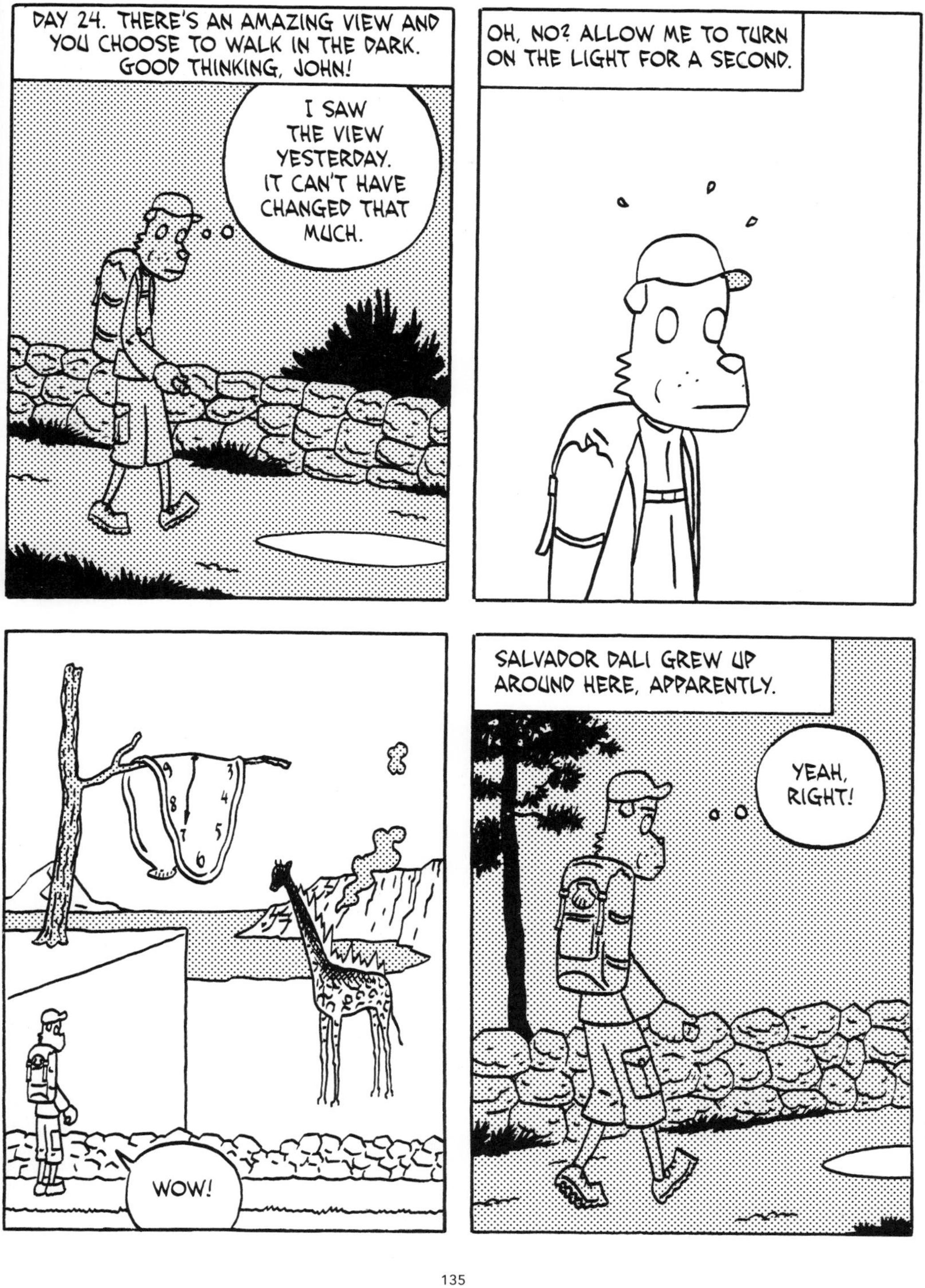
DAY 24. THERE'S AN AMAZING VIEW AND YOU CHOOSE TO WALK IN THE DARK. GOOD THINKING, JOHN!
I SAW THE VIEW YESTERDAY. IT CAN'T HAVE CHANGED THAT MUCH.
OH, NO? ALLOW ME TO TURN ON THE LIGHT FOR A SECOND.
WOW!
SALVADOR DALI GREW UP AROUND HERE, APPARENTLY.
YEAH, RIGHT!

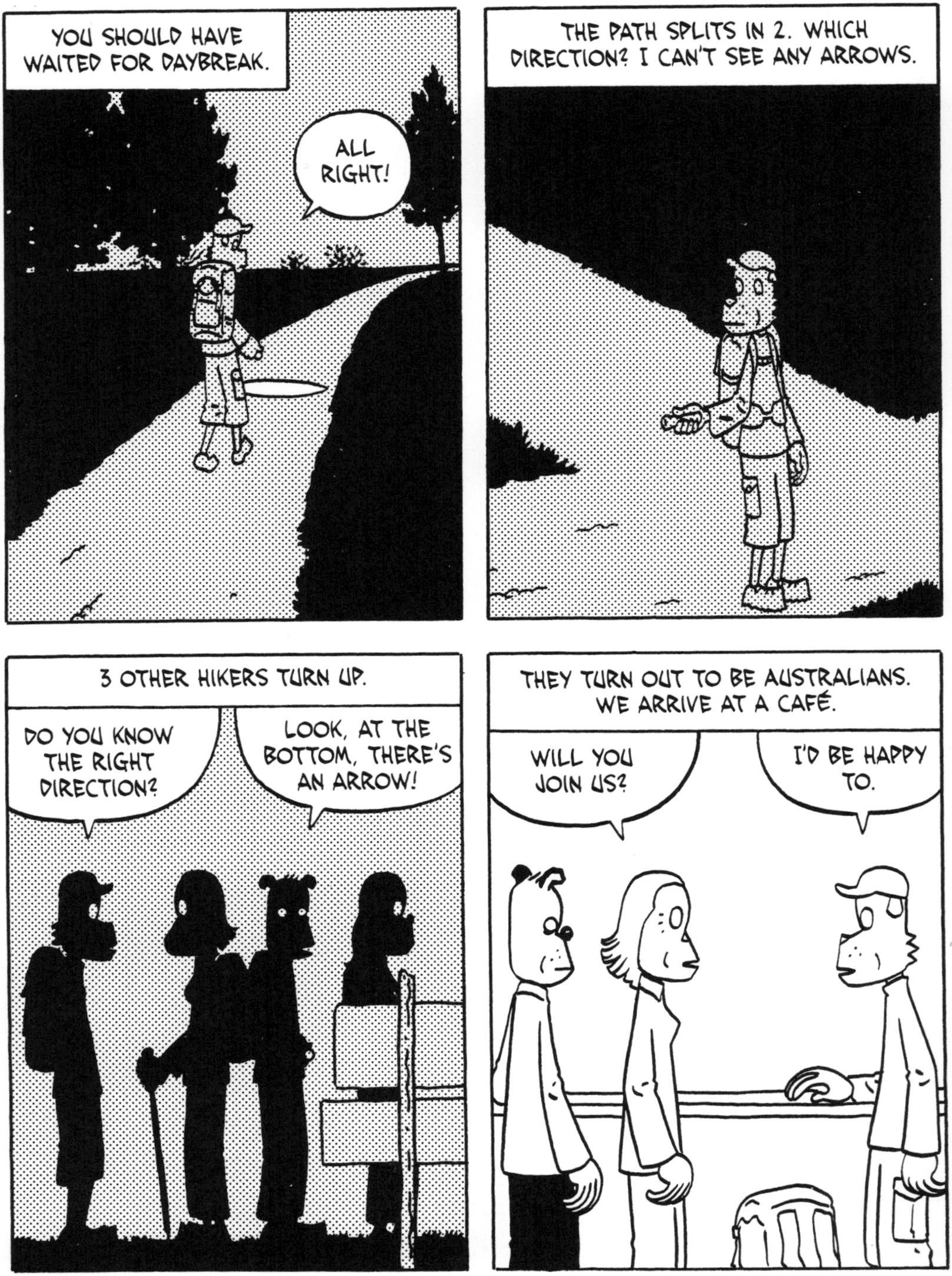
YOU SHOULD HAVE WAITED FOR DAYBREAK.
ALL RIGHT!
THE PATH SPLITS IN 2. WHICH DIRECTION? I CAN'T SEE ANY ARROWS.
3 OTHER HIKERS TURN UP.
DO YOU KNOW THE RIGHT DIRECTION?
LOOK, AT THE BOTTOM, THERE'S AN ARROW!
THEY TURN OUT TO BE AUSTRALIANS. WE ARRIVE AT A CAFÉ.
WILL YOU JOIN US?
I'D BE HAPPY TO.

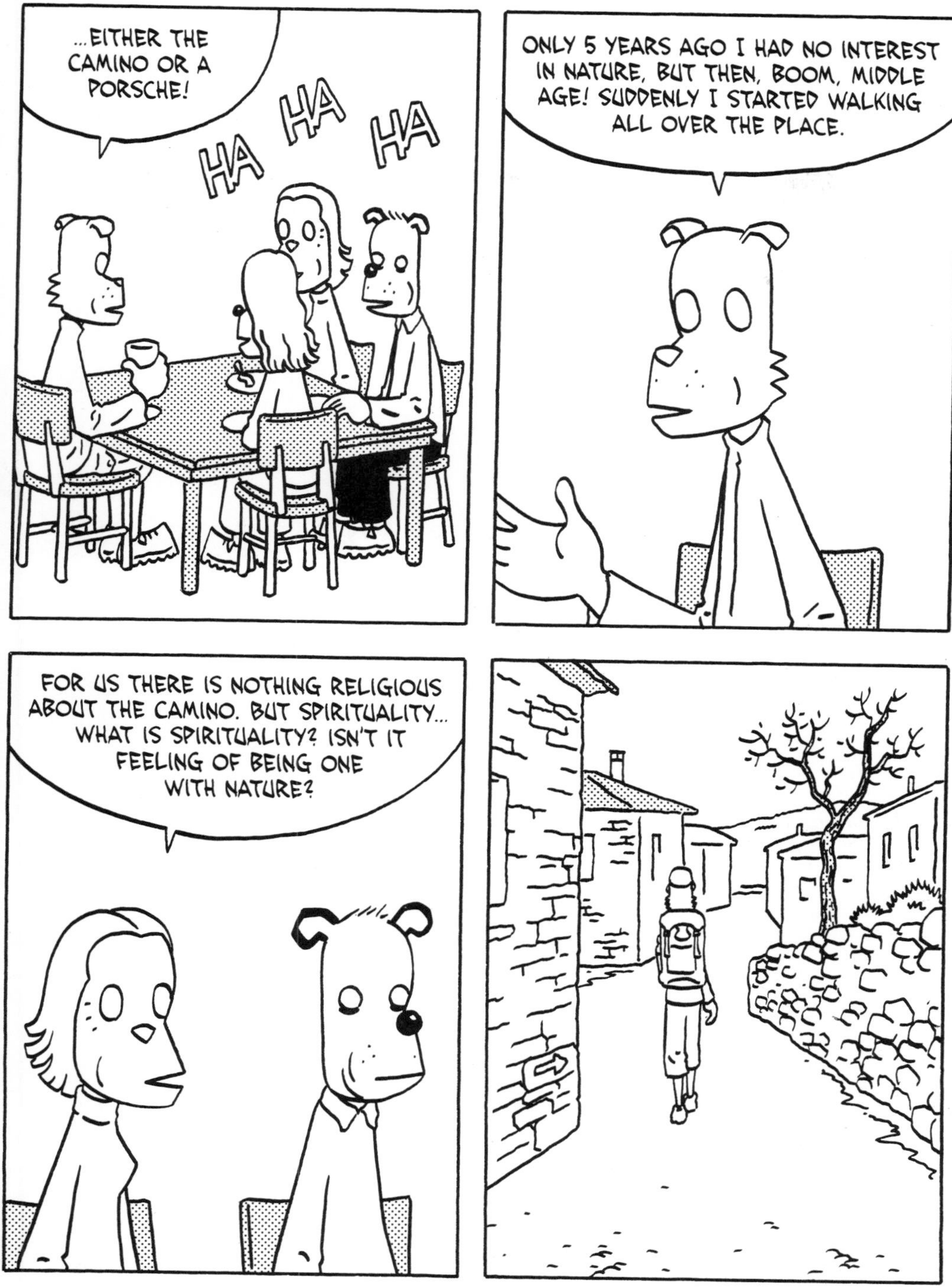
...EITHER THE CAMINO OR A PORSCHE!
HA HA HA
ONLY 5 YEARS AGO I HAD NO INTEREST IN NATURE, BUT THEN, BOOM, MIDDLE AGE! SUDDENLY I STARTED WALKING ALL OVER THE PLACE.
FOR US THERE IS NOTHING RELIGIOUS ABOUT THE CAMINO. BUT SPIRITUALITY... WHAT IS SPIRITUALITY? ISN'T IT FEELING OF BEING ONE WITH NATURE?

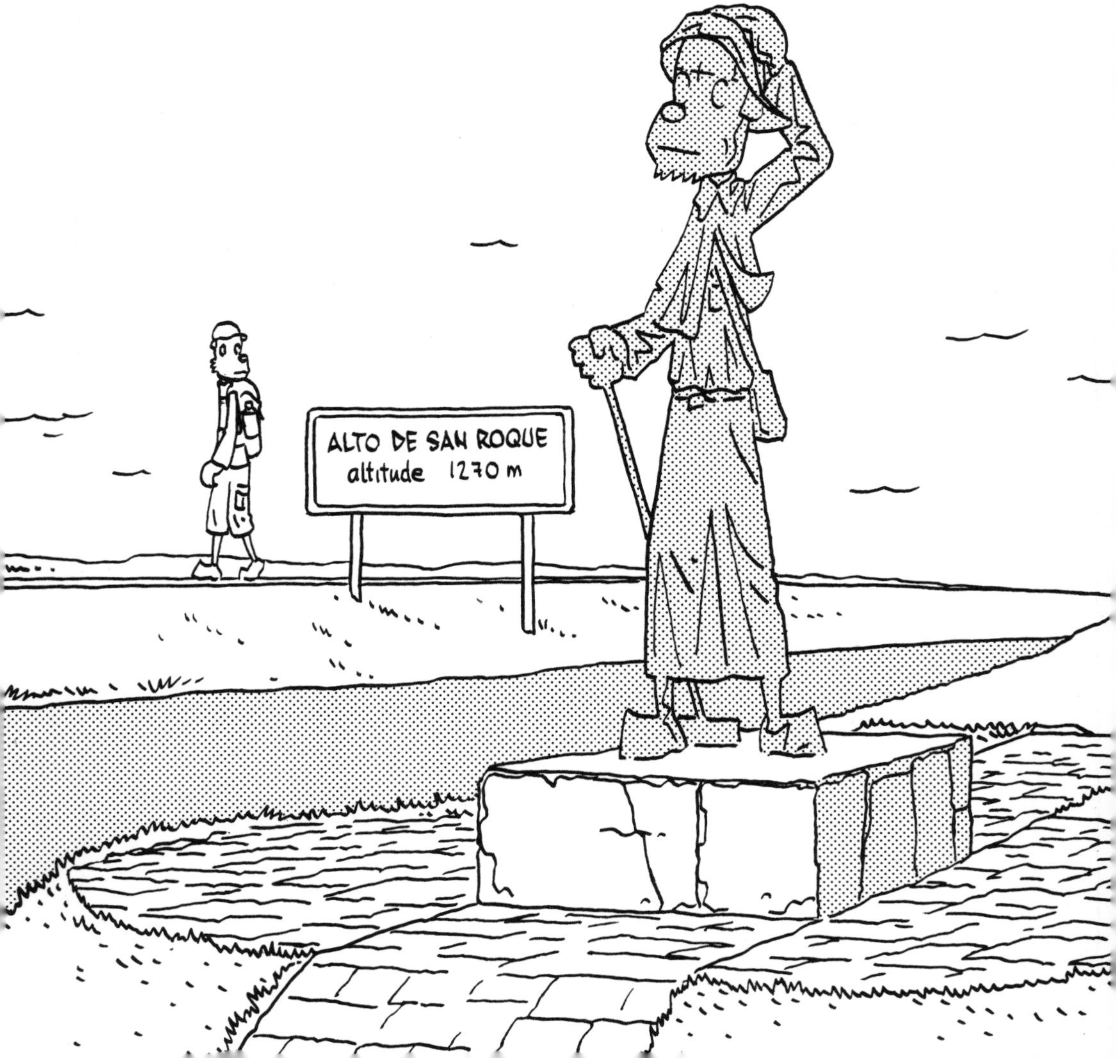
ALTO DE SAN ROQUE
altitude 1270 m

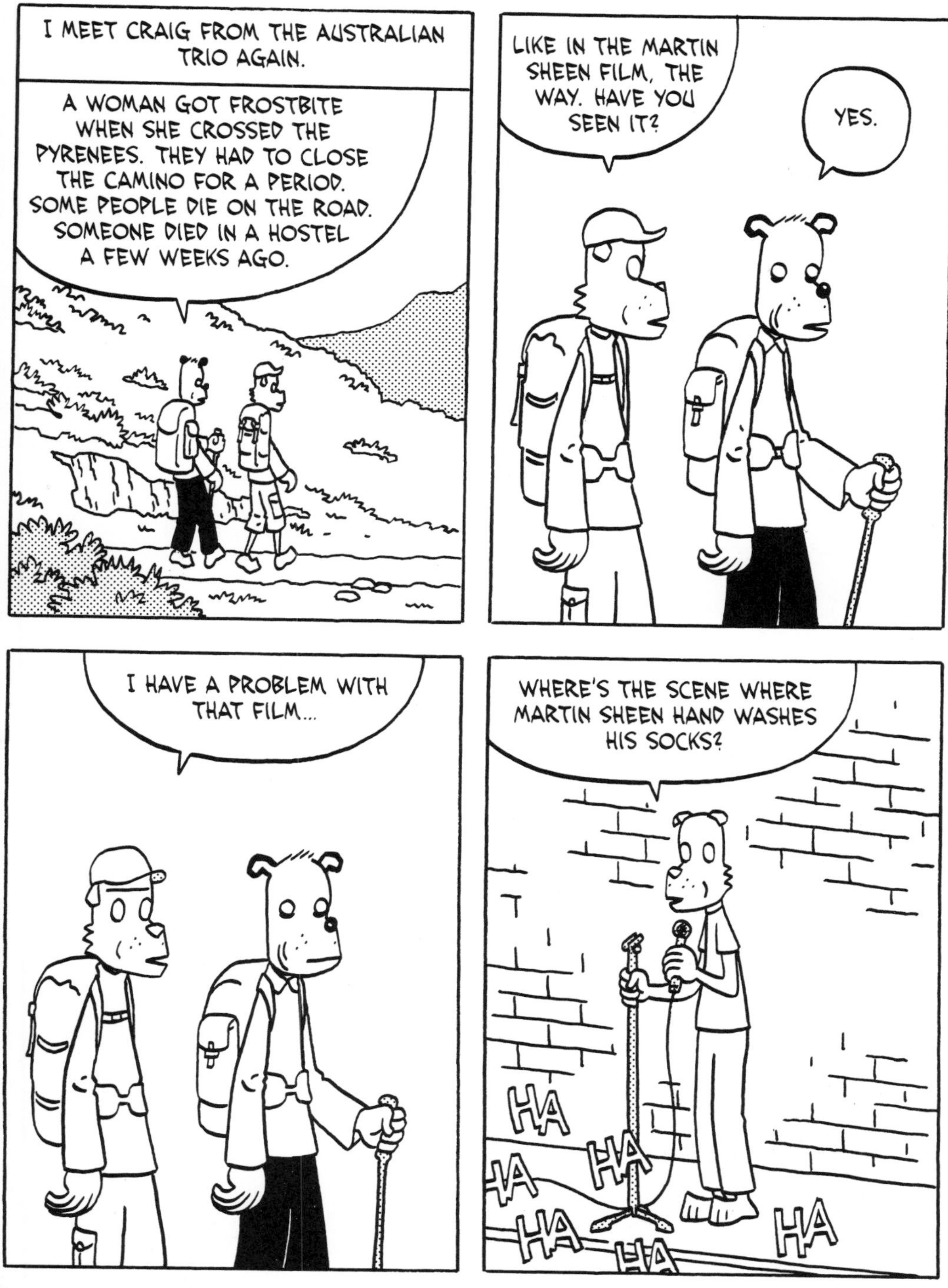
I MEET CRAIG FROM THE AUSTRALIAN TRIO AGAIN.
A WOMAN GOT FROSTBITE WHEN SHE CROSSED THE PYRENEES. THEY HAD TO CLOSE THE CAMINO FOR A PERIOD. SOME PEOPLE DIE ON THE ROAD. SOMEONE DIED IN A HOSTEL A FEW WEEKS AGO.
LIKE IN THE MARTIN SHEEN FILM, THE WAY. HAVE YOU SEEN IT?
YES.
I HAVE A PROBLEM WITH THAT FILM...
WHERE'S THE SCENE WHERE MARTIN SHEEN HAND WASHES HIS SOCKS?
HA
HA
HA
HA
HA
HA

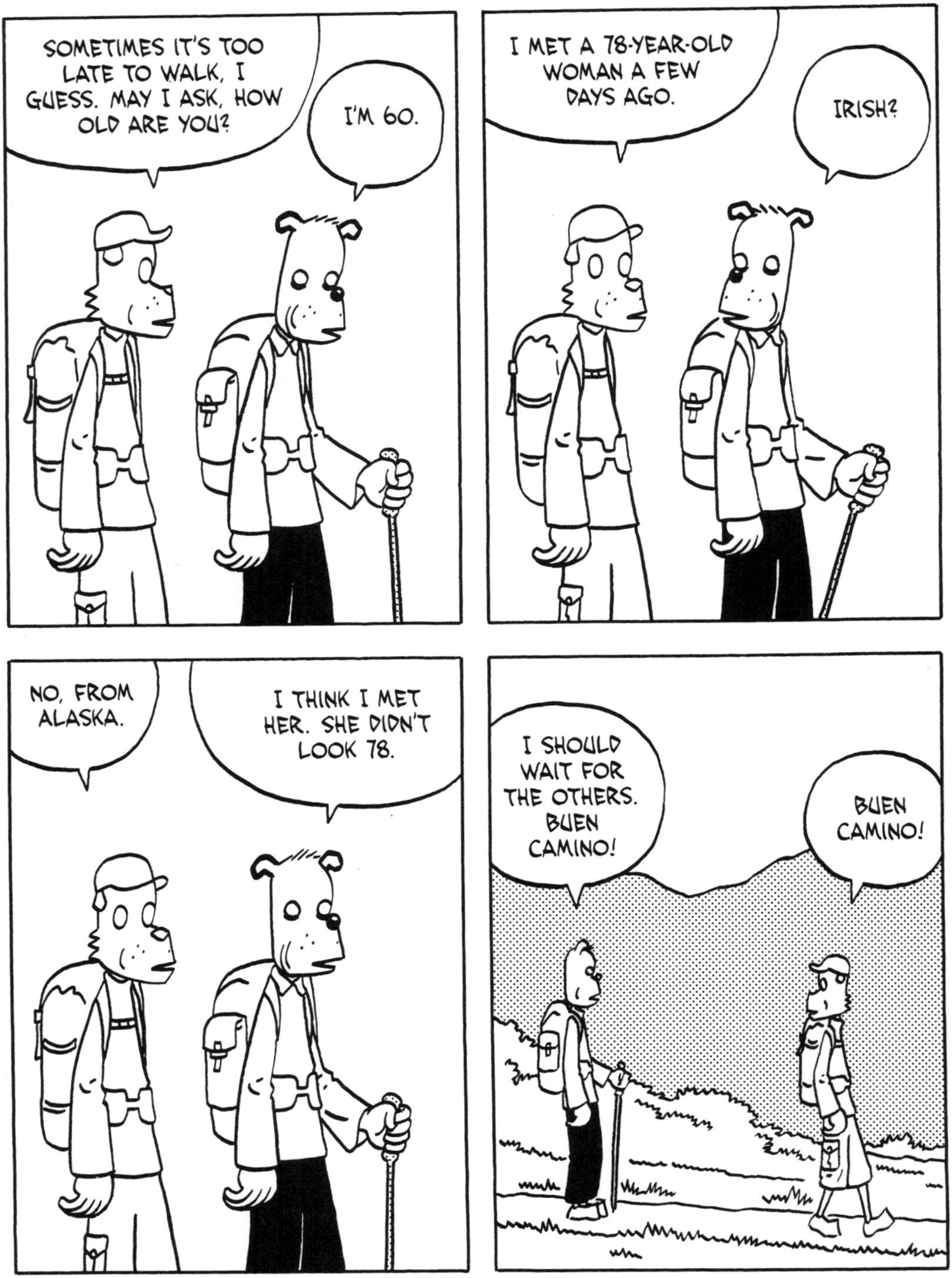
SOMETIMES IT'S TOO LATE TO WALK, I GUESS. MAY I ASK, HOW OLD ARE YOU?
I'M 60.
I MET A 78-YEAR-OLD WOMAN A FEW DAYS AGO.
IRISH?
NO, FROM ALASKA.
I THINK I MET HER. SHE DIDN'T LOOK 78.
I SHOULD WAIT FOR THE OTHERS. BUEN CAMINO!
BUEN CAMINO!

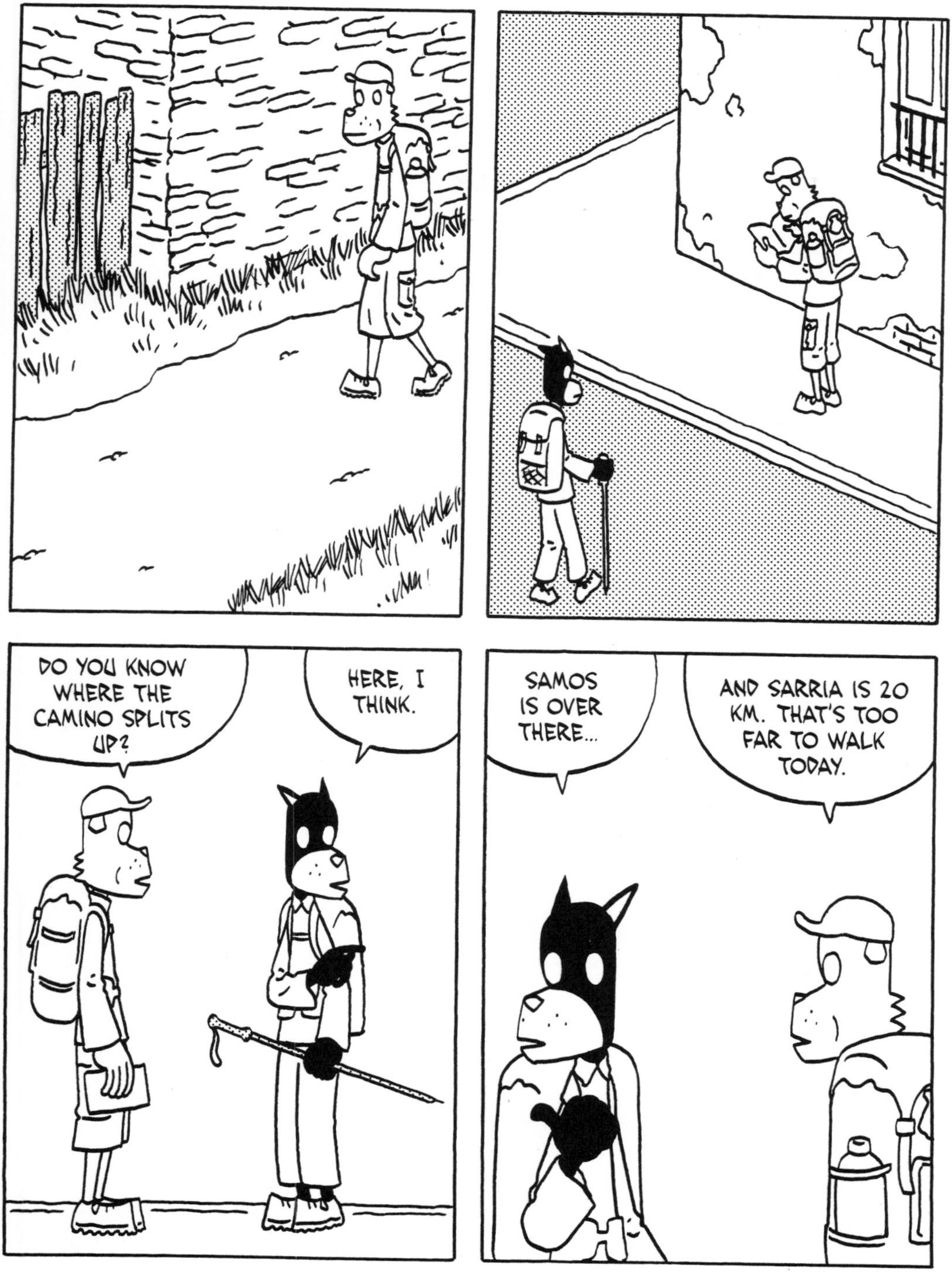
DO YOU KNOW WHERE THE CAMINO SPLITS UP?
HERE, I THINK.
SAMOS IS OVER THERE...
AND SARRIA IS 20 KM. THAT'S TOO FAR TO WALK TODAY.

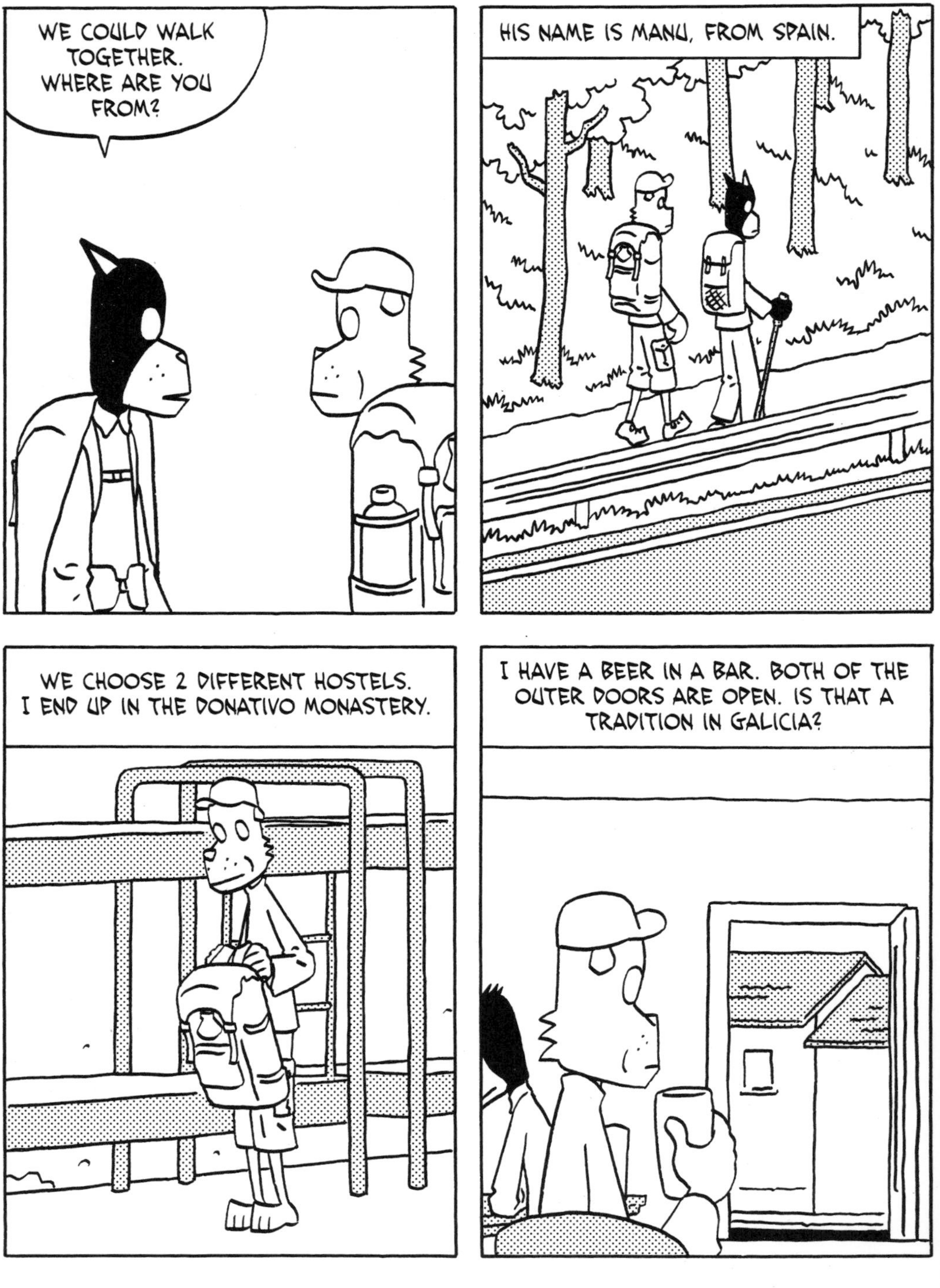
WE COULD WALK TOGETHER. WHERE ARE YOU FROM?
HIS NAME IS MANU, FROM SPAIN.
WE CHOOSE 2 DIFFERENT HOSTELS. I END UP IN THE DONATIVO MONASTERY.
I HAVE A BEER IN A BAR. BOTH OF THE OUTER DOORS ARE OPEN. IS THAT A TRADITION IN GALICIA?

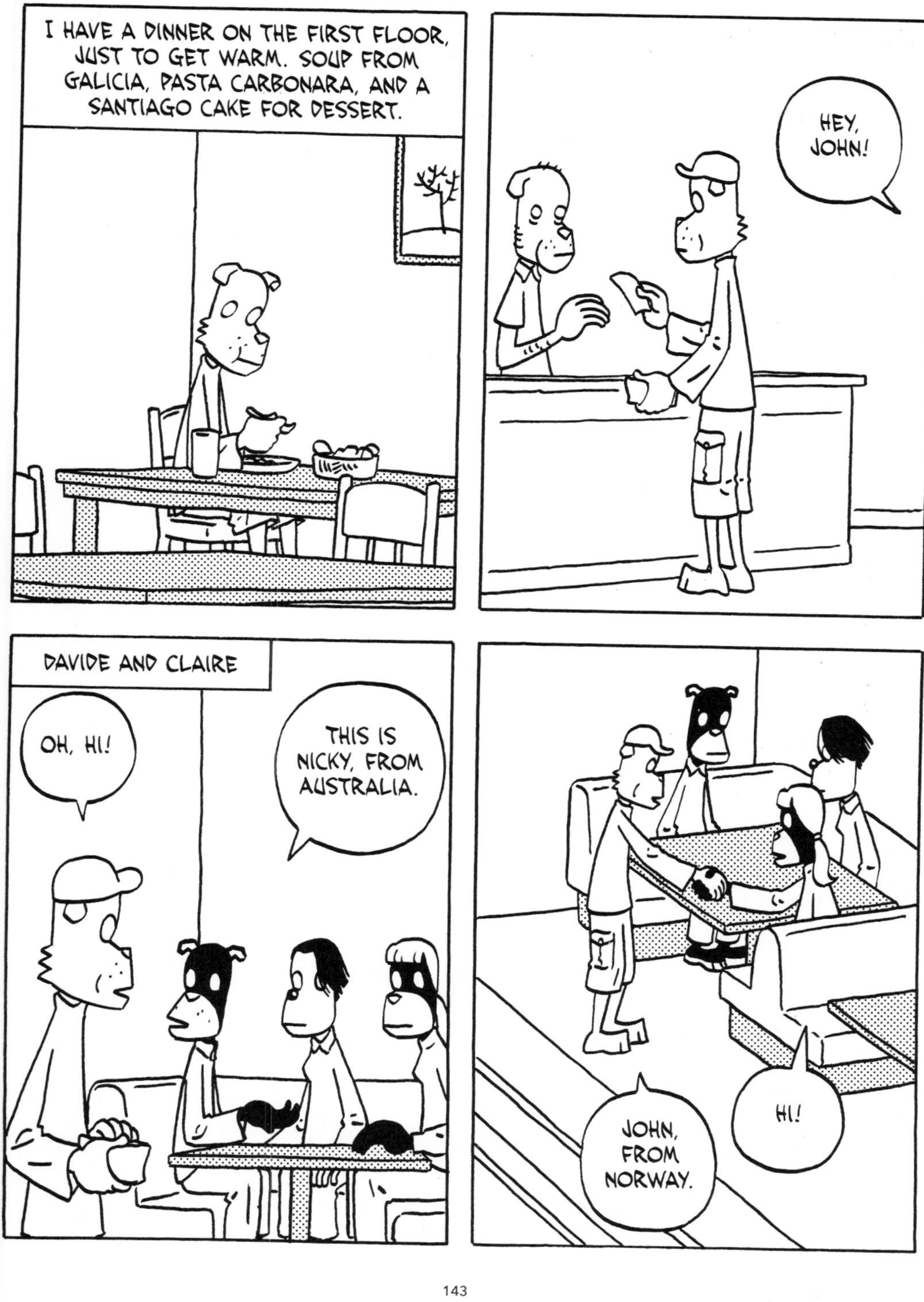
I HAVE A DINNER ON THE FIRST FLOOR, JUST TO GET WARM. SOUP FROM GALICIA, PASTA CARBONARA, AND A SANTIAGO CAKE FOR DESSERT.
HEY, JOHN!
DAVIDE AND CLAIRE
OH, HI!
THIS IS NICKY, FROM AUSTRALIA.
JOHN, FROM NORWAY.
HI!

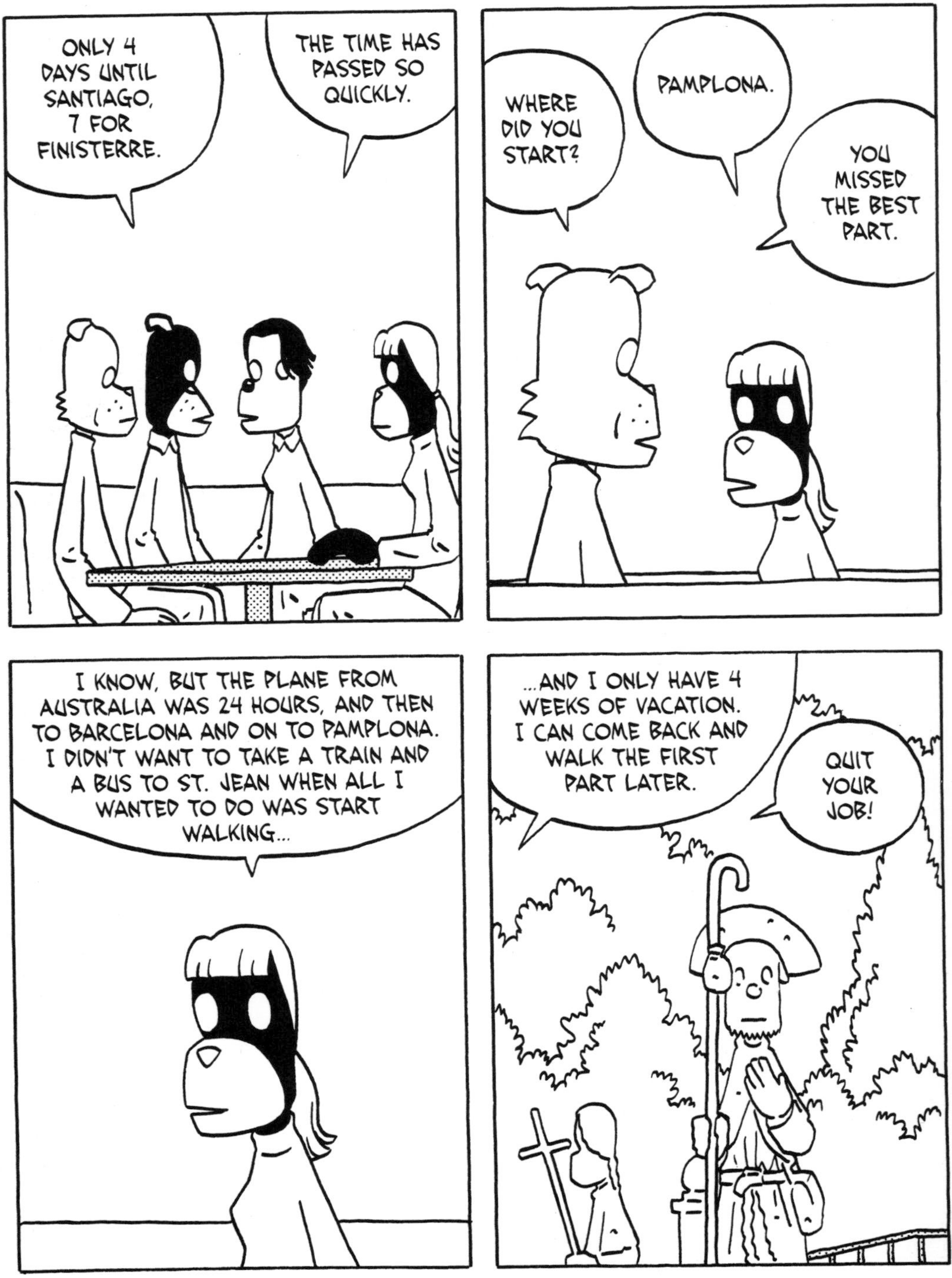
ONLY 4 DAYS UNTIL SANTIAGO, 7 FOR FINISTERRE.
THE TIME HAS PASSED SO QUICKLY.
WHERE DID YOU START?
PAMPLONA.
YOU MISSED THE BEST PART.
I KNOW, BUT THE PLANE FROM AUSTRALIA WAS 24 HOURS, AND THEN TO BARCELONA AND ON TO PAMPLONA. I DIDN'T WANT TO TAKE A TRAIN AND A BUS TO ST. JEAN WHEN ALL I WANTED TO DO WAS START WALKING...
...AND I ONLY HAVE 4 WEEKS OF VACATION. I CAN COME BACK AND WALK THE FIRST PART LATER.
QUIT YOUR JOB!

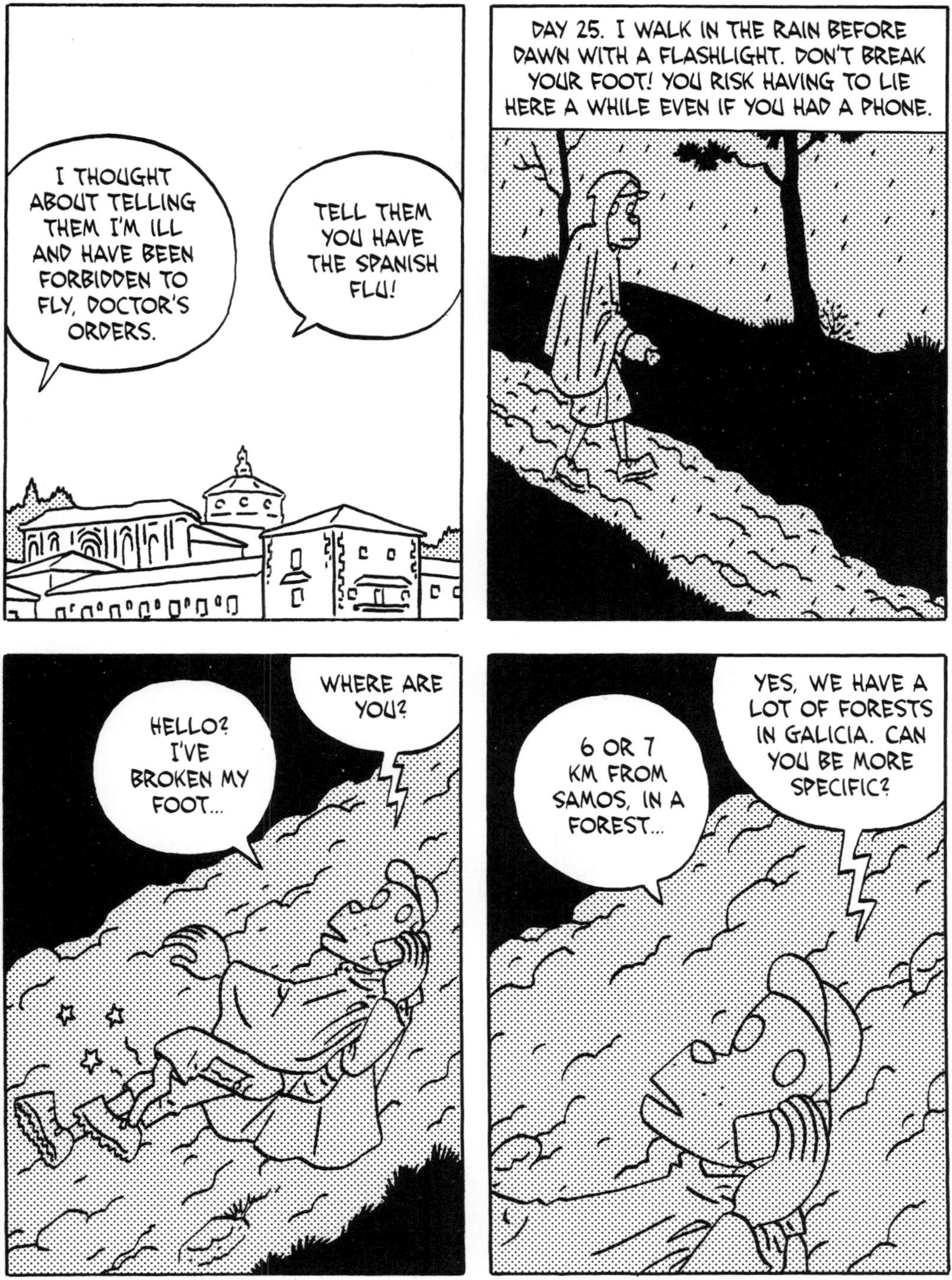
I THOUGHT ABOUT TELLING THEM I'M ILL AND HAVE BEEN FORBIDDEN TO FLY, DOCTOR'S ORDERS.
TELL THEM YOU HAVE THE SPANISH FLU!
DAY 25. I WALK IN THE RAIN BEFORE DAWN WITH A FLASHLIGHT. DON'T BREAK YOUR FOOT! YOU RISK HAVING TO LIE HERE A WHILE EVEN IF YOU HAD A PHONE.
HELLO? I'VE BROKEN MY FOOT...
WHERE ARE YOU?
6 OR 7 KM FROM SAMOS, IN A FOREST...
YES, WE HAVE A LOT OF FORESTS IN GALICIA. CAN YOU BE MORE SPECIFIC?

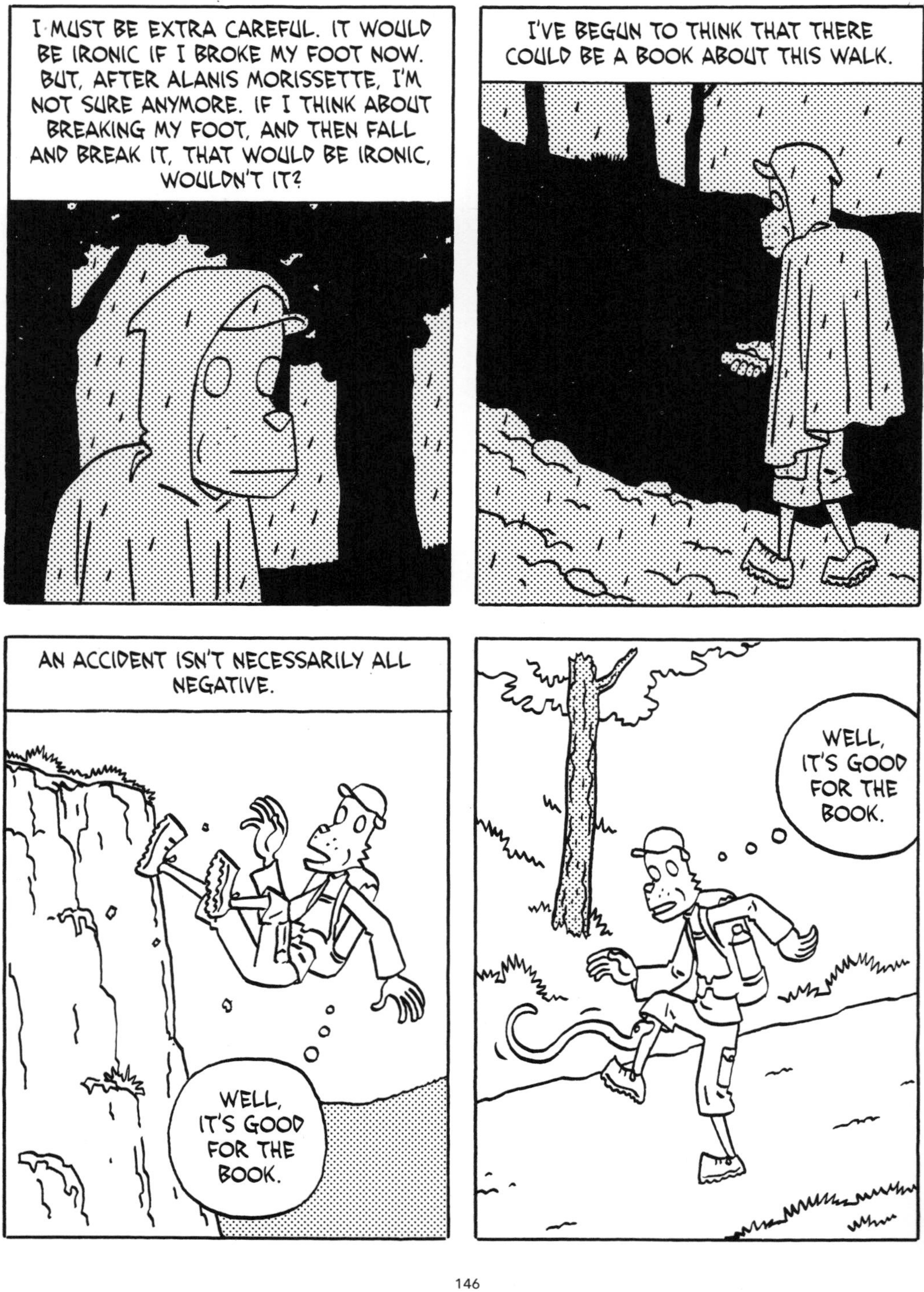
I MUST BE EXTRA CAREFUL. IT WOULD BE IRONIC IF I BROKE MY FOOT NOW. BUT, AFTER ALANIS MORISSETTE, I'M NOT SURE ANYMORE. IF I THINK ABOUT BREAKING MY FOOT, AND THEN FALL AND BREAK IT, THAT WOULD BE IRONIC, WOULDN'T IT?
I'VE BEGUN TO THINK THAT THERE COULD BE A BOOK ABOUT THIS WALK.
AN ACCIDENT ISN'T NECESSARILY ALL NEGATIVE.
WELL, IT'S GOOD FOR THE BOOK.
WELL, IT'S GOOD FOR THE BOOK.

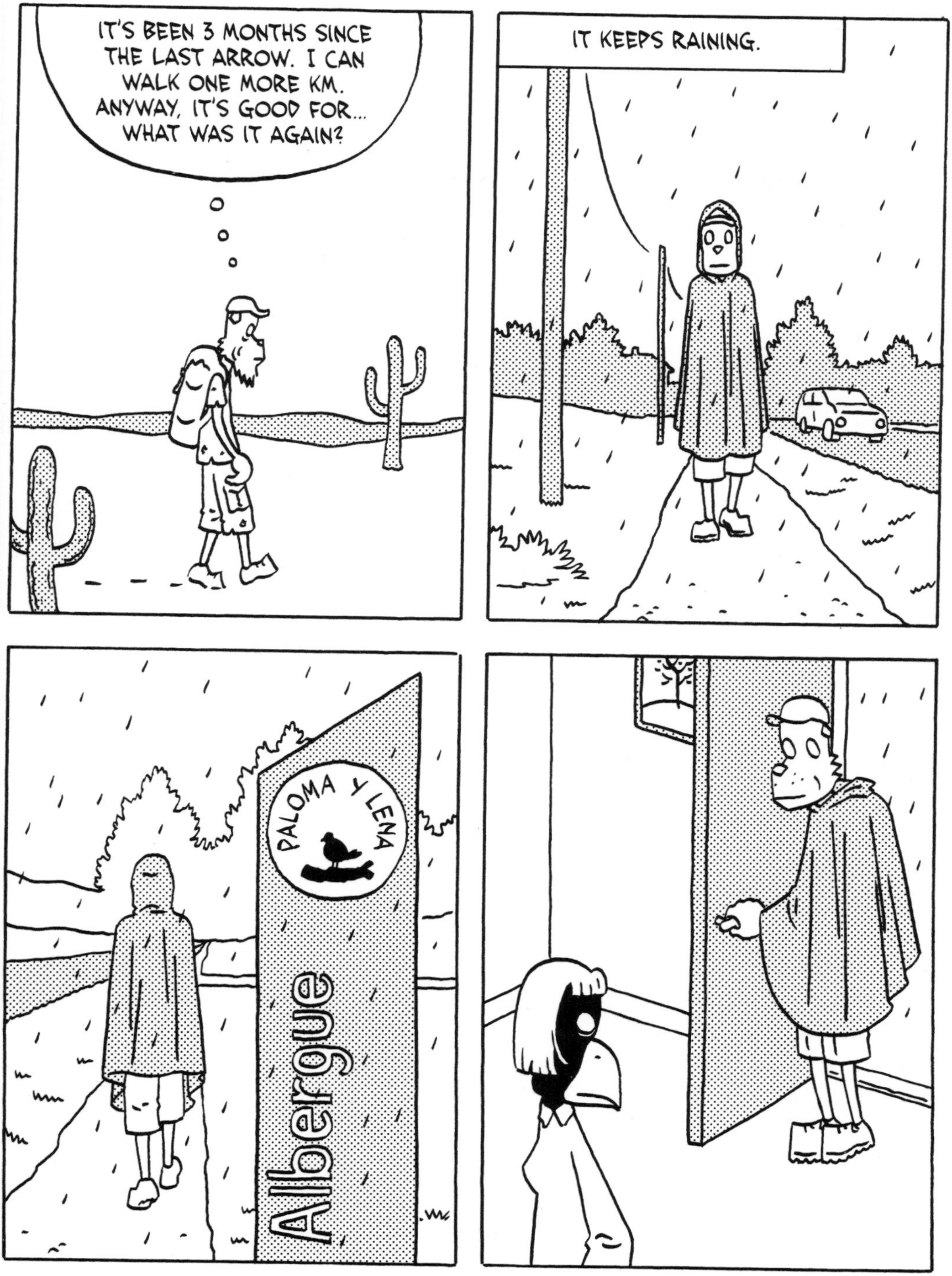
IT'S BEEN 3 MONTHS SINCE THE LAST ARROW. I CAN WALK ONE MORE KM. ANYWAY, IT'S GOOD FOR... WHAT WAS IT AGAIN?
IT KEEPS RAINING.
PALOMA Y LENA
Albergue

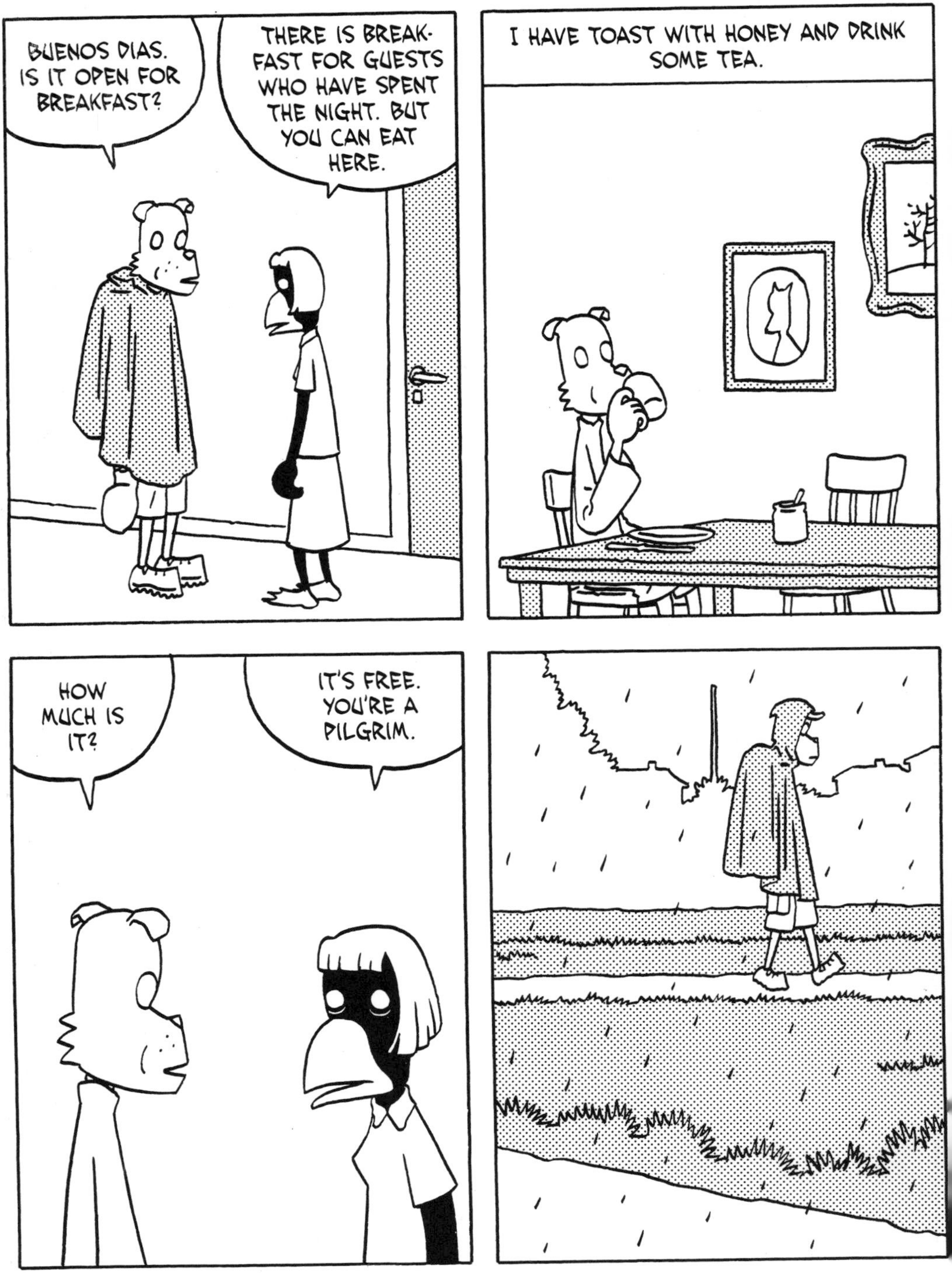
BUENOS DIAS. IS IT OPEN FOR BREAKFAST?
THERE IS BREAKFAST FOR GUESTS WHO HAVE SPENT THE NIGHT. BUT YOU CAN EAT HERE.
I HAVE TOAST WITH HONEY AND DRINK SOME TEA.
HOW MUCH IS IT?
IT'S FREE. YOU'RE A PILGRIM.

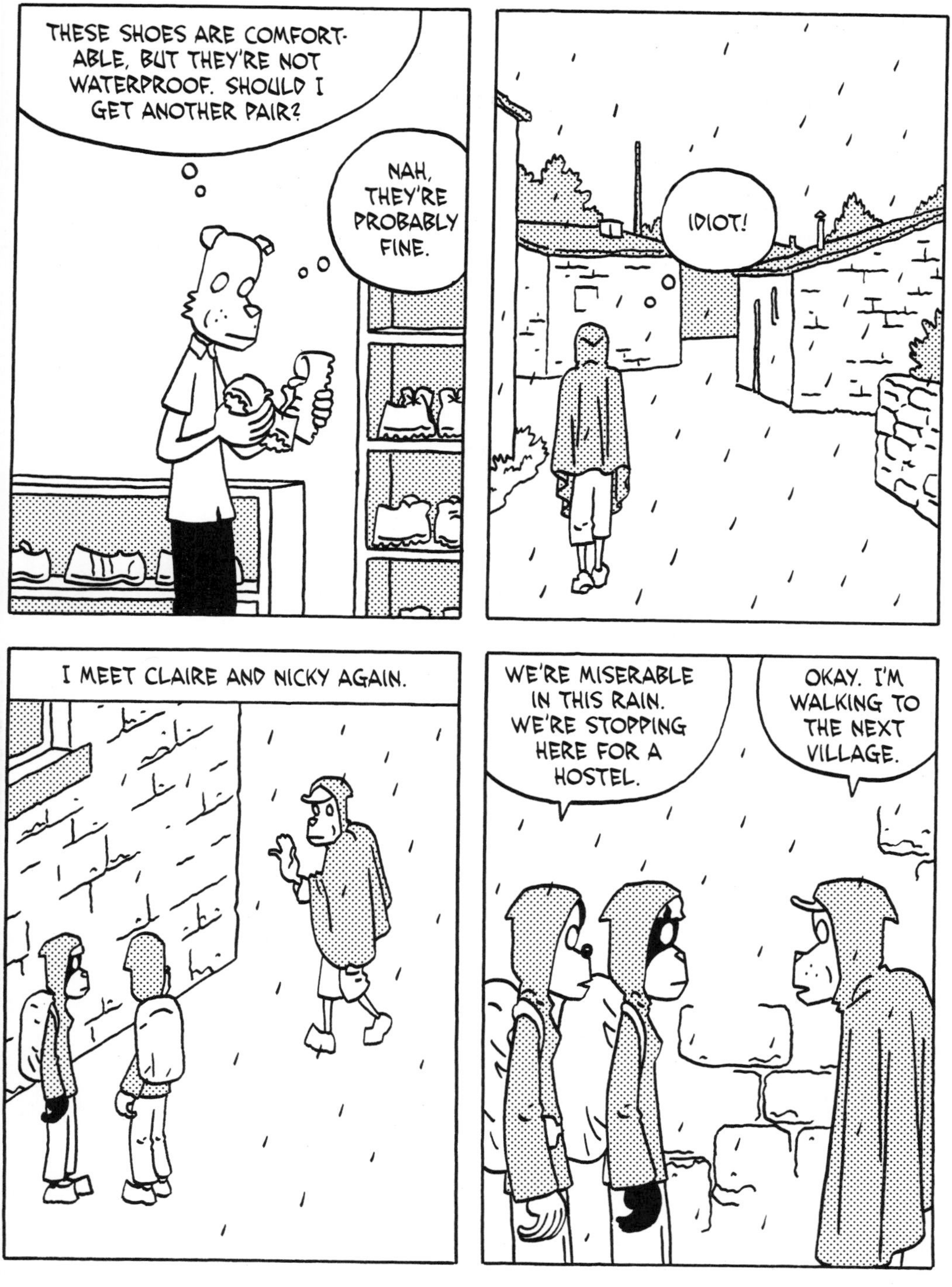
THESE SHOES ARE COMFORTABLE, BUT THEY'RE NOT WATERPROOF. SHOULD I GET ANOTHER PAIR?
NAH, THEY'RE PROBABLY FINE.
IDIOT!
I MEET CLAIRE AND NICKY AGAIN.
WE'RE MISERABLE IN THIS RAIN. WE'RE STOPPING HERE FOR A HOSTEL.
OKAY. I'M WALKING TO THE NEXT VILLAGE.

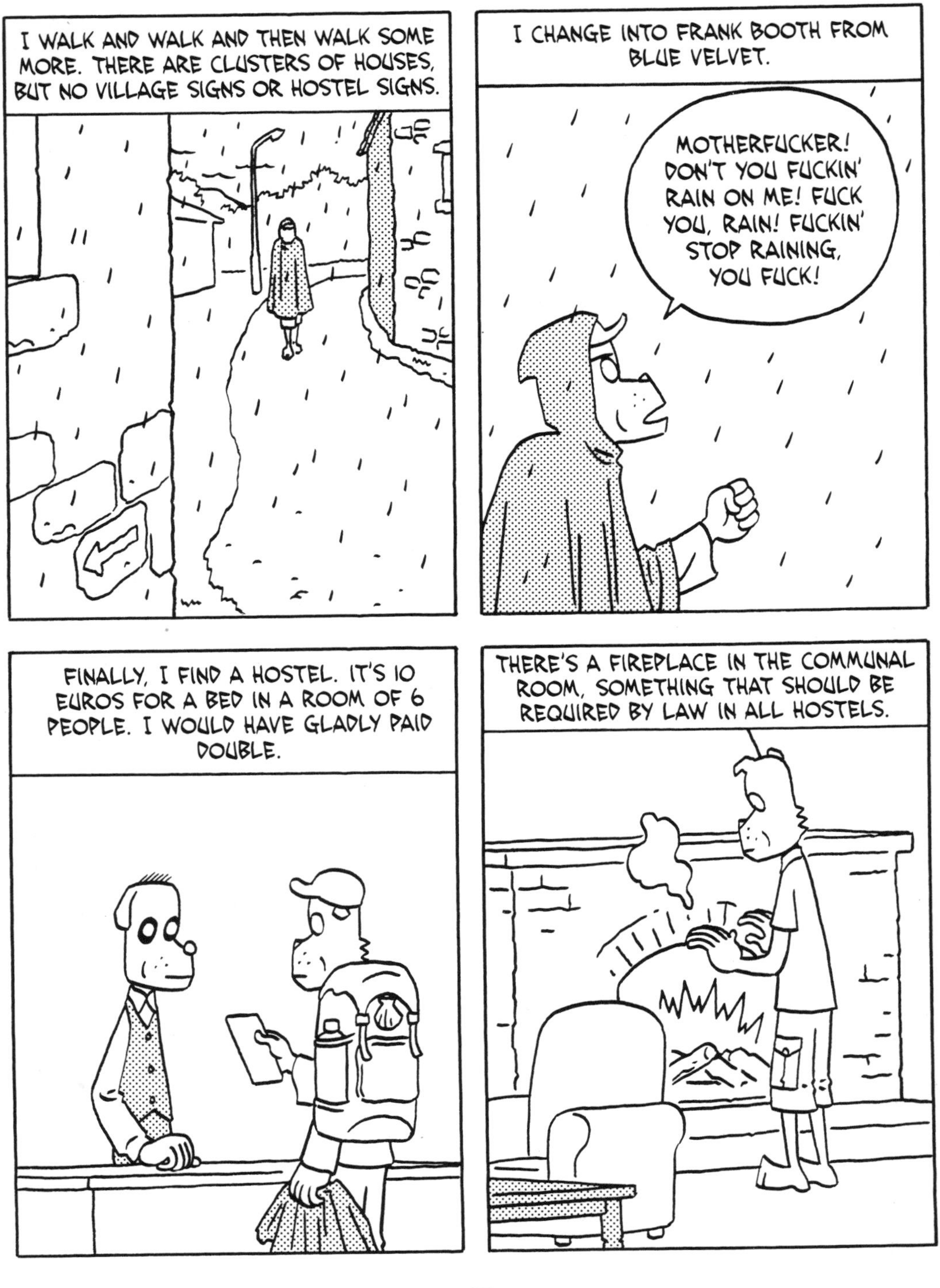
I WALK AND WALK AND THEN WALK SOME MORE. THERE ARE CLUSTERS OF HOUSES, BUT NO VILLAGE SIGNS OR HOSTEL SIGNS.
I CHANGE INTO FRANK BOOTH FROM BLUE VELVET.
MOTHERFUCKER! DON'T YOU FUCKIN' RAIN ON ME! FUCK YOU, RAIN! FUCKIN' STOP RAINING, YOU FUCK!
FINALLY, I FIND A HOSTEL. IT'S 10 EUROS FOR A BED IN A ROOM OF 6 PEOPLE. I WOULD HAVE GLADLY PAID DOUBLE.
THERE'S A FIREPLACE IN THE COMMUNAL ROOM, SOMETHING THAT SHOULD BE REQUIRED BY LAW IN ALL HOSTELS.

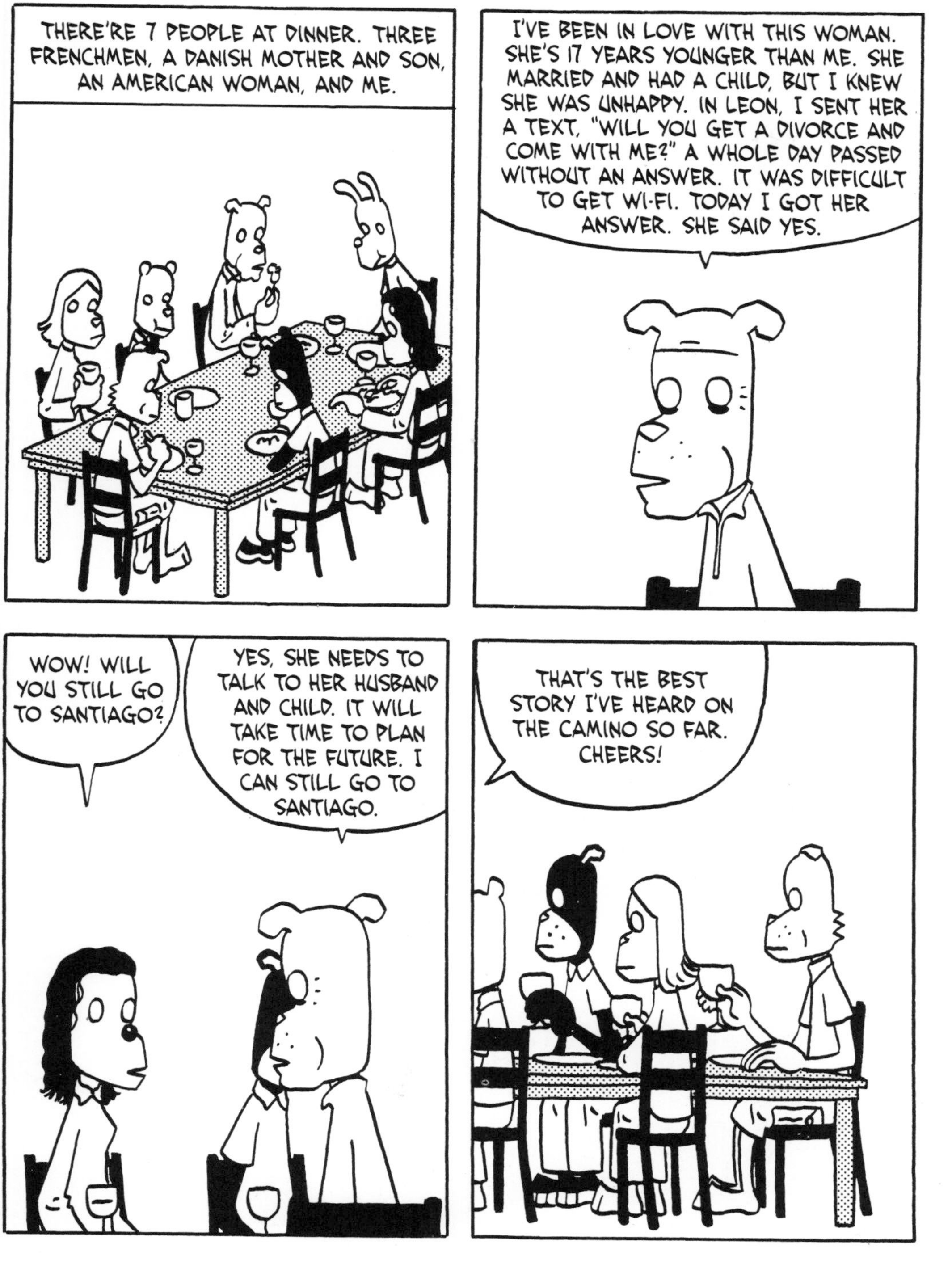
THERE'RE 7 PEOPLE AT DINNER. THREE FRENCHMEN, A DANISH MOTHER AND SON, AN AMERICAN WOMAN, AND ME.
I'VE BEEN IN LOVE WITH THIS WOMAN. SHE'S 17 YEARS YOUNGER THAN ME. SHE MARRIED AND HAD A CHILD, BUT I KNEW SHE WAS UNHAPPY. IN LEON, I SENT HER A TEXT, "WILL YOU GET A DIVORCE AND COME WITH ME?" A WHOLE DAY PASSED WITHOUT AN ANSWER. IT WAS DIFFICULT TO GET WI-FI. TODAY I GOT HER ANSWER. SHE SAID YES.
WOW! WILL YOU STILL GO TO SANTIAGO?
YES, SHE NEEDS TO TALK TO HER HUSBAND AND CHILD. IT WILL TAKE TIME TO PLAN FOR THE FUTURE. I CAN STILL GO TO SANTIAGO.
THAT'S THE BEST STORY I'VE HEARD ON THE CAMINO SO FAR. CHEERS!

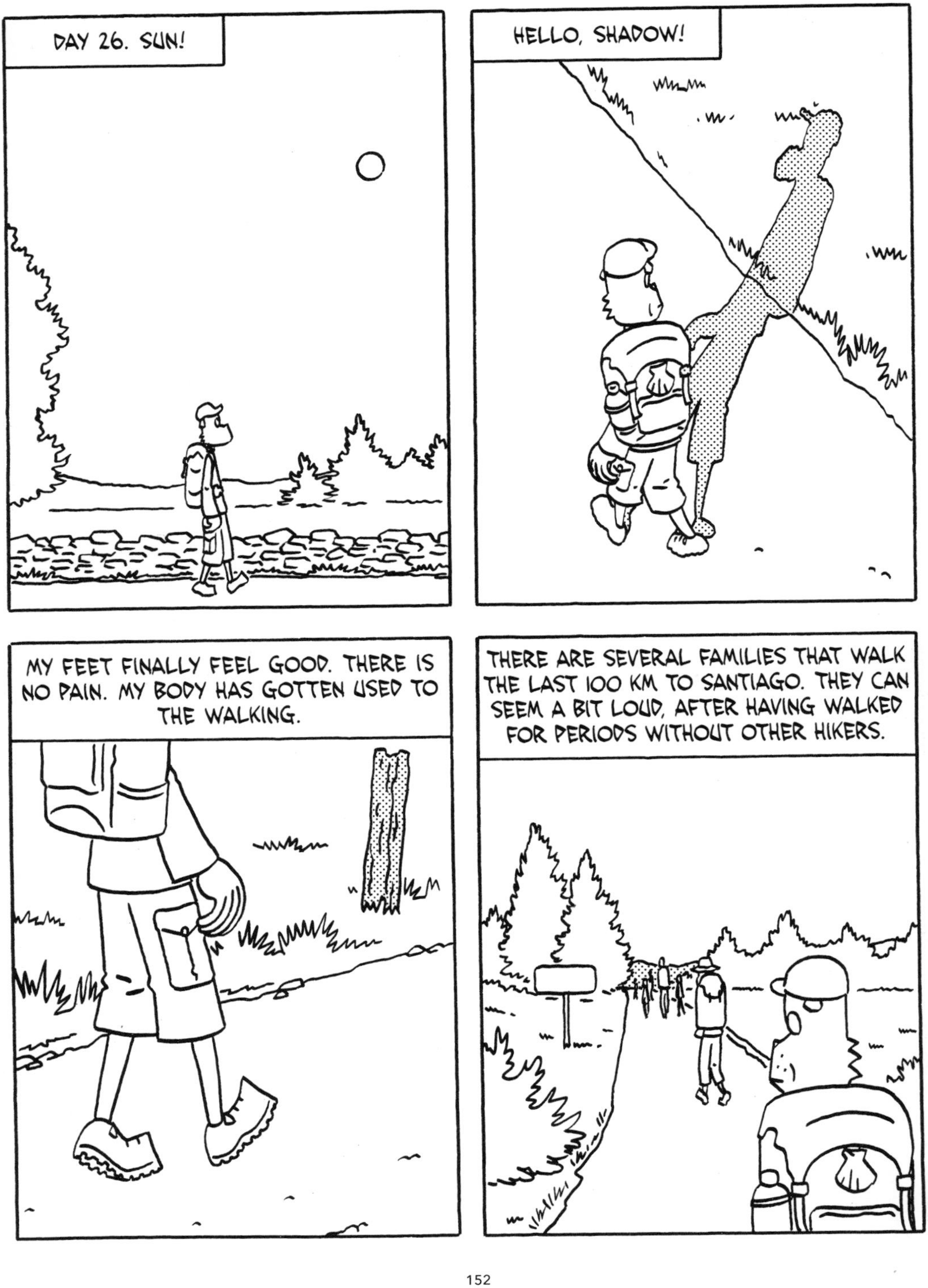
DAY 26. SUN!
HELLO, SHADOW!
MY FEET FINALLY FEEL GOOD. THERE IS NO PAIN. MY BODY HAS GOTTEN USED TO THE WALKING.
THERE ARE SEVERAL FAMILIES THAT WALK THE LAST 100 KM TO SANTIAGO. THEY CAN SEEM A BIT LOUD, AFTER HAVING WALKED FOR PERIODS WITHOUT OTHER HIKERS.

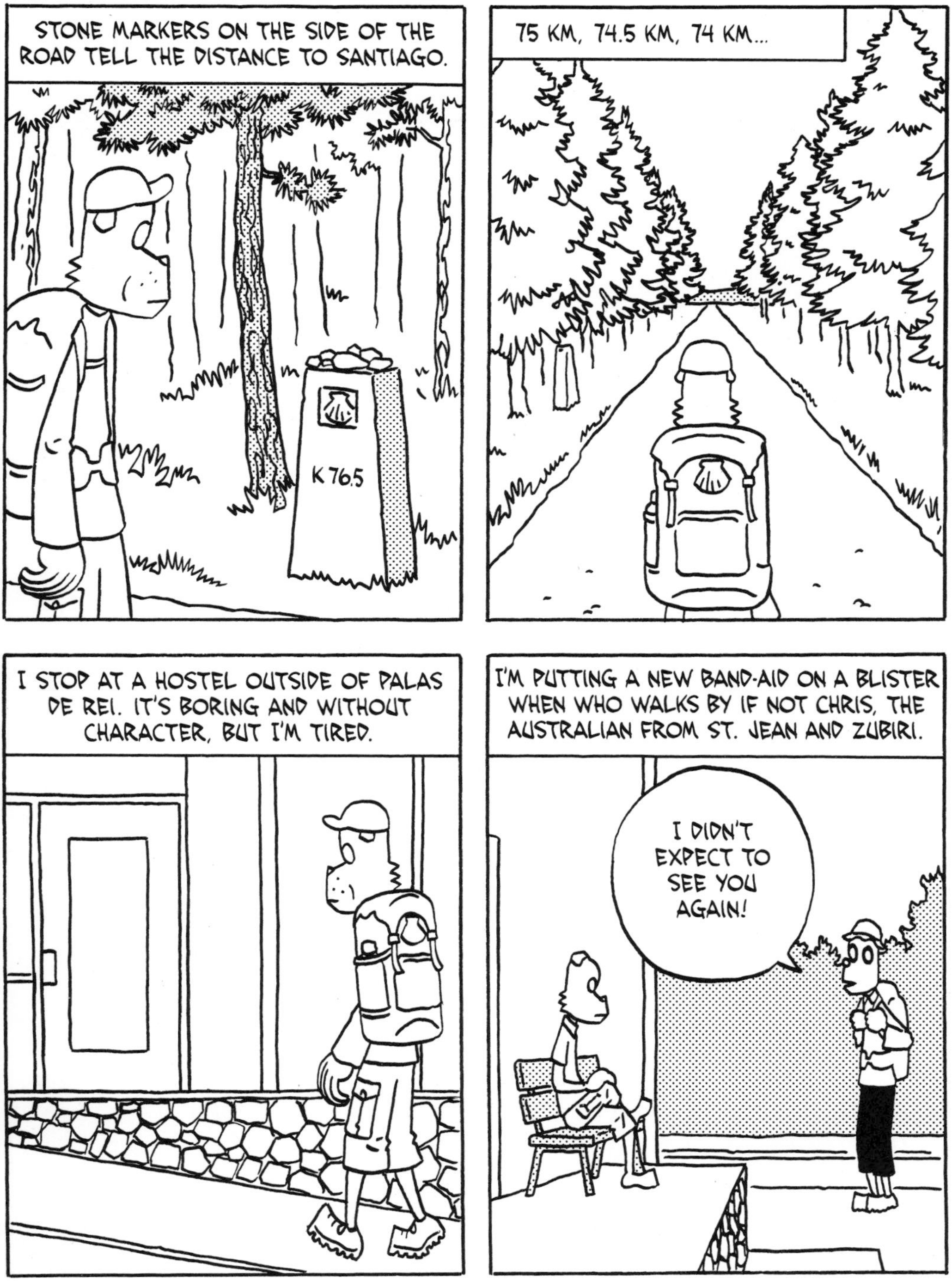
STONE MARKERS ON THE SIDE OF THE ROAD TELL THE DISTANCE TO SANTIAGO.
K 76.5
75 KM, 74.5 KM, 74 KM...
I STOP AT A HOSTEL OUTSIDE OF PALAS DE REI. IT'S BORING AND WITHOUT CHARACTER, BUT I'M TIRED.
I'M PUTTING A NEW BAND-AID ON A BLISTER WHEN WHO WALKS BY IF NOT CHRIS, THE AUSTRALIAN FROM ST. JEAN AND ZUBIRI.
I DIDN'T EXPECT TO SEE YOU AGAIN!

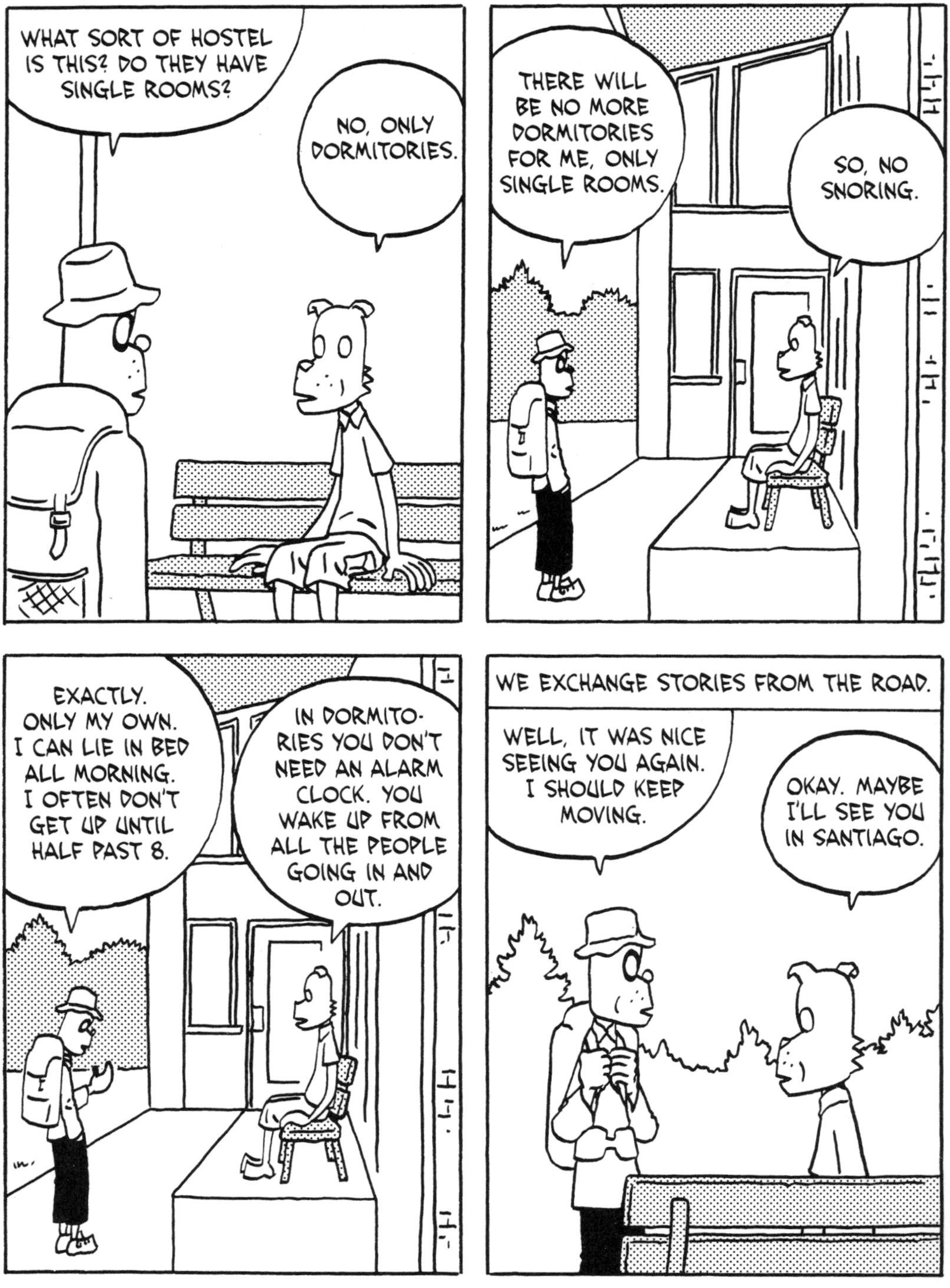
WHAT SORT OF HOSTEL IS THIS? DO THEY HAVE SINGLE ROOMS?
NO, ONLY DORMITORIES.
THERE WILL BE NO MORE DORMITORIES FOR ME, ONLY SINGLE ROOMS.
SO, NO SNORING.
EXACTLY. ONLY MY OWN. I CAN LIE IN BED ALL MORNING. I OFTEN DON'T GET UP UNTIL HALF PAST 8.
IN DORMITO-RIES YOU DON'T NEED AN ALARM CLOCK. YOU WAKE UP FROM ALL THE PEOPLE GOING IN AND OUT.
WE EXCHANGE STORIES FROM THE ROAD.
WELL, IT WAS NICE SEEING YOU AGAIN. I SHOULD KEEP MOVING.
OKAY. MAYBE I'LL SEE YOU IN SANTIAGO.

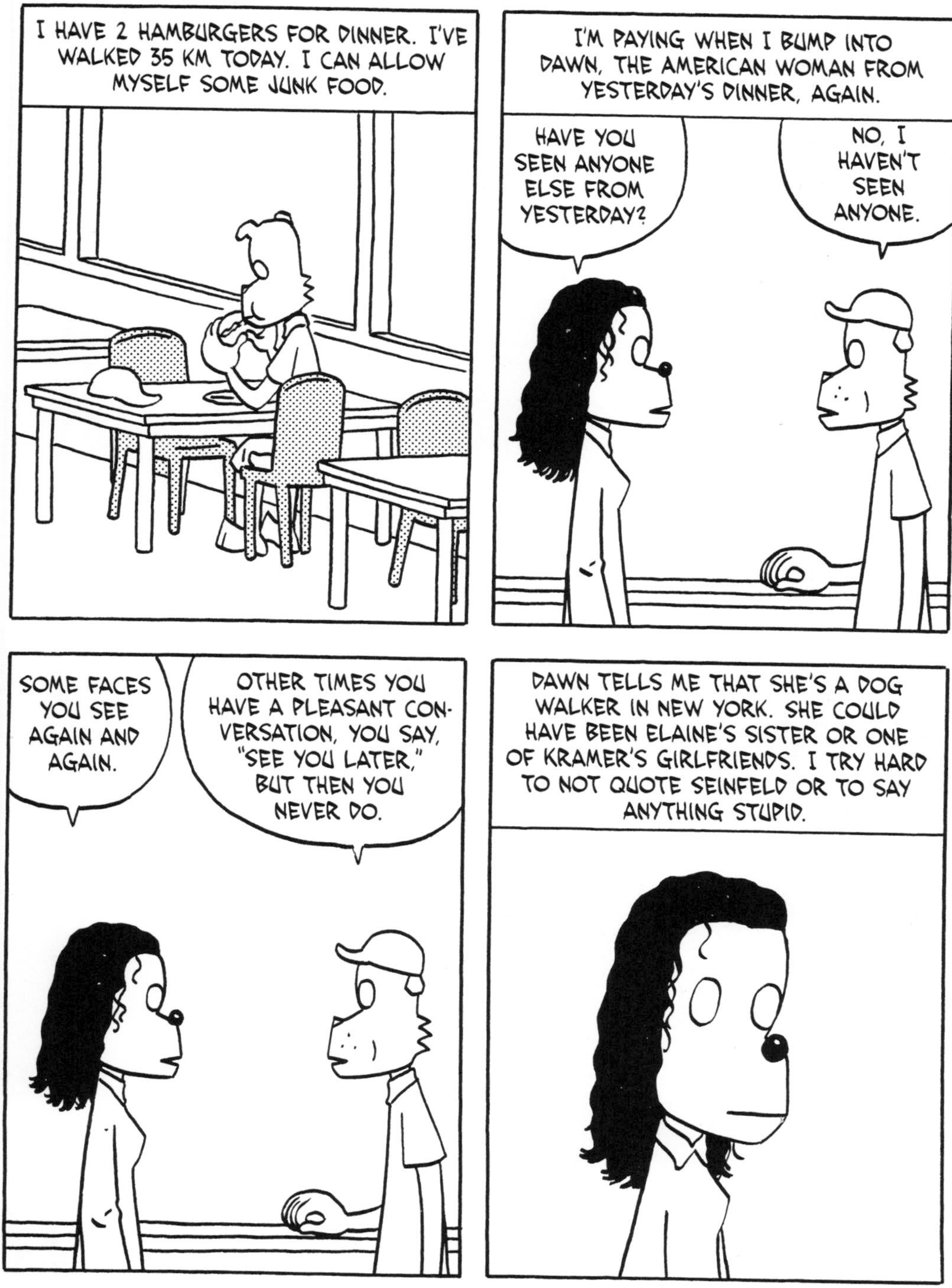

I HAVE 2 HAMBURGERS FOR DINNER. I'VE WALKED 35 KM TODAY. I CAN ALLOW MYSELF SOME JUNK FOOD.
I'M PAYING WHEN I BUMP INTO DAWN, THE AMERICAN WOMAN FROM YESTERDAY'S DINNER, AGAIN.
HAVE YOU SEEN ANYONE ELSE FROM YESTERDAY?
NO, I HAVEN'T SEEN ANYONE.
SOME FACES YOU SEE AGAIN AND AGAIN.
OTHER TIMES YOU HAVE A PLEASANT CON-VERSATION, YOU SAY, "SEE YOU LATER," BUT THEN YOU NEVER DO.
DAWN TELLS ME THAT SHE'S A DOG WALKER IN NEW YORK. SHE COULD HAVE BEEN ELAINE'S SISTER OR ONE OF KRAMER'S GIRLFRIENDS. I TRY HARD TO NOT QUOTE SEINFELD OR TO SAY ANYTHING STUPID.

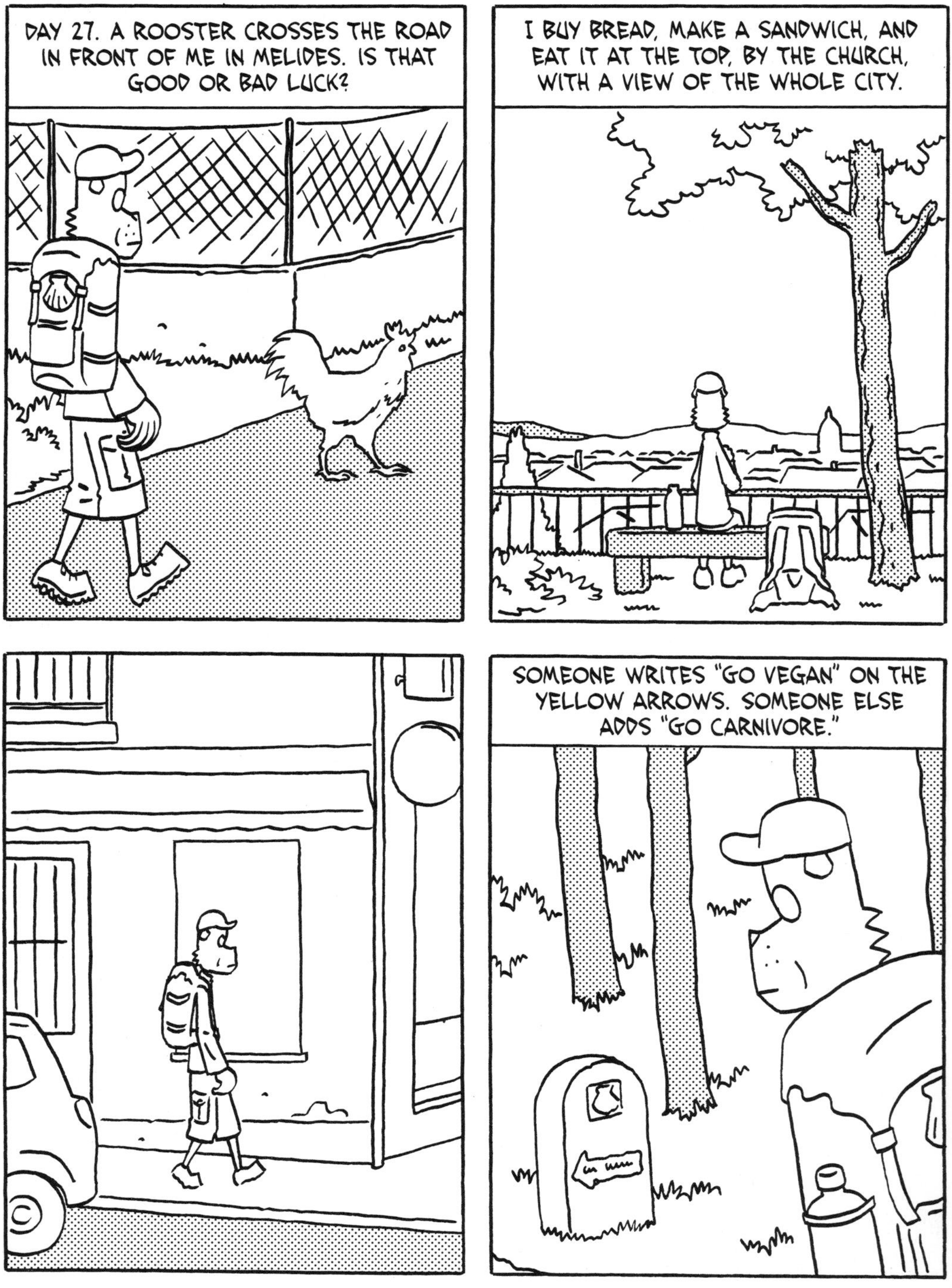
DAY 27. A ROOSTER CROSSES THE ROAD IN FRONT OF ME IN MELIDES. IS THAT GOOD OR BAD LUCK?
I BUY BREAD, MAKE A SANDWICH, AND EAT IT AT THE TOP, BY THE CHURCH, WITH A VIEW OF THE WHOLE CITY.
SOMEONE WRITES "GO VEGAN" ON THE YELLOW ARROWS. SOMEONE ELSE ADDS "GO CARNIVORE."

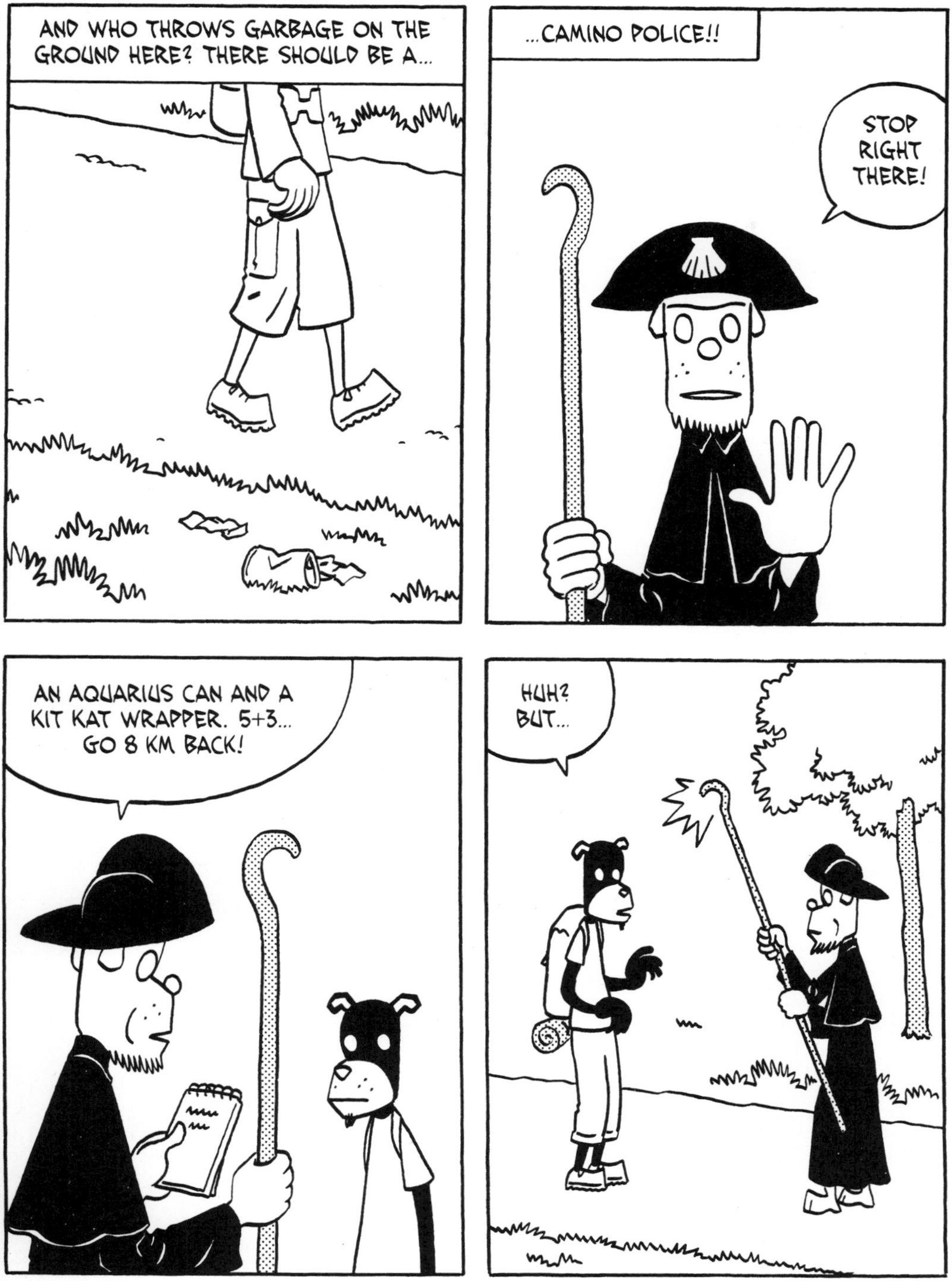
AND WHO THROWS GARBAGE ON THE GROUND HERE? THERE SHOULD BE A...
...CAMINO POLICE!!
STOP RIGHT THERE!
AN AQUARIUS CAN AND A KIT KAT WRAPPER. 5+3... GO 8 KM BACK!
HUH? BUT...

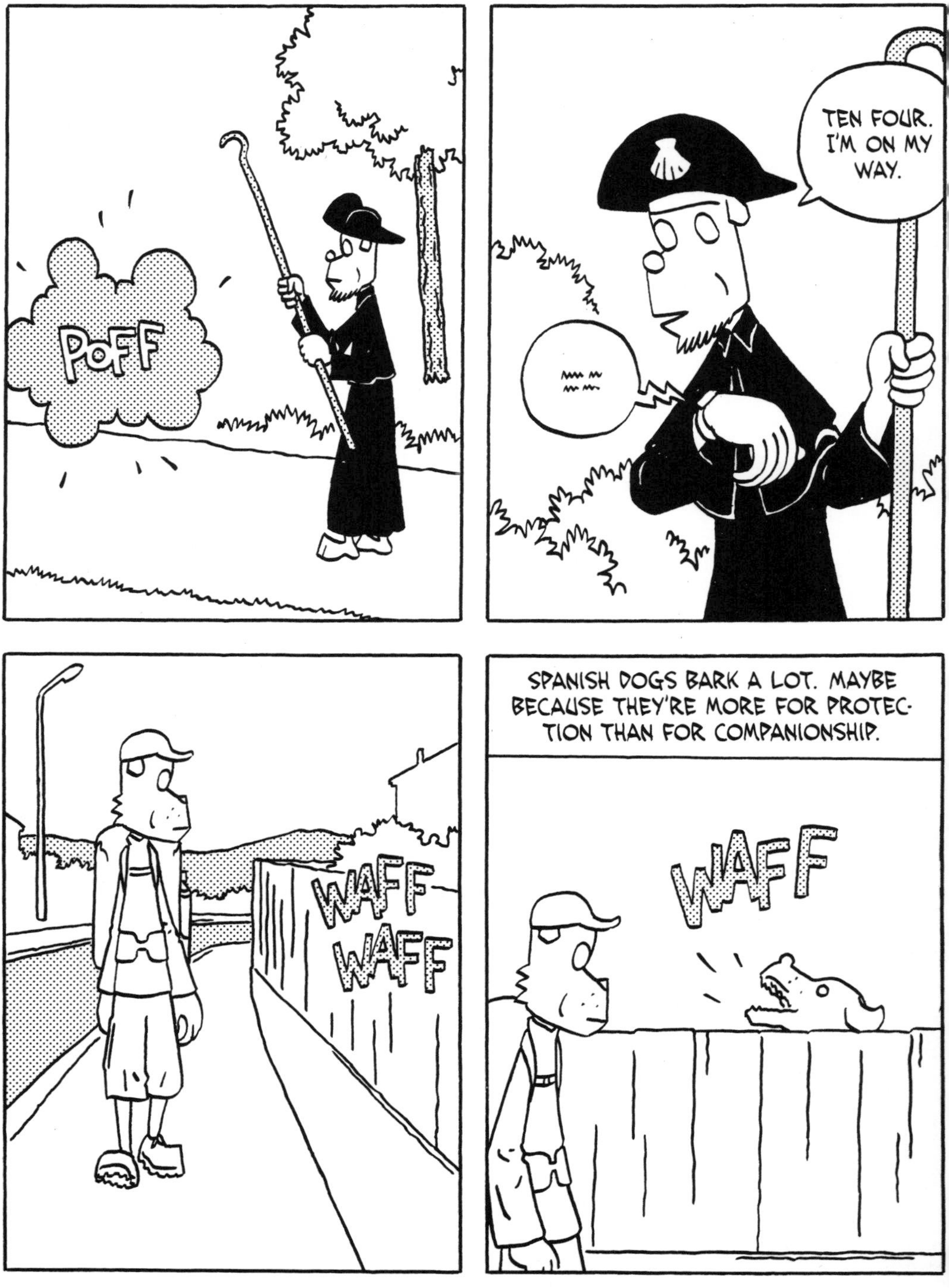
POFF
TEN FOUR. I'M ON MY WAY.
WAFF WAFF
WAFF
SPANISH DOGS BARK A LOT. MAYBE BECAUSE THEY'RE MORE FOR PROTECTION THAN FOR COMPANIONSHIP.
WAFF

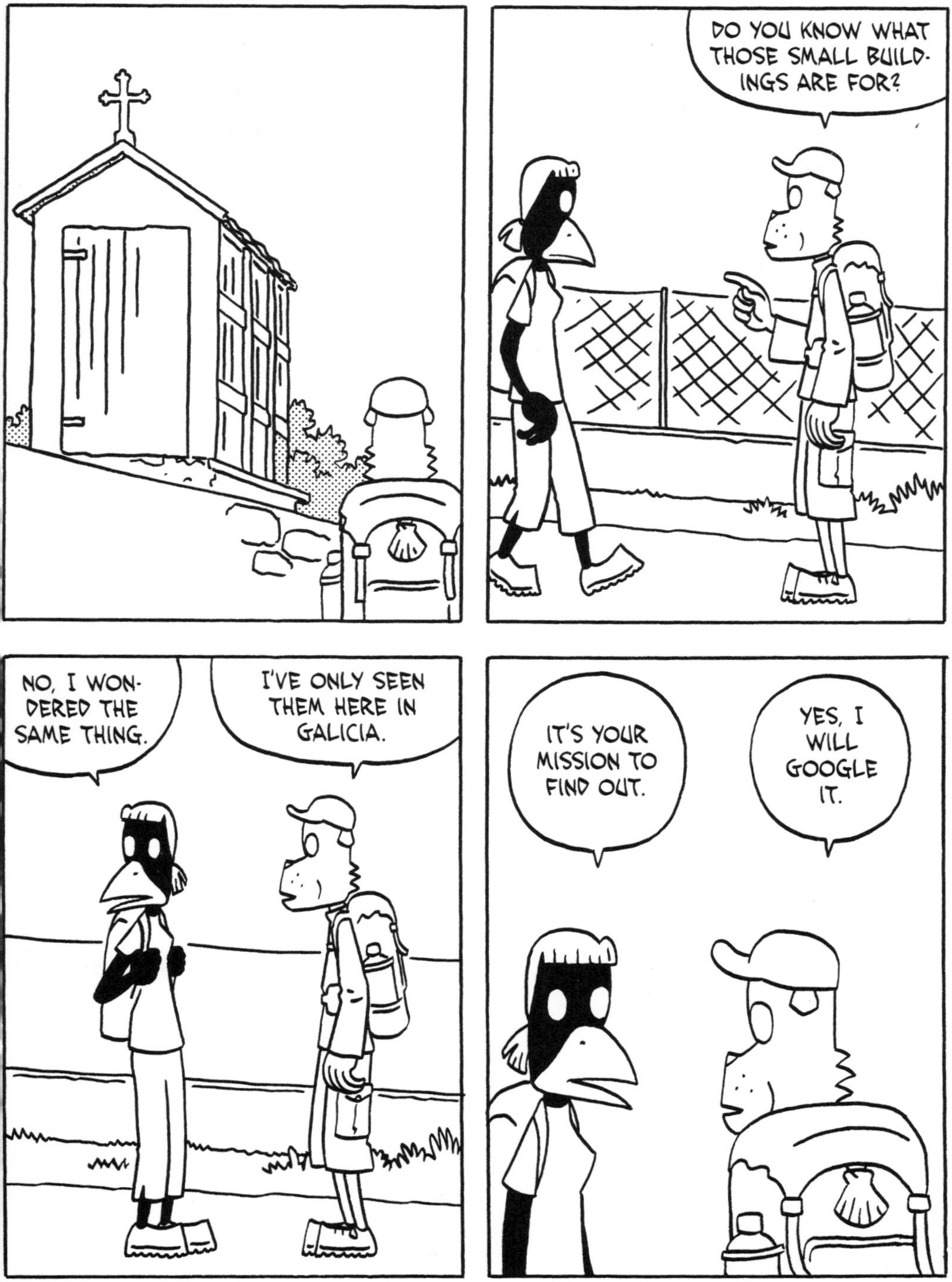
DO YOU KNOW WHAT THOSE SMALL BUILD-INGS ARE FOR?
NO, I WONDERED THE SAME THING.
I'VE ONLY SEEN THEM HERE IN GALICIA.
IT'S YOUR MISSION TO FIND OUT.
YES, I WILL GOOGLE IT.

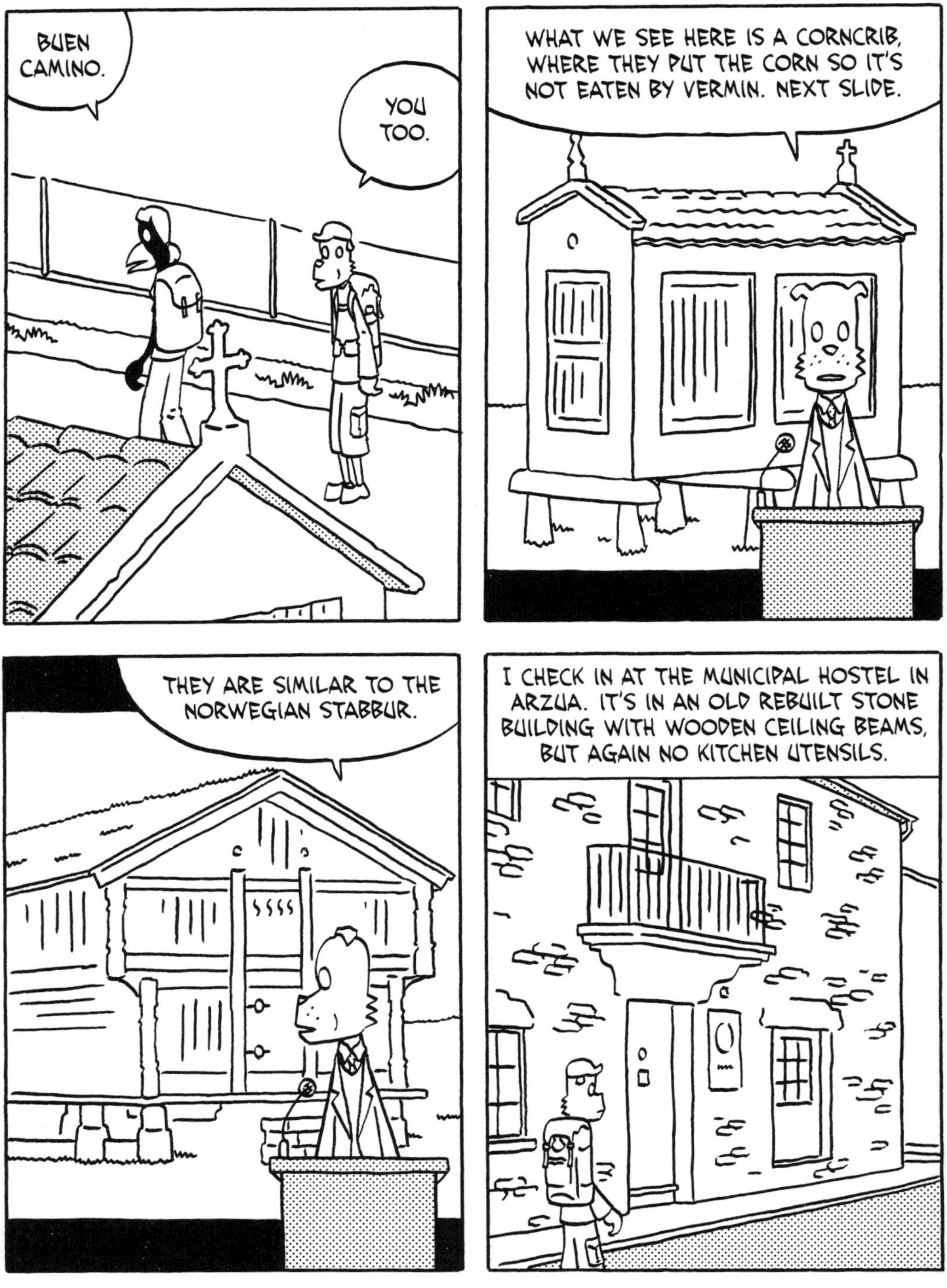
BUEN CAMINO.
YOU TOO.
WHAT WE SEE HERE IS A CORNCRIB, WHERE THEY PUT THE CORN SO IT'S NOT EATEN BY VERMIN. NEXT SLIDE.
THEY ARE SIMILAR TO THE NORWEGIAN STABBUR.
I CHECK IN AT THE MUNICIPAL HOSTEL IN ARZUA. IT'S IN AN OLD REBUILT STONE BUILDING WITH WOODEN CEILING BEAMS, BUT AGAIN NO KITCHEN UTENSILS.

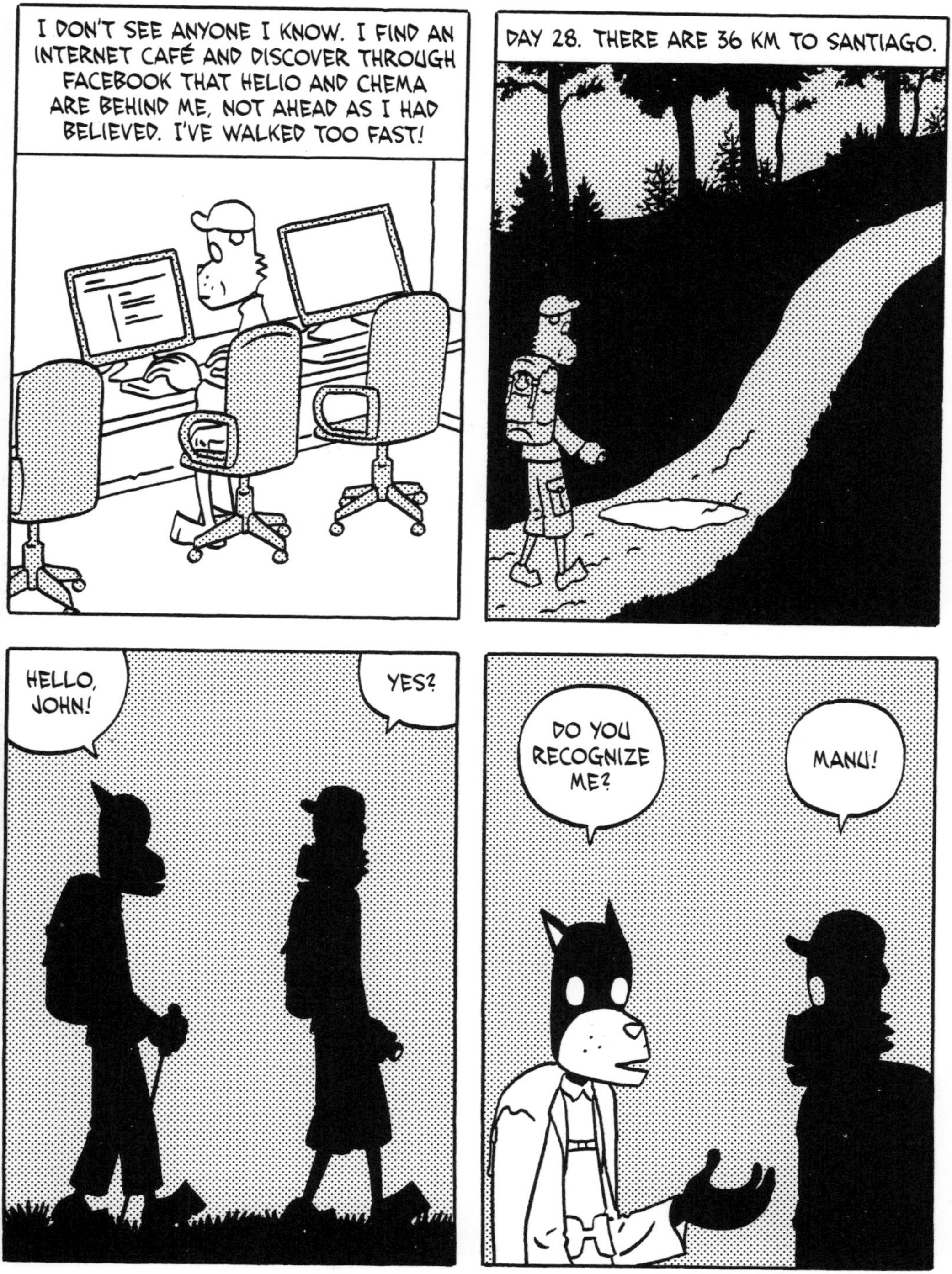
I DON'T SEE ANYONE I KNOW. I FIND AN INTERNET CAFÉ AND DISCOVER THROUGH FACEBOOK THAT HELIO AND CHEMA ARE BEHIND ME, NOT AHEAD AS I HAD BELIEVED. I'VE WALKED TOO FAST!
DAY 28. THERE ARE 36 KM TO SANTIAGO.
HELLO, JOHN!
YES?
DO YOU RECOGNIZE ME?
MANU!

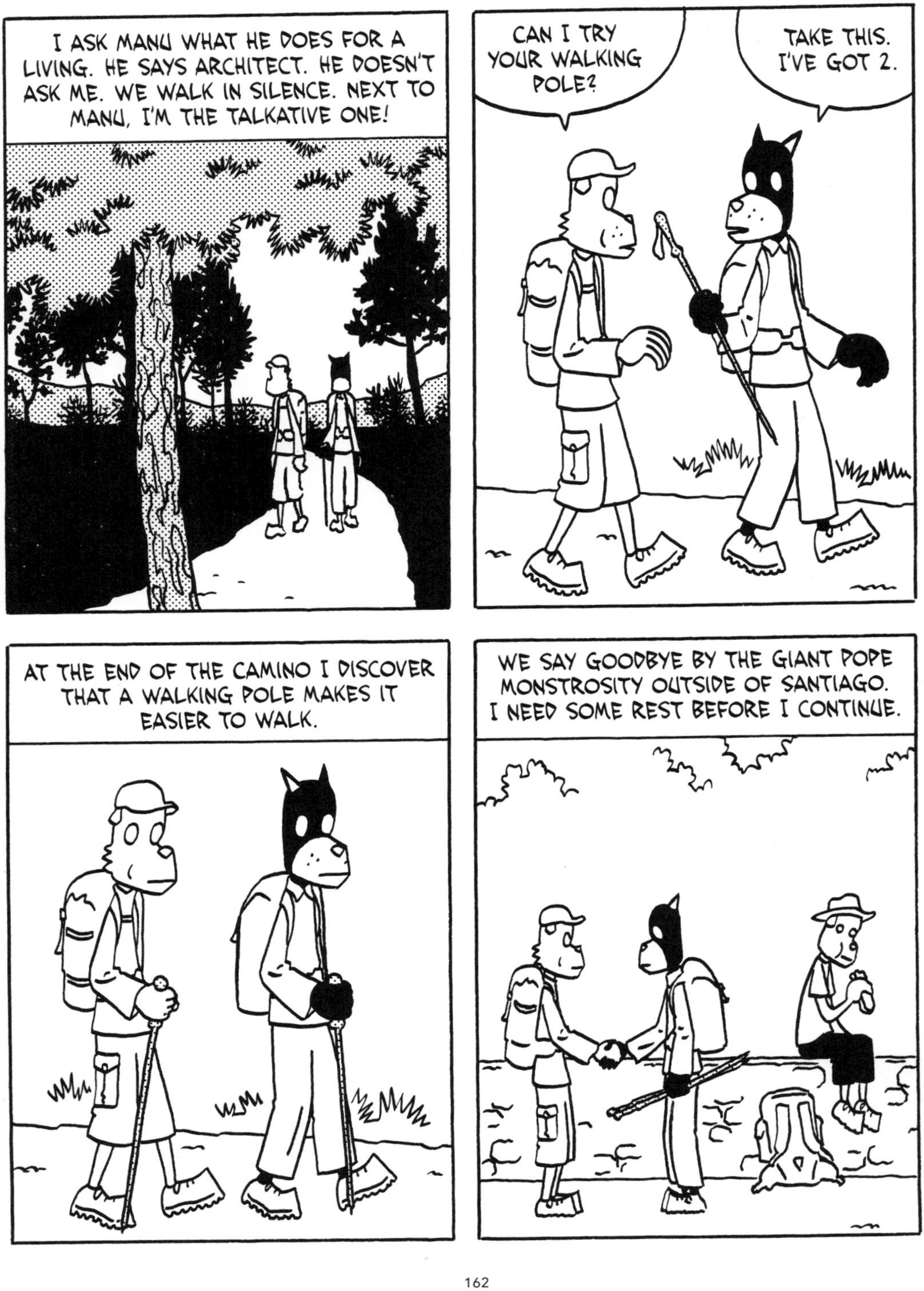
I ASK MANU WHAT HE DOES FOR A LIVING. HE SAYS ARCHITECT. HE DOESN'T ASK ME. WE WALK IN SILENCE. NEXT TO MANU, I'M THE TALKATIVE ONE!
CAN I TRY YOUR WALKING POLE?
TAKE THIS. I'VE GOT 2.
AT THE END OF THE CAMINO I DISCOVER THAT A WALKING POLE MAKES IT EASIER TO WALK.
WE SAY GOODBYE BY THE GIANT POPE MONSTROSITY OUTSIDE OF SANTIAGO. I NEED SOME REST BEFORE I CONTINUE.

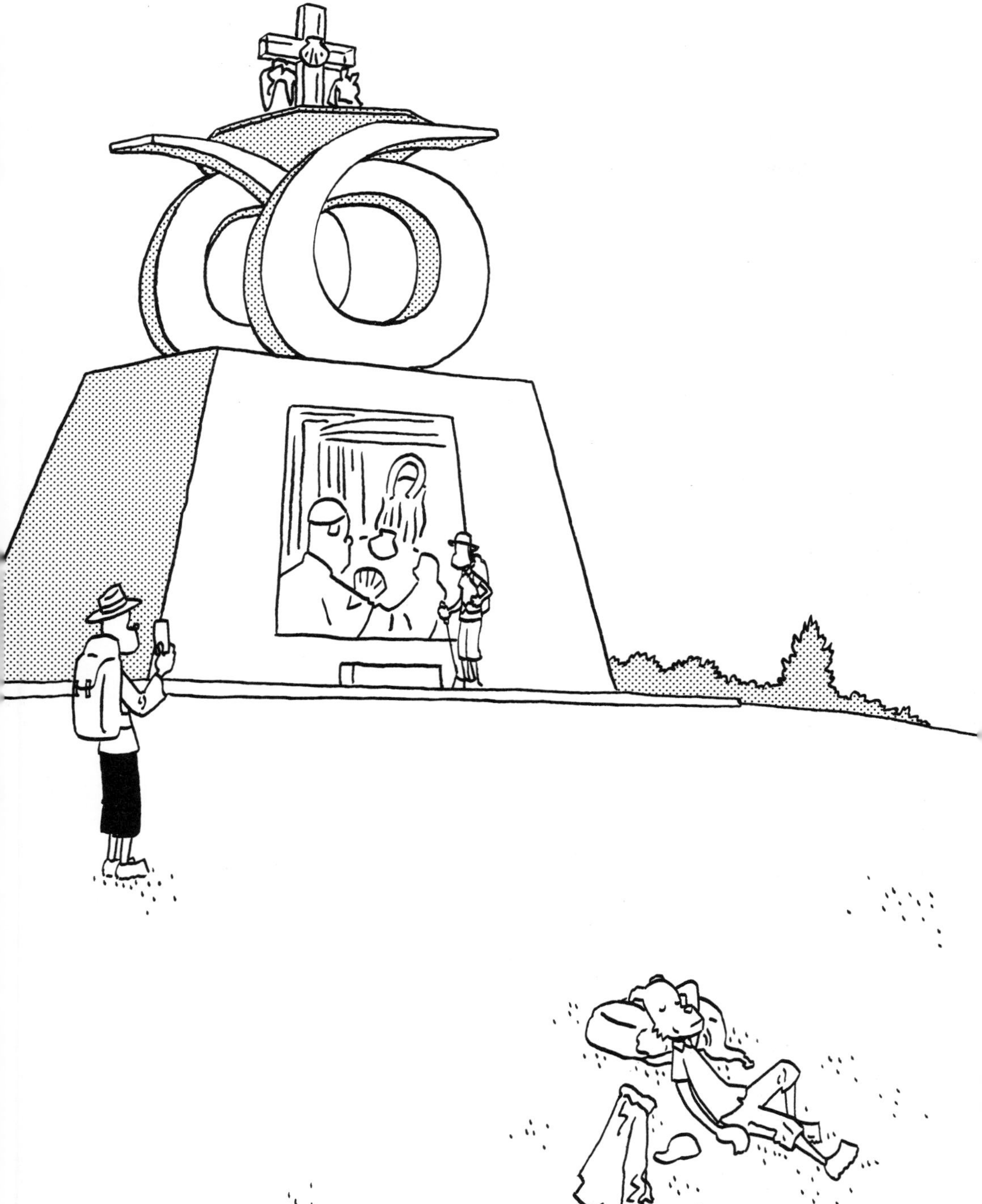

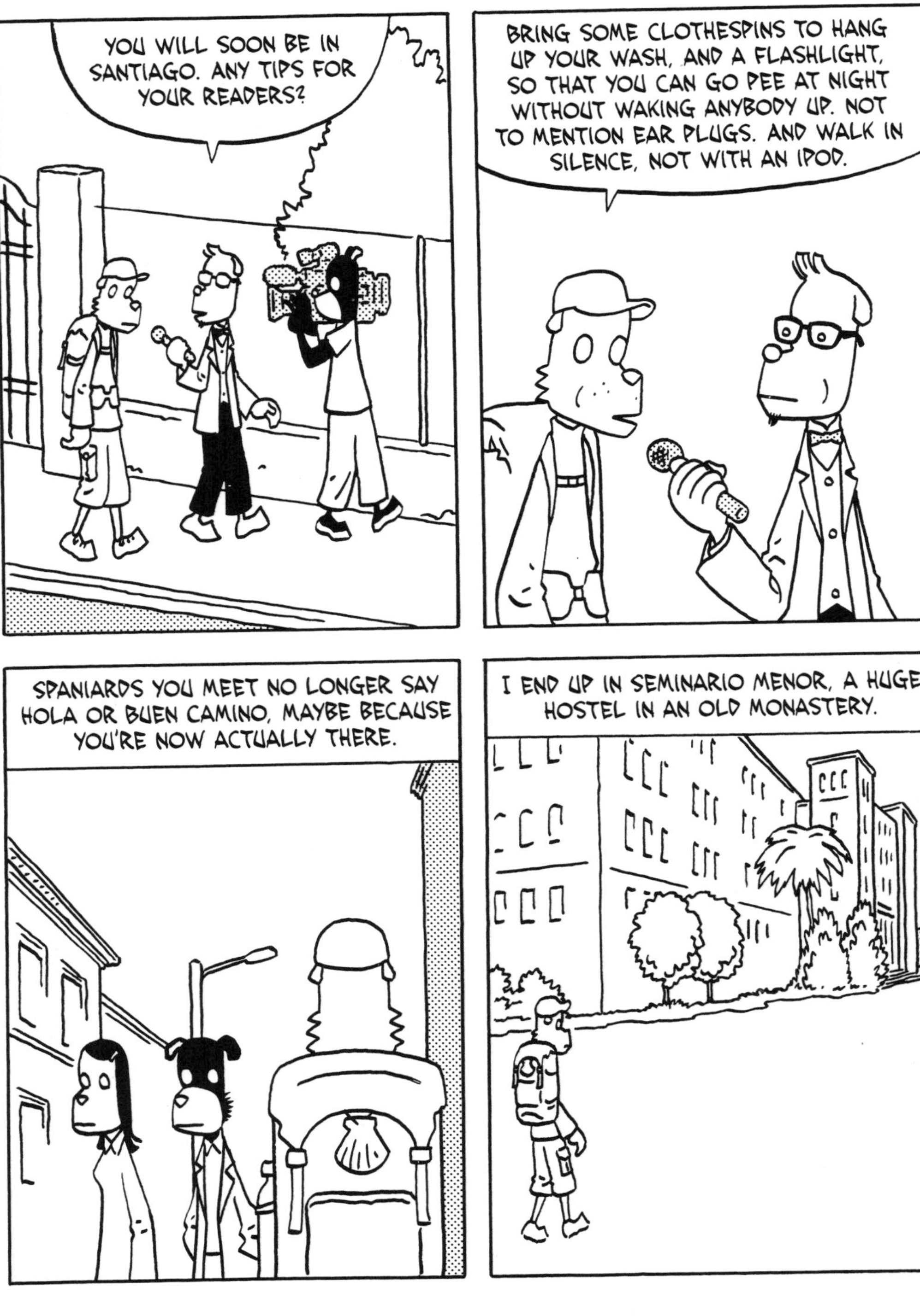
YOU WILL SOON BE IN SANTIAGO. ANY TIPS FOR YOUR READERS?
BRING SOME CLOTHESPINS TO HANG UP YOUR WASH, AND A FLASHLIGHT, SO THAT YOU CAN GO PEE AT NIGHT WITHOUT WAKING ANYBODY UP. NOT TO MENTION EAR PLUGS. AND WALK IN SILENCE, NOT WITH AN IPOD.
SPANIARDS YOU MEET NO LONGER SAY HOLA OR BUEN CAMINO, MAYBE BECAUSE YOU'RE NOW ACTUALLY THERE.
I END UP IN SEMINARIO MENOR, A HUGE HOSTEL IN AN OLD MONASTERY.

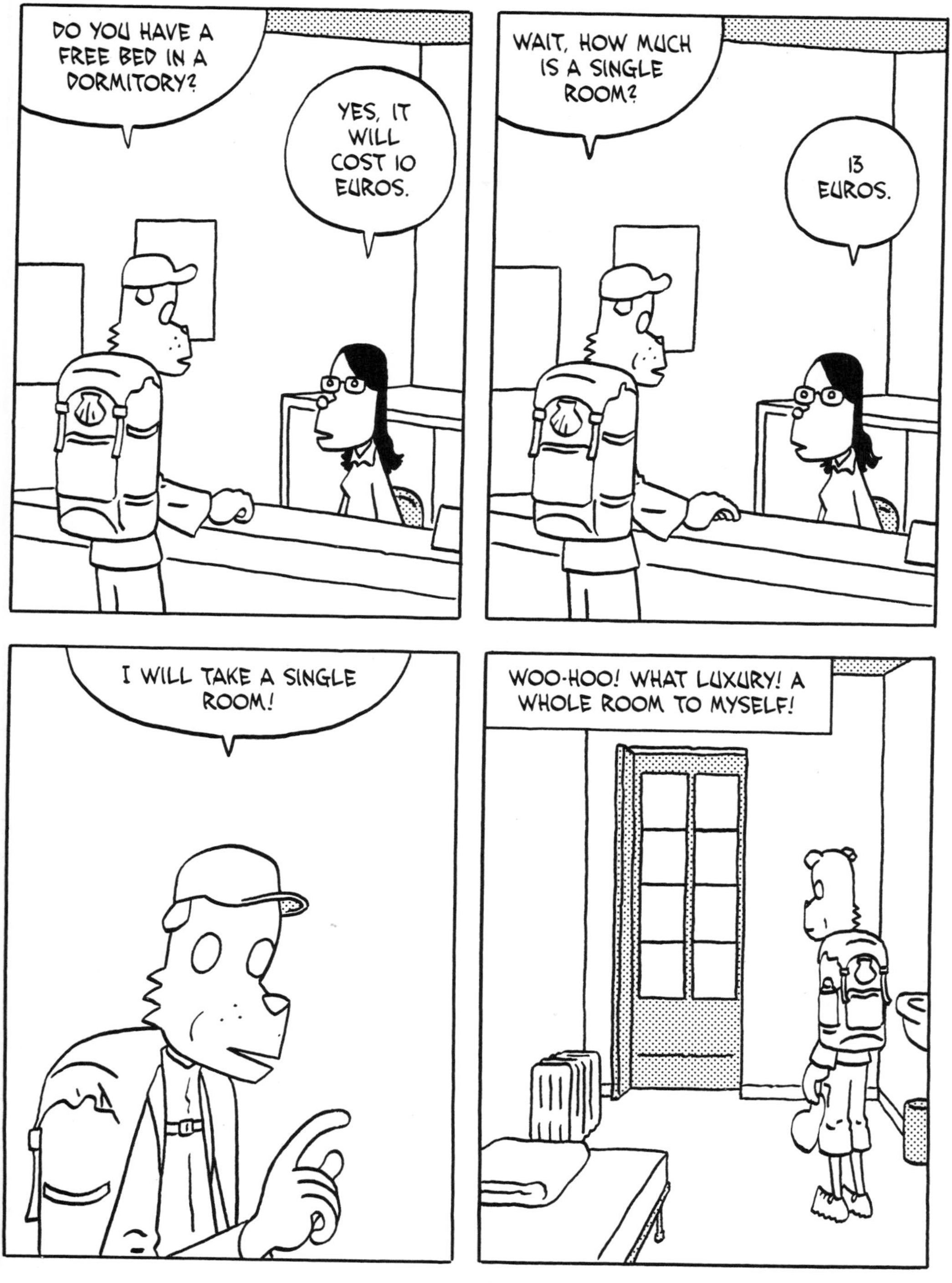
DO YOU HAVE A FREE BED IN A DORMITORY?
YES, IT WILL COST 10 EUROS.
WAIT, HOW MUCH IS A SINGLE ROOM?
13 EUROS.
I WILL TAKE A SINGLE ROOM!
WOO-HOO! WHAT LUXURY! A WHOLE ROOM TO MYSELF!

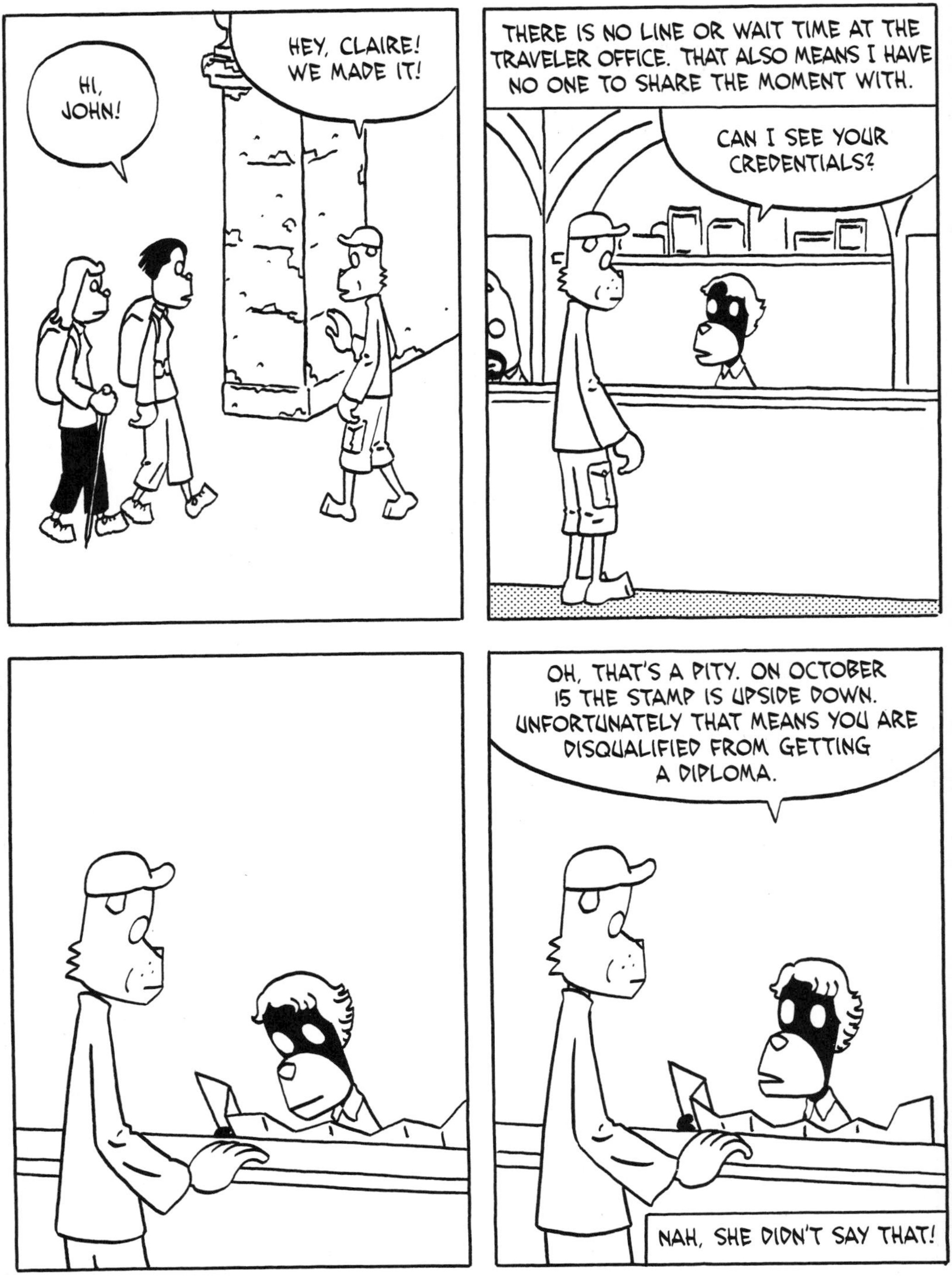
HI, JOHN!
HEY, CLAIRE! WE MADE IT!
THERE IS NO LINE OR WAIT TIME AT THE TRAVELER OFFICE. THAT ALSO MEANS I HAVE NO ONE TO SHARE THE MOMENT WITH.
CAN I SEE YOUR CREDENTIALS?
OH, THAT'S A PITY. ON OCTOBER 15 THE STAMP IS UPSIDE DOWN. UNFORTUNATELY THAT MEANS YOU ARE DISQUALIFIED FROM GETTING A DIPLOMA.
NAH, SHE DIDN'T SAY THAT!

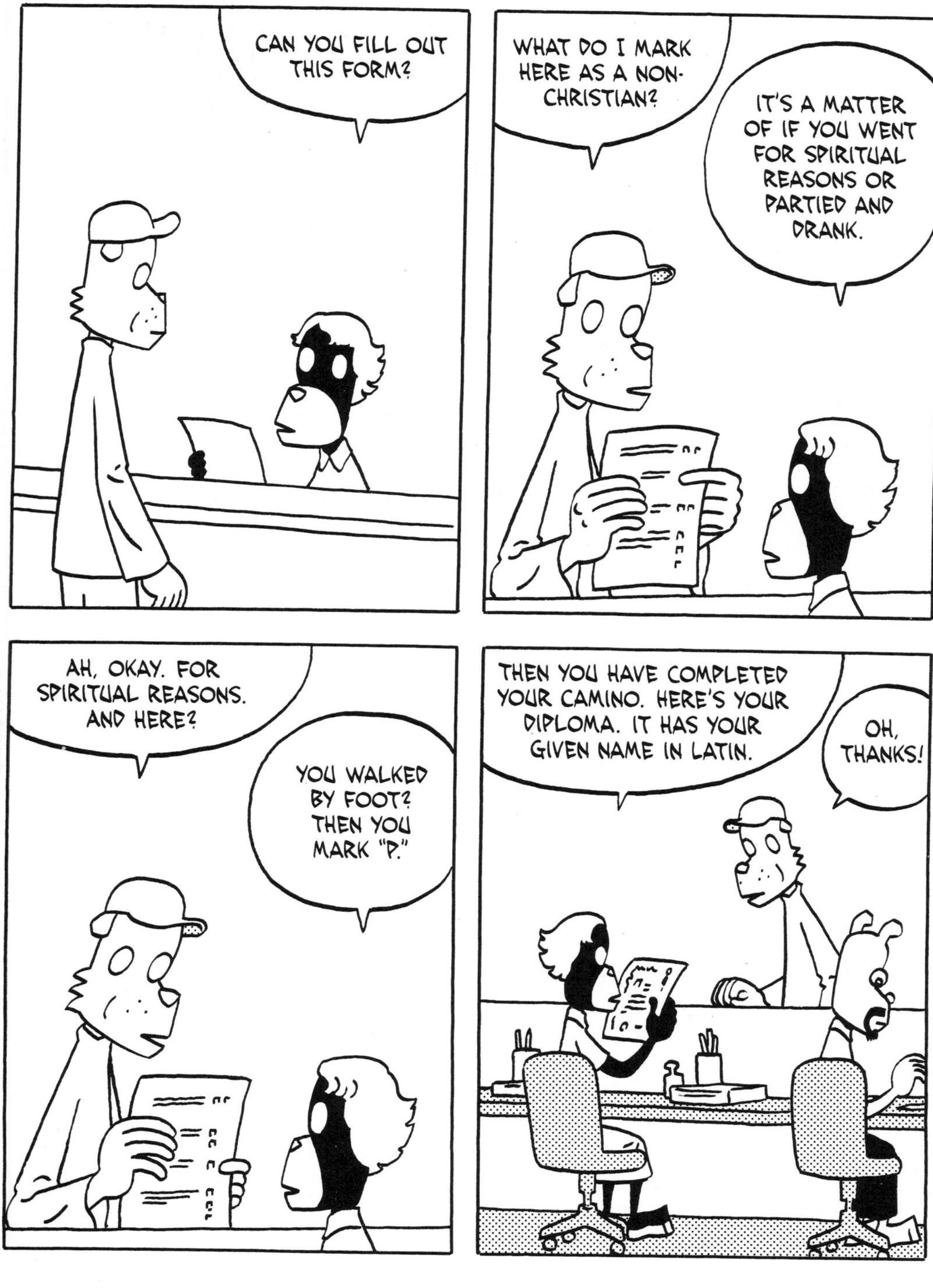
CAN YOU FILL OUT THIS FORM?
WHAT DO I MARK HERE AS A NON-CHRISTIAN?
IT'S A MATTER OF IF YOU WENT FOR SPIRITUAL REASONS OR PARTIED AND DRANK.
AH, OKAY. FOR SPIRITUAL REASONS. AND HERE?
YOU WALKED BY FOOT? THEN YOU MARK "P."
THEN YOU HAVE COMPLETED YOUR CAMINO. HERE'S YOUR DIPLOMA. IT HAS YOUR GIVEN NAME IN LATIN.
OH, THANKS!

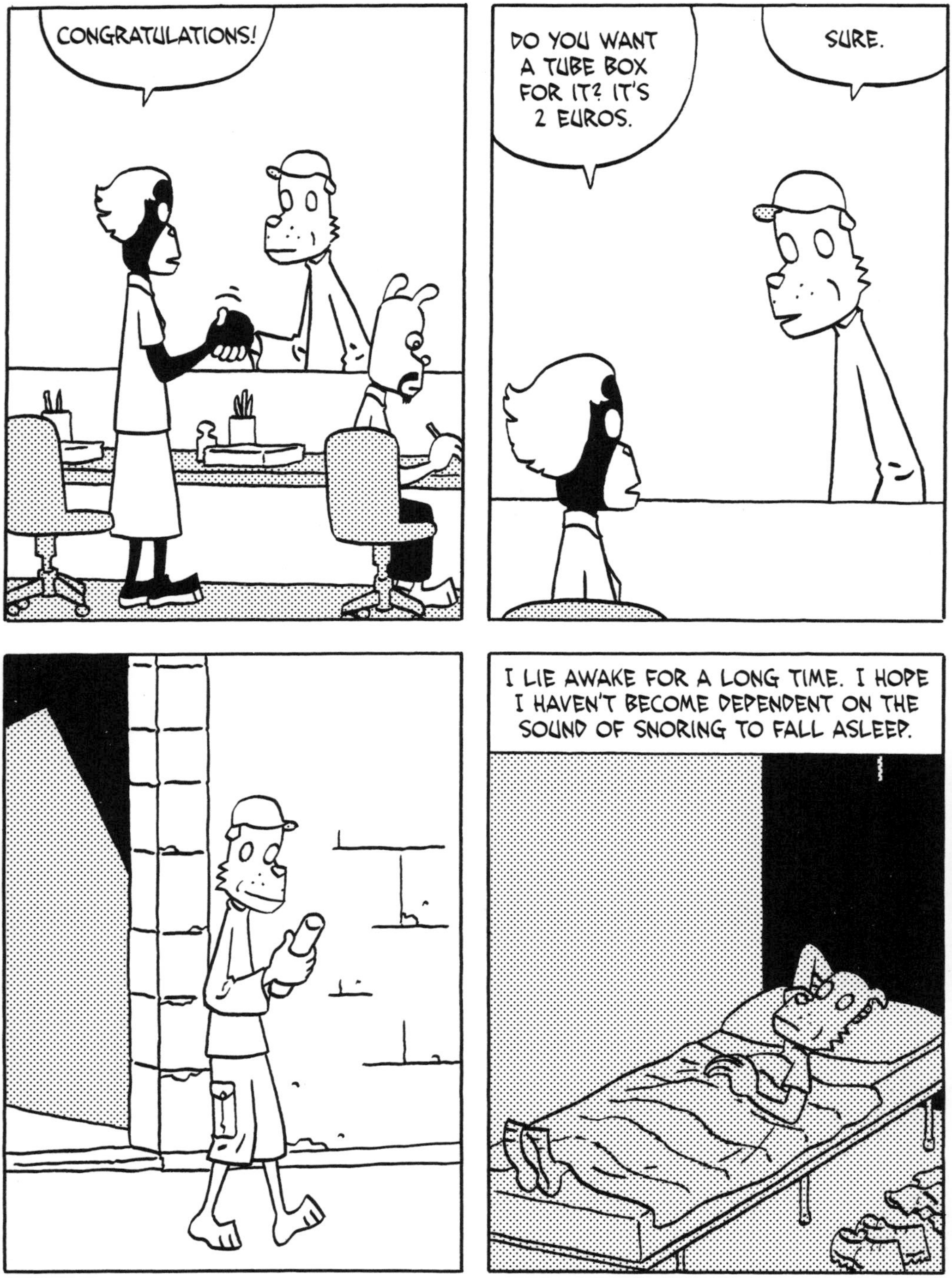
CONGRATULATIONS!
DO YOU WANT A TUBE BOX FOR IT? IT'S 2 EUROS.
SURE.
I LIE AWAKE FOR A LONG TIME. I HOPE I HAVEN'T BECOME DEPENDENT ON THE SOUND OF SNORING TO FALL ASLEEP.

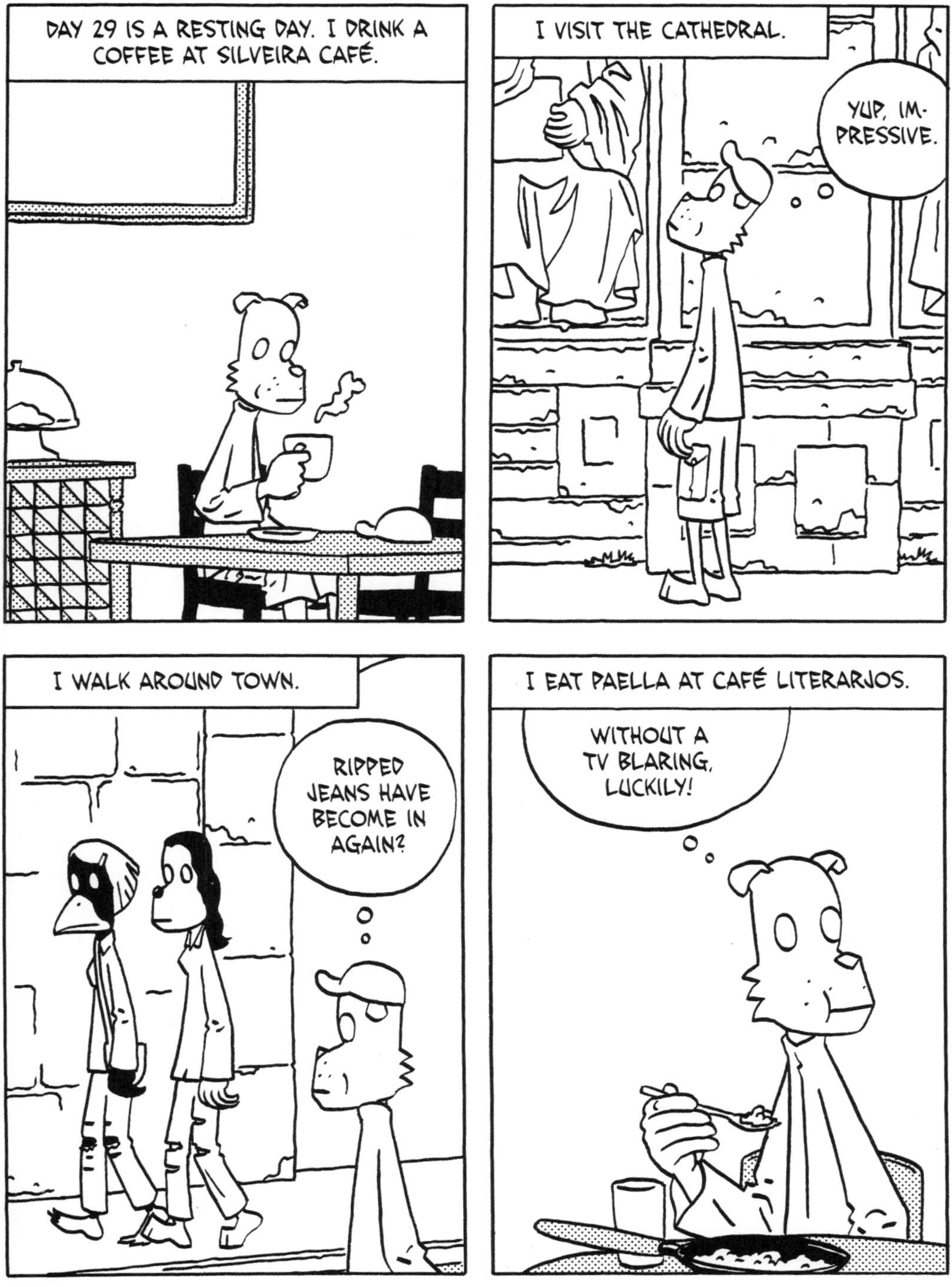
DAY 29 IS A RESTING DAY. I DRINK A COFFEE AT SILVEIRA CAFÉ.
I VISIT THE CATHEDRAL.
YUP, IM-PRESSIVE.
I WALK AROUND TOWN.
RIPPED JEANS HAVE BECOME IN AGAIN?
I EAT PAELLA AT CAFÉ LITERARJOS.
WITHOUT A TV BLARING, LUCKILY!

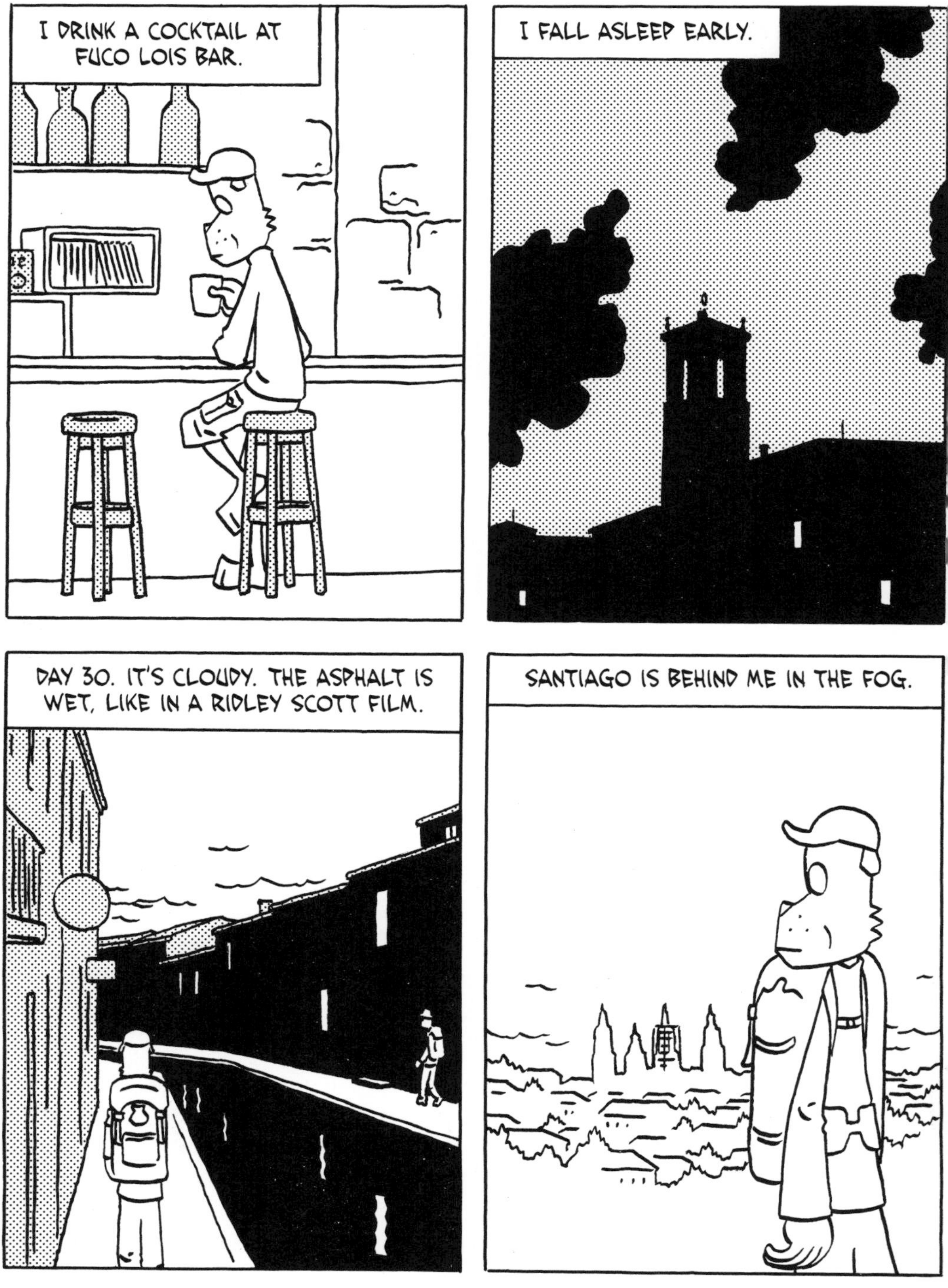
I DRINK A COCKTAIL AT FUCO LOIS BAR.
I FALL ASLEEP EARLY.
DAY 30. IT'S CLOUDY. THE ASPHALT IS WET, LIKE IN A RIDLEY SCOTT FILM.
SANTIAGO IS BEHIND ME IN THE FOG.

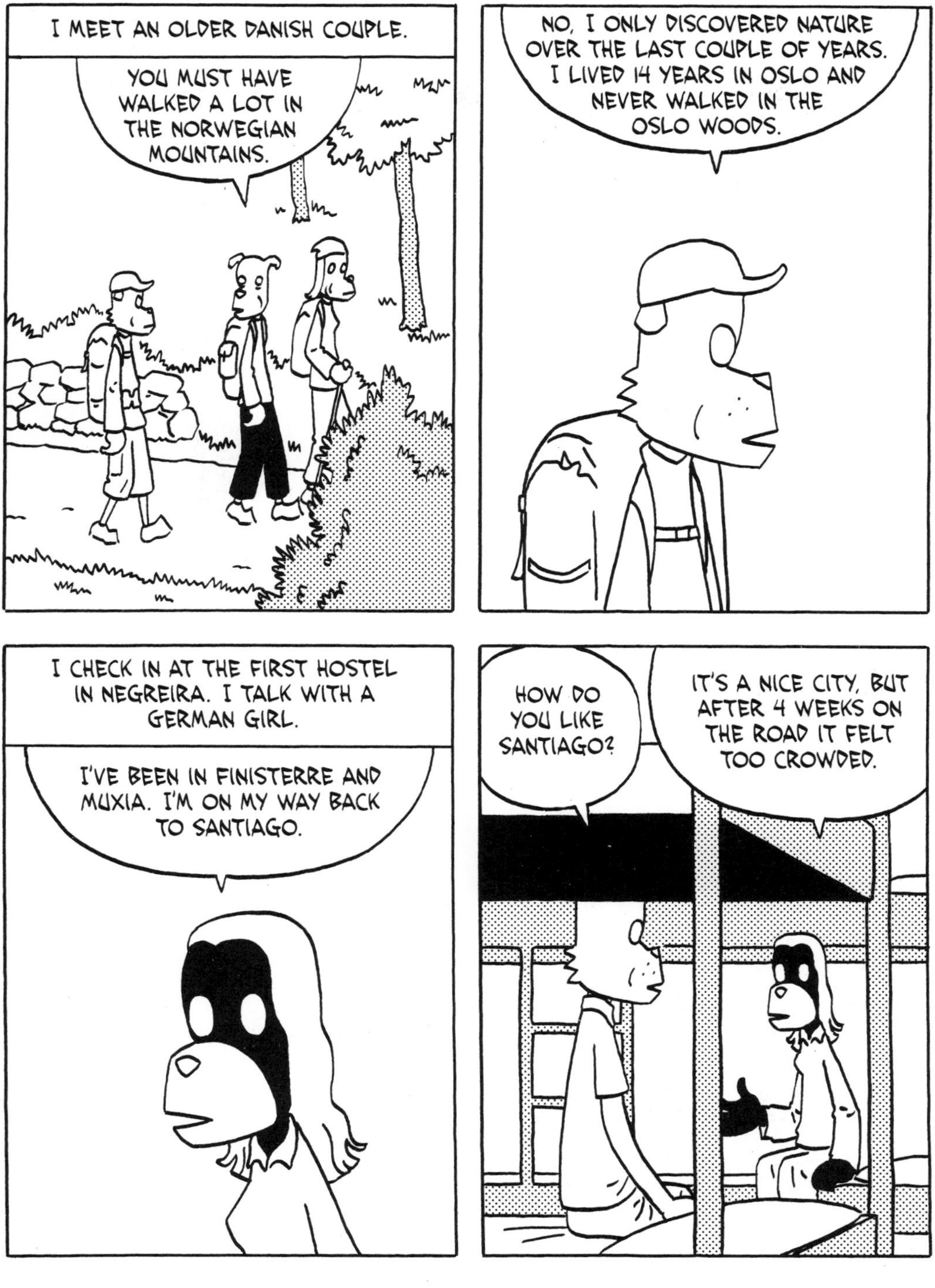
I MEET AN OLDER DANISH COUPLE.
YOU MUST HAVE WALKED A LOT IN THE NORWEGIAN MOUNTAINS.
NO, I ONLY DISCOVERED NATURE OVER THE LAST COUPLE OF YEARS. I LIVED 14 YEARS IN OSLO AND NEVER WALKED IN THE OSLO WOODS.
I CHECK IN AT THE FIRST HOSTEL IN NEGREIRA. I TALK WITH A GERMAN GIRL.
I'VE BEEN IN FINISTERRE AND MUXIA. I'M ON MY WAY BACK TO SANTIAGO.
HOW DO YOU LIKE SANTIAGO?
IT'S A NICE CITY, BUT AFTER 4 WEEKS ON THE ROAD IT FELT TOO CROWDED.

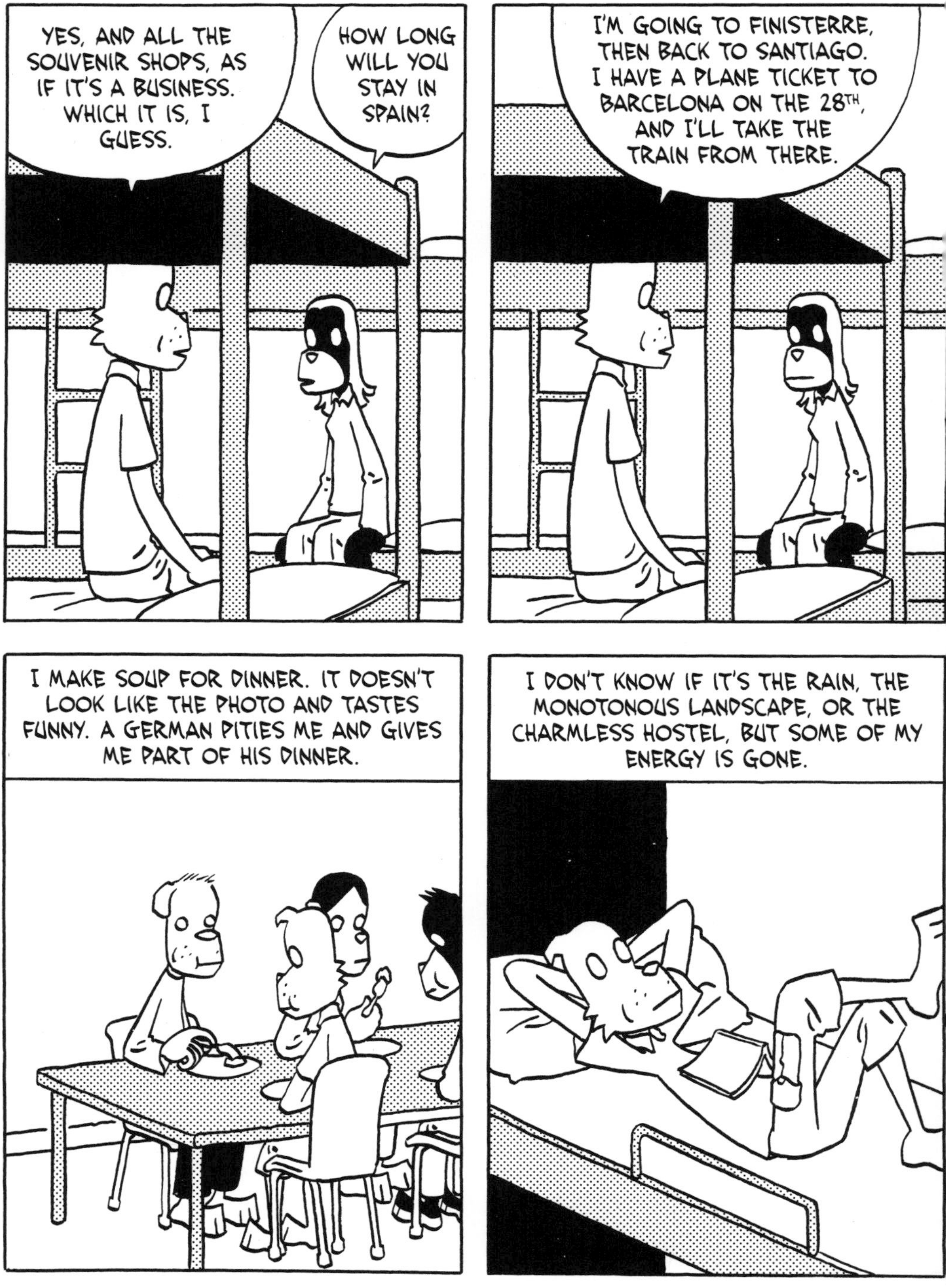
YES, AND ALL THE SOUVENIR SHOPS, AS IF IT'S A BUSINESS. WHICH IT IS, I GUESS.
HOW LONG WILL YOU STAY IN SPAIN?
I'M GOING TO FINISTERRE, THEN BACK TO SANTIAGO. I HAVE A PLANE TICKET TO BARCELONA ON THE 28TH, AND I'LL TAKE THE TRAIN FROM THERE.
I MAKE SOUP FOR DINNER. IT DOESN'T LOOK LIKE THE PHOTO AND TASTES FUNNY. A GERMAN PITIES ME AND GIVES ME PART OF HIS DINNER.
I DON'T KNOW IF IT'S THE RAIN, THE MONOTONOUS LANDSCAPE, OR THE CHARMLESS HOSTEL, BUT SOME OF MY ENERGY IS GONE.

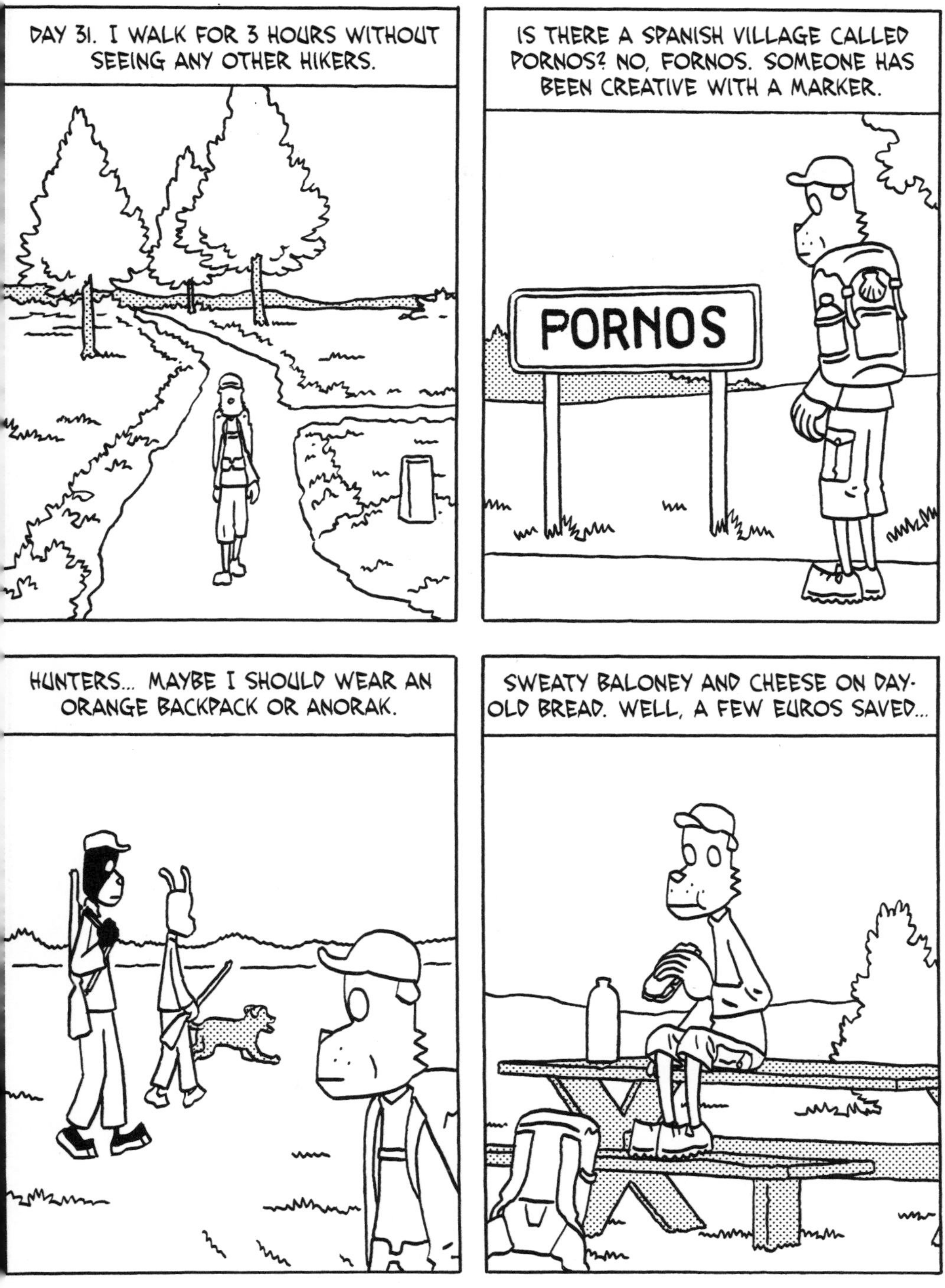
DAY 31. I WALK FOR 3 HOURS WITHOUT SEEING ANY OTHER HIKERS.
IS THERE A SPANISH VILLAGE CALLED PORNOS? NO, FORNOS. SOMEONE HAS BEEN CREATIVE WITH A MARKER.
PORNOS
HUNTERS... MAYBE I SHOULD WEAR AN ORANGE BACKPACK OR ANORAK.
SWEATY BALONEY AND CHEESE ON DAY-OLD BREAD. WELL, A FEW EUROS SAVED...

BLACK AND WHITE COWS AGAINST GREEN GRASS AND A CLOUDLESS SKY.

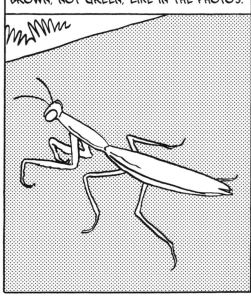

I SEE A PRAYING MANTIS FOR THE FIRST TIME IN MY LIFE. IT'S ABOUT 5 CM AND BROWN, NOT GREEN, LIKE IN THE PHOTOS.

I STOP IN OLVEIROA.

THE WOMAN WORKING AT THE HOSTEL WILL BE BACK AT 7. JUST CHOOSE A BED.

OKAY.

AFTER DINNER, I TALK WITH A MIDWESTERN AMERICAN COUPLE.

SO YOU HAVE NORWEGIAN ANCESTRY?

YES, MY DAD MADE LUTEFISK ON CHRIST-MAS AND MAY 17TH. IT TASTED AWFUL, BUT I ATE IT.

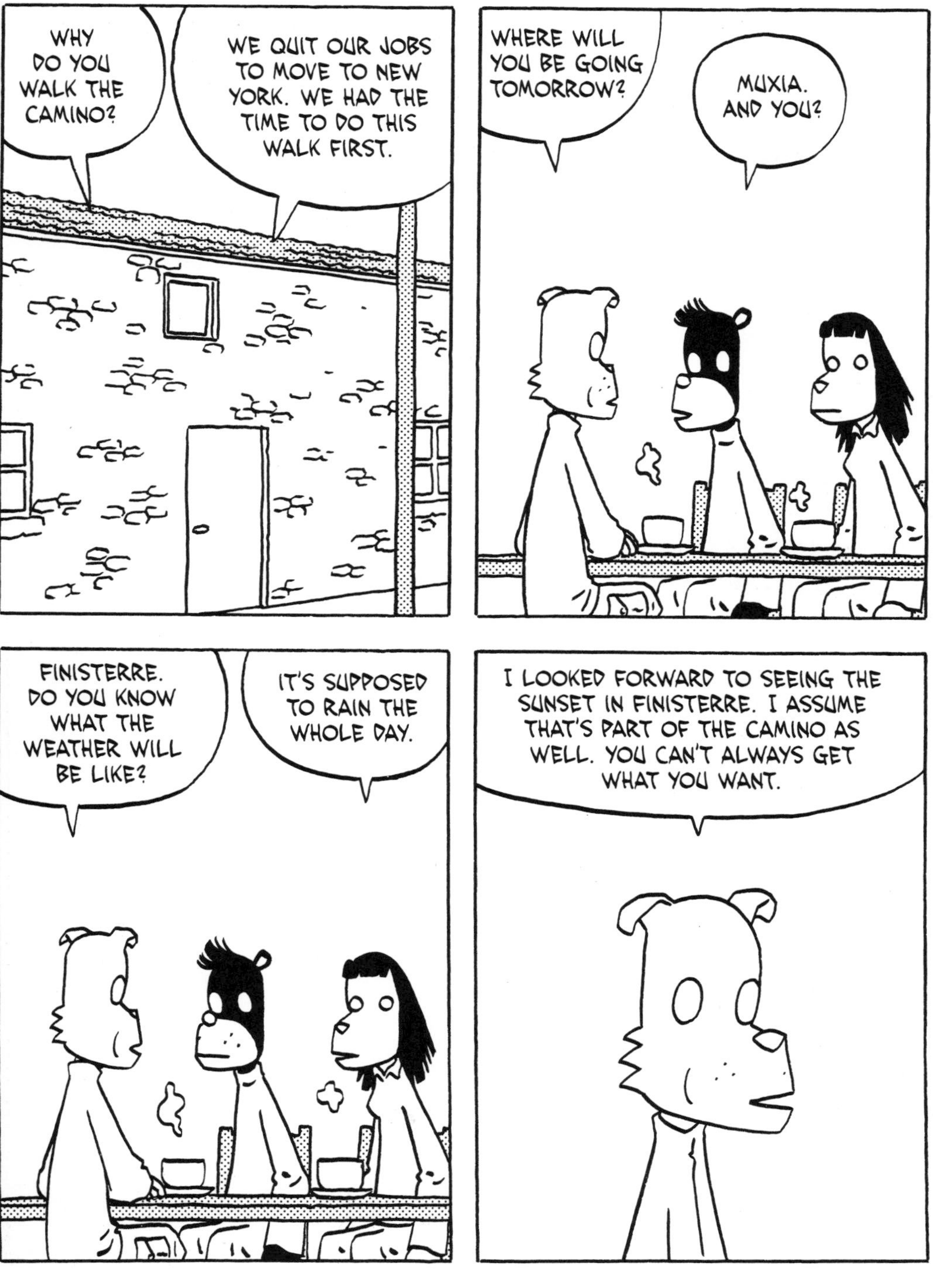
WHY DO YOU WALK THE CAMINO?
WE QUIT OUR JOBS TO MOVE TO NEW YORK. WE HAD THE TIME TO DO THIS WALK FIRST.
WHERE WILL YOU BE GOING TOMORROW?
MUXIA. AND YOU?
FINISTERRE. DO YOU KNOW WHAT THE WEATHER WILL BE LIKE?
IT'S SUPPOSED TO RAIN THE WHOLE DAY.
I LOOKED FORWARD TO SEEING THE SUNSET IN FINISTERRE. I ASSUME THAT'S PART OF THE CAMINO AS WELL. YOU CAN'T ALWAYS GET WHAT YOU WANT.

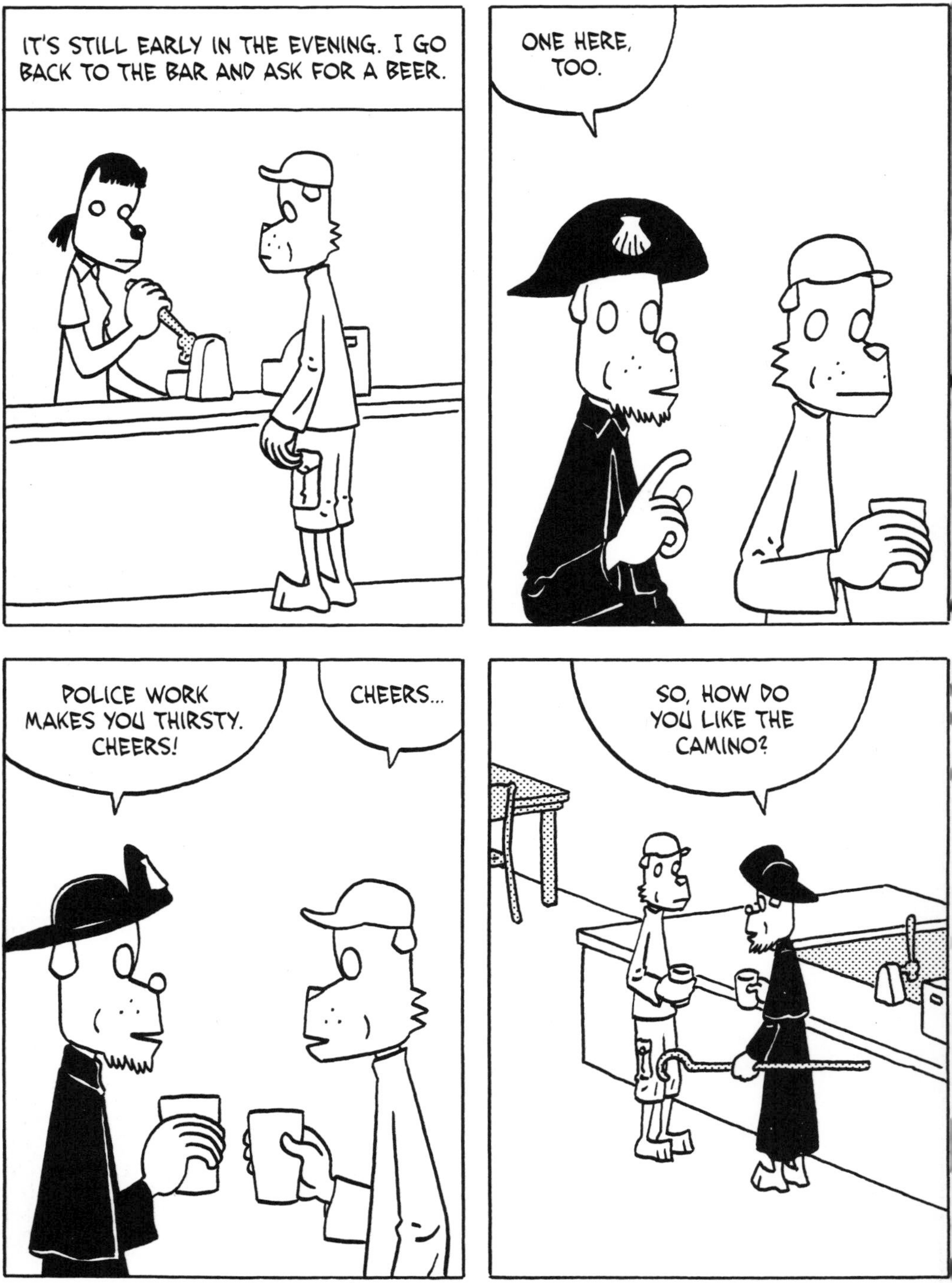
IT'S STILL EARLY IN THE EVENING. I GO BACK TO THE BAR AND ASK FOR A BEER.
ONE HERE, TOO.
POLICE WORK MAKES YOU THIRSTY. CHEERS!
CHEERS...
SO, HOW DO YOU LIKE THE CAMINO?

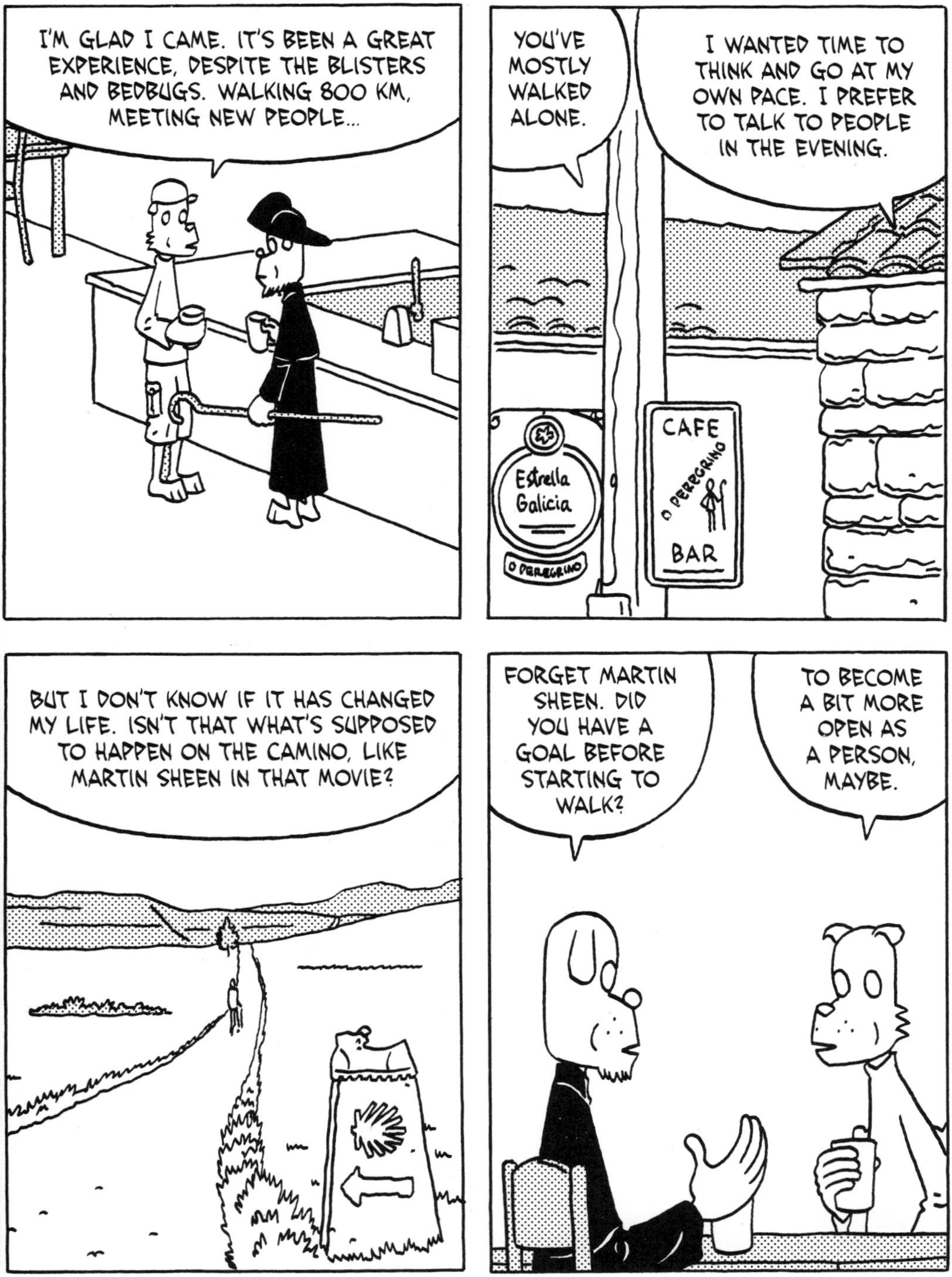
I'M GLAD I CAME. IT'S BEEN A GREAT EXPERIENCE, DESPITE THE BLISTERS AND BEDBUGS. WALKING 800 KM, MEETING NEW PEOPLE...
YOU'VE MOSTLY WALKED ALONE.
I WANTED TIME TO THINK AND GO AT MY OWN PACE. I PREFER TO TALK TO PEOPLE IN THE EVENING.
Estrella Galicia
O PEREGRINO
CAFE
O PEREGRINO
BAR
BUT I DON'T KNOW IF IT HAS CHANGED MY LIFE. ISN'T THAT WHAT'S SUPPOSED TO HAPPEN ON THE CAMINO, LIKE MARTIN SHEEN IN THAT MOVIE?
FORGET MARTIN SHEEN. DID YOU HAVE A GOAL BEFORE STARTING TO WALK?
TO BECOME A BIT MORE OPEN AS A PERSON, MAYBE.

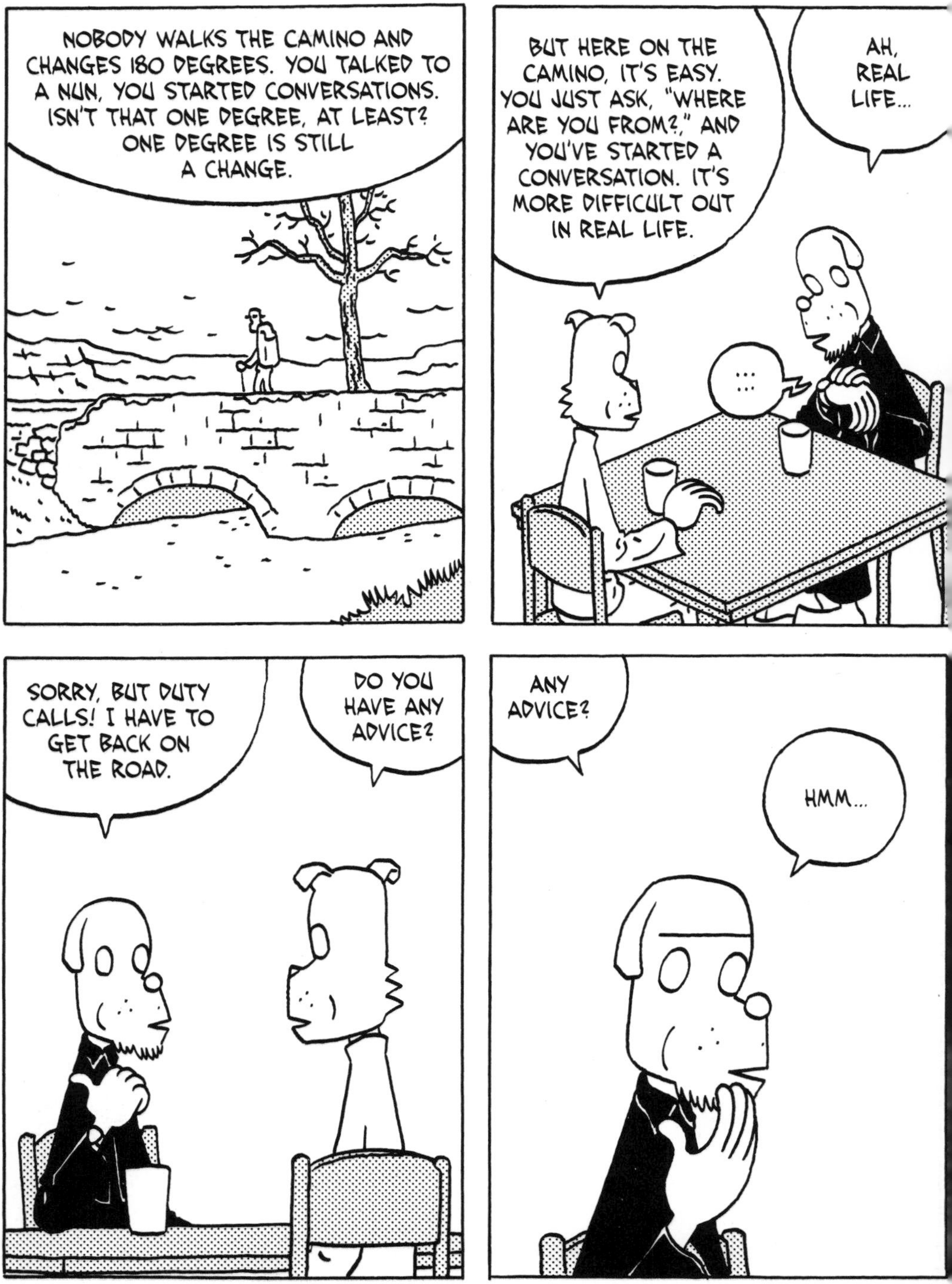
NOBODY WALKS THE CAMINO AND CHANGES 180 DEGREES. YOU TALKED TO A NUN, YOU STARTED CONVERSATIONS. ISN'T THAT ONE DEGREE, AT LEAST? ONE DEGREE IS STILL A CHANGE.
BUT HERE ON THE CAMINO, IT'S EASY. YOU JUST ASK, "WHERE ARE YOU FROM?," AND YOU'VE STARTED A CONVERSATION. IT'S MORE DIFFICULT OUT IN REAL LIFE.
AH, REAL LIFE...
...
SORRY, BUT DUTY CALLS! I HAVE TO GET BACK ON THE ROAD.
DO YOU HAVE ANY ADVICE?
ANY ADVICE?
HMM...

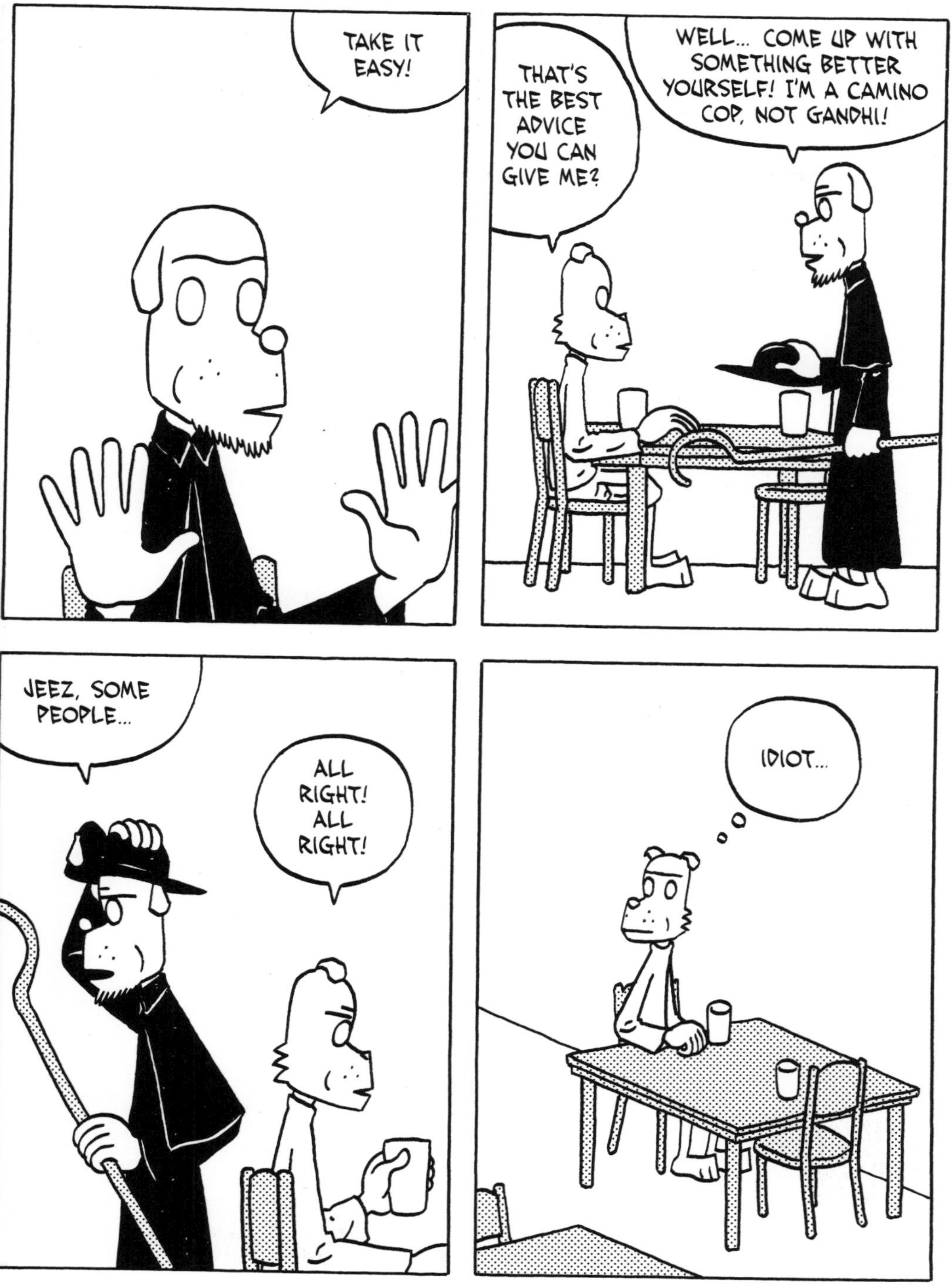
TAKE IT EASY!
THAT'S THE BEST ADVICE YOU CAN GIVE ME?
WELL... COME UP WITH SOMETHING BETTER YOURSELF! I'M A CAMINO COP, NOT GANDHI!
JEEZ, SOME PEOPLE...
ALL RIGHT! ALL RIGHT!
IDIOT...

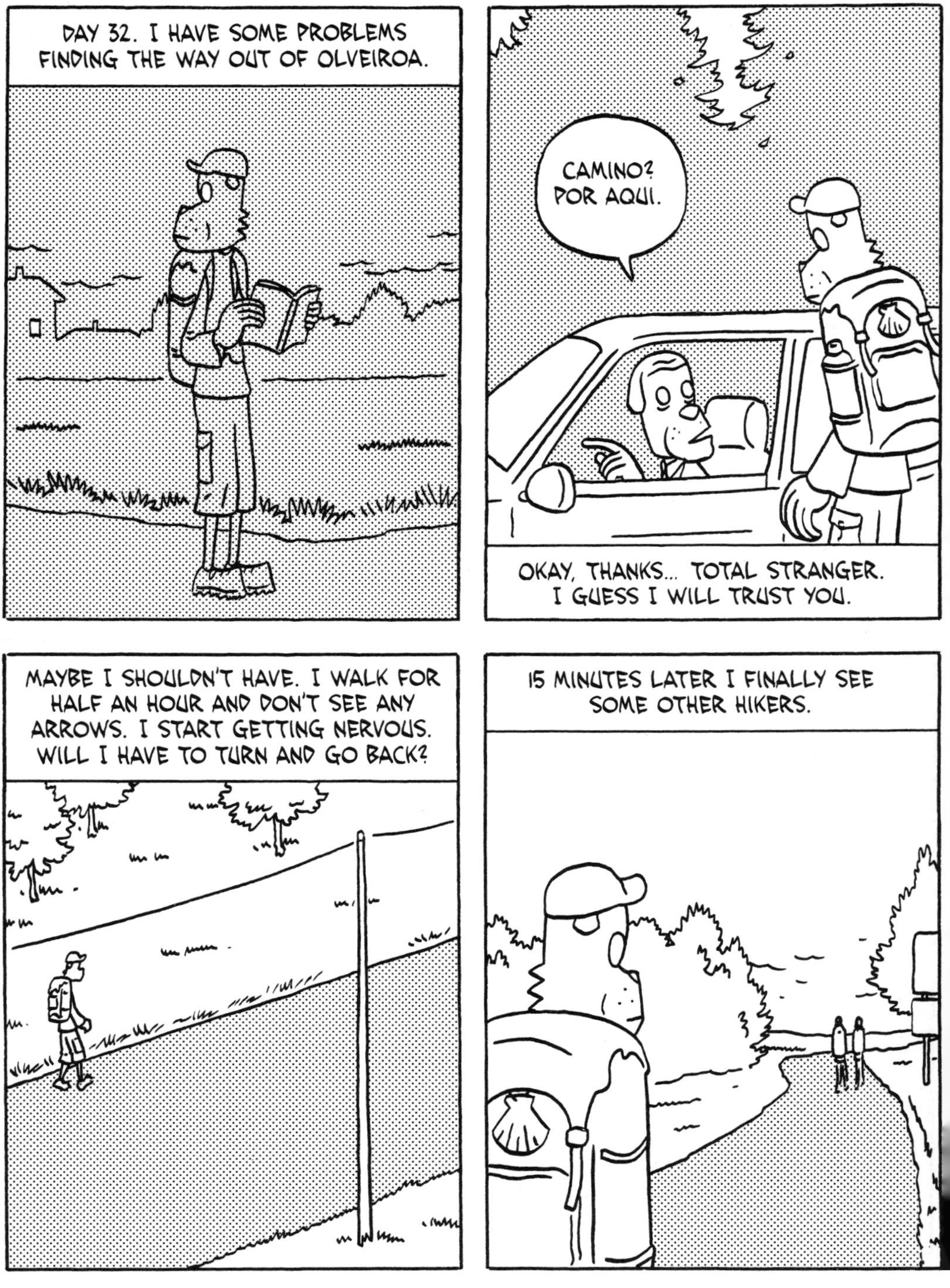
DAY 32. I HAVE SOME PROBLEMS FINDING THE WAY OUT OF OLVEIROA.
CAMINO? POR AQUI.
OKAY, THANKS... TOTAL STRANGER. I GUESS I WILL TRUST YOU.
MAYBE I SHOULDN'T HAVE. I WALK FOR HALF AN HOUR AND DON'T SEE ANY ARROWS. I START GETTING NERVOUS. WILL I HAVE TO TURN AND GO BACK?
15 MINUTES LATER I FINALLY SEE SOME OTHER HIKERS.

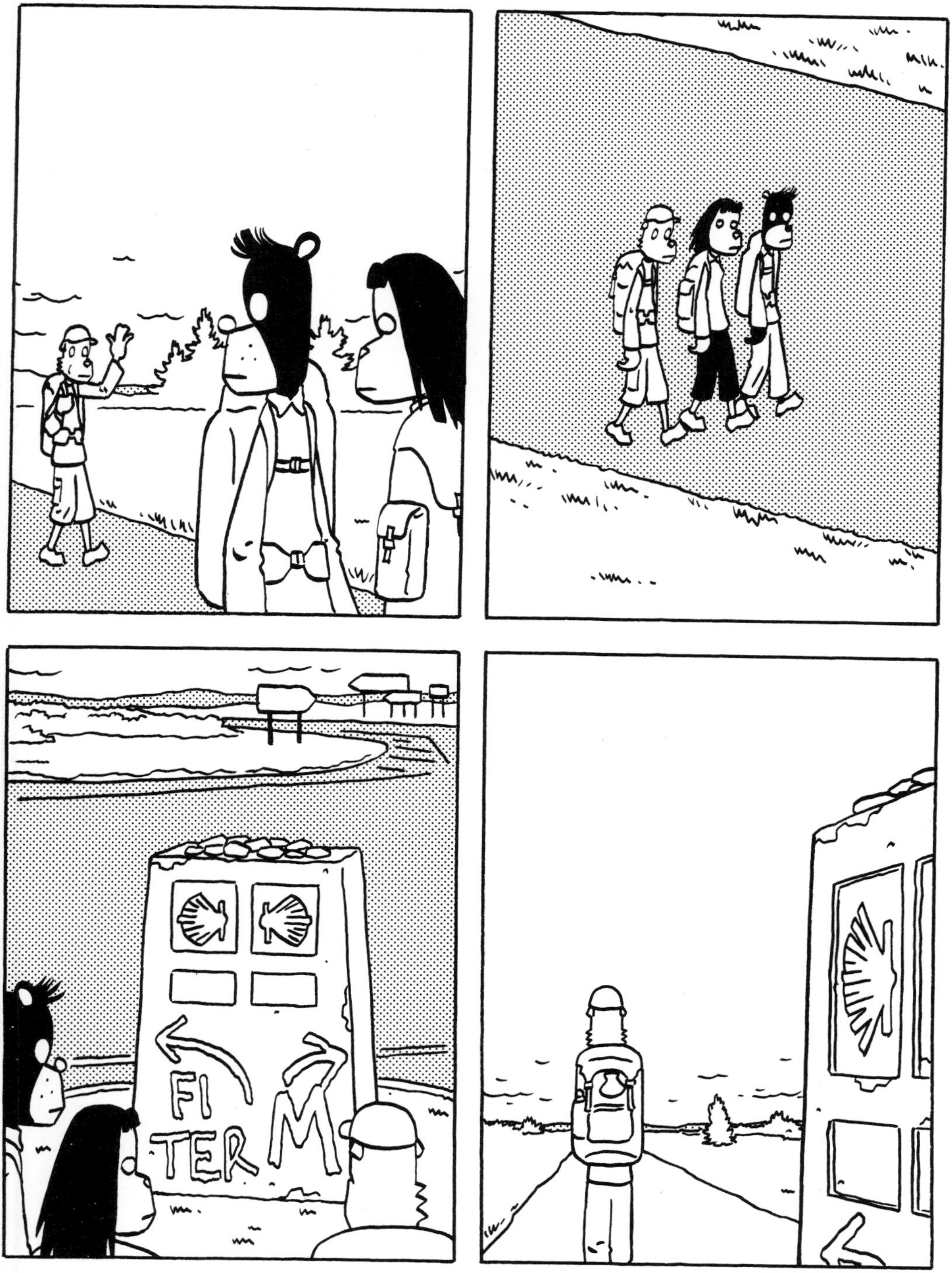
FI
TER
M

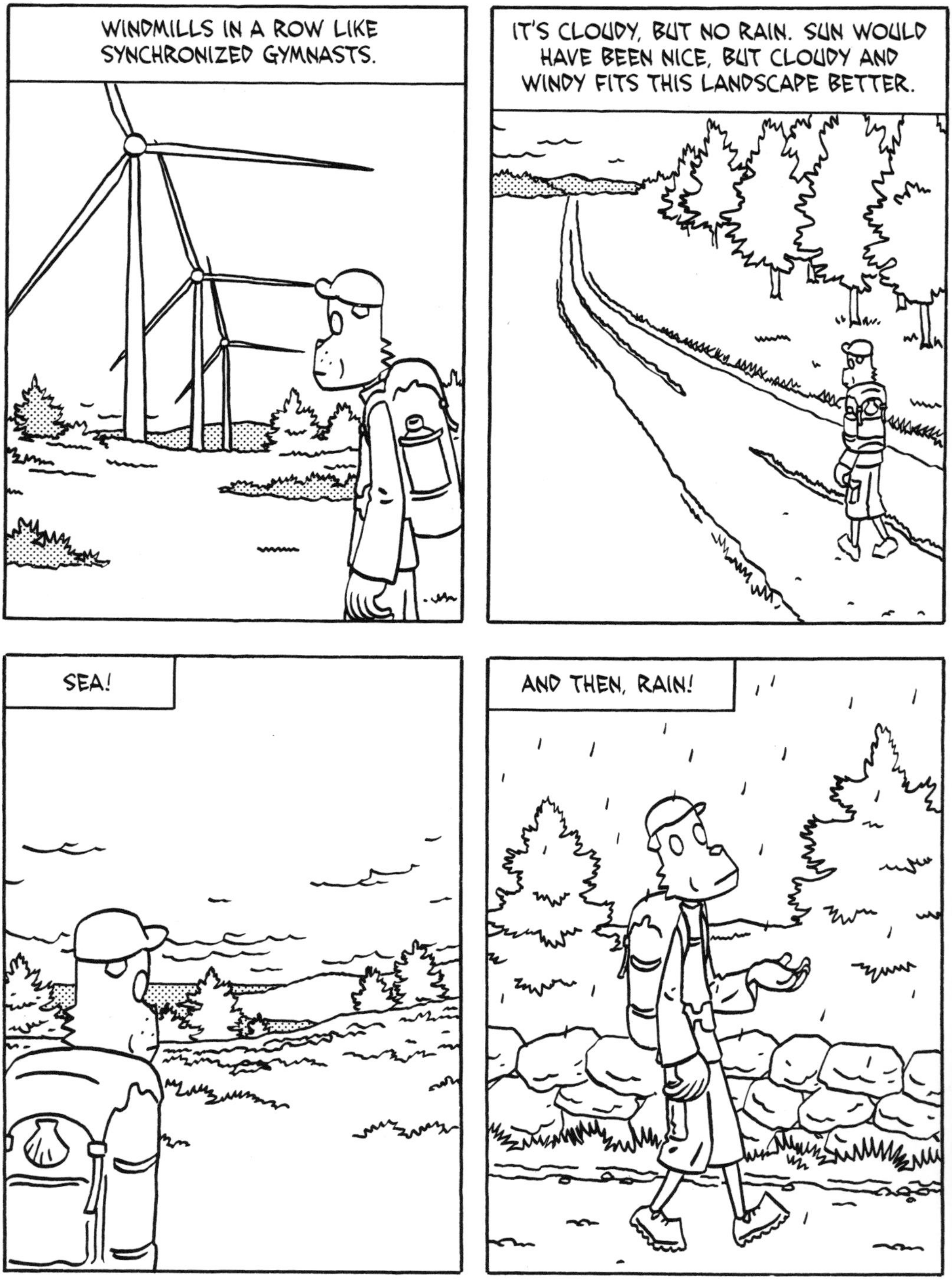
WINDMILLS IN A ROW LIKE SYNCHRONIZED GYMNASTS.
IT'S CLOUDY, BUT NO RAIN. SUN WOULD HAVE BEEN NICE, BUT CLOUDY AND WINDY FITS THIS LANDSCAPE BETTER.
SEA!
AND THEN, RAIN!

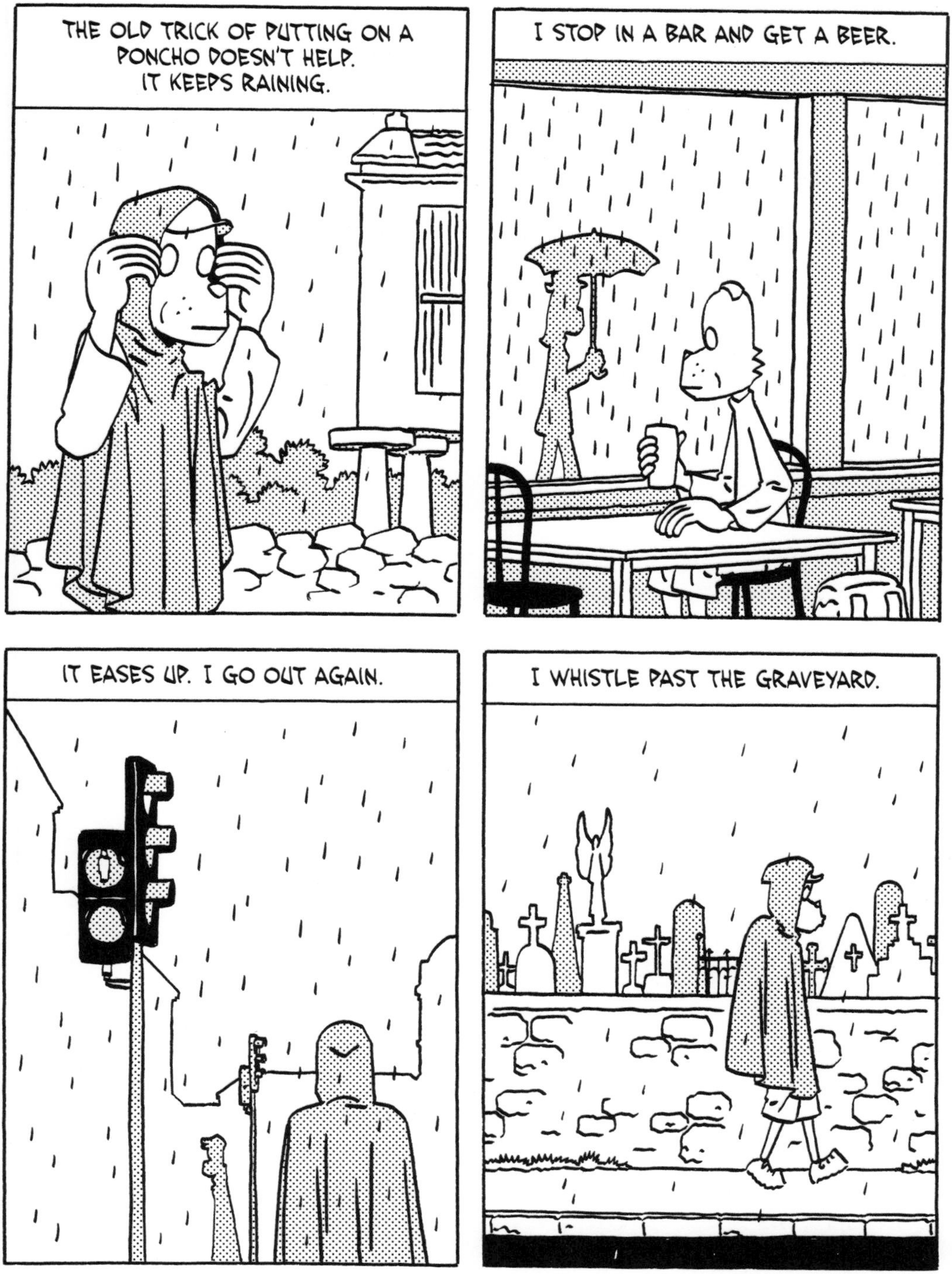
THE OLD TRICK OF PUTTING ON A PONCHO DOESN'T HELP. IT KEEPS RAINING.
I STOP IN A BAR AND GET A BEER.
IT EASES UP. I GO OUT AGAIN.
I WHISTLE PAST THE GRAVEYARD.

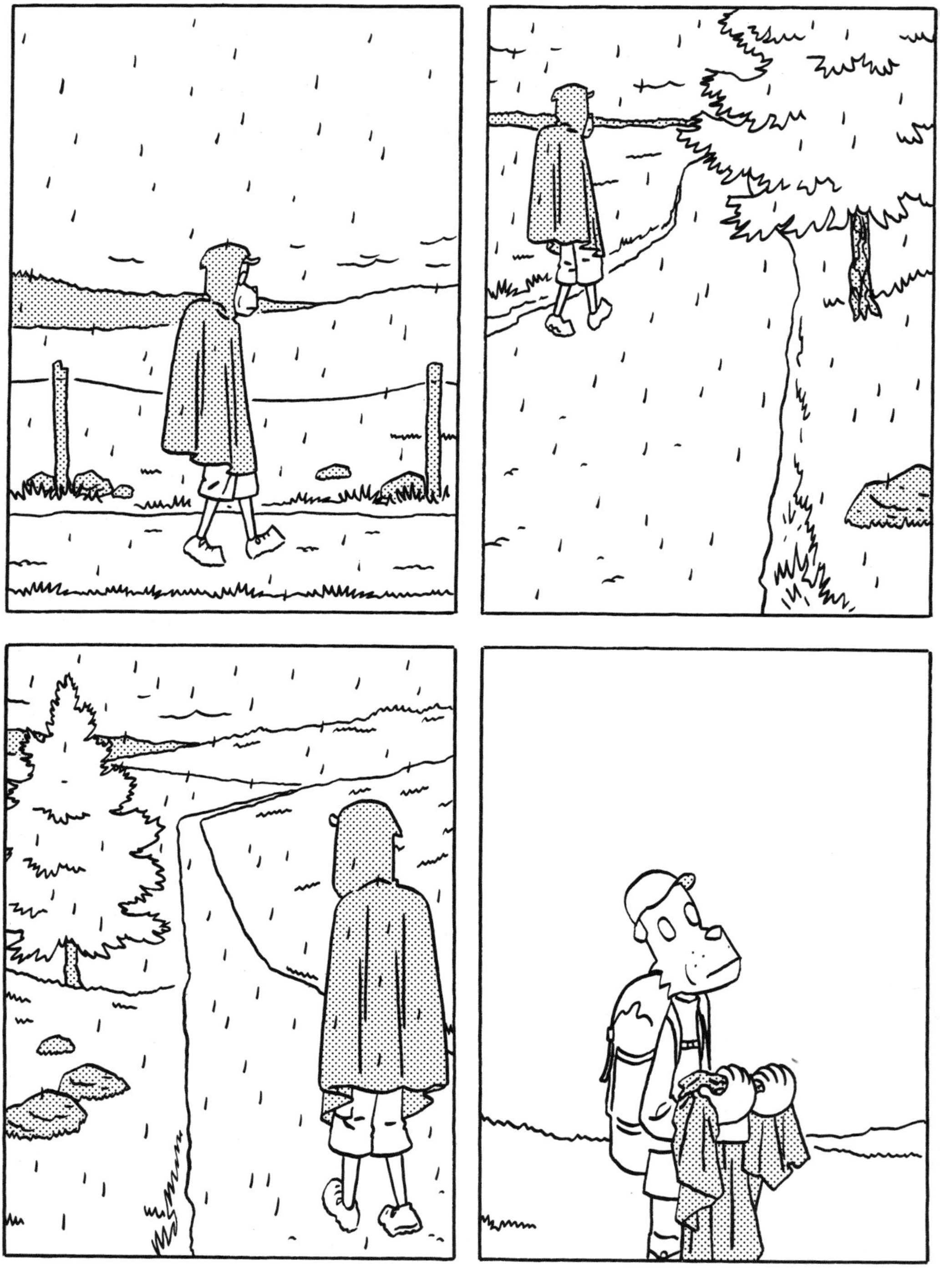

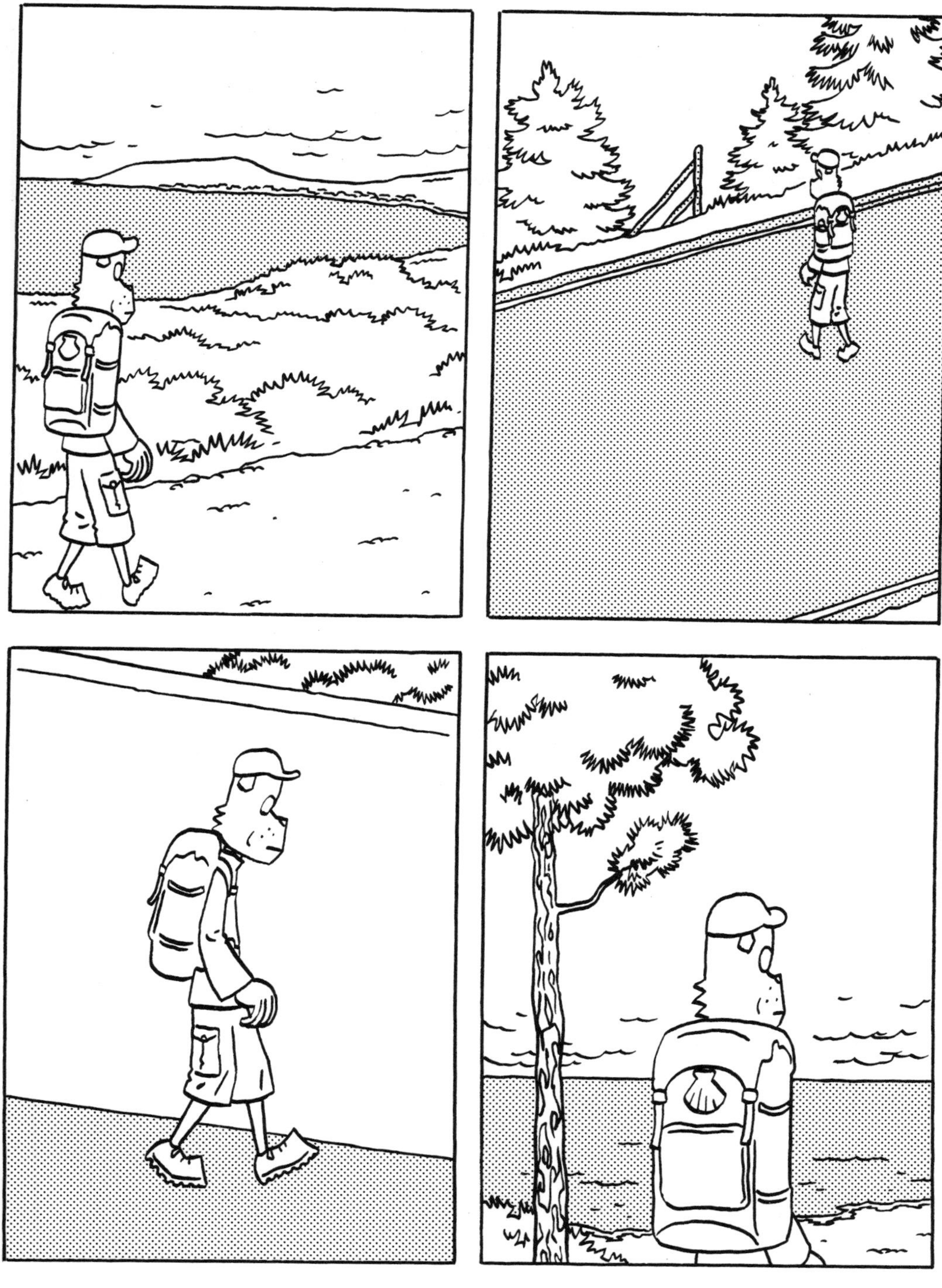

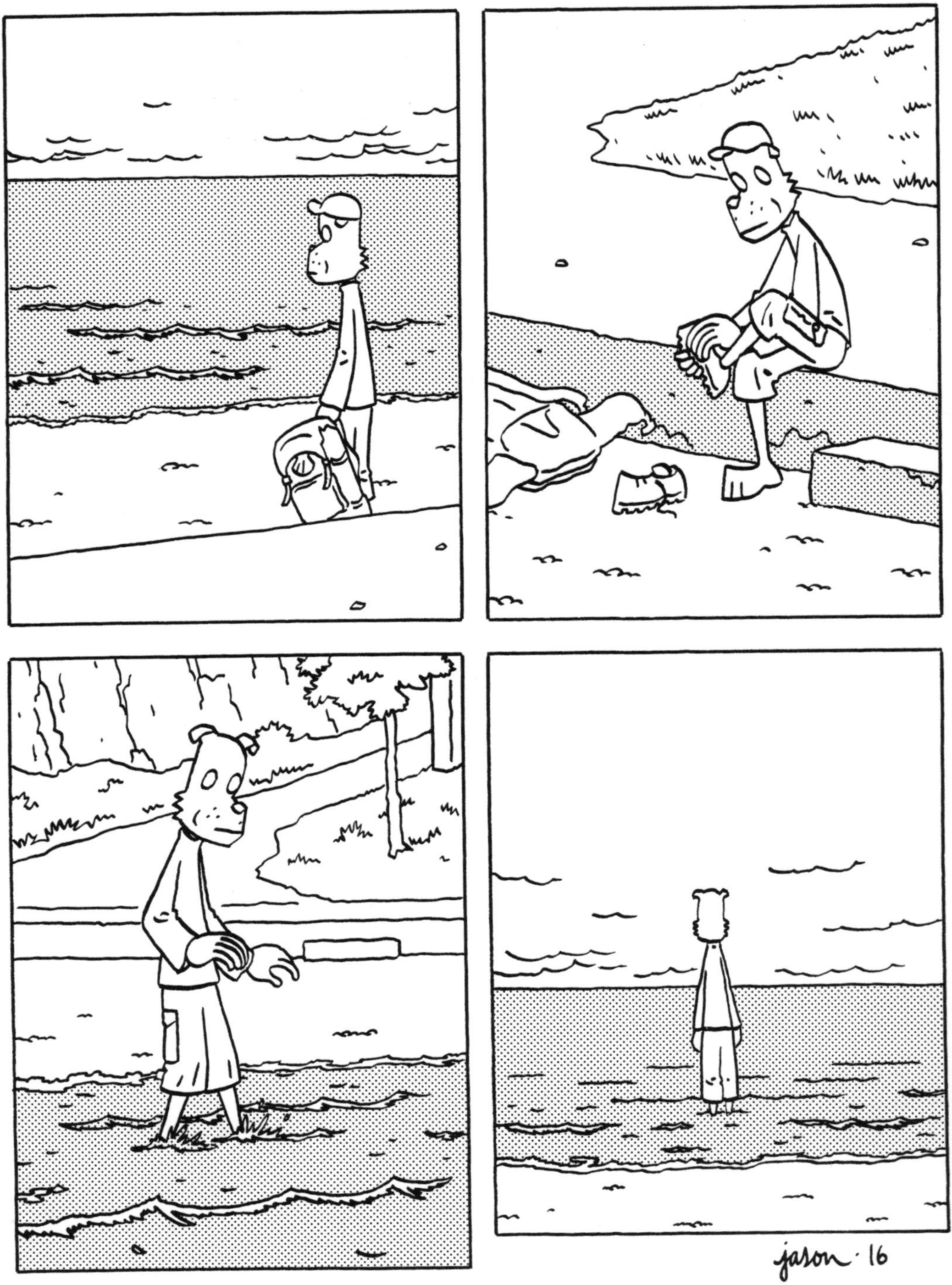
jason · 16

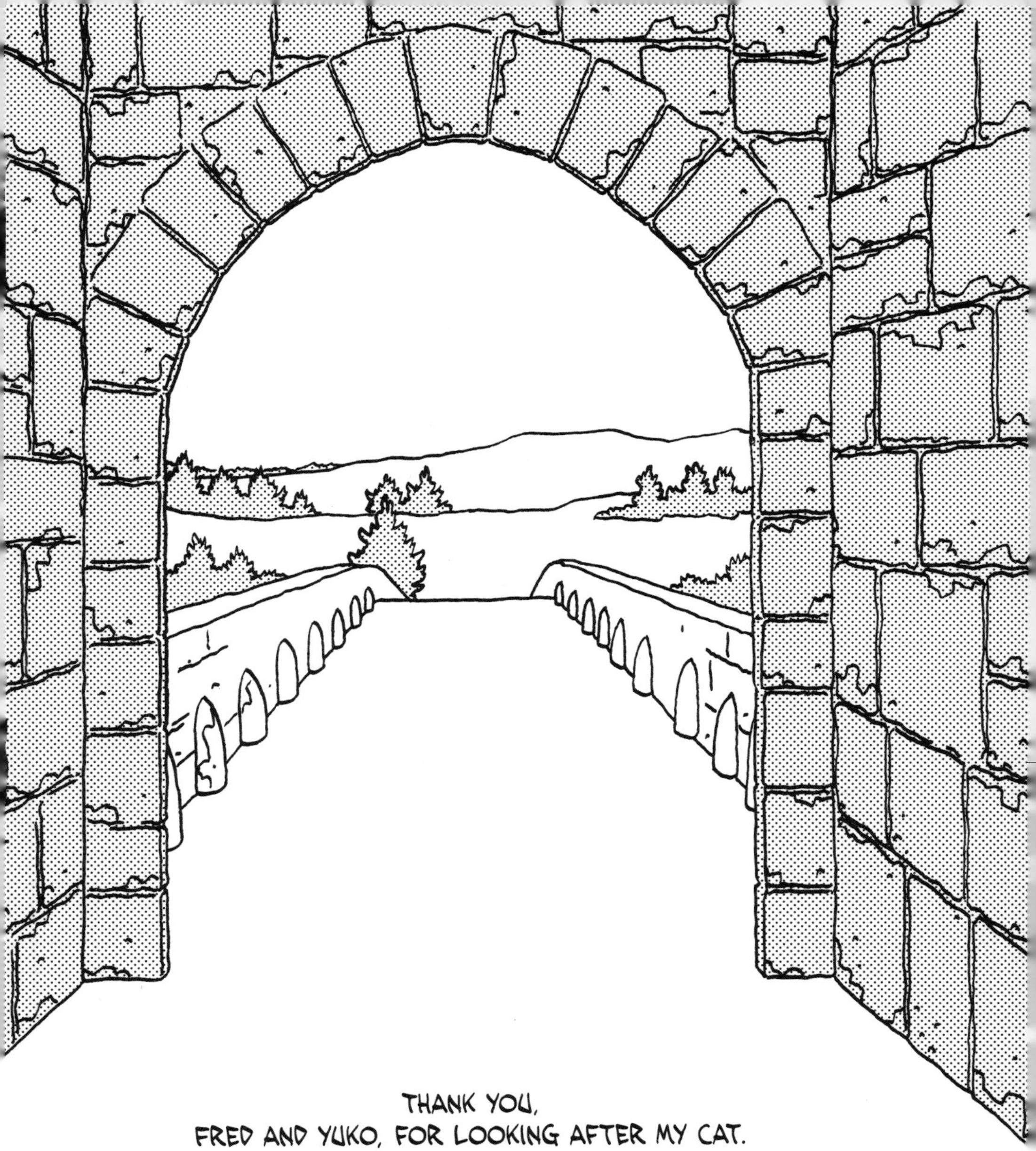

THANK YOU,
FRED AND YUKO, FOR LOOKING AFTER MY CAT.
LAUREANO DOMINGUEZ, FOR THE TAPAS.
AND LEWIS TRONDHEIM, FOR HIS PATIENCE.

THANK YOU,
EVERYBODY I MET ON THE WAY. BUEN CAMINO!

FANTAGRAPHICS BOOKS • 7563 Lake City Way NE • Seattle, WA 98115 • Designed by Jacob Covey • Production and lettering by Paul Baresh • Copy Editor: Conrad Groth Proofreader: R.J. Casey • Associate Publisher: Eric Reynolds Publisher: Gary Groth All characters, stories and artwork © 2017 Jason • This edition © 2017 Fantagraphics Books Inc. • All rights reserved; permission to quote or reproduce material much be obtained from the the author or publisher

Visit us online at www.fantagraphics .com • Purchase Jason original artwork at www.beguiling.com

First edition: May 2017 • ISBN 978-1-68396-021-8 • Printed in China

Jason is not actually a cat or a dog.
He was born in Norway in 1965, but
currently lives in the south of France.
He walked the Camino de Santiago in
2015. One day he will walk it again.

OTHER BOOKS BY JASON:

Why Are You Doing This? (2005)

The Left Bank Gang (2006)

I Killed Adolf Hitler (2007)

The Last Musketeer (2008)

Pocket Full of Rain (2008)

Low Moon (2009)

Werewolves of Montpellier (2010)

Almost Silent (2010 compilation)

What I Did (2010 compilation)

Isle of 100,000 Graves (2011)

Athos in America (2012)

Lost Cat (2013)

If You Steal (2015)

On the Camino (2017)